TK

Young Living

SEVENTH EDITION

Nanalee Clayton

GLENCOE

McGraw-Hill

New York, New York   Columbus, Ohio   Mission Hills, California   Peoria, Illinois

Teacher Reviewers

Glencoe/McGraw-Hill

A Division of The **McGraw-Hill** *Companies*

Editorial services provided by Visual Education Corporation, Princeton, NJ.

"Mama Is a Sunrise" by Evelyn Tooley Hunt is reprinted by permission from the author.

Send all inquiries to:
Glencoe/McGraw-Hill
3008 W. Willow Knolls Drive
Peoria, IL 61614-1083

ISBN 0-02-642816-4   (Student Text)
ISBN 0-02-642817-2   (Teacher's Wraparound Edition)

Printed in the United States of America.

2 3 4 5 6 7 8 9 10 VHJ   03 02 01 00 99 98 97

Table of Contents

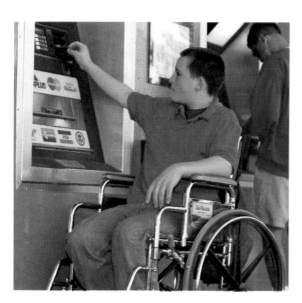

Features

CONNECTIONS

UNIT - 1 Personal Development

Chapter 1:
The Unique You

Chapter 2:
Everyday Living Skills

Chapter 3:
Steps to Success

Chapter 4:
Careers

x

The Unique You

TEENS MAKING A DIFFERENCE
Say Cheese, Please

Raj Patel loves the school fair. It's an opportunity to show off his hard work. Raj has been entering photography competitions for several years. Two years in a row, he won an award for his color photographs of nature.

Last year, Raj started taking black-and-white photographs and developing the film himself in his father's darkroom. Raj enjoys being able to see the pictures as they develop. Whether he wins an award for his photographs this year doesn't matter to Raj, because he has had so much fun processing the film and making his own prints.

Try THIS!

What about you? What are your interests and abilities? What achievements make you feel good about yourself and build your self-confidence? Discuss your answers with a classmate.

LESSON ONE
The One and Only You

WORDS TO KNOW

unique

heredity

environment

acquired

culture

role

role models

DISCOVER...

- why people are alike and different from everyone else.
- the difference between inherited and acquired characteristics.
- the influence of role models.

Nicole and Amanda are identical twins. Most people think that the teens are exactly alike, but, in fact, they are quite different. Nicole likes to listen to rock music, while Amanda prefers jazz. Nicole loves outdoor activities. Amanda, on the other hand, would rather read a mystery book. The teens even look slightly different from each other. In fact, no two people—not even identical twins—are exactly alike. There is something special about each person. You also are **unique**—*one of a kind.* You are special and different from all others.

You probably share some interests, such as camping or watching movies, with family members or friends. During your teen years you will also begin to develop other interests on your own. You are entering the stage in your life when you will establish your individuality and become your own person.

Try This!

Think of a new activity you would like to try, such as playing tennis, starting a baseball card collection, or playing chess. Then make a list of ways you could find out more about the interest.

Traits in Common

Although people are different from each other, they are also alike in many ways. Everyone must have food, water, and a place to live. Everyone needs to feel loved and accepted by others. All people need to feel safe. You, like others, have the desire to express your creativity and independence. However, the way you satisfy your needs may be different from that of other people. Like Nicole, you may enjoy outdoor activities. Your best friend may be more like Amanda and prefer playing board games and watching old-time movies.

Being an Individual

No two people act, think, or feel the same way. This is because everyone comes from a different background and has different experiences. Everything you do, everywhere you go, and everyone you know—especially your family members and friends—have influenced who you are. **Figure 1.1** on the next page shows the many influences on you that make you unique.

Heredity and Environment

Some of the characteristics that make you an individual are a result of your heredity. **Heredity** (huh-RED-i-tee) is *the passing on of traits or characteristics from parents to their children.* These traits include your eye and skin color, your facial features, and your body build.

You have other qualities that make you a unique individual. These are traits that are a result of your **environment,** or *all the living and nonliving things that surround you.* Do you live in a small town, in a big city, or in the country? Imagine how different you would be if you had been raised in a different climate or a different country.

Figure 1.1
Influences on You
Many factors influence
who you are. Which of
these factors have
influenced you the most?

Think about your interests, hobbies, and abilities. Some of them are **acquired,** or *learned from the people and things around you.* Perhaps your sister taught you how to skate. Maybe a friend sparked your interest in computers. These are examples of acquired skills or interests. Name three abilities that you have acquired or learned.

You have some characteristics that are influenced by both heredity and your environment. For example, body build may be inherited, but the athletic skill to play a particular sport is acquired.

Culture

Your culture also influences the person you become. **Culture** refers to *the ways of thinking, acting, dressing, and speaking shared by a group of people.* Cultures may be based

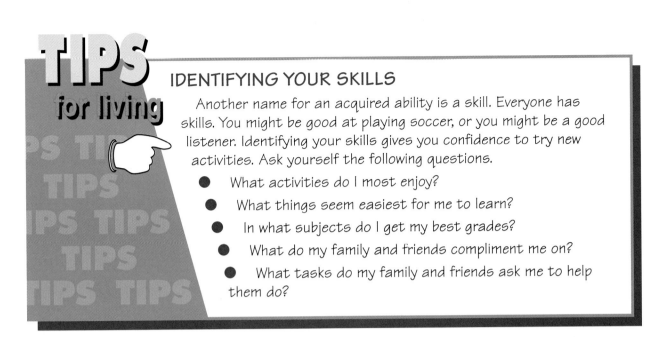

TIPS for living

IDENTIFYING YOUR SKILLS

Another name for an acquired ability is a skill. Everyone has skills. You might be good at playing soccer, or you might be a good listener. Identifying your skills gives you confidence to try new activities. Ask yourself the following questions.

- What activities do I most enjoy?
- What things seem easiest for me to learn?
- In what subjects do I get my best grades?
- What do my family and friends compliment me on?
- What tasks do my family and friends ask me to help them do?

on race, ethnic group, geographic location, or social class. You may not even think about your culture until you meet someone who speaks a different language at home or celebrates other holidays from yours.

Your culture may influence the food you eat or the holidays you celebrate. What might be some benefits of learning about other cultures?

Family Background

Your family has one of the strongest influences on the person you become. Are you an only child, or do you have brothers or sisters? Are you the oldest, the youngest, or in the middle? What activities do you do with family members? How important is spending time together with family members? These questions suggest some of the ways you are influenced by your family.

Experiences

Each person has a unique set of experiences. For example, you may have moved several times, and perhaps you have learned to play the flute. Your best friend has lived in the same house since she was born and excels in sports. These experiences affect a person's attitudes, achievements, and outlook on life. Experiences not only include the activities you do, but also the places you go and the friends you have. During your teen years, new experiences help you grow into a unique individual.

Roles

You may be a role model for someone else. How can you make sure that your role is a positive one?

What roles do you have? A **role** is *the way you behave when you interact with another person.* The roles you have determine how you relate to other people and how you act in various situations. For example, you may act silly when you are with your best friend but very mature when you are babysitting. You have many roles. At home you may be a daughter or a son and a brother or a sister. At school you may be a student, a best friend, and a team member. In the community you may be a volunteer for a recycling center or a member of a Scout troop. Your role varies, depending on whom you are interacting with.

You learn your roles by talking to and watching people who are important to you. **Role models** are *people who help you see what is expected of you and show you how to act in certain situations.* Role models can be parents, older siblings, relatives, teachers, coaches, or religious leaders. Who are some of your role models? How do you act as a role model to a younger sibling or neighbor?

One of a Kind

You share some traits—including the need for food, shelter, and love—with other people. You also have dreams, ideas, habits, and traits that are yours alone. All of the people, places, and events in your life have influenced the person you are now and the person you will become. Whether you are shy or outgoing, funny or serious, quiet or loud—you are a special, interesting, and unique person.

Although you share some things in common with other teens, you are a unique individual. What qualities do you have that make you different from your friends?

LESSON ONE *Review*

Using complete sentences, answer the following questions on a separate sheet of paper.

Reviewing Terms and Facts

1. Identify What are four influences that give you a unique identity?

2. List What are three ways your family influences the person you become?

3. Explain What effect do experiences have on people?

Thinking Critically

4. Distinguish What is the difference between inherited traits and acquired abilities? Give two examples of each.

5. Analyze Choose a person you think of as a positive role model. Explain what you admire about this person.

Applying Concepts

6. List ten of your most important characteristics. Decide what percentage of these traits are inherited, what percentage have been acquired with help from other people, and what percentage are a little bit of both. Draw a pie chart showing your results.

Understanding Yourself

WORDS TO KNOW

adolescence

personality

emotions

DISCOVER...

- how to understand yourself better.
- how adolescence is a time of change.
- constructive ways of dealing with emotions.

Ben is worried about himself. Some days he feels happy and cheerful one moment, and sad and restless the next. He is also concerned because he is shorter than most of his classmates. Do you ever have feelings like Ben's? These are normal feelings that occur during **adolescence** (a-duhl-E-suhns), *the period of great growth and change between childhood and adulthood.*

As you grow up, you will get to know yourself better and be comfortable with yourself. You will also become aware of how you see yourself and how others see you. This helps you understand your strengths and weaknesses. It gives you confidence to show off your positive qualities and encourages you to improve the things about yourself that you want to change.

Your Personality

Personality is *the sum total of a person's traits, feelings, attitudes, and habits.* Your personality shows in the way you look, the way you communicate, and the way you act. It is the part of you that you reveal to other people.

Your personality continues to grow and change throughout your life. It changes as you have new experiences and meet new people. You become a more interesting person when you develop your skills and talents, learn to do new things, and participate in school and community activities.

Everyone's personality is different. Perhaps you are very outgoing and friendly, while some of your friends are quiet and reserved. Do you enjoy spending time indoors reading a book, or do you prefer to be outdoors playing basketball? There is no right or wrong way to be. Learning more about yourself will help you appreciate and respect the differences in yourself and in other people.

Your Emotions

Do you remember how proud you felt when you scored the winning goal in a soccer game or got a good grade on your science project? Perhaps you remember how happy you were

No two people have the same personality. Why is it important to understand your own personality?

when your father praised you for keeping your room neat. An important part of your personality is related to your emotions. **Emotions** are *feelings, such as happiness,* *fear,* or *love.* By understanding your emotions and why they change, you will better understand yourself.

You have many emotions. You may feel pleased and excited when you do something well. Learning how to use a computer program or completing an English report, for example, would give you a feeling of pride and satisfaction. At other times you may feel sad or frustrated, such as when you have a disagreement with a friend or you cannot figure out a math problem. Depending on the situation, you may feel joyful, angry, proud, jealous, hurt, or loved. When was the last time you experienced each of these feelings?

One of the difficult things about emotions is that you may experience different ones at the same time. You may feel both excited and scared about being in the school play. You may feel proud that your sister was accepted by a college, yet sad that she will be going away. Having two different emotions at the same time makes it hard to sort out your feelings. It is a natural part of life that you sometimes feel confused or mixed up.

During adolescence you may develop close relationships with friends. What other emotional changes take place during adolescence?

Changes in Your Emotions

During adolescence you will be adjusting to many changes—both physical and emotional. Don't be surprised if your emotions seem stronger and harder to control. This is common, because your body systems are developing and changing. Your feelings may be hurt more easily. You may feel ignored or become irritated easily. Positive feelings can be stronger, too. For example, you may develop a closer relationship with a friend of the opposite gender.

Adjusting to new emotions can be challenging. Today you may laugh when someone teases you, but tomorrow teasing may upset you. Sometimes you will feel happy and want to share your joy with your friends. At other times you may want to be alone and not talk to anyone. When your moods are constantly changing like this, it may seem as if you lack control over your life. In fact, you can learn to handle your feelings. See Tips for Living, "Dealing With Your Emotions."

Controlling Your Emotions

Even though these new and changing emotions are difficult to understand, you should not let them rule your life.

TIPS for living

DEALING WITH YOUR EMOTIONS

It is normal to feel angry or sad sometimes. It's the way you handle your emotions that is important. Try these healthy ways to deal with your emotions.

- Admit how you feel. Try to figure out why you feel that way.
- Talk about your feelings with a family member, friend, teacher, or counselor.
- Write down your feelings in your journal.
- Work off your feelings by doing something physical, such as pounding a pillow or riding a bike.
- If you are angry with another person, wait until you have cooled off before speaking to him or her. Tell the person how you feel and what you need or want.

It is all right to feel angry, for example. However, if you yell at someone when you are angry, you may hurt that person's feelings and say something you will regret later. At times like these it helps to remember that you can have control over the way you react to situations.

Understanding Physical Changes

You must learn to adjust to not only the emotional changes that are taking place, but also the new physical changes. Physical changes in height, weight, and body shape occur rapidly during adolescence. You may have noticed that you or your friends seem to grow inches overnight. Sometimes the different parts of your body don't all grow at the same rate. Your feet may grow longer first. Other changes are taking place within your body, and the shape of your body changes.

Changes in Your Growth and Development

It can be frustrating when your body is constantly changing and growing. Just when you get used to it one way, it changes again. Adjusting to the rapid changes can be difficult. It can make you feel awkward and clumsy.

Everyone does not change and grow at the same rate. Some of your friends will grow taller before their bodies fill out. Others first put on weight and then grow taller. You might be concerned about being too tall or too short because your friends are medium height. Perhaps you wish your voice was deeper or your feet were smaller. Some people grow and change very quickly; others do so more slowly.

These changes can make you feel different from others around you. Since teens usually want to be like their peers, this can be a frustrating time. If you are the one who starts to grow first, you may feel embarrassed or out of place. Try not to worry—your classmates will soon catch up. On the other hand, if you are the one who starts to grow later, remember that you will soon catch up to the others.

Skills
IN ACTION

Getting Answers

You may wonder why you suddenly have acne, or why your moods are constantly changing. Where can you go for answers to your questions? Make a list of the names and phone numbers of adults you could ask for advice. Keep your personal "yellow pages" handy, and know there is always someone you can talk to.

Being Yourself

Although there are physical features that you can't change, such as your height, you can still look your best. By being well-groomed, showing good posture, and having a friendly attitude, you will emphasize your strengths.

While the teen years can often be confusing, they can also be exciting. During this time you are learning to control your varied emotions and to cope with rapid physical changes. You are learning more about yourself, which will prepare you for becoming an adult.

Everyone grows and changes at a different rate. What can you do to adjust to these changes?

LESSON TWO *Review*

Using complete sentences, answer the following questions on a separate sheet of paper.

Reviewing Terms and Facts

1. Vocabulary Define the term *adolescence*. Use it in an original sentence.

2. Vocabulary Define the term *personality*. What are three ways to develop your personality?

3. Describe List three physical changes that occur during adolescence.

Thinking Critically

4. List Identify three ways to control strong emotions, such as anger or jealousy.

5. Suggest What advice would you give to a friend who feels embarrassed because he is taller than his friends and classmates?

Applying Concepts

6. Think about a television show or movie you have seen in which a main character is an adolescent. What type of personality does the character display? Which emotions does he or she deal with? What, if anything, did you learn from this character? Write a paragraph or two in which you summarize your answers.

LESSON THREE
Your Self-Concept

WORDS TO KNOW

self-concept

self-esteem

self-confidence

constructive criticism

DISCOVER...

● how to build a positive self-concept.

● how to accept constructive criticism.

● how good health habits can contribute to a positive self-concept.

During the past month nothing seemed to go as Ramon planned. He did poorly on an important test and his baseball team lost the championship. Ramon is frustrated and discouraged. Have you ever had feelings similar to Ramon's?

How You See Yourself

During the teen years—and throughout your life—it is important to have a positive **self-concept,** or *mental picture of yourself.* Self-concept includes your views about your personality traits and about what activities you do well. Your self-concept is influenced by the people around you. It started forming when you were a child, and it continues developing throughout your life. Perhaps your sister teases you about the way you wear your hair, or your grandfather tells you that you are a good chess player. These comments affect your self-concept, or the image that you have of yourself.

Another term for self-concept is self-image. Your self-image does not always stay the same. It may change as the situation you are in changes. When you win a game or help a neighbor, for example, you feel really proud of yourself. On the other hand, if you get a poor grade or have an argument with a friend, you may not feel as good about yourself. Even people with a strong self-concept get discouraged with themselves when something does not work out as they planned.

Being recognized for an achievement makes you feel proud of yourself and gives your self-image a boost. In what other situations might your self-image improve?

A Positive You

Your success in life depends on developing a positive self-concept. It gives you the confidence to try new things. If you have a positive self-concept, you are willing to make new friends, go to new places, and try new activities. Why do you think that this is true?

Improving Your Self-Concept

It is possible to improve your self-concept, or the way you see yourself. Begin by concentrating on only a few traits at one time. Try to do something each day to help build the qualities you want to improve.

Here are some qualities that will help you build a positive self-concept.

- **Cheerfulness.** Being cheerful means being happy, friendly, and seeing the bright side of life.

- **Cleanliness and neatness.** Start each day by wearing fresh, clean clothes, and practicing good grooming habits. In addition to being neat with your personal appearance, take care of your possessions.

- **Honesty.** Telling the truth, being sincere, and being loyal are ways to show your honesty.

- **Thoughtfulness.** Think about how your actions affect other people. Help others without being asked. Use good manners, and remember to say "please" and "thank you."

When you have finished wearing your clothes or using your possessions, put them back where they belong. How do you think this will help your self-concept?

- **Responsibility.** Being responsible means doing your chores and your homework and coming home on time. It also involves accepting the consequences of your actions and decisions.

- **Resourcefulness.** Resourcefulness means knowing when to ask for help and where to find information when you need it.

- **Self-control.** Thinking before you act and setting limits are ways to practice self-control. It includes using your knowledge of right and wrong as a guide for your actions. Self-control could mean learning to control your anger or refusing to try tobacco, alcohol, or other drugs.

Building Self-Esteem

When you have a positive self-concept, you like yourself. In turn, you will develop **self-esteem,** or *the ability to respect yourself.* Respecting yourself helps you to use your own judgment, resist peer pressure, and set and achieve your goals. When you care about yourself, you do nothing to hurt yourself.

Gaining Self-Confidence

You need to have self-confidence to have a positive self-concept. When you have **self-confidence,** you have *faith in your abilities.* You gain self-confidence every time you do something well—even small daily achievements, such as improving your keyboarding skills or doing your homework.

You have probably noticed that success helps you gain confidence in your abilities. Learn to recognize the things you do well. Give yourself credit for your successes instead of dwelling on your mistakes. Be realistic about your expectations, and realize that no one does everything well.

Accepting Constructive Criticism

How do you feel when someone criticizes you? Do you become defensive or just ignore it? Learning to accept constructive criticism is a good way to improve your self-concept. **Constructive criticism** is *someone's evaluation of you that encourages you and helps you become a better person.* It helps you grow and improve yourself. For example, if your music teacher suggests a better song for your voice, you can follow the advice and improve your performance. Accepting and using constructive criticism will help you to improve your skills.

Taking Care of Your Health

Good health also promotes a positive self-concept. With good health habits you have energy and a healthful appearance, and you feel good. **Figure 1.2** on the next page shows ways to build good health habits.

Skills IN ACTION
Self-Image Booster

Take two minutes to list your strengths (honest), then your weaknesses (lazy). Begin by choosing which weakness you want to convert to a strength. Ask a friend for feedback as you practice your new skill.

Learning a new swimming stroke might give you the confidence to try out for the swim team. What activities do you do well?

Making Improvements

You can make a difference in your life by developing personal qualities. Getting to know yourself and accepting constructive criticism are two ways to begin. Once you identify the areas in your life that need improvement, you will be on your way toward a positive self-concept.

▲ Figure 1.2 Building Good Health Habits
Taking care of your health will contribute to your happiness and
well-being throughout your life.

LESSON THREE *Review*

Using complete sentences, answer the following questions
on a separate sheet of paper.

Reviewing Terms and Facts

1. Recall How does a positive self-concept
help you succeed?

2. List Name five qualities that help you
build a positive self-concept.

3. Identify What can you do to increase
your self-esteem?

Thinking Critically

4. Explain How is self-concept formed?

5. Apply Name qualities you have that help
promote a positive self-concept.

6. Analyze When might criticism not be
helpful?

Applying Concepts

7. Choose one health habit that you would
like to change. Make a list of ways that you
can work on changing the habit. For example, you might want to improve your health
by increasing your exercise or eating foods
low in fat. Then put your plan into action.

FRIENDS & FAMILY

YOUR OUTLOOK ON LIFE

You inherit physical characteristics from your parents. You may not realize it, but some of your attitudes as well as your outlook on life may also come from family members. Your own outlook on life, however, is something you can work on and change.

TRY THIS!

Do you think that you have a positive outlook on life? Why or why not? Make a list of ways you could become more of an optimist.

A Gl**O**bal View

CULTURAL CELEBRATIONS

Your culture influences you in many ways. It may influence your personality; the way you speak, dress, and act; and the way you express your emotions. Your culture may also influence the way you celebrate birthdays, holidays, and special occasions.

TRY THIS!

What is your cultural heritage? In what ways has it influenced the way you celebrate special occasions? Write your answers in your journal.

Consumer Focus

Drugstore Dilemma

Melinda, age 13, decided to start using a moisturizer when her skin became dry and flaky. She went to the drugstore, only to find half an aisle lined with moisturizers. Melinda was overwhelmed by all the possibilities. Which brand was the best?

Try This!

Discuss this problem with a small group of your classmates. Write a list of guidelines that teens could use when shopping for personal grooming products.

SCIENCE CONNECTION

PASS IT ON

You have probably heard people say things like "Mike has his grandfather's nose" or "Rosie looks just like her mother." These people were talking about heredity—the passing on of physical and mental traits from parents to their children.

Follow Up

1. Make a list of your physical characteristics. Which traits can you identify as coming from a parent? If you have brothers and sisters, which traits do you have in common with them?

2. Which of your abilities or skills did you inherit? Which have been influenced by your environment? Explain your answers.

Chapter Summary

- You are a unique individual.

- Your individual characteristics are a result of your heredity and environment, culture, family background, experiences, and roles.

- You have many roles in life—daughter or son, brother or sister, student or friend.

- Adolescence is a time of many changes, both physical and emotional.

- Your personality is a blend of all your traits, feelings, attitudes, and habits.

- Understanding and learning to handle your emotions can help to give you control over your life.

- A positive self-concept, or mental picture of yourself, is important for success in life.

- Having self-confidence and self-esteem will help you reach your goals.

- Learning to accept and use constructive criticism will help you improve your skills.

Words to Know

Using complete sentences, answer the following questions on a separate sheet of paper.

1. What is an *acquired* characteristic?

2. What is a *culture?* On what are cultures based?

3. Why is *adolescence* sometimes considered a mixture of childhood and adulthood?

4. List ten *emotions*.

5. What is the difference between *self-concept* and *self-esteem?*

6. Give an example of *constructive criticism.*

Review Questions

Using complete sentences, answer the following questions on a separate sheet of paper.

1. In what ways are people unique as well as similar?

2. Give an example of a characteristic that is influenced by both heredity and environment.

3. Why are role models important?

4. Why is it sometimes difficult to understand yourself during adolescence?

5. How does your personality grow and change throughout your life?

6. How can you gain control over your emotions?

7. Why is it important to build a positive self-concept?

8. How can you develop a positive self-concept?

9. How does a person with a positive self-concept react to compliments? Constructive criticism? Making mistakes?

10. In what way are good health habits related to a positive self-concept?

Thinking Critically

Using complete sentences, answer the following questions on a separate sheet of paper.

1. **Analyze** Why might teens be considered a cultural group?

2. **Apply** Give an example of a role you hope to have in the future. How might you prepare yourself for that role?

3. **Interpret** Why might teens' emotions be compared to a roller coaster?

4. **Explain** What might happen to your self-concept if you didn't deal with your emotions in a healthy way?

5. **Analyze** Why might teens with a poor self-concept use tobacco, alcohol, or other drugs?

Cooperative Learning

1. As a class, choose one aspect of a culture— such as food, clothing, jewelry, celebrations, or customs regarding learning from elders. In groups of three or four, select one culture and research this aspect of it. Share your findings with the class.

2. In small groups, discuss your favorite television characters. Make a list of their desirable and undesirable personality traits. Then discuss what each character could do to improve his or her personality.

Family & Community

1. Teens can be role models for younger brothers or sisters or children in the neighborhood. Think of ways you could set a good example for someone younger than yourself. Write a pledge to be a good role model, and then be sure to live up to your promise.

2. Families share inherited traits. They also share a cultural heritage. Learn more about traditions, customs, or events that are important to your family. With your family's permission, show the class an object that represents your cultural heritage.

Building A Portfolio

1. Divide a large sheet of paper into ten sections. In each section, write, draw, or paste something that illustrates a different aspect of your life. You might have a section for your hobbies, another for your achievements, another for your family, and so on. Add the illustration to your portfolio.

2. Write a letter to a real or imaginary teen who lives in a different part of the city, state, country, or world. Describe what life is like where you live and how you think your environment influences your personality. Your letter might be in the form of an audiotape or a videotape. Put a copy of your letter in your portfolio.

2

Everyday Living Skills

TEENS MAKING A DIFFERENCE
Improving a Neighborhood

Twelve-year-old Tanya Jenkins lives in a large city. When Tanya was younger, she played in a playground near her home. In the past few years, though, the playground fell into disrepair. The lot became overgrown with weeds and littered with trash. The swing set and jungle gym were no longer safe for children to use.

Tanya decided to do something about cleaning up the playground. With the permission of her teacher, Tanya got the help of her entire English class. The class spent one Saturday cleaning up the trash and pulling the weeds. To raise money for new playground equipment, the class held a bake sale and a flea market.

Today Tanya feels proud that she played an important part in helping to improve her neighborhood.

Try THIS!

Do you know of any volunteers who are working to make life better for the people in your community? Bring in newspaper articles describing their activities, or write your own account of their work.

25

Making a Good Impression

WORDS TO KNOW

impression

first impression

stereotype

maturity

empathy

DISCOVER...

- how to make a good impression.
- the disadvantages of stereotypes.
- the effects of a positive attitude.

Kelly and her brother Dan just moved to a new town. On their first day at school Kelly was polite and friendly. She wanted to make a good impression. Dan, on the other hand, started showing off and claiming to be the world's greatest soccer player. He was trying to impress people. Can you see the difference between trying to impress people and making a good impression? An **impression** is *an image you present or others present to you*. When you try to impress people, you pretend to be someone other than who you really are. When you make a good impression, you have presented yourself in the best way possible.

First Impressions

People form an opinion about you the first time they meet you. This *instant opinion, or image,* is called a **first impression.** It is based on certain clues, such as the way you look and talk and act. First impressions are important because they help people decide whether they want to know you better. What type of first impression do you make when you are considerate of others? In contrast, what do people think if you have poor manners?

When people judge you by only a few clues, the clues may be misleading. For example, you may wear a baseball cap but not like to play baseball. What other kinds of clues may mislead people about you?

First impressions are not always accurate. When people have a chance to get to know you better, they may change their opinion. Sometimes, however, the first impression is the only chance you have to make a good impression.

Try This!

General statements such as "All people who wear glasses are smart" or such descriptions as "Dumb jocks" are stereotypes. List stereotypes that you have heard people use. Then write a paragraph explaining why stereotypes should be avoided.

Avoiding Stereotypes

Sometimes people form opinions about you without even knowing you. They may expect you to act a certain way. *An idea or image formed in advance about all members of a group* is called a **stereotype.** The belief that all teens like rock music or that all elderly people are hard of hearing is an example of stereotyping. Some stereotypes are based on gender. For example, some people may think that all boys like sports or that all girls like to cook.

When people form their opinions of you based on a stereotype, their idea or image is usually unfair, untrue, or exaggerated. The only way for people to learn what you and others are really like is to get to know each person as an individual.

By talking and listening to someone, you can get to know that person as an individual. Why is this important?

Showing Good Behavior

You can make a good impression on others by being pleasant and sincere. Showing that you have confidence in yourself will make you more interesting to others.

Using good manners and being thoughtful of others help you create a good impression. Having good manners means more than just saying "please" and "thank you" or using the right fork when you eat. It means respecting other people's rights and helping them feel comfortable. Thinking about how your behavior affects others will help you practice good manners.

Being Mature

When you act maturely, you make a good impression on other people. **Maturity** means *making wise decisions, practicing self-control, and acting responsibly*. It means learning to express your feelings in a positive way and accepting responsibility for your actions. If you make a mistake, you don't get angry or defensive. Instead you know that making mistakes is part of the learning process.

Having a Positive Attitude

Have you ever wondered, "Why does this have to happen to me?" Most people feel that way sometimes. You can't

TIPS for living

BREAKING BAD HABITS

Bad habits, such as tapping your fingers or interrupting other people when they're talking, make a poor impression. Try the following tips to help you break a bad habit.

- Ask family members and trusted friends to help you identify a bad habit that you may not be aware of. Then have them give you a secret signal every time they see you practicing your habit.

- Figure out why you have the habit. Maybe you twist your hair around your finger when you're nervous. Try to remove the reason for the habit. For example, studying more for a test will help you feel less nervous.

- Find an acceptable substitute behavior. For example, try breath mints in place of biting your nails.

When something goes wrong, try to keep a positive attitude. How is this teen showing a positive attitude?

always control the things that happen to you. However, you can control how you react to the things that happen. When something unpleasant happens, you can choose to be positive and look on the bright side. You can choose to make the best of a bad situation. For example, if you don't make the school band, you might decide to spend more time practicing and try again next year. You might decide to try out for the school play instead. A positive attitude will help you make a good impression on teachers, friends, and parents.

Getting Along with Others

Getting along well with other people is an important part of the impression you make on others. If you can get along with your family, friends, classmates, teachers, and community members, you will make a good impression on them. Here are some qualities that will help you get along with other people.

- **Consideration.** Think about other people and their feelings. Treat people the same way you would like to be treated.

- **Friendliness.** Be pleasant and friendly. Greet people. Invite new students to join you and your friends for lunch. Let others know that you want to be a friend.

- **Cooperation.** Pitch in and do your share of work. At home you can keep your room clean. At school you can do your part on group assignments.

- **Reliability.** Do you do what you say you will do? People like to know they can depend on you. Prove to them that you will keep your word.

- **Understanding.** Try to understand how other people feel. Show **empathy,** or *the ability to put yourself in another person's place.* Respect that person's viewpoint and feelings.

Cooperating is an important part of getting along with others. How do you cooperate with others at home and at school?

A Lasting Impression

As you have learned, people form an impression of you as soon as they meet you. Often that first impression lasts for a long time. You can see why it is important to make sure that the first impression is positive. You can continue to make a good impression by having a positive attitude and practicing the skills for getting along well with other people.

LESSON ONE *Review*

Using complete sentences, answer the following questions on a separate sheet of paper.

Reviewing Terms and Facts

1. Compare What is the difference between making a good impression and trying to impress someone?

2. Vocabulary Define the term *stereotype.* Give an example.

3. Describe What does it mean to have good manners?

4. Identify What are three characteristics of a mature person?

5. List Name five qualities that can help you get along with other people.

Thinking Critically

6. Explain Why is a first impression so important?

7. Evaluate In general, do you think that you have a positive attitude? Why or why not? How could you develop one?

Applying Concepts

8. Look through magazines and newspapers to find examples of cartoon characters who are stereotyped. Identify the feature the cartoonist has exaggerated to produce the stereotype, and share your findings with the class.

Communicating with Others

DISCOVER...

- skills that will help you communicate better with others.
- verbal and nonverbal communication techniques.
- the importance of being an effective listener.

Dylan likes to talk on the telephone. Jason smiles and waves to his next-door neighbor. Amber confides all her hopes and dreams to her best friend, Rachel. How do you communicate with other people? Learning how to communicate effectively takes effort, but it has many rewards.

WORDS TO KNOW

communication

nonverbal communication

body language

conversation

gossip

Types of Communication

There are many forms of communication. **Communication** is *the process of sending and receiving messages*. Communication can be verbal or nonverbal.

Verbal Communication

Verbal communication begins with selecting the right words to express yourself. Next, it is important to be honest. Say what you really think and feel, but be polite. Other guidelines for effective verbal communication include the following:

- **Speak for yourself.** Make "I" statements. Talk about your own experiences and feelings. Don't assume that other people know what you think, how you feel, or what you want. You have to tell them.

- **Avoid speaking for others.** Don't assume that you know what other people think, how they feel, or what they want. Ask them.

- **Be clear and direct.** Tone of voice reveals your feelings. You send mixed messages if your tone does not match the words you are using. Mixed messages are confusing.

- **Be aware of your listener.** Check to see that your listener understands what you are saying.

  - **Ask questions.** Ask "who," "what," "where," "when," and "how" questions. These help others share their thoughts and feelings.

Talking on the telephone is one way to communicate verbally. Why do you think that it is especially important to speak clearly when using the telephone?

Nonverbal Communication

Much of our communication is **nonverbal communication,** or *messages sent without using words*. When you use nonverbal communication, you show how you feel about yourself and others. **Figure 2.1** shows some forms of nonverbal communication.

Touching. Touching communicates through physical contact. A pat on the back says, "Good job!"

Body language. You communicate a lot through body language, or the look on your face, gestures, and body stance. Sometimes you use body language as a substitute for words.

Personal space. Your personal space is like an invisible bubble that surrounds you. You use the space around you to communicate how you want to relate to others.

Physical appearance. Your posture and appearance are some of the most powerful forms of nonverbal communication. Your appearance can convey your self-image.

Figure 2.1 Forms of Nonverbal Communication

Nonverbal communication is an important way to convey messages. What forms of nonverbal communication do you use?

The Importance of Listening

The ability to listen is just as important as the ability to express yourself. Studies indicate that 60 percent of the time that you are communicating is spent listening. If you are a poor listener, you are probably a poor communicator. Listening is not the same as hearing. When you hear, you are aware of the words being said. When you listen, you try to understand the message.

Listening is one of the hardest communication skills to learn. You can improve your listening skills by using the following guidelines.

- Give your full attention to the speaker, and make eye contact.

- Concentrate on what the speaker is saying, not on what you will say next.

- Show your interest by leaning toward the speaker and nodding.

- Listen for the overall meaning, not just the details.

- Remember to notice nonverbal cues.

- Avoid making quick judgments.

- Resist distractions.

- Do not interrupt. Ask questions only when necessary.

- Give active feedback to indicate you have understood.

Having a Conversation

Conversation is *the sharing of ideas, thoughts, and feelings*. It is a two-way street. You must be willing to express yourself as well as to listen to others.

For a conversation to be interesting, it is important for each person to have a chance to talk. You have probably been bored by a situation in which one person took over the conversation. Keep it lively by including others.

Asking Questions

You can draw others into conversation by finding out what their interests are. Most people like to talk about television, movies, and current events. They usually like to talk about their own experiences, too.

When someone is speaking, give that person your full attention. Why is listening such an important skill to learn?

Asking good questions helps you find out about other people's interests. Ask questions that give people something definite to talk about. Consider the following example: Rena asks, "Do you like baseball?" Eric answers, "Yes." End of conversation. It has nowhere to go.

Suppose Rena asks, "What did you think of the game today?" If Eric is interested in baseball, he will have something definite to say. The conversation is off to a good start.

Avoid asking "why" questions. A question such as "Why did you change your mind?" forces the other person to explain or defend his or her actions. You also should avoid questions that lead the other person. For instance, the question "Don't you think that...?" is really a statement of what you think. It is designed to get the other person to agree with you.

Avoiding Problem Areas

Do you know people who gossip? **Gossip** is *talking about other people and their personal lives*. Gossip can destroy friendships and ruin a person's reputation. Gossip can also turn into rumors that spread and can lead to violent confrontations. By avoiding gossip and rumors in your conversations, you can show that you are a mature and responsible person.

Gossip can cause many problems in relationships. What would you do if someone wanted you to spread gossip?

LESSON TWO *Review*

Using complete sentences, answer the following questions on a separate sheet of paper.

Reviewing Terms and Facts

1. List Name four forms of nonverbal communication.

2. Vocabulary Define the term *body language*. Give an example.

3. Explain Why are gossip and rumors dangerous?

Thinking Critically

4. Evaluate Which of the listening skills do you think you do well? Which do you need to work on? Explain your answers.

5. Analyze Why is it important to avoid asking "why" questions?

Applying Concepts

6. Divide into groups of three or four students. One student should locate and read aloud the first paragraph or two from a newspaper article. After listening, the other students in the group should write down answers to the following questions: "Who, what, where, when, how?" Compare your answers to those of the other people in your group to see who was listening effectively.

LESSON THREE
Being a Citizen and a Leader

DISCOVER...

- ways to build and demonstrate your citizenship and leadership skills.
- how group members can work together to achieve goals.

On Saturdays Selena helps out at a community recycling center. Kyle picks up groceries for his elderly neighbor. Have you ever volunteered? A **volunteer** is *a person who donates time and energy without pay to do a service for others*. Being a volunteer has many benefits. The most important one is that it makes you feel good about yourself. Volunteers also gain valuable experience and the sense of accomplishment that comes from a job well done.

Being a Citizen

Why does being a volunteer make you feel good? When you have helped out, you discover that what you have given of yourself is helpful to another person. This gives you a sense of self-worth. Many organizations, including museums, hospitals, and nursing homes, rely on help from volunteers.

There are many ways you can help others and volunteer your talents and skills. For example, you can collect used clothing for the needy or hand out magazines and newspapers to people in a hospital or nursing home. Teaching computer skills or giving piano lessons to a neighbor is another way you can volunteer.

When you volunteer, you show that you are a good citizen. A **citizen** is a *member of a community, such as a city, state, or country.* There are many other ways to be a good citizen, such as offering to work as part of a team. When people use **teamwork,** *everyone in the group cooperates and works together to reach a goal.* For example, you use teamwork and demonstrate your citizenship skills when you

- participate in a school fund-raiser.

- join the student council.

- pitch in to help your family do yard work.

- take part in a walkathon.

This teen is volunteering his skills by reading to young children. What are some other ways to volunteer?

37

The examples just mentioned are ways of showing your citizenship skills by working as part of a team. However, some things that you do by yourself also show your citizenship skills. For example, you can

- take a moment to pick up litter and discard it in the proper place.

- return lost items to the lost-and-found department or to the rightful owner.

- care for pets when neighbors go out of town.

You can show your citizenship skills by pitching in and doing your share of the work. In what community-sponsored events have you participated?

What other ways can you think of to show your citizenship skills?

Whether you demonstrate your citizenship skills in a group or alone, being a good citizen helps you in many ways. It gives you a sense of belonging and a feeling of pride. You are able to share community facilities, such as libraries, parks, and museums. In addition, you are able to develop skills that will help throughout your lifetime and possibly even lead you into a career.

Citizenship Skills

It is easy to be a good citizen if you remember these three guidelines:

- **Do your share.** Offer to pitch in and help. Look for ways that you can lend a hand to family members, neighbors, teachers, and friends. Volunteer to help at school or in your community. Get involved in a community-sponsored event, such as a park cleanup, Neighborhood Watch, or recycling campaign. Ask teachers and neighbors what you can do to lend a hand.

- **Show respect for others.** Treat them as you—and they—would like to be treated. For example, wait your turn instead of trying to get to the front of a line. Give others in your family a chance to use the telephone. Speak respectfully to adults, such as grandparents, teachers, and police officers. Greeting adults and calling them "Mr.," "Ms.," or "Mrs." is another way to show your respect. What other ways to be courteous can you think of?

Remember to show respect to everyone, not just people you know well or especially like. Help all students. Make new students feel comfortable, and introduce them to other people. If someone holds different values from yours, be open and accepting. If you disagree with someone, give that person a fair chance to explain his or her opinion.

- **Take good care of shared property.** Be as careful with a library book or park equipment as you would be with your own possessions. Then the next person will be able to use and enjoy them too. The same is true for other property that you share, such as recreation areas, the school building, and streets and sidewalks.

Being a Leader

Every group needs a **leader,** *a person with the ability to guide and motivate others.* Leadership is the direction, or guidance, from the leader that helps a group accomplish its goals.

Sometimes leaders are chosen or elected. For example, the captain of your hockey team, your student body officers, and the mayor of your community were probably elected.

At other times the job of a leader is not a formal one. For example, when you organize a birthday party for a friend or get your siblings to help rake the leaves without being asked, you are being a leader.

Leadership Skills

Sometimes leaders are out in front of the team, showing the way. At other times they may be in the background, encouraging others. At all times leaders must use good communication skills and know how to work with people. **Figure 2.2** on the next page shows some ways to build leadership skills.

Skills IN ACTION

Volunteering

Volunteering gives you a chance to meet new people and learn new things. Make a list of your skills and interests. Then match your skills and interests with a volunteer job.

- Do you enjoy exercise? Mow lawns or shovel walks for an elderly neighbor.
- Can you play a musical instrument? Play your instrument for residents of a nursing home.
- Do you like to be outdoors? Deliver flyers for community organizations.

> **Serve as part of the team, not the boss.** Get everyone involved. Ask for and listen to everyone's opinion. Let group members help set goals and make decisions.

Figure 2.2
Building Leadership Skills
Being a good leader involves working with others to accomplish a goal.

Working as a Team

A group, such as a family, a school, or a community, needs all of its members to work together successfully to achieve its goals. Without the cooperation and support of all members, a group cannot operate effectively.

It is up to you to decide how you can best contribute. For example, if your club is organizing a fund-raiser, think of a few of the tasks involved: deciding on the date, deciding on the type of fund-raising event, getting people to help.

Ask yourself: "How can I best contribute to this effort? Then volunteer your services!

Developing Your Skills

Developing your team-member and leadership skills is an important part of becoming an adult. When you use your skills to help others, you feel good about yourself and also gain valuable experience.

Encourage team spirit. Be enthusiastic and positive. Use effective communication skills.

Show appreciation. Thank people who help the group reach its goal. Tell people that you appreciate their efforts.

LESSON THREE — *Review*

Using complete sentences, answer the following questions on a separate sheet of paper.

Reviewing Terms and Facts

1. Identify What are some benefits of being a volunteer?

2. Vocabulary Define the term *teamwork*. Use it in an original sentence.

3. Explain Why is it important to take good care of shared property?

4. Identify List three ways to build leadership skills.

Thinking Critically

5. Give Examples Name two ways that you show your citizenship skills.

6. Analyze Why is being a good team member just as important as being a good leader?

Applying Concepts

7. Select a person whom you consider to be a leader. Write a list of the leadership qualities that you think the person has. Is this person a formal or informal leader? Write a list of guidelines that other people could use to develop leadership skills.

LESSON FOUR
Managing Your Life

management

evaluate

resource

talent

prioritize

procrastinate

DISCOVER...

- the basic steps of the management process.
- resources that can be used to help you reach your goals.
- time-management tools and techniques.

Megan and her friend Theresa are opposites. While Theresa always has her homework done on time, Megan is often working on hers until the last minute. Theresa is never late to student council meetings, but Megan usually rushes in and is often unprepared. Theresa gets more accomplished than Megan because Theresa practices good management skills. **Management** is *using what you have to get what you want, being organized, and planning ahead.*

Learning Management Skills

People who manage well accomplish more with greater ease. They use their time, money, and energy wisely. Theresa is a good manager. So are Katie and Hassan. Katie has learned to save money by putting part of her earnings into a savings account. Hassan gets to school a half hour early so that he can work in the computer lab.

Management Steps

You can be a good manager if you learn to follow certain basic steps. These steps can be followed if you are writing a report or organizing a bake sale for the school band.

- **Step 1: Decide on your goal.** Determine what your goal is, and write it down on a piece of paper. Maybe you want to earn $50 or complete your science project. Writing down your goal helps you commit to it.

- **Step 2: Make a plan.** Decide how you want to achieve the goal. Maybe the goal can be broken into smaller parts, or short-term goals, that are easier to reach. For example, if you want to earn $40, perhaps you will plan to earn $20 this week and $20 next week.

- **Step 3: Put the plan into action.** Begin working on your plan. If you are going to try out for the cheerleading squad, don't just talk about it—practice.

- **Step 4: Evaluate the results.** The last step is to evaluate the outcome of your plan. When you **evaluate,** you *determine the value of what you accomplished.* Are you satisfied with the way your plan worked? If not, what would you do differently the next time?

By learning the basic steps of management, you can accomplish tasks more easily. What is the first step of management?

Managing Your Resources

To be a good manager you must make full use of the resources that you have. A **resource** is *a source of information or expertise that you can use to help you meet your goals.* The three types are personal resources, material resources, and community resources.

Your skills and talents are part of your personal resources. How can you improve your skills?

Personal Resources

Personal resources are time, energy, knowledge, skills and talents, and people. How well you use your personal resources makes a difference in how successful you are and how much you accomplish.

- **Time.** Everyone has 24 hours a day. Much of this time is spent eating, sleeping, grooming, studying, working, and playing. The time that is left over can be used for special activities. Learn to use time wisely.

- **Energy.** Energy is the power or ability to be active. It has to do with the strength of the body and mind to do things—to work and play. Much of your energy depends on getting enough sleep, eating nutritious foods, and following a regular exercise program. Your attitude toward what has to be done also affects how energetic you may feel.

- **Knowledge.** Knowledge is information and understanding. Throughout your life you will continue to learn.

- **Skills and talents.** A skill is an ability that comes from training or practice. You have reading, writing, math, and computer skills. You may also have other skills, such as the ability to play the piano, which you learned from taking lessons. Talents are different from skills. A **talent** is *natural ability*. You may have a talent for drawing, singing, or playing tennis. In order to develop your talent, however, you need to practice and train.

- **People.** People are valuable resources. Strong relationships with family and friends will provide help and support all your life. The encouragement of family and friends can help you gain confidence and strengthen your self-concept.

Material Resources

Material resources are possessions, objects, and money. They make it easier to do what you want to do. Your personal possessions might include a bike, a stereo, or books. Objects might include a refrigerator, a table, or a microwave oven.

How do these possessions and objects help you do what you want to do? Personal possessions give you enjoyment and satisfaction. Riding your bike and listening to your stereo are a few ways that you gain enjoyment from your possessions. Objects make life easier. For example, using a washing machine to wash clothes is easier than washing them by hand.

Community Resources

Every community provides a variety of resources for its citizens to use. These include schools, hospitals, and police and fire departments. Among other community resources are youth programs, parks, and recreational facilities. Some communities have interesting places to visit, such as museums or important historic buildings.

Communities also provide resources for people who have special kinds of problems. Most communities offer programs for the homeless, the elderly, people with low income, and people who have problems with alcohol and other drugs. There are also programs to protect battered spouses and abused children.

Using Resources

There are several ways to obtain resources that you may not have. Resources can be traded or substituted. For example, you can use your time and energy to mow lawns for pay. Then you can use the money to buy a CD player. You might trade your knowledge and skill by tutoring a friend in math in exchange for guitar lessons.

Sometimes you can substitute one resource for another. If you want some posters for your room, for example, you could

Communities provide resources, such as parks, where people can enjoy many types of activities. What resources does your community provide?

use your money resources to buy them. You could also substitute your personal resources of time, energy, and skills for money and make the posters yourself.

Managing Your Time

Using good time management skills will help you in all areas of your life. You will have more time for special activities that you want to do, such as playing basketball or starting a stamp collection. You won't constantly be late or forget to do important tasks. You will have more time for yourself and others.

Time Management Tools

Calendars, lists, and schedules help people keep track of activities and get more done. It doesn't matter what method you use as long as it works well for you.

- **Calendars.** On the calendar make a note of upcoming activities or appointments; important dates, such as birthdays and holidays; and other events that you want to remember. At a glance you can check to see what upcoming events are planned.

- **Lists.** Some people use a list each day as a reminder of tasks to complete. Once a day or once a week, you can make a "To-Do List" for the next day or week. As you complete each task, you can cross it off the list and see how much you have accomplished.

- **Time Schedules.** A time schedule is a list of hours in the day with tasks to be done filled in at the right time. It could also be a chart that combines the days of the week and the hours of the day.

Time Management Problems

Time management includes dealing with problems that may arise. You may find that two activities occur at the same time. If you cannot make room for both or change the time for one, you may have to make a choice. This will be difficult if

Making a "To-Do List" is one way to keep track of the tasks you need to accomplish. How do you keep track of your activities?

you must choose between two things you really want to do. Your choice may be between play rehearsals and gymnastics practice. Think about what is most important to you, and make a choice. Then act on your decision.

Sometimes you have several things you want to accomplish during a day. It may be difficult to know where to begin. In this case, you can *rank the tasks in order of importance,* or **prioritize** them. If you are using a "To-Do List," put an **A, B,** or **C** next to each task. Activities marked with an **A** are top-priority items. They need to be done first. **B** activities are completed next. **C** activities are the least important activities. If they are not done, they can wait until the next day.

Another challenge is dealing with unexpected changes. Sometimes schedules and lists do not work out exactly as planned. A friend may have to cancel the shopping trip to the mall you had scheduled. The rain may prevent you from raking leaves. Whatever the case, stay flexible. Make the most of your time by having ideas for alternate activities.

Figure 2.3 Timesaving Techniques
There are many ways to save time. What other ways can you think of?

Establish daily routines for eating and sleeping. Set a specific time each day for study and exercise.

Avoid interruptions. If a friend calls while you are doing your homework, tell your friend that you will call back when you have finished.

Learn to say no. If your friends want you to go to the movies but you haven't finished writing your report, you need to say no.

Divide big jobs into small tasks. For example, you can study for a test for 30 minutes before dinner and 30 minutes after dinner.

Simplify work. If something takes too much time, try to figure out ways to reduce the time.

Stick with a task until it is done. When you're cleaning your room, don't stop to read a magazine you picked up off the floor.

Do two tasks at the same time. For example, you can memorize a poem for English class while washing the car.

Saving Time

As you begin to pay more attention to time, you will find many ways to save it. **Figure 2.3** on page 47 gives some suggestions that can save you time each day.

Making Time Count

Have you ever turned on the television to watch one show and later realized that you were watching television for hours? Perhaps you have spent a lot of time looking for your math book, only to find it under a stack of papers. Precious time can be lost. Here are some ways to avoid wasting time.

- **Avoid putting things off.** If you **procrastinate,** or *put things off,* you can waste a lot of time thinking and worrying about the task you need to do. Usually the job itself doesn't take very long when you finally do it.

- **Get organized.** Almost any task goes faster when you are organized. Before you begin the task, gather the tools or equipment you need and find out how to do the task.

- **Take care of yourself.** If you have ever thought that you could make more time by sleeping less, you have probably found out that it doesn't work. It is hard to concentrate when you are tired. Often you end up getting less done, instead of more, because you are tired.

You can avoid wasting time by organizing everything you need before you start a task. What are some other ways to avoid wasting time?

LESSON FOUR *Review*

Using complete sentences, answer the following questions on a separate sheet of paper.

Reviewing Terms and Facts

1. List Name the four steps of the management process.

2. Identify What are three types of resources?

3. Vocabulary What is the difference between *skills* and *talents*?

4. Name List three time management tools.

5. Recall Name four timesaving techniques.

Thinking Critically

6. Explain What can you do if you don't have the resources that you need?

7. Analyze What are some reasons why people might procrastinate?

Applying Concepts

8. Think of a project you want to complete in the next few weeks. Write a plan for how you will manage the project. Include the resources you will use and a time schedule.

Consumer Focus TECHNOLOGY

CASCADE RECYCLED LEGAL PAD

Saving Time

Not long ago a television ad showed nervous, upset people rushing into a bank and asking to withdraw time. "I need another 24 hours," a worried customer says to the bank teller.

Try This!

Do you use time wisely? Keep a list for one day of exactly how you spend your time. Then think of ways that you might manage your time more effectively.

"Netiquette"

People who communicate via on-line computer services and the Internet are expected to follow certain guidelines, called "netiquette." For example, before asking a basic question, polite online users should "FAQ-check," or look up "Frequently Asked Questions."

Try This!

Find out more about modern technology and good manners. Write your own rules of etiquette for renting videos, talking on cellular phones, or listening to portable stereos. Share the guidelines with your classmates.

FRIENDS & FAMILY

THE EXPERIENCE GAP

Teens don't always understand their parents' world, and parents sometimes forget what it's like to be a teen. You can help to close "the experience gap."

TRY THIS!

Try taking a few minutes each day to exchange experiences with your parents. It may help you and your parents to communicate and understand each other better.

SOCIAL STUDIES CONNECTION

EVERYDAY CITIZENS

Citizens of the United States have many rights, including freedom of speech and freedom of religion. In exchange for these rights, they have certain responsibilities. The government, for example, requires citizens to obey laws and pay taxes. Citizens have other responsibilities that are not required by law. These include the duty to vote and the duty to keep informed.

Follow Up

1. What things can you learn in school that will help prepare you for participating in your community?

2. As a class or in small groups, identify a problem, such as graffiti. Find out if anything is being done about it. If so, join the effort. If not, plan a way to meet the need or help solve the problem and carry out your plan. Write an account of the group's efforts for a local newspaper.

2 REVIEW

Chapter Summary

- Making a good first impression is important. Being mature, having a positive attitude, and getting along with others are all ways of making a good impression.

- To get along with other people, show consideration, friendliness, cooperation, reliability, and understanding.

- By practicing good communication skills—choosing the right words and using appropriate nonverbal communication—you send a clear, direct message.

- Nonverbal communication is any message sent without words. It may be body language, the use of personal space, touching, or physical appearance.

- Conversation is a two-way street that involves listening as well as talking.

- Doing volunteer work is a good way to show your citizenship and to develop team-member and leadership skills.

- Being a good citizen and leader means using teamwork.

- Being a good citizen includes doing your share, showing respect for others, and taking good care of shared property.

- Good management requires deciding on a goal, making a plan, putting the plan into action, and evaluating the results.

- Using your personal, material, and community resources will help you achieve your goals.

- Time management tools, such as calendars, lists, and time schedules, can help you make the best use of your time.

▶ Words to Know

Using complete sentences, answer the following questions on a separate sheet of paper.

1. What is the relation between a *stereotype* and a *first impression?*

2. How might you show *empathy* for a friend who didn't make the team?

3. What are three types of *body language?*

4. Describe the characteristics of a good *conversation.*

5. Give an example of *volunteers* in your community.

6. Name the three types of material *resources.*

7. What does it mean to *prioritize* tasks?

▶ Review Questions

Using complete sentences, answer the following questions on a separate sheet of paper.

1. How could a teen with the latest clothes and hairstyle still make a poor impression?

2. Why is it important to treat people as individuals rather than stereotyping?

3. Why is listening such an important communication skill?

4. How does asking questions promote good conversation?

5. Why is being able to work in a group an important part of being a good citizen?

6. How does being a good citizen benefit you?

7. In what ways can other people be a resource in meeting your goals?

8. What are the benefits of good time management?

Thinking Critically

Using complete sentences, answer the following questions on a separate sheet of paper.

1. **Describe** In what types of situations would it be especially important for teens to make a good first impression?

2. **Analyze** What stereotypes might adults have of teens? What can be done to break these stereotypes?

3. **Contrast** In what ways does a conversation on the telephone differ from a conversation that takes place in person?

4. **Explain** What responsibilities do citizens have to their leaders?

5. **Suggest** How could you show your consideration for other people's time?

Cooperative Learning

1. In small groups, role-play ways in which teens might make a good impression in various situations. The situations might include showing understanding and empathy for a new student or meeting a friend's parents

for the first time. Try to show good communication skills.

2. As a class or in small groups, plan and carry out a project to meet a need in your school. Use the management process to guide your planning.

Family & Community

Try having a family "roundtable" discussion once a week. Gather everyone in one room. Go around the group and give each person a chance to report on his or her activities during the past week. Encourage family members to talk by using good listening skills and body language.

Building A Portfolio

1. Have a conversation with a parent or other adult. Ask the person about his or her experiences as a teen. Tell the person about your life as a teen. You might share photos and other souvenirs, such as school yearbooks. With the other person's permission, tape-record the conversation. Put the tape in your portfolio and listen to it again in the next few weeks. Reviewing the tape will remind you of how to use your communication skills.

2. Take an inventory of your resources. Divide a sheet of paper into three columns: Personal Resources, Material Resources, and Community Resources. List the resources you have in each column. Place the inventory sheet in your portfolio. The next time you have a goal to accomplish, use your inventory sheet to remind you of your resources.

3

Steps to Success

TEENS MAKING A DIFFERENCE
Helping Others

Thirteen-year-old Keesha James and her friends are popular visitors at the Twin Oaks Nursing Home. When Keesha's grandmother moved to the nursing home, Keesha started visiting her. She spent time playing cards with her.

One Saturday, Keesha brought a few friends with her. When some of the other people in the nursing home saw Keesha's grandmother and the girls playing cards, they joined in the game too. Everyone had such a good time that the teens decided to visit the nursing home every other Saturday.

The teens have made many new friends at the nursing home. They enjoy making the residents happy and seeing their smiling faces.

Try THIS!

Start a collection of newspaper articles that show teens helping others. Put the articles in your portfolio. Circle the activities that you would like to do.

LESSON ONE
What's Important to You?

WORDS TO KNOW

needs

potential

wants

values

refusal skills

DISCOVER...

- the difference between wants and needs.
- the importance of identifying your personal values.
- the influence of your values on your actions.

Can you list the things that are important to you? You might think of a good family life, close friends, and enough food each day. Other teens might add having enough spending money or the chance to play on the hockey team to their list of things that are important to them. If you know what is important to you, it is easier to set goals and to achieve happiness in life.

Basic Needs

You share the same basic needs that all people have. **Needs** are *things that you have to have in order to live*. There are different types of needs. Physical needs are basic to your survival and well-being. They include air, food, water, sleep, a place to live, and clothing.

Remember how pleased you were to see all your friends on the first day of school? You have emotional needs, too. Emotional needs include your need to belong and to be accepted by other people. Getting along with other people is an important need that everyone has. Another emotional need is the need to be safe and secure. That means feeling comfortable and protected from harm. The need to be loved and the need to be respected and recognized for your work and your actions are also emotional needs. When your emotional needs are met, you feel good about yourself.

Another need that you share with other people is the need to reach your full potential. **Potential** is *the capacity to grow and develop*. When you strive to reach your full potential, you use your skills, talents, and abilities to try to be everything you are capable of becoming.

Wants

Wants are different from needs. **Wants** are *things that you would like to have but that are not necessary for survival*. You may want the latest CD, but you can live without it.

Sometimes people confuse wants and needs. Have you ever wanted something so much that you convinced yourself that you really needed it? Perhaps you felt that you could not live without a new camera. Did you really need it, though, or was it something you simply wanted to have? Wants are not basic to your survival as food and water are.

Values

The way you satisfy your needs and wants is based on your **values,** *ideas about right and wrong and about what is important in your life*. Most people share common values, such

Skills IN ACTION

Acting on Your Values

It's not always easy to act on your values—to do the right thing. One helpful idea is to practice what you will say or do in difficult situations. Think of a situation in which your values might be challenged. Then write a short skit to show how you stand up for what you believe is important.

as a good family life, freedom, honesty, trust, and health. Other values are individual, such as being a good student and playing a sport well.

Sharing Values

Many of your values come from your family and from other people who are important to you, such as teachers and religious leaders. Like most young people, you probably grew up sharing your family's values. You learned values from your family related to such things as food, money, religion, education, and marriage. Perhaps your family placed a value on traditions, such as how birthdays and holidays are celebrated.

A good family life is a common value shared by most people. What are some other common values?

As you get older, you may begin to add other values. Some of these values will come from your environment, the people and the things around you. For instance, if your community starts a recycling campaign, you may learn to value reusing and recycling in your home.

Differences in Values

People have different values because their interests and experiences vary and because they come from diverse backgrounds. What values do you have that differ from the values of your friends?

The way you prioritize, or rank, your values may also be different from the way others rank their values. For example, some people put a high priority on exercising regularly; some don't. Some of your friends may work extra hard at getting good grades; some may care little about grades. You can learn to respect other people's values and priorities even though these values and priorities are different from yours. In return, other people should respect your values and priorities.

Your Own Value System

It is important to develop your own set of values based on what you believe to be right or wrong. Knowing what is important to you will help you make decisions about your personal life and your career.

As you develop your value system, you may notice that some of your values are in conflict with each other. For example, if getting good grades is important to you, you may want to spend the afternoon finishing your math assignment. What if your friends are going to the movies and they encourage you to join them? You will have to decide which value is more important—completing your math homework and turning it in on time or being with your friends.

At times, your values may also be in conflict with other people's values. To remain true to what you believe is right and wrong, you may need to use **refusal skills,** or *ways to say no effectively*. **Figure 3.1** gives examples of refusal skills.

**Figure 3.1
Refusal Skills**
Sometimes you will need to use refusal skills to stay true to your beliefs and values.

- ➤ State exactly how you feel, directly and honestly.
- ➤ Do not apologize for your decisions—or for your values.
- ➤ Use direct eye contact to show that you mean what you say.
- ➤ Use a firm yet friendly tone of voice.
- ➤ Use the other person's name.
- ➤ Suggest an option that is more acceptable to you.
- ➤ Avoid compromise, which can be a slow way of saying yes.

Try This!

Most people have only a few real needs but lots of wants. Practice telling the difference by making a back-to-school shopping list. Divide the list into two columns—"Needs" and "Wants." Estimate how much money you would save if you bought only the items in your "Needs" column.

Some of your values—such as freedom and health—will be important to you all your life. Other values may become more or less important as you have new experiences and meet new people. For example, you may learn to value the outdoors as a result of taking a science class in school. You will want your life to include the values that are the most important to you.

Your values serve as guides to your actions. For example, if you value honesty, you will not lie to a friend. If you value your family, you will help out at home. If you value excellence as a singer, you will practice. Your values help you decide what to do and how to act.

Your Values and Your Life

Your values are influenced by your family, friends, and environment. When you decide on your personal values, you will be able to satisfy your needs and wants in ways that contribute to a happy, successful life.

LESSON ONE *Review*

Using complete sentences, answer the following questions on a separate sheet of paper.

Reviewing Terms and Facts

1. Identify List three kinds of basic needs, and give an example of each.

2. Explain What does reaching your full potential mean?

3. Vocabulary What is the difference between *needs* and *wants*?

4. List Name three common values that most people share.

Thinking Critically

5. Evaluate Which has influenced your values more—your family or the environment? Explain your answer.

6. Explain Why does each individual have a unique set of values?

7. Relate Give an example of how your values determine your actions.

Applying Concepts

8. Write a description of what a perfect day would be like for you. How would you spend your time, what would you eat, and with whom would you spend the day? Compare your description with those of your classmates. How does the description reflect your values?

Acting Responsibly

Everybody...
We will treat people with
courtesy and respect.
3. We will include people who are left out.
4. Stopping violence is everyone's job.

DISCOVER...

- the meaning of responsibility.
- ways you can act responsibly.
- the importance of acting responsibly.

During the teen years you will have more opportunities to act responsibly. Acting responsibly earns you the trust of other people and builds good relationships. It makes you feel good about yourself and helps you keep safe.

What Is Responsibility?

Responsibility means *making choices and being able to answer for those choices.* As you get older, you will have more opportunities to make your own choices. It is important to know how to handle the responsibility that comes with those choices. This is an important part of becoming an adult.

Responsibility for Yourself

You are responsible for your own behavior and actions. Each day you make many choices. You can show responsibility for yourself by making wise choices. For example, you can take care of your health by choosing to eat healthful foods, to exercise, and to get enough rest. At school you can choose to complete your schoolwork on time and to try to do your best.

Responsibility to Others

In addition to being responsible for yourself, you have a responsibility to other people. These people include your family members, your friends, and the members of your community. By being honest and dependable, you show that you care about other people.

One way to show your family that you are dependable is to do your chores without being asked. What other ways can you think of?

Your Family

Showing responsibility to your family means being polite, arriving home on time, and being reliable. You can show your family that you are reliable by doing the chores and other tasks that are expected of you.

Acting responsibly at home also includes following the rules and showing **respect,** or *consideration,* for other people's feelings and concerns. Showing respect for family members means asking permission before using their things, calling home to let someone know if you are going to be late, and cleaning up after yourself.

Your Friends

An important part of friendship is showing responsibility to your friends. This includes honoring your **commitments,** or *promises*. If you said that you would help paint scenery for the school play, your friends can count on you to be there.

You can also act responsibly by helping a friend in need. Sometimes this means simply comforting a friend who is sad. Other times, however, a friend may have a serious problem or may be involved in something dangerous. In these situations you should try to get your friend to talk to an adult, such as a parent or teacher. If this doesn't work, you should tell an adult about the problem so that your friend can get professional help.

Your Community

In your community, your responsibilities include respecting public and private property and showing concern for the environment. Acting responsibly can be as simple as making sure that your garbage goes into a trash can instead of onto the street, and not destroying community property.

You can also show responsibility by helping out in your community. You might volunteer to collect food for the needy, or take part in a walkathon. When people act responsibly, they help to make their community a better place to live.

Being a volunteer in your community is a good way to show responsibility. Have you ever been a volunteer?

Showing Responsibility

The more you show that you are accountable now, the more freedom and trust you will be given in the future. Here are a few of the many ways to show responsibility.

- **Obey rules.** Families, schools, and communities have rules that help maintain order and keep people safe. Your parents probably have rules about what time you must be home after school. Your school most likely has rules against running in the halls. You act responsibly when you follow the rules.

- **Help others.** Responsible people look out for their families, friends, and neighbors—not just for themselves. If you see someone in trouble, try to help.

- **Carry out tasks or duties.** If it is your job to clear the table, do it without being told. If you see other tasks that need to be done, take the initiative. **Initiative** is *taking action without being asked.*

- **Keep your promises.** If you told a friend that you would help him study for a test, you have an obligation to keep that promise. In this way you will show friends and others that they can count on you.

- **Have a positive attitude.** If there are chores to be done, do them without complaining.

- **Show maturity.** There are many ways to show maturity. One way is to be honest and admit your mistakes. If you forgot that it was your turn to walk the dog, apologize and offer to do it the next time.

Helping others will make you feel good about yourself. Why do you think this is true?

Characteristics of Responsible People

Certain characteristics go along with being responsible. Responsible people

- are reliable.

- admit their mistakes and don't blame others.

- are trustworthy.

- show respect for other people and their property.

- keep their word.

Learning Responsibility

Not everyone has the same responsibilities, and people's responsibilities change over time. As a young child, your main task may have been to take care of your toys. As a young teen, however, you will be expected to assume more complex jobs, such as preparing dinner.

Learning responsibility can be hard, but it has many rewards. You will feel good about yourself, and other people will respect you and start treating you like an adult. Try following these guidelines.

- **Find out what is expected of you.** Listen carefully. Ask questions if you don't understand.

- **Look to adults as role models.** Ask them to help you learn the right thing to do.

- **Take on new tasks gradually**. You will avoid stress if you don't take on too much at once.

- **Be patient with yourself.** If you forget to do something or do it wrong, learn from your mistake and try harder the next time.

Try **This!**

Check the Yellow Pages for charitable organizations in your community. Choose one and find out how you can lend a helping hand. Report your findings to the class.

LESSON TWO *Review*

Using complete sentences, answer the following questions on a separate sheet of paper.

Reviewing Terms and Facts

1. Recall In what ways can you act responsibly at home?

2. Vocabulary Define the term *respect*. Use it in an original sentence.

3. Vocabulary What is another word for *commitment*?

4. Identify Name three characteristics of responsible people.

Thinking Critically

5. Describe Give two examples of ways that you could take the initiative at home.

6. Predict What do you think would happen if people did not act responsibly in their community?

Applying Concepts

7. An important way to show responsibility is to help others. Think of an opportunity you have to lend a helping hand to someone, and then act on it. Describe your experience to a small group of your classmates.

LESSON THREE
Using the Decision-Making Process

WORDS TO KNOW

decision

default

habit

options

consequences

DISCOVER...

● the difference between routine and major decisions.

● how to use the six-step decision-making process.

● how to make responsible decisions.

You have many choices in your life. Each day you have the choice of what to eat for lunch, what to do with your free time, and how hard to study. In fact, life is made up of all kinds of decisions. A **decision** is *a choice a person makes about what action to take*.

Types of Decisions

Decisions are made in several different ways. Sometimes you make decisions by responding to something that has happened, such as deciding to start an exercise routine after doing poorly in gym class. You also make decisions that cause something to happen, such as deciding to be honest so that your family can trust you. Even if you decide not to decide, such as not responding to an invitation to a party, you have made a decision—by default. Making a decision by **default** means *failing to make a decision and leaving the outcome to chance.*

Making Routine Decisions

Some decisions are minor or routine. These are choices that you make every day. They usually do not require a lot of time or thought. Deciding what clothes to wear is a routine decision. It is important to you at the time, but it really does not affect your life very much.

Some routine decisions become habits. A **habit** is *a behavior pattern that is repeated without thinking about it.* You probably have habits like taking a shower every morning and doing your homework each evening.

Making Major Decisions

Major decisions are the choices that have long-term effects on your life. They require much time and thought and may be difficult to make. You do not make major decisions as often as you make routine decisions.

Some of the major decisions you will make as a teenager are what classes to take in school, whether to get a part-time job, or who your friends will be. Some major decisions, such as whether or not to go to college, can be life changing.

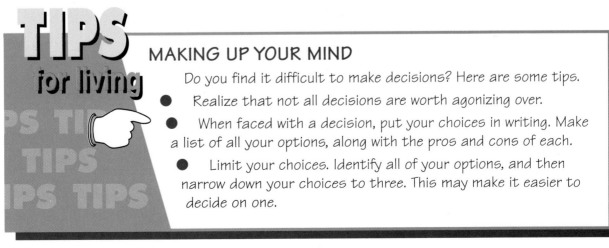

TIPS for living

MAKING UP YOUR MIND

Do you find it difficult to make decisions? Here are some tips.

● Realize that not all decisions are worth agonizing over.

● When faced with a decision, put your choices in writing. Make a list of all your options, along with the pros and cons of each.

● Limit your choices. Identify all of your options, and then narrow down your choices to three. This may make it easier to decide on one.

When making decisions, try writing down all of your options and comparing them. How might this help you? ▶

Why Decision Making Is Important

You will find that being successful in life depends a lot on your ability to make wise decisions. Learning to make routine decisions will help you develop the self-confidence to make more difficult decisions as you get older. The ability to make decisions gives you a sense of freedom and independence.

The decisions you make now will affect the choices you have in the future. For example, deciding now to explore different careers will make you aware of your options and will expand your choices later. What other ways can you think of in which the decisions you make now will affect your future choices?

Steps in Decision Making

Making a decision is easier if you break the problem into smaller parts. If you approach decision making as the six-step process shown in **Figure 3.2,** you will learn to make wise decisions. This process is particularly helpful when you need to make major decisions. The decision-making process includes the following six steps.

1 State the situation

Identify the decision you must make. You need to be clear about the real question facing you before you can find the best answer. Stating the situation also allows you to concentrate on one decision at a time.

Figure 3.2 The Six Steps of Decision Making

It is helpful to use the six-step decision-making process if you have to make an important decision.

2 List the options

Options are possible choices. Usually more than one choice is available to you. You may have several options.

3 Weigh the possible outcomes

Think about the advantages and disadvantages of each possible choice. Ask yourself, "What would happen if I…?" Consider your needs, wants, and goals. Thinking through all the possibilities will help you make better decisions.

4 Consider your values

Use your beliefs, or what is important to you, as guidelines in your decision making. You will not be happy with a decision that goes against your values or your family's values.

6 Evaluate the decision

Making a decision and then acting on it is not the end of the decision-making process. You must judge whether the decision you made was the best one. Analyzing the outcome of your decision will help you in future decision making.

5 Make a decision and act

This is the point where you actually decide. A decision is not a real decision until you take action on your choice. After you have made your decision, you must take the responsibility to see it through.

When faced with a difficult decision, ask for advice from your parents or other trusted adults. Why is their advice valuable?

Making Responsible Decisions

Learning to make responsible decisions will give you a sense of control over your life. Instead of accepting whatever happens to you, you can help control how things happen. Here are some suggestions to help you make responsible decisions.

- **Make your decisions at the right time.** Avoid making quick decisions. Give yourself time to consider all the facts. On the other hand, don't put off a decision too long. If you do, you may find that some of your options are no longer available.

- **Consider the consequences. Consequences** (CON-suh-kwen-sez) are *the results of your choice*. Think about how your choice will affect your life now and in the future. How will it affect your family members or friends?

- **Be willing to take risks.** Any time you make a decision, there is a risk involved. There is always a chance that you will make a mistake. You must have the courage to act on your decisions despite the risk.

- **Seek advice when you need it.** Advice from family members and friends can help you make the right decisions. Sometimes they have had to make similar decisions. Listen to others and use their advice if it is helpful.

- **Accept responsibility for your decisions.** Making your own decisions means accepting responsibility for the choices you make. You cannot make excuses or blame others when you make a poor decision. Accepting responsibility for your decisions and the consequences of those decisions is a sign of maturity.

Your Decisions

Decisions will become more complex as you grow older. Knowing how to handle routine decisions can give you practice and help you feel confident when you have to make major decisions. The six-step decision-making process will help you explore your options and make responsible decisions that you can feel pleased with.

LESSON THREE *Review*

Using complete sentences, answer the following questions on a separate sheet of paper.

Reviewing Terms and Facts

1. Vocabulary Define *habit* and give an example.

2. Recall How are routine decisions different from major decisions?

3. Recall Why is it important to learn how to make decisions?

4. List Name the six steps of the decision-making process.

5. Identify What are four tips for making responsible decisions?

Thinking Critically

6. Analyze Why do people sometimes make decisions by default?

7. Predict What might be the consequences of deciding to smoke cigarettes?

Applying Concepts

8. Write a list of ten decisions you make in an average day. Next to each item on your list, note whether it is a minor decision or a major decision. Then number each decision in order of importance, with 1 being the most important and 10 being the least important.

LESSON FOUR
Setting Goals

WORDS TO KNOW

goal

realistic goal

resource

trade-off

DISCOVER...

● short-term and long-term goals.

● how to set realistic goals.

● resources that will help you reach your goals.

What do you want to achieve in life? Do you want to be a guitar player? An Olympic gymnast? An architect? Knowing what you want to do makes life more interesting and rewarding. It gives purpose to your life and helps you do your best.

Setting Personal Goals

Goals are essential for success in life. A **goal** is *something you want to achieve*. Your goal may be becoming the class treasurer, learning how to fly a plane, or earning a college degree. A goal serves as a guide for what you do and gives you something to work toward. Personal goals help you do your best and achieve the things you want in life.

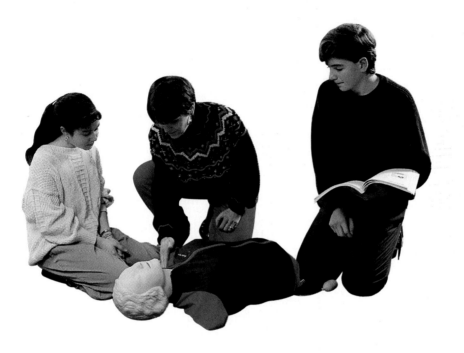

Setting short-term goals, such as completing a CPR course, can prepare you for your long-term goal of becoming an emergency medical technician. What are your short-term goals?

Long-Term and Short-Term Goals

Even though you may not often think about setting goals, you do it all the time. Some of your goals may take a long time to reach—months or even years. These are called long-term goals. Your long-term goals may include learning to drive a car, going to college, or saving enough money to buy a computer.

Short-term goals can be reached more quickly, perhaps in a few days or weeks. Your short-term goals might include completing a science project or getting an A on a math test. Short-term goals are usually specific and can be met in a definite time period.

Sometimes short-term goals can help you achieve a long-term goal. For example, a long-term goal of making the school choir could be broken down into the following short-term goals.

- Take voice lessons to improve your singing.

- Plan time each day to practice your singing.

- Sign up for an audition.

- Choose a song to use at the audition.

- Practice the song.

- Audition for the choir.

In this example, reaching each short-term goal is one step toward achieving the long-term goal.

Setting Realistic Goals

When you set goals, you need to make sure that they are realistic. A **realistic goal** is *one that you can reach*. If your goals are too hard to reach, you may become discouraged and give up. If they are too easy, you may lose interest in them. Realistic goals are both reachable and challenging.

Achieving Your Goals

Achieving your goals is not something that just happens. You have to plan how you will reach each goal. Writing the goal down is a good first step. This will help you get a clear picture of what you want to accomplish.

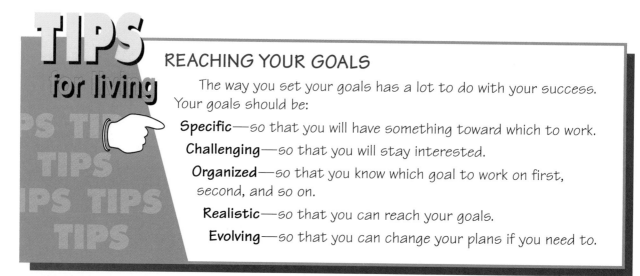

TIPS for living

REACHING YOUR GOALS

The way you set your goals has a lot to do with your success. Your goals should be:

Specific—so that you will have something toward which to work.

Challenging—so that you will stay interested.

Organized—so that you know which goal to work on first, second, and so on.

Realistic—so that you can reach your goals.

Evolving—so that you can change your plans if you need to.

You need to determine what resources will be required to reach your goal. A **resource** is *something you need to accomplish a goal*. Your resources include your time, money, energy, knowledge, and skills. Your family and friends are also resources that are available to you. Using your resources wisely helps you achieve the goals you set for yourself.

You also need to plan more than one way to reach your goal in case your first plan doesn't work. For example, suppose that you want to take up a new sport. If you find that you don't like team sports, you could try an individual sport such as swimming, jogging, or biking.

Your Attitude

A positive attitude goes a long way toward helping you achieve your goals. Your attitude is the way you feel about something. A positive attitude helps you do your best even if the task is something you do not enjoy. It helps you tackle a difficult job rather than putting it off. It also helps you be flexible when things don't go exactly as you had planned. A positive attitude will help you to be successful in whatever you try to accomplish.

Your family and friends are valuable resources that can help you achieve your goals.

Setting Priorities

Some of your goals will be more important to you than others. You may even find that two or more goals are in conflict with each other. When this happens, you need to set priorities for your goals. This will let you concentrate on the goals that are most important to you.

Setting priorities for your goals may involve making trade-offs. A **trade-off** is *something that you give up in order to get something more important*. For example, if being on the debate team is very important to you, you may need to give up other after-school activities and put off trying out for the band.

Having Successful Experiences

Have you ever heard the expression "Nothing succeeds like success"? True success is made up of many little successes along the way. Having successful experiences will help you grow and develop during your teen years. As you experience success in reaching your goals, you will begin to feel good about yourself. You will want to set new goals and to try new things. This will add to your sense of personal worth.

There may be times when you do not achieve all the goals you set for yourself. If you fail to reach a goal, try to figure out what went wrong. Was your goal realistic? Did you have a clear picture of what you wanted to accomplish? Did you use your resources wisely and plan alternative ways to reach your goal? Did you have a positive attitude? Did you set priorities? Knowing what went wrong will help you improve your chances for success the next time.

Having successful experiences as a teen will help you achieve success throughout your life. Why do you think this is so?

LESSON FOUR *Review*

Using complete sentences, answer the following questions on a separate sheet of paper.

Reviewing Terms and Facts

1. Compare What is the difference between a long-term goal and a short-term goal?

2. Vocabulary Define the term *realistic goal*. Use it in an original sentence.

3. Identify List five resources that can help you achieve your goals.

4. Explain Why is it necessary to set priorities for your goals?

Thinking Critically

5. Explain Why is it important to set goals?

6. Illustrate Give an example of a trade-off you have had to make.

Applying Concepts

7. Write down one long-term goal you are interested in working toward. Then list all the short-term goals that could help you achieve your long-term goal.

Chapter 3 Activities

A Global View — FAMILY VALUES

Many people in the United States belong to families that came here from other countries. Sam's great-grandparents, for example, came from China. Katerina's parents were born in Germany. Although these teens may seem very different, they share many of the same values.

TRY THIS!

Find out about ethnic or cultural celebrations with your friends. Then analyze what common values these celebrations represent.

FRIENDS & FAMILY

SCORING GOALS

Having goals, or something to shoot for, gives purpose and direction to life. Just as in sports, scoring life goals takes strategy and skill. Others can help you achieve your goals. Just as in sports, you will feel a sense of accomplishment when you reach your goal.

TRY THIS!

Talk to your family and friends about the goals they have for their lives, and share your goals with them.

Consumer Focus

The Appeal of Advertising

Advertising—especially for clothes and personal care products—often appeals to people's emotions. Advertising may appeal to people's desire to be attractive to others, to be loved, or to fit into a group.

Try This!

Find a magazine advertisement for a product you want, or think about a TV ad for the product. Write a paragraph analyzing how the advertiser appealed to your emotions.

TECHNOLOGY CONNECTION

TECHNOLOGY AND YOUR FUTURE

Nearly any job you choose will require technology skills. To be prepared for the future and to reach your full potential, you should learn as much about technology as you can. Take advantage of the opportunities you have in school to learn about it and to work on the computer.

Follow Up

1. Make a list of your computer skills that you could show an employer. Include the training you have had and the systems and software you have used. Find out ways you could improve your skills.

2. Think of a job you might like to have. Use a reference book on occupations to find out how technology is used in that job. Report your findings to the class.

Chapter Summary

- Needs are those things that are necessary for survival, such as air, food, clothing, and shelter.

- Wants are things that you would like to have but that are not necessary for survival.

- Values are ideas about right and wrong and about what is important in your life. Some common values are honesty, trust, a good family life, and good health.

- Acting responsibly means making choices and being answerable for those choices.

- You can show responsibility in many ways, including obeying rules, helping others, and keeping promises.

- A good way to learn responsibility is by following the example of an adult role model.

- You make many decisions each day. Decisions are made in response to an event, by default, and by habit.

- Use the six-step decision-making process for major decisions, and make your decisions responsibly.

- To be successful, you must set realistic goals throughout your life. You will have both long-term and short-term goals.

- Planning how to reach your goals requires using your resources.

Words to Know

Using complete sentences, answer the following questions on a separate sheet of paper.

1. The U.S. Army uses the slogan "Be all that you can be" to encourage young people to join the military. What term from this chapter fits this slogan?

2. What are some major *commitments* that most people make during their lives?

3. Sports teams sometimes win games by *default*. What does this mean?

4. What are *consequences*? Give an example.

5. List two personal *resources* that most teens have.

Review Questions

Using complete sentences, answer the following questions on a separate sheet of paper.

1. Why do some of your values change over time?

2. Why is it important for you to define your own values?

3. What are some rewards for acting responsibly?

4. Give an example of a decision you might make now that could affect your life in the future.

5. How can short-term goals contribute to long-term goals?

6. Why is it important to set realistic goals?

Thinking Critically

Using complete sentences, answer the following questions on a separate sheet of paper.

1. **Suggest** Why might a "value" in one culture be considered an undesirable quality in another culture? Give an example to support your answer.

2. **Explain** Why is it important to learn responsibility at an early age? What would you teach a five- or six-year-old child about acting responsibly?

3. **Analyze** Sometimes friends make decisions by saying "I'll go if you go" or "I'll do it if you do it." What is wrong with this approach to decision making?

4. **Apply** How might achieving an important goal affect your self-concept? How might it affect your attitude toward other goals?

Cooperative Learning

1. In groups of four or five, share the plot of a movie, television show, or book you have read in which one of the main characters holds two conflicting values. Discuss the character's solution to the problem. Justify the decision with explanations of goals, wants, needs, and values.

2. Goal setting can provide direction to groups as well as to individuals. Along with your classmates, decide on a project you would like to accomplish. Some ideas for a long-term goal include improving the school grounds by planting flowers or a tree, or purchasing new equipment for the school.

Plan together the short-term goals, or steps, you will need to reach your long-term goal. Decide on the resources you have for accomplishing your long-term goal. If possible, put your plan into action.

Family & Community

1. Talk to your family members about the goals you have as a family. Choose one of your family's goals, and draw a newspaper ad for it. Use the title "Go for the Goal!" for your ad. Ask for permission to display the ad in your home.

2. Write an article about yourself or a friend showing responsibility. Post a copy of your article on the classroom bulletin board.

Building A Portfolio

1. Put a small object or a picture in your portfolio that represents a value you have. Include a paragraph describing your value.

2. Think of a major decision you made recently. Apply the six steps of the decision-making process you followed to make the specific decision. On a piece of paper, write the process you used, and keep the paper in your portfolio as a model for future decision making.

3. Look over your written work on personal goal setting. Select one of your goals (a long-term goal plus short-term goals) to include in your portfolio. Once a week, look at your goal and check your progress. Assigning a completion date for each short-term goal will help keep you on track.

CHAPTER 4

Careers

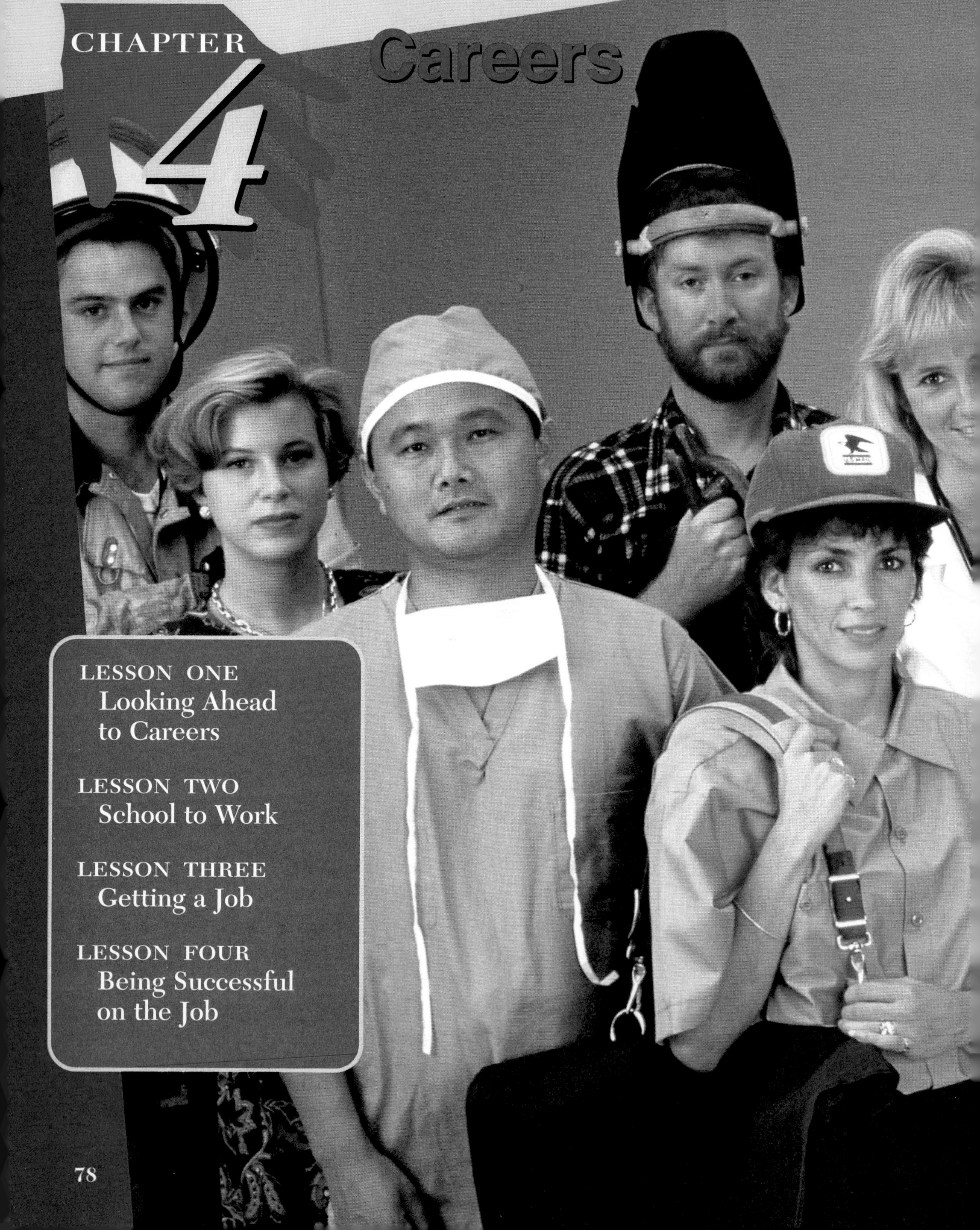

LESSON ONE
Looking Ahead to Careers

LESSON TWO
School to Work

LESSON THREE
Getting a Job

LESSON FOUR
Being Successful on the Job

TEENS MAKING A DIFFERENCE

Junior Entrepreneur

Bobby Vasek started a car-cleaning service when he was 13 years old. His business was inspired by his love of cars and his need to earn some spending money. Now, at age 17, Bobby and three of his friends still wash, wax, and polish cars after school and on weekends.

Bobby is an entrepreneur—a person who runs his own business. Bobby's hard work is paying off: he will soon have enough money saved to buy his own car.

Try

THIS!

Is starting a business something you would like to do? List five personal characteristics that you think a successful entrepreneur needs.

79

LESSON ONE
Looking Ahead to Careers

WORDS TO KNOW

aptitude test

career research

job preparation

apprenticeship programs

DISCOVER...

- reasons why people work.
- considerations for choosing a career.
- various ways to prepare for work.

"What do you want to be when you grow up?" You have probably heard that question many times. Have you really thought about your answer? Perhaps you are interested in becoming a gourmet chef or a fashion designer. Maybe you have always dreamed of a career in computers or medicine. You have many choices, and it is not too soon to start thinking about some careers you might want to pursue.

The World of Work

People work for many reasons. The main reason, of course, is to earn a living, but there are other benefits. People take pride in their work and get a feeling of accomplishment from a job well done. Work is a way to meet people and make friends.

Most people choose jobs based on their interests and skills. Some people enjoy physical tasks, such as repairing machinery or installing new roofs. Others prefer creative work, such as taking photographs or designing homes. Still others want jobs in which they can help people: responding to medical emergencies, for example, or caring for young children.

Most people spend a large part of their lives working. They may spend 40 or more years in the workforce. Wouldn't you rather spend that time doing something you enjoy?

If you enjoy science and have an aptitude for it, there are many careers to explore in scientific fields. What is one career you might like to know more about?

Thinking About Careers

It is a good idea to begin planning a career path while you are still in school. Thinking ahead will give you time to learn some of the specific skills that will help you get a job. It will also help you determine what kind of training and education you will need for the career you choose.

Matching Yourself to a Job

It can be a challenge to match yourself to a job. A few people decide early in life what they want to do and begin to prepare for a career right away. For example, if they enjoy math or science in school, they may choose careers in accounting or medicine.

Try This!

You will be happiest if you choose work that matches the interests and skills you already have. Make a list of your skills and interests.

Now match each skill on your list with a job that uses that skill. Look in career books for ideas. If possible, use a computer software program to match your skills and interests with various jobs.

You will probably have several jobs during your lifetime. One of the first steps in finding work that will satisfy you is to consider what you are interested in. Do you have special skills that could be useful in a particular type of work? Could you volunteer or work part-time to strengthen those skills?

When considering a career, you should also think about your values and goals. What do you want to do with your life? What is important to you? Do you want to help other people? Consider a career in health services. Do you like to build things? Look into construction or architecture. Knowing your values and goals will help you focus on an area that suits the sort of person you are.

If you still can't decide, there are special tests that can help you discover your aptitudes. Aptitudes are natural abilities or talents. An **aptitude test** is *a test that predicts a person's ability to learn certain skills.* A test of this kind can help by revealing your strengths.

Researching Careers

When you have chosen a few possibilities, you can look for answers to questions you may have about various kinds of jobs. **Career research** is *the process of finding out all you can about a field of work that interests you.*

Looking for Answers

If you know what to expect from a job, it will be easier to decide which kind is best for you. Here are some of the points you will want to research about various jobs:

- Education required for the job

- Responsibilities or duties expected

- Salary or wages for entry-level and experienced workers

- Chances for promotion

- Working conditions, including protection against safety hazards

- Possible need for more workers in this field in the future

You can learn about careers through computer programs or on-line services. Ask your librarian to recommend some.

You can find out some of these facts about various careers by talking with people who work in the fields in which you are interested. You can also look in the library for books on careers; *The Occupational Outlook Handbook* or the *Dictionary of Occupational Titles (DOT)* are useful references. The *DOT* lists 20,000 different kinds of jobs.

Choosing a Career

You might find that there are two or three career areas that really interest you. If so, over the next few years try to find out more about each of them. Talk over the possibilities with family members, school counselors, and teachers. They can advise you or answer questions.

Preparing for Work

The learning required to get and keep the kind of job you want is called **job preparation.** You will need to be willing to study and work for specific jobs as well as for promotions. Here are some of the benefits of preparing for work.

- Job preparation means a better life for you and those you might have to support.

- You will have a better chance for success and financial security.

• If a job is one you really like, it will give you enjoyment and satisfaction.

Without a high school education, your job opportunities are limited. Many fields of work require education beyond high school.

Many skilled workers learn their jobs by participating in a formal apprenticeship program.

Continuing to Learn

There are many ways to continue your education after high school. You may want to:

• attend college. Community colleges, four-year colleges, and universities offer courses and degrees in a wide variety of fields.

• enroll in a course at a vocational trade center. A vocational program can teach you skills for specific occupations, such as computer programming, plumbing, or the food industry.

• get a job with a company that teaches its employees the special skills they need. Some companies have **apprenticeship programs,** which are *formal programs that use on-the-job training to teach job skills.*

TIPS for living

READING THE WANT ADS

You can find a job by looking at help-wanted ads. Here are some tips to remember.

● The Sunday paper has the largest number of job ads.

● Most newspapers divide job listings into sections, such as "Part-Time."

● Newspaper ads use abbreviations. For example, "PT" means part-time.

● Note the qualifications for a job, the hours required, and other information. Make sure that the job is right for you before answering an ad.

Working Part-Time

Before you look for a full-time job, you will probably have worked at part-time jobs. You can get valuable experience by working in restaurants, businesses, and stores, or by baby-sitting or delivering newspapers.

Part-time employment can be part of your preparation for full-time employment. Part-time work helps you:

- learn to get along with your supervisor and coworkers.

- find out how you like a certain type of work.

- gain work experience that will be helpful when you apply for a full-time job.

- become aware of job requirements and other qualities that you need to acquire for full-time work.

By asking other people how they got started in a career, you might get ideas for your own life. With whom could you talk about a career that interests you?

Exploring Your Options

It is a good idea to start exploring career opportunities now. That way you will be better prepared to make a career choice. When you think about your options, consider your interests, abilities, values, and goals. Decisions based on these factors will lead you to work you enjoy.

LESSON ONE *Review*

Using complete sentences, answer the following questions on a separate sheet of paper.

Reviewing Terms and Facts

1. List Name three reasons why people work.

2. Recall What should you consider when matching yourself to a career?

3. Vocabulary Define the term *apprentice-ship program.* Use it in an original sentence.

Thinking Critically

4. Analyze When you begin to research careers, which three factors do you feel will be most important to you?

5. Explain How can you narrow down possible career choices?

6. Interpret Why is part-time employment valuable?

Applying Concepts

7. Using some item such as a toy, a book, or a box of cake mix, work with a group of students to make a list of as many jobs as you can think of that would be involved in the creation of the product. Find out what training is needed for the job that interests you.

School to Work

DISCOVER...

- how basic skills—reading, writing, math, science, speaking, and listening—contribute to success in life.
- why computer skills are essential in the workplace.

Imagine what your life would be like if you did not have reading, writing, math, science, speaking, and listening skills. You would not be able to read a magazine article, a CD cover, or a store advertisement. You could not complete your class assignments. How would you count your spending money? You would have trouble communicating with your friends, family, and classmates.

Developing Basic Skills

The most important key to your success is developing skills in the basics: reading, writing, math, science, speaking, and listening. These skills are called *basic* because they serve as tools to help you function in life. More and more, computer skills are considered basic, too.

Basic skills are important to you not only now but also in the future, especially at work. For example, you will need reading and writing skills to fill out a job application or write a résumé. To understand the information on your paycheck and to budget your money, you will need math skills. Skills in science will help you understand how technology affects people and their environment. Listening and speaking skills will be essential when you meet with prospective employers.

Using your reading, writing, math, science, speaking, and listening skills every day is the best way to develop them. When you leave your language arts, math, and science classes, continue to use your basic skills. Find ways to apply them in practical situations. What ways can you think of to do this?

Reading

Reading is one of the most important basic skills. It provides a foundation for other skills. Without reading skills, you could not write, read directions, understand and solve math problems, or use a computer.

By using your basic skills every day, you will continue to improve them. How is this teen using basic reading skills?

Building your vocabulary is one way to develop your reading skills. Use a dictionary to learn to pronounce words correctly and find out what they mean. You must also learn how to follow written directions. For example, if you are reading an instruction manual in a computer class, you must be able to follow the directions in order to do the work correctly.

The main goal of reading is comprehension. **Comprehension** means *understanding what you read*. With practice, you can improve your comprehension. You can even think beyond the facts that are given. For example, you can read advertisements for competing products and decide which one is probably the best.

Writing

Writing is a way to express your ideas. Your writing is a reflection of you. Developing writing skills will help you feel good about yourself and make a positive impression on others. The ability to express yourself clearly in writing will improve your chances for getting and keeping a job.

You can improve your writing skills by taking time to organize your thoughts. Think about the purpose of what you are going to write. Perhaps you are writing a letter to a prospective employer. How can you convince the employer to call you in for an interview? If the letter is long, first outline the major points. Use a dictionary to be sure that you are using the right words and spelling them correctly.

TIPS for living

IMPROVING YOUR STUDY SKILLS

Good study skills can improve your learning and your grades. A good school record is important for getting a job. Here are some ways to improve your study skills.

● Arrange a study area. Keep supplies within easy reach, including a dictionary.

● Set aside a specific time each day for studying.

● Be sure that you understand all assignments.

● Avoid distractions such as TV and stereo. If you get a phone call, arrange to call back later.

Write a rough draft, and reread it to see if it can be improved. Does it say what you want it to say? **Proofread,** or *check for errors in your grammar, punctuation, and spelling.* Retype or input a final copy, and check to be sure that your work is neat and accurate. You want to make a good first impression with your letter.

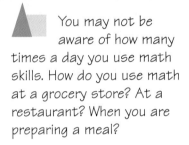

Math and Science

You use math and science skills every day in ways you may not even think about. For example, you use math and science when you compare prices, prepare a meal, or remove stains from your clothes.

Some of the math skills you must develop are the basic processes: addition, subtraction, multiplication, and division. You also need to master fractions, decimals, and percentages. These basics will help you figure out your weekly earnings if you are paid by the hour, or the cost of getting to work. Correct use of a calculator is another essential math skill. Developing good math skills now will open the door to many opportunities later.

Whether or not you plan to become a scientist, you can use science skills every day. Knowing how chemical and physical reactions occur is useful in many practical situations. For example, what happens when food is cooked or frozen? Science skills will also help you develop an appreciation for nature and your environment. You will understand how to select clothing that will protect you in extreme weather.

Speaking

Communication takes place between a sender and a receiver. The speaker is sending a message to the receiver, or listener. However, just speaking to another person does not guarantee good communication. If someone talks too fast, for instance, the message may not get through. Speaking and listening are basic skills that need to be learned and practiced.

You may not be aware of how many times a day you use math skills. How do you use math at a grocery store? At a restaurant? When you are preparing a meal?

Speaking is just as important in the workplace as reading and writing. Developing the ability to express your thoughts clearly will help you perform well on the job, no matter what career you choose. You can improve your speaking skills by:

- thinking before you speak in order to organize your ideas.

- speaking in a direct and straightforward manner.

- making sure that the other person understands what you are saying.

- finding a different way to express your idea if your listener does not understand you.

Listening

The second part of good communication is listening. To be an effective listener, you need to hear, think about, and respond to what the speaker is saying. On the job, you will need to make a real effort to understand what others say to you. If you do not understand what your employer wants you to do, you may not do the job correctly. You can improve your listening skills by:

- concentrating on what the other person is saying.

- allowing the other person to finish talking without interrupting.

- listening even if you do not agree with everything the other person is saying.

- letting the other person know that you are listening.

Could this trainee learn to do the job if it were not explained clearly? What could be done to improve understanding?

Computer Skills

Computers are changing the way we live and work. Today computers are used for many purposes, including education, communication, and entertainment. Knowing how to use a computer is essential for certain jobs in almost every field.

Computers have a great impact on your life. They are used almost everywhere, including factories, offices, restaurants, stores, and repair shops. At home, people use computers to manage finances, write reports, locate information, and communicate with others.

If you have not spent much time using a computer, now is a good time to practice your skills. You can learn to use **software,** which is *a computer program or set of instructions.* Most computer software is "user-friendly." That means that it is designed to help you make computers work for you even if you know little about them.

Such skills as speaking a foreign language may not be basic, but they can contribute to your qualifications for a job. What jobs can you think of in which you could use foreign language skills?

Your Future Success

All workers need basic skills to be successful. You need reading and writing skills to read a job posting and apply for a promotion. Your math and science skills will help you keep up with technological advances. When you work with other people, you use speaking and listening skills. Computer skills are required in just about every occupation.

LESSON TWO *Review*

Using complete sentences, answer the following questions on a separate sheet of paper.

Reviewing Terms and Facts

1. Recall What is the best way to develop your reading, writing, math, science, speaking, and listening skills?

2. Vocabulary What do you do when you *proofread?*

3. Explain Why might computer skills be considered basic?

Thinking Critically

4. Analyze Why is it important to develop basic knowledge and skills?

5. Apply Give three examples of ways in which you use math and science skills in your daily life.

6. Integrate Name a specific work skill you would need for a particular job.

Applying Concepts

7. Keep a record of how often you use math, reading, writing, and communication skills during a single day. Did you use science or computer skills? Make a graph to show which skills you used most often.

Getting a Job

WORDS TO KNOW

job opening

job application

references

job interview

job applicant

DISCOVER...

● how to find and apply for a job.

● how to prepare for a job interview and make a good impression.

Getting a job requires good management skills. Marla learned about these skills when she looked for an after-school job. Her mother told her that the first thing she needed to do was to gather the required forms. Next Marla had to learn how to find the kind of job she wanted. Then she had to apply for the job and get an interview. Marla decided that getting a job was not going to be easy. By following the guidelines in this lesson, however, she got a part-time job at a garden center.

Looking for a Job

No matter what type of work you have done before, perhaps yard work or babysitting, you will eventually need to seek out possible employers—businesses that can offer you a job. By learning job-hunting skills now, you will be prepared to find a part-time job while you are still in school or a full-time job when you have finished school.

Getting Organized

Before you look for a job, you need to get organized. You must get a social security card if you do not already have one. You will need a copy of your birth certificate or other proof that you are a United States citizen. Depending on where you live, you may also need a work permit, or employment certificate, if you are under the age of 16 or 18. Your school counselor can help you get one.

Finding employers who have jobs available is only one part of looking for a job. Why is it important to learn job-hunting skills now?

Once you have the necessary papers, you are ready to plan your job hunt. First, decide what kind of job you want. A look at your career goals, favorite subjects and activities, and past experiences should help you focus your attention on jobs that would be most suitable for you. Next, decide when and for how many hours you can work. For example, can you work after school or on weekends only? Now decide when you should look for a job. If you want a summer job, you should start looking in the spring. If you want a job during winter or spring vacation, start looking before the vacation begins. If you want an after-school job, look for it after school. Do not miss school to apply for a job. An employer may think you will also miss work if you want to do something else.

Speak with family and friends.

Read newspaper help-wanted ads.

Call companies directly.

Check with your school placement office.

Visit an employment agency.

Use computer on-line job listings.

**Figure 4.1
Ways to Find
Job Openings**

What other ways can you think of to find a job opening?

Finding a Job Opening

Now you are ready to look for job openings. A **job opening** is *a job that is not filled*. **Figure 4.1** shows some common ways to find job openings.

Applying for a Job

When you find a job opening that interests you, contact the employer to apply for the job. You may be asked to fill out a job application and come in for an interview when you apply for a job.

A **job application** is *a form on which you supply information about yourself that will help an employer make a hiring decision*. You will need to write down information about your education, skills, activities and interests, and work experience. If you fill out the application at the job site, you will need to have that information with you. Be sure to complete the application form neatly without skipping any questions.

On an application form, you may be asked to give the names of several references. **References** are *people who can tell an employer about an applicant's character and quality of work.* Your references should be adults (not parents or other relatives) who know and like you. You might choose teachers, counselors, family friends, coaches, previous employers, club leaders, or religious leaders. Be sure to ask their permission before you use their names as references. Sometimes you can get adults to write letters of reference for you. The employer may call or write to your references to ask questions about your character or your abilities.

If the employer thinks that you might be suitable, you will be invited to interview for the job. A **job interview** is *a face-to-face meeting between an employer and a job applicant.* A **job applicant** is *a person who wants a job.* The interview gives the employer a chance to meet you and learn more about your qualifications for the job. The interviewer may ask, "Why do you think you can do this job well?" or "What are your strengths and weaknesses?" The interview also gives you a chance to learn more about the job and the business. It is an opportunity to ask questions about the job or about the place of employment. You might ask where and when you would work and what your duties would be.

TIPS for living

FILLING OUT A JOB APPLICATION

The way you fill out a job application can make a lasting impression. Here are some rules to follow.

- To avoid putting information in the wrong place, read the application form carefully before you start filling it in.
- Read the instructions, and follow them exactly.
- Print as neatly as possible, using blue or black ink.
- Answer all questions that apply to you. If a question does not apply, write "NA" (not applicable) in the space.
- Be prepared to describe your education, skills, past work experience, and references.
- Check to make sure that you have answered every question.

An interview gives you a chance to see if you are really interested in the job. What questions would you ask during an interview?

The Job Interview

You can improve your chances of getting a job by making a good impression during the job interview. The moment you walk through the door for an interview, you start making an impression on the employer. The first thing the employer usually notices is the applicant's appearance—dress, hair, and grooming.

Your posture and manners are also important parts of the first impression. Employers look for an applicant who has good posture, walks confidently, and looks people in the eye. They are impressed by an applicant who smiles, speaks clearly, and seems friendly and enthusiastic.

You can prepare for a job interview by learning all you can about the employer and practicing for the interview. Practice by having a friend ask you questions; respond as if you were really being interviewed.

Dressing for the Interview

Plan carefully what you will wear to a job interview to make a good first impression. Your clothes should be appropriate for the interview, clean, and neatly pressed. Be sure that your shoes are also clean and polished.

Pay attention to details as you dress for a job interview. Be sure that you have a clean body, shiny hair, white teeth, and clean fingernails. Many interviewers notice these details. An effort to appear neat and clean tells an employer that the job is important to you.

Using Your Skills to Get a Job

It is easier to find a job if you organize your search. When you find a job opening that interests you, be prepared to fill out an application and go to an interview. Your chances for a successful interview improve if you are well-groomed and neatly dressed. If you make a good impression on the employer, you will be more likely to get the job.

Which job applicant do you think will make a better first impression? Which one would you hire?

LESSON THREE *Review*

Using complete sentences, answer the following questions on a separate sheet of paper.

Reviewing Terms and Facts

1. Recall What papers must you have before you look for a job?

2. Vocabulary Define the term *job application.*

3. List Name the three things that contribute to an employer's first impression of you.

4. Describe How can you prepare for a job interview?

Thinking Critically

5. Summarize What do you need to do when planning your job hunt?

6. Explain What are the purposes of a job interview?

7. Suggest What would you wear to an interview for a job in an office? For an interview for babysitting? For a fast-food job?

Applying Concepts

8. With a classmate, take turns role-playing the parts of an applicant and an employer in a job interview. Be sure to agree on the type of job the applicant is looking for. Analyze your performance in each role.

Being Successful on the Job

WORDS TO KNOW

coworkers

supervisor

employee manual

flexibility

teamwork

work record

promotion

entrepreneur

DISCOVER...

- steps to becoming a responsible employee.
- why building a good work record is important.
- how you can advance at work.

Caitlyn is a junior in high school. She has always dreamed of becoming a professional photographer. When she heard about a part-time job as an assistant in a photography studio, she jumped at the opportunity. She filled out a job application and went for an interview. The employer was impressed by Caitlyn's good grades and her positive attitude. Caitlyn got the job and now works one day a week after school and every Saturday. She enjoys her work, and her **coworkers,** *the people she works with,* and customers like her enthusiasm. Each week Caitlyn puts part of her paycheck into a savings account. She hopes to open her own photography studio someday.

Becoming a Responsible Employee

The key to success in any job is to be a responsible employee. You are a responsible employee when you know what your job responsibilities, or duties, are and you fulfill them.

There are some responsibilities that every employee has in every job situation. These responsibilities include having a positive attitude and using good communication skills. It is also important to be a good team member.

If you think about it, these job responsibilities are similar to your responsibilities at school. At work, as in school, you need to arrive on time, follow rules, and do your share of the work. Of course, you also know that you should always be honest and do your best. What other general responsibilities can you think of?

To become a responsible employee, follow these three steps.

- **Step 1: Know your job responsibilities.** Besides general job responsibilities, every job also has specific

Skills that you develop in school, such as working as a member of a team, will help you in your future career. What other skills do you need to be a responsible employee?

You will have many opportunities to use communication skills at work. Here are a few examples:
• Finding out customers' needs and wants
• Getting acquainted with coworkers
• Handling problems
Think of an on-the-job situation requiring good communication skills. Ask a classmate to role-play the situation with you.

duties. If you work in a flower shop, for example, your duties might include making flower arrangements, dealing with customers, and operating the cash register.

How do you know what your responsibilities are? You will probably learn about some of them during your job interview. In your first week of work, your specific responsibilities will be explained to you by your **supervisor,** *the person who checks your work and evaluates your performance.* You may be given an **employee manual,** *a book of rules that employees must follow.* You will have to understand and obey these rules.

• **Step 2: Fulfill your job responsibilities.** A key to success at work is just to *do* your job. This sounds simple, and it is. You would be surprised, though, at how many people fail to follow this simple rule.

Sean had a part-time job as a salesperson at a music store in the mall. Sean's friends would often visit him at work. When Sean was talking to his friends, he would ignore customers. Because Sean didn't do his job, he was fired. The lesson to learn from Sean's experience is that you are at work to do your work. Arrive on time, ask questions if you do not understand something, and make your job responsibilities your top priority.

• **Step 3: Evaluate yourself.** At the end of each workday you should evaluate your performance on the job. Did you fulfill your responsibilities? How could you have done your job better? Did you use good communication skills?

Success on the job requires hard work. Following these steps, however, will help you become a good employee and reach your career goals.

Flexibility

Even when you plan carefully, you cannot always control the ways things turn out. People who are flexible accept that plans may be affected by forces they cannot control. **Flexibility** is *the ability to adjust easily to new conditions.* Because conditions on the job can change often, most work situations requirc flexibility. For example, computer technology is constantly changing, and as a result, workers must learn new skills and new ways to accomplish tasks.

Flexibility is also important when dealing with coworkers. You cannot always control the ways tasks are done. Sometimes coworkers must each give in a little to reach an agreement.

Team Spirit

When you go to work, you become part of a team. As a member of a team, you should work with and listen to others and have a helpful attitude. That builds **teamwork,** or *cooperation while working together to reach a goal.* When coworkers cooperate with one another and share feelings of pride in their work, they get along better and can reach their goals more effectively. **Figure 4.2** shows some ways to be a good team member.

Figure 4.2 Working as a Team Member

Sharing goals and responsibilities as part of a team is an experience that is valuable to everyone.

- Show loyalty.
- Be flexible.
- Have a positive attitude.
- Focus your attention on each task.
- Speak in a pleasant way to others.
- Listen attentively to others.
- Do your full share of the work.
- Be truthful.

Try This!

Employers want workers who manage their time, energy, and material resources wisely. With a group of your classmates, make a list of good work habits such as "Get to work on time" or "Be honest."

Getting Along with Others

Relationships are an important part of every job. You have to learn to get along with your employer, supervisor, and coworkers, and perhaps customers or clients. The better your relationships are with these people, the more you will enjoy work and experience success.

Your Work Record

Do you know someone who has a reputation as a nice person? Maybe you know someone with a reputation for good grades. What kind of reputation do you have? You probably know that once you get a reputation, it's hard to change it.

As you work, you will develop a reputation based on your work record. A **work record** is *a written record of how well an employee performs on the job.* Your work record shows how well you have fulfilled your job responsibilities. It mentions how often you were late and how often you missed work. You can also expect to find comments about your attitude and how well you followed instructions.

TIPS for living

GETTING ALONG WITH COWORKERS

You will do a better job and enjoy your work more if you get along with your coworkers. To build good working relationships:

- **Do your share.** If you don't, others may resent getting stuck with extra work.

- **Be prompt.** Arrive at work early, and return from breaks on time.

- **Help others.** If you finish your work early, offer to help someone else.

- **Accept differences.** Keep an open mind, and see what you can learn from others.

- **Stay positive.** People like to work with others who smile and think positively.

- **Avoid gossip.** Stay neutral and don't get involved when people gossip or spread rumors at work.

If you apply for a job with a new company, that employer will probably check your work record along with other references. A good work record will improve your chances of being hired. You can see that your work record will follow you like your reputation, so it pays to build a good one.

Advancement Opportunities

As you know, to be promoted means to move forward. In the world of work, a **promotion** is *a move up to a better job with more responsibility.* For example, you might be promoted from stock clerk to assistant manager. A promotion usually includes a raise in salary. Another way to advance is to accept a better job—one with more responsibilities and higher pay—with another company.

Becoming an Entrepreneur

For some people, the way to begin a career or to advance is to strike out on their own. An **entrepreneur** is *a person who starts and runs his or her own business.* Running your own business has many advantages. You are your own boss. You get credit for all of your successes. Of course, when you are an entrepreneur you are also responsible for every part of the business. If the business does not do well, you lose money. Do you know anyone who is an entrepreneur? If you were an entrepreneur, what type of business would you have?

You can gain experience as an entrepreneur by starting a business at home. For example, a neighbor might agree to pay you for doing chores.

Taking Initiative

Everyone who is successful on the job has one thing in common: initiative. Initiative means starting something on your own and working to complete it. You will use your initiative to get a job and to advance in your career. By taking initiative, you will gain the self-esteem that comes from success in your work.

Managing Your Income

Have you ever heard of a millionaire who went bankrupt? It does happen. Earning an income is not enough; you have to manage your money carefully. Managing your income is a way to get what you want out of life. If you make a habit of saving part of every paycheck, you will be able to set and reach financial goals. Perhaps you want to save enough money to buy a computer or a stereo. It is not too early to start saving now for a future goal, such as buying a car or going to college. Remember that how you manage your income is as important as how much money you earn.

By managing your income carefully, you can save money to reach a goal. What would you buy with your savings?

LESSON FOUR *Review*

Using complete sentences, answer the following questions on a separate sheet of paper.

Reviewing Terms and Facts

1. List Identify three steps you can take to become a responsible employee.

2. Explain Define the term *flexibility*. Use it in an original sentence.

3. Vocabulary Define the term *work record*. Then write a sentence explaining what it includes.

4. Explain Why is it important to manage your income?

Thinking Critically

5. Contrast Write a paragraph contrasting the advancement of an employee who has a good work record with that of an employee who has a poor work record.

6. Apply Describe your dream job, and explain how two skills you learned in this lesson might help you achieve it.

Applying Concepts

7. Interview the owner of a small business. Write a paragraph explaining the steps that person took to achieve success. Share your findings with the class.

Chapter 4 Activities

Consumer Focus

Career Information

Helping people find satisfying work has become a big business. Stores sell a wide range of books, videos, and software on career planning. Now a growing number of educators are developing career awareness materials for middle school students.

Try This!

Begin looking for information on careers that interest you. Start a job file where you can keep the materials you find.

TECHNOLOGY

Job Search

Did you know that you can use a computer to help you choose a career? Special software packages let the computer match your answers to questions about your personal job preferences with the characteristics of hundreds of jobs.

Try This!

Ask for a more detailed description of any of the jobs. In this way, you can learn about jobs that might be right for you.

A Global View

GLOBAL MARKETPLACE

You live in a global marketplace. In the past, marketplaces tended to be close to customers' homes. Today, however, modern transportation and communication systems make it easier to buy and sell goods and services around the world. What do you think that you can do now to get ready for a job in the global marketplace?

TRY THIS!

Find out the name of a company that does business worldwide. Read about the types of jobs available in that business's global marketplace.

MATH CONNECTION

GROSS PAY VERSUS NET PAY

Clearing tables at The Heritage Diner was Zach Ryan's first "real" job. After two weeks, he looked forward to receiving his first paycheck. Zach soon learned that his earnings, or *gross pay,* would not be the same as his take-home pay, or *net pay.* Zach's gross pay was $166.25, while his net pay was $136.58. What is the reason for the difference? Deductions!

Follow Up

1. Alicia earns $6.25 an hour as a cashier at Martin's Variety Store. Last week she worked 38 hours. She had the following deductions: F.I.C.A.—$18.17, federal income tax—$6.49, state income tax—$4.00, and medicare—$3.44. What was Alicia's gross pay? What was her net pay?

2. Interview a self-employed person to find out how he or she pays taxes and insurance. Write a paragraph or two on your findings.

Chapter Summary

- Your choice of a career will be one of the most important decisions you will ever make. Since you will be spending a large part of your life working, you should choose work you will enjoy.

- You can prepare for your future career by setting goals, researching careers, continuing your education, and working part-time.

- In school you learn the basic skills of reading, writing, math, science, speaking, and listening. Knowing how to use a computer is also an important basic skill.

- Job hunting requires organization. Before starting your search, decide what kind of job you want and when you can work.

- You can find job openings by asking family and friends, looking at the help-wanted ads, calling possible employers, and visiting employment agencies.

- Dressing appropriately is important for a job interview. Your appearance is usually the first thing an employer notices.

- Good communication skills, flexibility, and team spirit will help you succeed on the job.

- Your work record includes a description of your work habits and how well you handled problems.

- Getting promotions or finding new employment will depend on a good work record.

▶ Words to Know

Using complete sentences, answer the following questions on a separate sheet of paper.

1. What is the purpose of an *aptitude test?*

2. How might *proofreading* help you in a job?

3. Whom should a person list as *references* on a job application?

4. At work, what words might mean the same as *supervisor?*

5. Give an example of *flexibility* on the job.

6. Describe what an *entrepreneur* does.

▶ Review Questions

Using complete sentences, answer the following questions on a separate sheet of paper.

1. Why is it important to decide on career goals while you are in school?

2. How can you find a job or career that is right for you?

3. Why are reading, writing, math, science, speaking, and listening skills called basic skills?

4. Describe the process of getting a job.

5. What can you do to promote good team-work on the job?

6. Give three examples of good work habits.

Thinking Critically

Using complete sentences, answer the following questions on a separate sheet of paper.

1. **Explain** Why might aptitude tests give people an incomplete picture of career possibilities?

2. **Analyze** Do you think that computers make learning to read, write, and do math less important? Why or why not?

3. **Apply** What questions would you ask an employer at a job interview?

4. **Describe** Why is team spirit such an important quality for employees to have? When might it not be very important?

5. **Apply** What would you do if a coworker was not doing his or her job?

Cooperative Learning

1. With a group of your classmates, make an employment guide for young teens. Include descriptions of jobs suitable for teens, information on how to find jobs in your community, and tips on how to succeed on the job. Each member of the group can be responsible for writing a different section of the guide. Make your guide available to other students in your school.

2. Gather information about a career that interests you. Find out the education required for jobs in that field, responsibilities or duties to be expected, working conditions, and

employment outlook. Exchange information with a small group of your classmates.

Family & Community

1. One reason why teens may not know much about their parents' jobs is that they rarely see their parents at work. Arrange to spend some time with a parent or any adult family member at his or her workplace during a vacation from school. Find out about the adult's duties and responsibilities and how he or she uses basic skills at work. Report your findings to the class.

2. Look for resources in your community that help teens start their own businesses. You might find books on teen entrepreneurship at the public library or in bookstores. Programs such as Junior Achievement or Future Business Leaders of America provide teens with business training.

Building A Portfolio

1. Parent-teacher-student conferences and report cards provide a "performance review" of the job you are doing in school. Use information from these sources to list some goals for improving your performance. Place a copy of your list of goals in your portfolio, and use it to measure your progress.

2. Write a business letter to a nearby college, vocational school, community college, or technical school. Request information about available training for careers that interest you. Place a copy of your letter and the information you receive in your portfolio.

UNIT 2

Relationships

Chapter 5:
Your Family and Friends

Chapter 6:
Parenting and Children

108

5
Your Family and Friends

TEENS MAKING A DIFFERENCE

Story Time

One Monday, in creative writing class, Tara could not think of any ideas for her next story. Tara's teacher suggested that Tara think about the children she has met through her volunteer work at the hospital.

Tara thought about a little girl named Cindy who was very scared about being in the hospital. When Cindy's mother was not there, Tara would read stories to the girl.

Just then, Tara got an idea. She asked, "Could our class write a collection of stories for the children?" Everyone thought that it was a great idea. When the collection was finished, the class dedicated it to the children at the hospital.

Try THIS!

What could you do to help a young friend or family member who was scared about something? Write down five ideas, and share them with a classmate.

Getting Along with Others

WORDS TO KNOW

belonging

security

cooperation

considerate

DISCOVER...

- the importance of relationships.
- the skills needed to develop strong relationships.
- ways to practice relationship skills.

People often take relationships for granted. They may not realize how important another person is to them until something changes in their relationship. For example, if your brother went away to college or your best friend went to summer camp, you would miss that person a great deal.

Why Are Relationships Important?

Relationships are important because they help you meet your social and emotional needs. Everyone needs to feel accepted and liked by others. How well your relationships meet these needs influences your feelings about yourself and others.

Belonging

Relationships with friends and family members give you a sense of **belonging,** or *feeling included.* Belonging helps you feel good about yourself and builds your self-esteem. It allows you to feel at ease and comfortable.

To feel that you belong, you need to feel loved and accepted by others. This gives you a sense of **security**—*feeling safe and protected.* When you know that you can count on family and friends to love and accept you the way you are, you feel that you are secure and that you belong.

You can add to your own feelings of security by making others feel loved and secure in turn. When you care for others, their needs become as important as your own. If you comfort your younger sister after a classmate has said something mean to her, you make her feel that she is secure and that she belongs. If you bring your dad a glass of lemonade when he is washing the car, you make him feel loved. Showing others that you care about them makes you feel giving and unselfish.

Approval

The approval and recognition of family and friends also build your self-esteem. Think about how good you feel when someone compliments or thanks you. "Great haircut!" or

Skills
IN ACTION

Using "I" Messages

The next time you're upset with a family member or a friend, try sending an "I" message instead of saying, "You always…" You might say, for example, "I feel angry because…" "I" messages allow you to express how you feel without putting others down or making them feel defensive. With a partner, role-play sending "I" messages.

When family members help each other, they build strong relationships. In what ways do you help members of your family?

Try This!

Are you looking for that perfect gift for a family member or a special friend? Sometimes the best choice isn't something that costs a lot of money. For example, make a gift certificate that says "This certificate entitles (name) to 'one car wash' or 'three games of checkers.'"

"Thanks for your help" are comments that everyone likes to hear. Such comments make you feel good about yourself.

You have probably heard little children shout, "Look at me!" when they build a tower with blocks or run a race. Their need for recognition is so great that they persist until you look at them and say, "Very good!" When you show others a special art project or a poem you wrote, you are also seeking approval. It is natural to feel happy when you receive a compliment for something you are proud to have done. Likewise, you can make your family members or friends happy by complimenting them on their accomplishments.

Developing Relationship Skills

There are several skills that can make your relationships more satisfying. These skills will help you get along better with both your family and your friends. They will also help prepare you for future relationships.

Communication

A key to good relationships is practicing communication skills. That means learning to express your thoughts clearly and listening to what others say. Good communication brings people closer together. Share your problems or concerns with your family and friends. Express your joys and dreams. When family members and friends are talking, listen closely to what they are saying. Try to understand the message from their point of view. Use positive body language, such as a smile or a nod of approval, to show that you are listening.

When you cooperate with others, you do your share of the work. What are some other ways to show that you are cooperative?

Cooperation

For relationships to work, the people involved need to cooperate with one another. **Cooperation** is *working together for the* *good of all.* At school, cooperation may involve sharing equipment in gym class or doing your share of the work on a social studies project. At home, cooperation may mean taking turns using the telephone or helping out by preparing dinner.

Building Trust

The ability to build trust is also necessary in relationships. To earn the trust of parents, adults, and friends, you need to show them that you can handle new experiences and responsibilities. For instance, taking out the trash without being reminded or getting up on time are ways of showing that you are trustworthy.

Another way to earn trust is to be reliable and honest with people. This means that you do what you say you are going to do. For example, if you say that you will take care of a new kitten, it is important to keep your word.

Showing consideration for others is an important relationship skill. How is this teen being considerate of someone else?

Being Considerate

It takes practice to consider others' needs and feelings. Being **considerate,** or *thoughtful,* is an important part of getting along with others.

How do you act around your family and around your friends? Is there a difference? Using a pleasant, friendly tone of voice and thinking before you speak will make others feel accepted and respected. Your actions show how considerate you are. Here are some ways to show your family and friends that you care. Can you think of other ways?

- **Respect others' privacy.** Don't listen to their conversations or borrow things without asking.

- **Be thoughtful about noise.** Make sure that your music or television isn't disturbing others.

- **Notice others' feelings.** If your father is tired or your friend is upset, find ways to help out.

- **Show your appreciation.** Say thank you or return the favor when someone has done something nice for you.

- **Help people with disabilities.** Open a door for someone in a wheelchair, or offer to carry a package for someone with crutches.

The Value of Relationships

You can see why good relationships are important to people. Strong relationships give you a sense of security, acceptance, and approval. Practicing relationship skills at home, at school, and with friends is worth the effort. You will be happier, make those around you happier, and feel better about yourself.

Learning how to develop strong relationships is a skill that will help you throughout your life. Why do you think that this is so?

LESSON ONE *Review*

Using complete sentences, answer the following questions on a separate sheet of paper.

Reviewing Terms and Facts

1. Name What two types of needs do relationships fulfill?

2. Vocabulary Define the term *security*. Use it in an original sentence.

3. List Name four skills that help people develop strong relationships.

4. Recall How can you earn trust?

5. Explain What are some ways to show family and friends that you care about them?

Thinking Critically

6. Analyze What might happen if team members did not cooperate?

7. Apply Give two examples of ways you could show appreciation at home.

Applying Concepts

8. List ten ways in which you could be more considerate of family members or friends. Put a star next to five ideas that you could start doing immediately. Make plans to carry out the other ideas on your list.

Family Relationships

DISCOVER...

- several types of family structure.
- the importance of family ties and traditions.
- ways to get along with family members.

What comes to mind when you think of *family*? Can you create a description of what a family is? Is it being together for a holiday? Is it the group of people next door? Perhaps you think of a family you see on a favorite television program. There are many groups of people that function as families.

WORDS TO KNOW

family

siblings

traditions

What Is a Family?

A **family** is *a group of two or more people who care about each other and are committed to each other.* Usually, the members of a family live together, and in most cases they are related by marriage, birth, or adoption. **Figure 5.1** describes some of the common family structures.

The Importance of Families

Regardless of the structure, a healthy family life is a source of pleasure and growth for its members. Healthy families consist of people who care about each other and work together as a team. Family members work together to

- provide food, clothing, and a place to live.

- create a loving environment.

- encourage independence.

- teach values and life skills.

- give friendship, guidance, and emotional support.

In what ways do you and the members of your family meet these needs?

Try **This!**

Every family has special stories and memories. Try one or more of the following to preserve your family memories.
- Volunteer to organize family photos into a photo album.
- Videotape special family events.
- Tape-record a collection of family stories.
- Put together a scrapbook that highlights vacations.

Figure 5.1
Family Types
These are some common types of families.

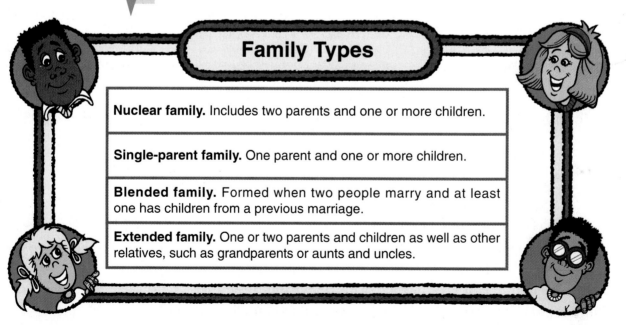

Family Types

Nuclear family. Includes two parents and one or more children.

Single-parent family. One parent and one or more children.

Blended family. Formed when two people marry and at least one has children from a previous marriage.

Extended family. One or two parents and children as well as other relatives, such as grandparents or aunts and uncles.

Strengthening Family Relationships

Families can become closer when they spend time together. By becoming involved in each other's daily lives and participating in similar activities, hobbies, and interests, family members strengthen their ties with each other.

Think about the activities you like to share with your mother, father, and **siblings,** or *brothers and sisters.* Perhaps you like to go biking or hiking with your parents or shopping with your sister. Even sharing daily events, such as talking about what happened at school or fixing dinner, can help build long-lasting and satisfying family relationships. Other ways to enrich family life include the following:

- sharing games or hobbies

- attending religious services

- planning holiday celebrations

- discussing books, movies, and current events

What do you enjoy doing with your family? What other activities might you suggest to them?

In healthy families, members do things with and for each other. When her mother had a baby, Maya helped out by making dinner each night until her mother felt stronger. Maya's older brother pitched in and did the laundry. These actions increase the bonds of affection and provide emotional support for the family unit. They are especially helpful if members are faced with difficulties, such as someone losing a job or becoming ill. At times like these, it helps if everyone can join together to be supportive and make ends meet.

The traditions you practice with family members help make your family unique. What traditions does your family have?

Your Unique Family

The people who make up a family have different skills, talents, and possessions. For example, your father may be an artist. Your sister may play on the soccer team. Your brother may own a drum set and play in a band. The skills, talents, and possessions of its members make each family unique.

Families also have different ways of expressing themselves and their emotions. You have probably noticed that some show their love for each other more openly than others. They may show affection by hugging and kissing one another and saying, "I love you." This does not mean that families who hug and kiss less feel less love. They just express it in different ways.

It is not surprising that families have different ways of expressing themselves. Families have various **traditions,** *customs and beliefs handed down from one generation to another.* These traditions might influence, for example, how they celebrate holidays, the foods they like, and their religious beliefs. Even people in different parts of this country have their own customs. It is important to realize that customs can be different without being wrong. By sharing ideas with a variety of people, you can learn more about them. At the same time, they will learn more about you as well.

Talking openly with your parents will bring you closer together.

Getting Along with Family Members

Within your family, you practice the skills of communication, cooperation, trust, consideration, respect, and appreciation. These skills help you get along with other family members and prepare you for relationships with others.

You and Your Parents

As you move toward independence, it helps to understand that parents are people, too. They have strengths and weaknesses, interests, and skills. They, too, are working toward goals. Perhaps they are going back to school or saving for a family vacation. Sometimes they face trouble at work, financial difficulties, or health problems. In these cases, it helps to recognize your parents' point of view. Just like you, they have good days and bad days and worries and hopes. If you give

Choose a time when you can be alone and when your parent is not busy or upset.

Try to understand your parents' position.

Make it a habit to talk with your parents every day, not just when you have a problem.

UNFAVORABLE EMOTIONS

Keep your emotions in control. Do not raise your voice or lose your temper.

Begin the conversation with positive comments about what happened during the day.

them love, understanding, patience, and cooperation, your family life will go more smoothly.

Communicating with parents is especially important during your teen years. Talk openly to your parents about your problems and concerns. Many times this helps both you and your parents understand one another's feelings. Try the tips in **Figure 5.2** to improve communication with your parents.

Getting Along with Siblings

You may enjoy many activities with your brothers and sisters. However, sometimes you may have difficulty getting along with them.

Learning to get along with siblings helps you learn to get along with others away from home. Here are some suggestions to improve your relationships with siblings.

- Avoid teasing them. Accept the way they act and what they say.

- Share your belongings with them, and ask permission before you use or borrow theirs.

Figure 5.2
Improving Communication with Your Parents

Following these guidelines will help you communicate with your parents. Why is communication so important?

Take time to have fun with your family. Sharing activities can bring you closer together.

- Do your share of the work. Don't leave it for them to do.

- Compliment them when you can, and speak kindly about them.

Enjoying Family Life

Your family provides you with physical care and gives you love, guidance, and friendship. The ties and traditions that you share with them will influence your personal development and relationships for the rest of your life.

LESSON TWO *Review*

Using complete sentences, answer the following questions on a separate sheet of paper.

Reviewing Terms and Facts

1. Vocabulary What is the difference between a *blended family* and an *extended family*?

2. Identify Name three ways family members support one another.

3. Explain How are family ties strengthened?

4. Identify What are three guidelines that you could follow if you have a difficult time talking with your parents?

Thinking Critically

5. Analyze How can learning to get along with family members now help to improve your relationships in the future?

6. Discuss Why do siblings sometimes not get along with each other?

Applying Concepts

7. Discuss the guidelines for improving communication with one or both of your parents. Ask them which suggestion they believe would be most effective in your family.

LESSON THREE
Changes Within Families

DISCOVER...

- the changes that occur naturally throughout the life cycle of a family.
- how to adapt to change.
- how to cope with stress.

WORDS TO KNOW

life changes

stress

cope

Change is a normal part of life. Over the years, almost everything changes, from clothing to technology. Just as fashions and technology change, families also change. Sometimes it's easier to deal with a new computer in the classroom than it is to adjust to a divorce or the birth of a sibling. It helps to understand the change and know how to adapt to it.

Life Changes

Think of how you have changed over the years. Think of how your life has changed. Some changes are unimportant, but others are **life changes,** or *major ways your life is altered by events that you may or may not be able to control.* Sometimes these events present you with a new way of life.

Some life changes are the result of things you do, or don't do. For example, if you need to make up a class but do not go to summer school, you will not be promoted to the next grade.

Other life changes you cannot control. If your family moves to a new house, you may have to go to a different school. If your parents have a new baby, you are no longer an only child. An accident or serious illness can put you in the hospital. Whether you want to or not, you may experience changes.

Understanding Family Changes

Families undergo changes just as their members do. As each individual grows and changes, the rest of the family adapts and changes. This is called the life cycle of the family. Your roles change as members grow and change. If your older sister gets married, you may find that you have more chores to do at home. You may also find that you have more time to spend with your parents. Sometimes the changes are planned or expected, such as children gaining more responsibility as they get older. Other times they come as a surprise.

TIPS
for living

LAUGHTER IS THE BEST MEDICINE

Have you ever heard, "Laughter is the best medicine"? Humor is often a healthy way of dealing with emotions. Laughter even keeps your body fit. When you laugh, your chest, heart, lungs, and other body parts are exercised. Laughing can also increase your heartbeat. After a good laugh, all systems return to normal, resulting in less stress and an all-around good feeling. Here are some ways to add humor to your life.

● Read the cartoons and comic strips in the newspaper daily.

● Watch your favorite situation comedy on television.

● Find friends who have a good sense of humor. Some people have a talent for seeing the funny side of life.

Changing Family Roles

When Justin's father remarried, Justin was surprised at how many changes took place in his family. His stepmother brought her two young children to live with Justin and his father. Now Justin has found himself in a new role—as an older brother and sometimes as a babysitter.

Maria's family also has had changes in roles. Maria's mother has a new job in the city, and she often works in the evening. Now Maria must take care of her younger sister after school and make dinner for the family.

Both Justin and Maria have learned to accept their changing roles. They discovered that when someone in their family was adjusting to a new situation, they could help out.

Changes Within the Family

Sometimes changes occur in the structure of your family. Family members may be born or adopted. Older brothers or sisters may move out of the home.

Changes may result in your having to take on new roles and responsibilities at home. What roles do you have within your family?

Other changes are the result of separation and divorce. Families must learn to accept changes, even painful ones. After a divorce, one or both parents may remarry. This causes more changes. New stepbrothers or stepsisters may join the family.

One of the most difficult changes for a family to deal with is the death of one of its members. People find it hard to accept that a part of the family is gone. They sometimes feel guilty about what they did not say or do when the person was alive. These reactions are normal. Everyone in the family can support and comfort one another. Some families seek professional counseling to help them deal with the loss of a family member.

Changes Outside the Family

Some changes are the result of the economy. A job may be lost and the family has less money to spend. The increase in the number of women working outside the home has changed people's ideas about the roles of men and women. Men are helping more often with child rearing. Social issues, such as poverty, child or spouse abuse, and substance abuse, affect everyone.

Today both parents in many households work outside the home.

Adjusting to Change

Not all changes are sad, of course. Getting your own bedroom and making a new friend are examples of happy changes. No matter what changes occur in your life, though, you will have to adjust to them. Here are some positive ways to accept change.

- **Plan ahead.** If you know about the change in advance, prepare for it even if you do not want it to happen. For example, if you are transferring to a new school, you can find out about the school before your first day.

- **Talk about your feelings.** Your family and friends can be a great source of strength and encouragement. Teachers, school counselors, coaches, religious leaders, and family service agency workers can also help you understand and handle the new situation.

- **Discover something positive about the change.** Remember that changes are part of life and they will help you grow. It does not help to keep thinking about what is wrong or different. What can you learn from the experience?

- **Be supportive.** When your family faces changes, you can help just by being there. If your brother is nervous about going to a new high school, point out his strengths and help him to manage his weaknesses. If something goes wrong for the family, do not waste time and energy blaming or finding fault. Be patient and understanding. Listen and help one another.

Many teens would find this situation stressful. How would you cope with this kind of stress?

Understanding Stress

When change occurs in your life, you may experience stress. **Stress** is *the body's reaction to changes around it*. Both pleasant and unpleasant events cause stress. For example, performing a solo in a school concert may be stressful even though you enjoy singing. Whatever the situation, remember that stress is a natural part of life.

Effects of Stress

How much stress you feel depends on how much change there is in your life and how you see the event. For instance, adjusting to a new school and making new friends would be somewhat stressful to most people. To a person who has never changed schools before and feels scared, it would be more stressful. If the person is handling another major life change at the same time, such as the parents' separation, the stress would be even greater.

Stress can also motivate and challenge you. It can help you accomplish your goals in life. The stress of wanting to make

Figure 5.3 Managing Stress

Some techniques for managing stress are shown here. What other techniques can you think of?

Set priorities. Decide what is important, and concentrate on one task at a time.

Realize that you are not alone. Almost everyone your age is experiencing some kind of stress.

Keep a positive attitude. Don't worry about things you can't control.

Gather a support system. Friends, parents, relatives, and other people who care about you can provide insight and encouragement.

Practice good health habits. Eat well-balanced meals, and get enough rest and exercise.

the soccer team, for example, would motivate you to exercise and practice.

Constant stress, however, can have a negative effect on a person. It can cause depression and a lack of physical or mental energy. People who are unable to **cope,** or *adjust to a difficult situation,* may become unhappy, depressed, or seriously ill. Sometimes they try to run away from their problems by turning to alcohol or other drugs.

Coping with Stress

Learning to cope with stress in a positive way is important to your health and well-being. **Figure 5.3** shows some ways to manage stressful situations.

Researchers believe that exercise changes body chemicals that affect the brain, resulting in a feeling of well-being. Keeping the benefits of exercise in mind, choose a sport or physical activity that you enjoy. Then develop an exercise plan.

Living with Change

During your teen years, you will probably experience many changes in your life. Although you will not be able to control all of these changes, viewing them as challenges and opportunities to learn and to develop new skills may help you to avoid negative stress and keep a positive outlook.

LESSON THREE *Review*

Using complete sentences, answer the following questions on a separate sheet of paper.

Reviewing Terms and Facts

1. Vocabulary Define the term *life changes.* Use it in an original sentence.

2. Give Examples What are three examples of changes that can occur within the family?

3. Identify List four ways in which you can adjust to changes.

4. Recall What are three ways to manage stress?

Thinking Critically

5. Analyze In what ways can you benefit from changes?

6. Explain Why might two people experience different amounts of stress from the same event?

Applying Concepts

7. Imagine that a friend's parents are getting a divorce. Write a letter to the friend, offering support and making suggestions on how he or she might cope with the change.

Developing Friendships

WORDS TO KNOW

acquaintance

peers

peer groups

expectations

DISCOVER...

● what it means to be a friend.

● the qualities of a friend.

● why friendships may change.

Who are your friends? Are they people you can talk to about your secrets and ambitions? Are they other teens who also like to go to the movies? Are they your teammates or the people in your science club? Can you really define your friends in such simple terms? You probably can't. Friends may be all those things, but they are also much more.

What Is a Friend?

A friend is someone you like and who likes you. It is someone you can talk to. A friend is a person who shares similar interests, goals, or values with you. For instance, you may enjoy collecting stamps or working on the computer with your friend. Perhaps you study with your friend. You and your friend may have the same career goal of becoming a lawyer or a fire fighter. The important quality you have in common is that you care about one another's lives.

How Do Friendships Begin?

Friendships begin and develop when people meet and like each other. You do not automatically have a friend just because you meet someone. Some people are only acquaintances. An **acquaintance** is *a person you greet or meet fairly often but do not have a close relationship with.* It may be a neighbor, the librarian at school, or the bus driver.

Friendships usually develop from the acquaintances that you have. They are formed with people you are interested in knowing better. They grow into true and lasting friendships as people learn more about one another.

Give and Take

Good friendships are based on a give-and-take relationship. No two people are alike in what they give to you as a friend or in the benefits they receive from you. Some people may just be casual friends. You may enjoy their company at school or play street hockey with them in your neighborhood. Others may become close friends whom you know very well and in whom you confide. Almost all friends learn from each other. They have something to offer one another. Some of the ways that friends share and contribute to each other's lives are by

- giving companionship and happiness.

- sharing good times.

- demonstrating a feeling of acceptance.

As people get to know each other better, they often develop lasting friendships. How did you meet your friends?

- depending on each other to listen when they need to talk about their problems.

- offering help when it is needed.

- being loyal to one another.

What are some other ways that friends show that they care about each other?

Making New Friends

Beginning a new friendship is not always easy, but you can be successful if you make the effort. Everyone has to make new friends at times. Old friends may move away, or friendships may change as you grow and develop new interests. For example, you may want a new buddy to go swimming with or a person who shares your love of crafts. Making new friends is a skill that you can learn.

As you go through life, you will have many opportunities to develop new friendships. Some may begin easily. Others take more effort, and you may need to keep trying. However, not all the friendships will work out. The person with whom you hoped to be friends may be too busy or have different interests. With experience you will recognize what friendships are worth pursuing.

As you develop new interests, you will want to make new friends who share those interests. What interests do you have in common with your friends?

What Makes a Friend?

When friendships are formed, they are based on caring, sharing, and good communication. These qualities, along with trust and reliability, help to strengthen friendships. They show others that you want to be a good friend. However, in order to have friends, you cannot be on the receiving end all the time. You have to be willing to contribute something. Listening to your friend and offering your help when it is needed are signs of a good friend. For instance, have you ever helped

Your peer group can be a major influence on the way you feel about yourself. Why are peer groups important?

a friend practice for baseball tryouts or finish chores so that you both could go to the movies? Doing your part when working with others and praising your friends when they do well are also ways to show that you are a good friend.

Being Part of a Group

During adolescence, most teens seek approval from their peers. **Peers** are *people of the same age as you.* Your peers' acceptance and recognition help you develop a sense of belonging. Acceptance by your peers strengthens your self-esteem.

Most teens strive to become part of a peer group. **Peer groups** are *groups of people of the same age.* Your peer group helps to fill your need for companionship and support. Within the group, you practice skills that can be used in other groups throughout your life.

Changes in Friendships

Your friendships will probably change over the years. Some of your friends may move away or transfer to different schools. Some of your friends may have new responsibilities

Skills
IN ACTION
Making New Friends

Here are some suggestions for making new friends.

• **Be friendly.** Don't be afraid to smile and greet other people.

• **Take an interest in others.** Ask questions. Listen to what the other person has to say.

• **Enjoy yourself.** Your happiness will be contagious.

With your classmates, brainstorm a list of ways to meet people and make new friends.

after school. Friendships may also change, as you and your friends discover new interests and activities.

The important point to remember about changes in friendships is that you can grow and learn from them. You may not have chosen the changes, but you can use them to understand more about yourself and others.

Differences in Expectations

Has there ever been a time when a friend let you down? Some changes in friendships are due to changing expectations. **Expectations** are *a person's ideas of what should be or should happen.*

A common expectation in friendships is to have and to be a best friend. Best friends expect to be able to confide in and trust each other and share common interests. Changes in friendships may occur when someone who was your best friend develops different interests and no longer shares as much with you. Perhaps a new friend, someone you enjoyed being with

Friendships can change if one friend develops new interests. What are some other reasons why friendships change?

at summer camp, expects to become your best friend. During the early teen years, changes in best friends are common, as young people learn what to expect from certain friends and what their friends expect from them.

Expectations in friendships between boys and girls also change often during the teen years. Sometimes a boy and girl who have just been friends develop a boyfriend-girlfriend relationship. This usually means that they have special caring feelings for one another. Problems may arise when one friend expects more from the relationship than the other friend wants to give.

The Importance of Friendships

Friendships help you grow and learn more about yourself and other people. Sometimes, people form a childhood friendship that lasts a lifetime. More often they make new friends as they move to high school and beyond. As you expand your circle of friends, you will discover new ways to interact with others.

Try This!

If you or a friend must move away, it doesn't mean you have to stop being friends.
• Write a friendly letter. Ask questions that will encourage your friend to write back.
• Send greeting cards on special occasions. Make your own cards for a more personal touch.
• Make an audiotape or a videotape. Your friend will enjoy hearing your voice and seeing how you look.

LESSON FOUR *Review*

Using complete sentences, answer the following questions on a separate sheet of paper.

Reviewing Terms and Facts

1. Recall How do friendships begin and develop?

2. List Name four ways in which friends share and contribute to one another's lives.

3. Vocabulary Define the term *peer group*. Use it in an original sentence.

4. Identify What are some benefits of being part of a peer group?

Thinking Critically

5. Contrast What is the difference between an acquaintance and a friend?

6. Evaluate Which qualities are the most important ones in your friendships?

7. Analyze In what ways can you benefit from changes in friendships?

Applying Concepts

8. Make a collection of cartoons, quotations, captions, and articles about friendship. Put them in a scrapbook or file. Create your own poem, saying, or cartoon about friendship, and add it to the file.

LESSON FIVE
Peers and Decision Making

WORDS TO KNOW

peer pressure

popularity

addiction

assertive

DISCOVER...

● the positive and negative influences of peer pressure.

● ways to handle peer pressure.

● how to be assertive.

Everyone wants to be accepted and liked by peers. In many situations, the desire to belong to a peer group is a positive influence. There are times, however, when peers can be a negative influence in your life. Learning to recognize the differences between these types of influences will help you decide whether to go along with the group or act as an individual.

The Influence of Peers

Having good friends and being part of a peer group can be a positive influence in your life. Their attitudes toward school, sports, or after-school activities can encourage you to do your best. The support and confidence peers give you can help you gain confidence. At times, your peers may expect you to join in their actions and activities or adopt their beliefs. **Peer pressure** is *the influence you feel to go along with the behavior and beliefs of your peers.*

Positive Peer Pressure

The acceptance and recognition of your peers help you feel good about yourself. A peer group can give you a sense of belonging and strengthen your self-esteem. A peer group can give you support and encourage positive behavior. Suppose that you were competing in a tennis match. Wouldn't you feel good knowing that your friends were there cheering you on? You would feel confident and want to do your best. This type of peer pressure is a positive force.

Negative Peer Pressure

Sometimes peer pressure is a negative force. Some groups make outsiders feel uncomfortable, unpopular, or unwanted. It may be difficult for you to go against the wishes of your

Try This!

Recognizing peer pressure is the first step in deciding how to deal with it. With a partner, decide whether the following situations represent positive or negative peer pressure.
• Your friends urge you to run for student council president.
• A popular classmate wants to copy your math homework.
• Your friends tease you about getting good grades.

How have you used positive peer pressure to encourage your friends?

peers—for instance, to be friendly to someone the group has excluded. If one member of a group is critical or has a bad attitude, it may influence the entire group.

Another negative kind of peer pressure is when you feel pushed to participate in activities that go against your values. Maybe you have been faced with making a choice about skipping school, smoking, drinking alcohol, or doing something else that you think is wrong or know is dangerous or illegal.

Making Responsible Decisions

Eventually, most teens are faced with decisions about following the group or following their own conscience. When this happens, they need to ask: Are the wishes of a few people more important than what they believe is right? If they did something only because of peer pressure, would they regret it later?

Avoiding Harmful Substances

Everyone wants to be liked and accepted, but some people feel that gaining **popularity,** or *the state of being well liked,* is essential. Some people think that they can become popular by smoking cigarettes or using alcohol or other drugs. They may do these things to impress friends or because their friends have coaxed or dared them to take part. It is important to learn to use refusal skills (see page 57) when you feel pressured to engage in activities that you believe are wrong.

If you are faced with negative peer pressure, sometimes it is best just to say no and walk away.

TIPS
for living

HANDLING PEER PRESSURE

Here are some ways to deal with negative peer pressure.

- **Think ahead.** Decide in advance what you will do if certain situations arise. You might even practice what you will say and do.

- **Practice refusal skills.** If your friends suggest that you do something that is wrong or against your values, use your refusal skills.

- **Suggest other activities.** Think of things to do that are fun, healthy, safe, and legal. Let your friends know that you would like to be with them, but not if it means doing something that goes against your values.

- **Choose your friends carefully.** Develop friendships with peers who share your values and interests.

- **Talk to parents and counselors.** Let them know if you're having problems. They can give you the support and encouragement you need to resist giving in.

If you have ever thought about trying alcohol or other drugs, think again about the reasons why. Consider carefully the long-term effects of such a decision. Using alcohol and other drugs does not make a person popular, build up self-confidence, or solve problems. What alcohol and other drugs can do is trap a person. These harmful substances slow down the ability to act and think normally, and they weaken the ability to make sound decisions.

Many people who try tobacco, alcohol, or other drugs soon find themselves addicted. **Addiction** is *a person's physical or mental need for a drug or other substance.* Many people die each year from alcohol and drug abuse.

Avoiding High-Risk Behavior

Certain kinds of negative peer pressure cause more than just regrets. Accepting a ride from someone who has been drinking alcohol can result in injury or death from a serious accident. Sexual involvement can result in pregnancy or can have harmful, even life-threatening, results in the form of AIDS (acquired immunodeficiency syndrome) and other sexually transmitted diseases. Responsible people avoid such risks, knowing that a healthy future is at stake.

The next time you and your friends are looking for something to do, practice being assertive by suggesting a fun, healthy activity. What other ways can you think of to be assertive? ▶

Being Assertive

You will be better prepared to handle negative peer pressure if you learn how to use refusal skills and to act assertively. Being **assertive** means *standing up for yourself in firm but positive ways.* Assertiveness means speaking in a confident manner, not giving in to others when you feel something is wrong, and standing up for what you believe in. Assertive teens don't wait for someone else to decide what the group is going to do. They are the ones who suggest going in-line skating, renting a video, or playing a computer game. Learning how to act assertively will make you feel more in control of your life.

LESSON FIVE *Review*

Using complete sentences, answer the following questions on a separate sheet of paper.

Reviewing Terms and Facts

1. Recall Name an advantage of being part of a peer group.

2. Explain Why is it important to be yourself, no matter who your friends are?

3. Vocabulary Define the term *addiction.*

4. Identify List three qualities of an assertive person.

Thinking Critically

5. Analyze Why do you think that peer pressure is more common among teens than among adults?

6. Evaluate Do you consider yourself to be assertive? Why or why not?

Applying Concepts

7. With a classmate, role-play a situation involving negative peer pressure. One of you should act as the person who uses negative peer pressure, and the other should act as the person who resists the pressure. Use the refusal skills you learned in Chapter 3, Lesson 1. Then switch roles and try a different way of saying no. Which way worked best? Why?

LESSON SIX
Resolving Conflicts

DISCOVER...

- reasons why conflicts occur.
- ways to prevent conflicts.
- how conflicts can be resolved.

Do you get along with everyone all of the time? If you are like most people, your answer is probably no. In fact, you might even find that lately you are getting into more arguments than you did when you were younger. That's because you are developing more opinions and beliefs that are your own. Learning how to handle these differences in a positive way is an important part of becoming an adult.

WORDS
TO KNOW

conflict

prejudice

compromise

negotiation

peer mediation

What Are Conflicts?

A **conflict** is *any struggle, disagreement, or fight*. Conflicts can occur just about anywhere, and everyone experiences them at one time or another. You have probably had disagreements with both friends and family members. Conflicts don't just occur between individuals, though. They also happen on a large scale, such as when two countries disagree and go to war.

Causes of Conflicts

Think about the last time that you had a disagreement. Can you remember the cause? Maybe you felt that someone wasn't respecting your feelings. Perhaps you and the other person wanted two different things. Then again, maybe you wanted the same thing. Here are some reasons why conflicts occur.

When two people want the same thing, they may have a disagreement. How would you handle this situation?

- **Misunderstandings.** Arguments often occur when people don't communicate effectively. Sometimes one person doesn't take the time to listen closely to what the other person is saying.

- **Differing Beliefs or Opinions.** You have your own beliefs and opinions about a wide range of topics. If someone put down your favorite football team, for example, you might take that remark as an attack on you personally. You might feel a need to defend yourself.

- **Gossip and Teasing.** When people gossip about or tease someone, they usually hurt that person's feelings and may start a conflict. For instance, if a group of peers started teasing your best friend about his braces, your friend would probably feel hurt and angry. You might feel angry, too.

- **Jealousy.** When one person wants something that someone else has, a disagreement may occur. If you and a friend both tried out for the lead in the school play and your friend got the part, you might have a conflict.

- **Prejudice.** Some conflicts are caused by **prejudice** (PRE-juh-dis), *an opinion about people that is formed* *without facts or knowledge about those people.* Prejudice causes people to judge others without taking the time to get to know them. Prejudice often leads to heated arguments and angry clashes.

Preventing Conflicts

You can prevent some conflicts by heading off problems before they even start. The best way to do this is to pay attention to your own behavior. How do you treat others? Why do you say or do certain things? By exploring your actions, you may find that there are some qualities you can improve in yourself. For example, you might work on accepting other people as they are, even if they are different from you, and try looking at situations from their point of view.

Learning to control your anger is another important way to prevent conflicts. Controlling anger is not always easy and takes a great deal of practice. When you feel yourself getting angry, you can try one or more of the following.

- Take a deep breath and count to ten.

- Go for a walk or a bike ride.

- Take a few minutes to have a "talk" with yourself. Remind yourself of the reasons why you don't want to act angry.

- Think about why you are feeling angry.

Ways to Resolve Conflicts

If you do find yourself in a conflict, how do you handle it? Your heart may start to pound. You may have the urge to turn and run—or to leap in and fight. These are all very emotional reactions, and they are quite natural. They will not solve your problems, however.

Resolving a conflict means that you and the other person work out your differences in a way that satisfies both of you. To resolve a disagreement, you and the other person must

If you are angry, try doing something physical, such as exercising. What are some other ways to cool off?

work as a team. Instead of thinking of the situation as the two of you against each other, think of it as the two of you against the problem.

Communication

The first step in conflict resolution is to open the lines of communication. Choose a neutral location that is quiet and free of groups of people. You and the other person must both be willing to listen to each other and to explain your own point of view.

You should explain how you feel and how you see the problem. When you are talking, try not to start sentences with the word *you*. The other person might feel attacked and stop listening. Start sentences with the word *I* instead. See the "Skills in Action" feature in Lesson 1 of this chapter for more about "I" messages. Express your point of view as clearly as possible. Try to stay calm, and avoid using an angry tone of voice.

When you are talking, you want the other person to listen. You should do the same. When you listen, look directly at the speaker. Don't interrupt. If you have questions, save them for when the other person has finished. It is helpful if you sum up the other person's point of view to make sure that you understand it.

As you know, body language is another important part of communication. The way you look at a person, the way you stand, and the way you move your hands and arms all communicate your feelings to others. You want your body language to show the same feelings as your words.

Even if you are not involved in a disagreement yourself, you can help other people solve a problem through communication. Instead of taking sides in an argument or a fight, try to get the people involved to talk out their problems. Giving friends this kind of support will help them see that they don't have to fight to impress anyone.

Compromise

Resolving a conflict often means that the people involved must reach a compromise. A **compromise** (KAHM-pruh-myz)

Learning to Compromise

The ability to compromise is a skill that will help you in every relationship. Think of a situation in your life that calls for a compromise. Write a paragraph describing how you could work out an agreement with the other person.

is *an agreement in which each person gives up something in order to reach a solution that satisfies everyone.*

Negotiation is one of the best ways to compromise. **Negotiation** (ni-GOH-shee-AY-shuhn) is *the process of talking about a conflict and deciding how to reach a compromise.* This requires a lot of give and take, in which both people give up some demands and make promises.

For negotiation to work, both sides must be willing to stop asking for certain things or at least change their demands. For instance, Rachel gets angry when her younger brother, Mark, borrows her CDs without asking. Mark, however, cannot always ask because she is at basketball practice when he has time to listen to them. Perhaps Rachel could agree to let him borrow certain CDs when she is not home. In return, Mark could let her borrow his handheld electronic game without asking, when she wants to play it after he has gone to bed.

When you are negotiating you must also make sure that you can follow through with your promises. If you agree to behave differently, you must actually do so. Otherwise, your agreement might crumble. For example, if you have agreed to stop teasing a friend about her haircut and she has agreed to stop teasing you about your clothes, you must both keep your promises.

Sometimes compromises can best be reached with the help of a third person who is not involved in the conflict. This person may be a parent, teacher, school counselor, or other

Try This!

The idea behind peer mediation programs is that students often feel more comfortable discussing their differences in front of someone their own age rather than an adult. Find out more about peer mediation by asking the following questions:
- What training do mediators get?
- What kinds of situations are best handled by peer mediation?
- What are some typical rules for mediation sessions?

A specially trained peer mediator can work with teens to resolve a conflict. What personal qualities do you think that a peer mediator should have?

145

When you need help solving a problem, it is best to seek advice from an adult. Whom would you ask for help with a problem?

adult. Sometimes this third person is a peer. **Peer mediation** is *a process by which specially trained students help other students find a solution to a problem.* A peer mediator does not take sides in the conflict.

Avoiding Conflicts

Let's say that you have tried everything. You have made every effort to head off problems before they spark conflicts. You have tried to resolve problems through communication, negotiation, and compromise. Still, a conflict is growing to a dangerous point. You are at school and a classmate is bullying you. What do you do? Sometimes, as hard as it may be, the best response is to walk away. In such situations it is helpful to seek out an adult at school or at home to talk to. You can't solve every problem alone. No one can. What is important is that you do your best to behave in a way that reflects your values.

LESSON SIX *Review*

Using complete sentences, answer the following questions on a separate sheet of paper.

Reviewing Terms and Facts

1. **Identify** List five causes of conflicts.

2. **Vocabulary** Define the term *prejudice.* Use it in an original sentence.

3. **Explain** What does it mean to resolve a conflict?

4. **Vocabulary** What is the difference between *compromise* and *negotiation?*

5. **Describe** How can peer mediation be used to solve a problem?

Thinking Critically

6. **Analyze** Why might close friends have conflicts?

7. **Interpret** Give an example of one situation in which you had to negotiate.

Applying Concepts

8. In small groups, discuss a book or a story you have read in which two characters had a conflict. How did they solve the problem? Could they have benefited from the help of a peer mediator?

Chapter 5 Activities

TECHNOLOGY
The New Post Office

Writing letters has once again become fashionable. Many people stay in touch with friends through electronic mail, or E-mail. A computer and a phone line are all they need. They can send messages through the Internet, and their friends can receive them in seconds.

Try This!

Find out more about E-mail and the Internet. If possible, interview someone who uses them. Write a short report on your findings.

Consumer Focus

"I Just Have to Have..."

Did you ever buy shoes or another clothing item just to be like other teens your age? Wanting to follow fads is a normal part of adolescence.

The next time you want to buy something, however, think about whether it's right for you.

Try This!

Make a list of any items you bought simply to fit in with your peers. Analyze if they were right for *you*.

FRIENDS & FAMILY

SHARING A ROOM

Matt shares a bedroom with his brother, Josh. Over the last week they have been constantly arguing. Josh never finishes his homework early enough for Matt to have time to listen to music before going to bed. Matt's light bothers Josh when he is trying to sleep.

TRY THIS!

List three possible solutions for the problem that are fair for both Matt and Josh.

LITERATURE CONNECTION

MAMA IS A SUNRISE

When she comes slip-footing through the door,
she kindles us
like lump coal lighted,
and we wake up glowing.
She puts a spark even in Papa's eyes
and turns out all our darkness.

Evelyn Tooley Hunt

Follow Up

Reading literature can give you words to describe your feelings about the people closest to you.

Find another poem or a song about families or friends. It might describe how you feel about a relationship. It might describe relationships in an entertaining or a thought-provoking way. You could even try writing your own poem or song lyrics. Read your poem or lyrics to a small group of your classmates and explain what it means to you.

Chapter Summary

- Relationships, the bonds you form with others, give you a sense of belonging, security, and self-esteem.

- A successful relationship depends on communication, cooperation, trust, and consideration.

- There are many types of families. Examples include nuclear, single-parent, blended, and extended families.

- An important part of family life is learning to get along with family members.

- Change is a part of life. Changes occur in family roles and structure.

- Stress is the emotional and physical tension caused by change. Learning to manage stress is an important life skill.

- A friend is someone who shares your interests, goals, and values. An acquaintance is someone you see fairly often but do not know very well.

- Building and maintaining friendships means forming a give-and-take relationship. Friendships can change over time.

- Peer pressure can be either positive or negative. Being assertive and standing up for what you believe in will help you resist negative peer pressure.

- Conflicts in relationships occur for many reasons, including misunderstandings, differing beliefs or opinions, gossip and teasing, jealousy, and prejudice.

- Learning how to prevent or resolve conflicts peacefully is an important part of becoming an adult.

▶ Words to Know

Using complete sentences, answer the following questions on a separate sheet of paper.

1. How do you feel when you have a sense of *security?*

2. What does it mean to be *considerate?*

3. Describe an *extended family.*

4. Give an example of a *tradition.*

5. Give two examples of *life changes.*

6. What are some words that mean the same as *cope?*

7. What does it mean to have an *addiction?*

8. If you practice *assertiveness* when confronted with negative peer pressure, what do you do?

9. What is meant by *conflicts* in a relationship?

▶ Review Questions

Using complete sentences, answer the following questions on a separate sheet of paper.

1. Why are relationships important?

2. Give an example of a way to show cooperation.

3. In what ways are families different? In what ways are they alike?

4. Why is it important to learn to adjust to life changes?

5. How can stress be both positive and negative?

6. How can you be a good friend?

7. Explain how peer pressure can be either positive or negative.

8. How can you prevent some conflicts from occurring?

9. What is the first step to take in resolving a conflict?

Thinking Critically

Using complete sentences, answer the following questions on a separate sheet of paper.

1. **Analyze** Which do you think is the most important relationship skill: communication, cooperation, trust, or consideration? Explain your choice.

2. **Analyze** Why do you think that some teens use negative peer pressure on others?

3. **Suggest** What are some ways a teen could cope with a move to a new school or to a new community?

4. **Recommend** What do you think is the best way to deal with a conflict?

Cooperative Learning

1. As a class, make a friendship quilt. Each person should decorate a sheet of paper. Include your name and a drawing that reflects something about you, such as a hobby, pet, or favorite activity. Tape all of the sheets together, and hang the quilt on a bulletin board.

2. Read a short story. Think about the relationship between the main character and one of the other characters. Are these two people relatives, friends, or acquaintances? Did any changes occur in the relationship? Discuss your ideas about the story in small groups.

Family & Community

1. Gather information about clubs or organizations for teens in your community. Find out about activities and meeting times. Choose and join a group that interests you. Encourage your friends to go with you, or use the group to make new friends.

2. Make a poster that shows one way to prevent or resolve conflicts. If possible, display the poster in your school or community.

Building A Portfolio

1. Paste a photograph of your family at the top of a piece of paper, or draw a picture of your family. Underneath the picture, write a description of your family. Include names and ages of family members and information about each person's skills and talents. Describe an activity you like to do together. Keep your family portrait in your portfolio.

2. Make a time line to show the major changes that have happened to you over the years. Choose one of your life changes. Write one or more paragraphs describing how the change affected your life, how you coped with the change, and what you might have done differently. Place your time line and your description in your portfolio.

TEENS MAKING A DIFFERENCE
Friendship Matters

Two years ago, as a sixth grader, Ricky Rodriguez decided to participate in a cross-age peer mentoring program. Once a week the mentors spent an hour with elementary school children who needed one-on-one attention.

Ricky was paired with Josh, a shy and withdrawn first grader. Soon Ricky's visits became the highlight of Josh's week. In fact, Josh asked if Ricky could be his mentor again the next year.

The second year there was a noticeable difference in Josh. His schoolwork improved and he was more outgoing. Because of his experience with Josh, Ricky is thinking about becoming a teacher or a social worker.

Try
THIS!

Do you know any younger children who look up to you? Write a paragraph or two describing how you can be a good role model to them.

Parenting Skills

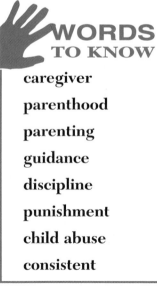

WORDS TO KNOW

caregiver

parenthood

parenting

guidance

discipline

punishment

child abuse

consistent

DISCOVER...

- the difference between parenthood and parenting.
- the commitment involved in becoming a parent.
- how parenting skills can help you interact positively with children.

Do you remember who taught you to ride a bike, tie your shoes, or tell time? Was it your mother, father, grandmother, grandfather, brother, or sister? You can probably think of many people who have taught you what you know today. These people have been your caregivers. A **caregiver** is *a person who takes care of a child or a sick or elderly person.* A caregiver can be a relative, babysitter, teacher, child care worker, nurse, or neighbor. Who are the caregivers who have had a major influence in your life?

Parenthood— A Lifelong Commitment

If you were asked to apply for a job that required a lifelong commitment, 24-hour duty, and some extra benefits, how would you respond? That job description fits **parenthood,** or *the function of being a parent.* Parenthood is a major decision and a lifelong commitment. It takes love, patience, guidance, and financial resources to be an effective parent.

Parents are the primary caregivers. They are responsible for providing a safe, loving, and stimulating environment for their children. They must fulfill a child's physical needs as well as provide emotional support. Can you see why this is a 24-hour job?

Many new parents are surprised to find how demanding parenthood can be in terms of time, energy, and money. Parents often have to make adjustments or give up their personal desires in order to provide for their children. For example, parents may have to give up traveling if their children are in school.

Parenthood can bring many joys, however. The special relationship that develops between a parent and child is a fulfilling and enriching experience. All over the world parents claim that parenthood brings them special extra benefits such as happiness, love, and pride.

Babysitting or caring for a younger sibling requires parenting skills. How can you improve your parenting skills?

Responsible Parenting

Parents and other caregivers need to use good parenting skills. **Parenting** is *the process of caring for children and helping them to grow and learn.* This process can be very rewarding, but it also takes a lot of hard work.

Do you use parenting skills? Perhaps you help care for a younger brother or sister, or

maybe you babysit for children in your neighborhood. You can improve your parenting skills by watching your parents, by taking a child development class, and by reading this chapter and other books on the topic. The more you know about children, the more comfortable you will be with them. You will find that the way you handle children affects the way they behave and their friendliness toward you.

Responding to Children's Needs

Young children, just like everyone, have physical, emotional, social, and intellectual needs that must be met. While you are caring for, playing with, and teaching children, it is up to you to fulfill these needs.

- **Physical Needs.** All children have basic physical needs. They need healthful food, appropriate clothing, good hygiene, rest and sleep, and a safe and stimulating environment. Babies and young children indicate their needs by crying. Crying is their way of telling you they are hungry, wet, tired, frightened, ill, or unhappy. As children become older and their language skills increase, they are better able to use words or sentences to communicate their needs.

Playing with children helps to improve their intellectual skills. What are some other ways to meet children's intellectual needs?

- **Intellectual Needs.** Children have intellectual needs, too. They need a stimulating environment, language activities, and opportunities to explore. Reading books, playing with puzzles and blocks, and selecting toys of different shapes and sizes helps to develop children's intellectual abilities.

- **Emotional and Social Needs.** Children also need to have their emotional and social needs met. They need to be held, cuddled, and comforted. Sometimes a kiss, hug, or gentle pat is all children need to be reassured that someone cares. Children are very sensitive to your feelings about them. Be warm and friendly with them. Speak kindly to them. They can tell by the way you touch, hold, or talk to them that they are loved.

Providing Guidance

Caregivers need to give children **guidance,** or *direction.* That is how children learn basic rules for behavior. These rules help children stay safe, learn self-control, and learn to get along with others.

Discipline is *the task of teaching a child which behavior is acceptable and which is not.* Children need guidance in learning appropriate behavior, and as they are learning they may use inappropriate behavior. **Punishment** is *a way of discouraging inappropriate behavior.* Some forms of punishment may be effective in helping a child learn self-control; others may not. *Physical or emotional mistreatment of a child* is called **child abuse.**

When guiding children, it is important to be **consistent,** which means *reacting the same way to the same situation each time it occurs.* It also means that you follow through and do what you say you will do. For example, if you say that you will take away a toy the next time a child throws it, you should do so. When you are consistent, children know what to expect.

In addition to being consistent, avoid making false threats. For example, telling a child that you will leave her at home alone if she misbehaves is a false threat, because you know that it would be unsafe to leave the child at home without supervision.

Communicating Positively

Children, like adults, respond better to positive statements than to negative ones. Keep your sentences simple. For instance, say "Let's play outside for awhile" instead of "Don't play in the living room." Emphasize what the children are allowed to do rather than what they should not do. You may also need to explain why. "Try to climb on the jungle gym this way, so you won't fall and get hurt."

Skills IN ACTION

Making Friends

Here are some tips to help children feel comfortable with you.

- When talking to children, sit or kneel so that you are at their eye level.
- Be patient—don't jump in to finish their sentences.
- Ask children how you can join in their play. "How about if I be the mailman who delivers mail to your store?"

Children will learn to look at life in a positive way if you set a good example. How can you use body language to communicate positively?

Praise is another way of focusing on the positive. You might say to a young child, "I think you did a terrific job finding all those marbles that spilled—you have really sharp eyes."

Encouraging Independence

Children want to become independent and be able to perform tasks by themselves. As they try to do new tasks on their

TIPS
for living

HELPING CHILDREN BECOME INDEPENDENT

As children perform more tasks for themselves, they learn to be more independent—an important part of growing up. Here are some ways to encourage independence.

- A step stool by the sink lets children reach the faucet and wash their hands by themselves.
- Child-size utensils encourage children to feed themselves.
- Child-size toothbrushes, combs, and hairbrushes help children learn to groom themselves.
- Allowing children to make choices about what story to read or what game to play makes them feel important. Even a choice between two options is better than no choice at all.

own, they will probably make mistakes at first. It takes practice to learn skills such as using a fork, brushing teeth, or tying a shoe. Just like you, they learn from their mistakes.

You can encourage children to become more independent. If you always help children with something they could do themselves, they will not think they can do it alone, or they may not want to try. If they make mistakes, encourage them to keep trying. Praise their efforts, even when the results are not perfect.

Positive Parenting

Because everything that happens to a child helps to shape the child's personality, it is important that you interact with children in a positive way. When you practice parenting skills, you will be able to respond to children's needs and help them feel secure. Your encouragement and consistent guidance will also help them grow to be healthy, caring, and secure individuals.

Encouraging children to become independent will help them grow and develop. What can you do to help encourage a child's sense of independence?

LESSON ONE *Review*

Using complete sentences, answer the following questions on a separate sheet of paper.

Reviewing Terms and Facts

1. Vocabulary Define the term *caregiver*. Give three examples of people who could be caregivers.

2. Recall What are some ways for teens to acquire parenting skills?

3. Identify What are ways that you can help fulfill a child's emotional and social needs?

4. Name Identify three ways that you could communicate positively with a young child.

Thinking Critically

5. Contrast What is the difference between parenting and parenthood?

6. Analyze Why is it important to be consistent when guiding young children?

Applying Concepts

7. Imagine that you are a parent and that you are looking for a caregiver for your child. Write a help-wanted advertisement listing the personal qualities that you are looking for in a caregiver.

LESSON TWO
Ages and Stages

WORDS TO KNOW

developmental
tasks

conscience

toddlers

preschoolers

DISCOVER...

- how infants and children develop.
- what to expect when interacting with infants and children.
- how to help children learn.

What comes to mind when you think about young children? Do you remember your two-year-old niece who is just learning to talk? Do you think of the children you babysit for who like the bedtime stories you read to them? Perhaps you think about your best friend's younger brother and how he enjoys playing games with you. Knowing what to expect of children at different ages and stages makes your time with them more enjoyable.

Developmental Tasks

The concept of developmental tasks is important to understand when caring for children. **Developmental tasks** are *achievements or milestones, such as walking and talking, that can be expected of children at various ages and stages of growth.*

The sequence, or order, of developmental tasks follows a set pattern. Infants crawl before they walk, for example. Some children achieve these milestones faster than others, however. Janie learned to walk by the age of 12 months, but Marta did not take her first step until 15 months. Both are normal. Toddlers babble sounds before they learn to say words. They say individual words before they speak in complete sentences.

Most toddlers enjoy activities that allow them to use their physical skills. What are some other physical tasks that children learn?

Developmental tasks are useful for explaining what the typical child can do by certain ages. However, each child is a unique individual. Just as children do not grow at the same rate physically, they do not all perform developmental tasks at the same time.

Types of Development

Children develop physically, intellectually, emotionally, socially, and morally. For example, walking and climbing are physical tasks. Talking and singing are intellectual tasks. Kissing and hugging are emotional tasks. Playing with others and sharing are social tasks. Understanding right from wrong and learning how to be fair are moral tasks.

- **Physical Development.** During the first 12 months of Anna's life, she put on weight, grew longer, and gained the muscle coordination to hold her head up, sit up, and crawl. Her first food was mother's milk, but by the age of 6 months she began eating solid foods.

- **Intellectual Development.** During the first few years of her life, Anna also developed the ability to think, reason, and solve simple problems. She learned to recognize familiar faces and places. As Anna learned to talk, that became another sign of her intellectual development.

- **Social Development.** During the first weeks of life, Anna began to learn how to relate to others. She began by smiling when she saw her mother's or father's face. During her toddler years, she learned to play with other children, make friends, and share toys.

- **Emotional Development.** When Anna was an infant, her needs were met as soon as she cried. Anna learned to trust her caregivers—the first stage of emotional

Although children master developmental tasks in the same order, each child develops at his or her own rate. What skills do toddlers learn? ▶

Infant (Birth to 1 year)
- Coos, Laughs (Birth–6 months)
- Grasps at Rattle (2 months)
- Smiles (2 months)
- Rolls Over (3–6 months)
- Puts Objects in Mouth (2 months)
- Sits Up Alone (4–6 months)
- Says Single Words (6–12 months)
- Crawls (7–9 months)
- Pulls Self Up (9–12 months)
- Plays Pat-A-Cake, Peek-A-Boo (10–12 months)

Toddler (1–3 years)
- Walks
- Learns Meaning of "No"
- Follows Simple Instructions
- Feeds Self with Spoon
- Identifies Pictures
- Climbs Stairs
- Undresses Self
- Plays Beside Others
- Puts Words into Sentences
- Begins Toilet Training

Preschooler (3–5 years)
- Opens Doors
- Dresses Self
- Recognizes Colors
- Rides a Tricycle
- Repeats Rhymes, Songs
- Brushes Teeth
- Speaks in Sentences
- Begins Cooperative Play

Figure 6.1
Patterns of Children's Development
At what stage do most children learn how to use a spoon? Throw a ball? Brush their teeth?

development. As she gets older, Anna will also learn to express her feelings in acceptable ways to parents, siblings, and others.

- **Moral Development.** Anna's parents are teaching her a system of rules to guide her behavior. They want her to develop a sense of right and wrong, fairness, justice, and consideration for others. Around the age of four or five, Anna will begin to develop a **conscience,** *the internal moral code that directs people's behavior.*

What to Expect of Children

It is important to treat each child as an individual. Even children who have the same parents experience different growth rates and patterns. After you spend some time with children and get to know them, you will have an idea of what you can expect from each child. **Figure 6.1** shows some of the tasks learned by children at various stages of development.

Guiding Preschoolers

Preschoolers are ready to learn appropriate behavior and to follow rules. With a small group of classmates, compile a list of ways to guide preschoolers. Here are some ideas to get you started.

- Set a good example.
- Stick by any limits you set.
- Give brief, simple reasons for the rules you set.

Infants

Katrina, a newborn baby, eats every few hours. She sleeps 16 to 20 hours each day. As she gets older, she will stay awake longer and eat less often. In the first few months, her parents will gradually develop a schedule so that Katrina can learn to have a regular time for eating, bathing, sleeping, and playing.

Katrina will have many developmental tasks to learn, such as how to eat, sit alone, pick up objects, and crawl. She will learn how to play with toys and be comfortable with different people and places. Katrina will also need a great deal of love and attention.

Toddlers

Toddlers are *children who are one to three years old.* The name comes from the unsteady way they walk, or toddle. Toddlers are usually full of energy and ideas. They are learning to be more independent by doing tasks for themselves and by being less dependent on the people who care for them. As a part of this new independence, they often use the word *no.* These are some tasks that toddlers can learn to do:

- Come to the table for meals when called.

- Eat food without dawdling or being bribed.

- Follow safety rules such as not touching something hot.

Preschoolers

Preschoolers are *children who are three to five years old.* Preschoolers interact more with their playmates and like to play with children of all ages. They like to talk. Preschool children may carry on a conversation with make-believe playmates or dolls. They might imitate their heroes or pretend to be superhuman.

Children with Special Needs

Some children have special needs. Jake walks with a leg brace. Peter wears a hearing aid. Joanna has emotional problems. Each of these children has a particular disability, yet what they need most is to learn how to develop their abilities and enjoy a good life. For example, they need to learn to be as independent as possible, and they need encouragement to develop a positive self-concept. The attitudes of people around them are important in making this possible.

How Young Children Learn

Young children learn from exploring their environment with their five senses— sight, hearing, taste, touch, and smell. Children learn something from everyone and everything around them, including toys. Their first toys might help them develop their body and coordination or help them learn to focus, perhaps on a brightly colored object. As children grow, activities and toys can help them improve their intellectual abilities. Some toys teach shapes, colors, letters, numbers, and others teach reasoning skills.

Children with special needs benefit from caregivers who encourage their independence.

TIPS for living

SPARKING A CHILD'S IMAGINATION

Try these ideas to jump start a youngster's journey into imagined worlds.

● Ask open-ended questions—questions that don't have a yes or no answer. "What do we need to build a dream castle?"

● Write a group story. Start off the story in some such way as, "Once upon a time there was a frog who didn't have any friends." Ask each child to contribute a sentence.

● Here's a rainy day idea: Ask children to help plan a make-believe outing in their home. Maybe they will go camping and make a tent out of a blanket spread over a table. Encourage as many ideas from the children as possible.

Young children also learn by practicing tasks over and over again, observing and imitating others, and exploring objects in their environment. They also learn from being exposed to such interesting places outside the home as an aquarium, a science museum, a historic house, a children's theater, or a pick-your-own strawberry patch.

Young children learn through hands-on discovery, using the five senses: touch, taste, smell, sight, and hearing.

Understanding Children

Although every child is unique, most children go through a similar pattern of growth and development. As an older brother or sister or as a babysitter, you can help children learn and discover new things by interacting with them. Show children that you are interested in them and that what they say matters to you.

LESSON TWO *Review*

Using complete sentences, answer the following questions on a separate sheet of paper.

Reviewing Terms and Facts

1. Vocabulary Define the term *developmental tasks.* Give two examples.

2. Explain Why don't all children of the same age perform developmental tasks at the same time?

3. List Name the five main areas of development.

4. Identify What are five ways in which children learn?

Thinking Critically

5. Analyze Why is it helpful to understand when young children should accomplish certain developmental tasks?

6. Describe Give an example of each of the five main areas of development.

7. Compare How are toddlers and preschoolers similar? How are they different?

Applying Concepts

8. Divide into groups of four or five. Review the section in this lesson called "How Young Children Learn." Think of one simple game or activity for young children for each of the five senses. Try to make one or two of your activities appropriate for outdoors. Have someone in the group take notes. Compile the activities from all the groups into a babysitter's activity guide.

Child's Play

DISCOVER...

- how infants, toddlers, and preschoolers learn through play.
- how to select safe toys.
- the different types of play activities.
- the advantages of quiet play.

Beep, beep! Gabrielle's school bus honks at the cars and trucks in the traffic jam on the floor. Gabrielle is working hard at an important job for a child—learning through play. Through play with other children and with toys, children develop physically, intellectually, emotionally, socially, and morally. Play teaches children about sizes and shapes, colors, and numbers. It teaches them about their world and helps them grow.

WORDS TO KNOW

attention span

solitary or independent play

parallel play

cooperative play

group play

How Infants Learn Through Play

As a class, prepare a display of toys that are safe for babies—no parts small enough to be swallowed. Here's how you can do it without actually buying anything.

- Borrow a toy.
- Draw a toy.
- Bring in a picture from a toy catalog.

Allow class members to evaluate each selection.

Baby Nicholas is happy waving his arms and kicking his legs. He likes to have someone play with him and enjoys being moved from place to place so he can look at new sights. A walk outside or to the grocery store is very interesting to him.

Nicholas does not stay with one toy for very long. He, like other infants, has a short **attention span,** *the length of time a person can concentrate on any one thing.* This means that toys and other objects hold his interest for only a short amount of time.

When infants discover their hands and can hold a toy, play becomes more important to them. They gradually learn to pick up a toy and hold it. It is natural for them to play happily, picking up first one toy, then another. Playing with toys is one way babies learn about the world around them. For example, when they shake a rattle, it causes a sound.

Playing helps infants get the exercise they need. When they first throw a toy, it may go in any direction. They keep trying until they finally learn to control their muscles enough to toss the toy toward another person.

Toys for Infants

Infants engage in **solitary** or **independent play**—*playing alone and showing little interest in interacting with other children.* Infants play with their hands, toes, toys, or other objects. Toys that are easy to pick up and hold with tiny fingers are best for first toys. Infants like toys that are pleasant to touch, see, and chew on.

Infants develop their senses by playing with toys. Which senses is this baby developing?

Musical toys, squeeze toys, and stacking and nesting blocks are good toys for a baby. Even small kitchen items, such as plastic measuring cups and spoons and pots and pans, can be entertaining toys. **Figure 6.2** provides suggestions for choosing toys for infants as well as for toddlers and preschoolers.

Playtime for Toddlers

Play is toddler's work, and toys are their tools. Playing helps children develop their minds, bodies, and social skills.

Toddlers are curious about everything and spend much of their time exploring. They pull out various toys, look them over, and go on to something else. Most toddlers play alone or

Figure 6.2 Choosing Toys for Children

What kinds of toys are good choices for a child who is six months old? Two years old? Five years old?

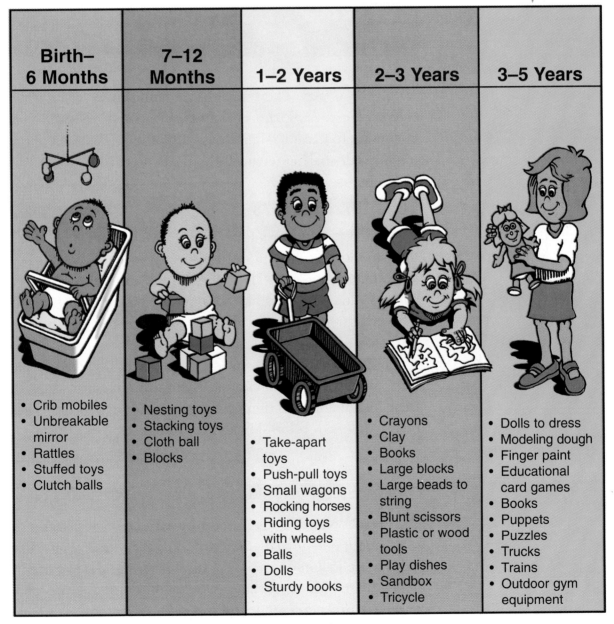

Birth–6 Months	7–12 Months	1–2 Years	2–3 Years	3–5 Years
• Crib mobiles • Unbreakable mirror • Rattles • Stuffed toys • Clutch balls	• Nesting toys • Stacking toys • Cloth ball • Blocks	• Take-apart toys • Push-pull toys • Small wagons • Rocking horses • Riding toys with wheels • Balls • Dolls • Sturdy books	• Crayons • Clay • Books • Large blocks • Large beads to string • Blunt scissors • Plastic or wood tools • Play dishes • Sandbox • Tricycle	• Dolls to dress • Modeling dough • Finger paint • Educational card games • Books • Puppets • Puzzles • Trucks • Trains • Outdoor gym equipment

Toddlers do not yet have the social skills to play with other children. Instead, they play alongside other children. What is this type of play called?

watch others play. They engage in **parallel play,** or *play that occurs alongside of, rather than with, a friend.* They are just beginning to learn to share toys with others. The idea of taking turns or sharing means little to a two-year-old.

Toys for Toddlers

Toddlers need toys for both active and quiet play. Their toys should help them develop socially and physically. Toys for toddlers should also help them think and use their imagination. Older toddlers like toys that do something, but they may be startled by toys like a jack-in-the-box or toys that move too fast.

Toddlers also enjoy vehicle toys. Toy cars, bulldozers, tractors, and airplanes will capture their attention and stimulate their imagination. Action toys, such as riding toys and balls, help toddlers develop skill and coordination.

Playtime for Preschoolers

Preschoolers engage in **cooperative play**—*playing together with one or two other children and sharing toys.* Play helps preschoolers learn to take turns, share, and make friends with other children. As they get older, they enjoy **group play,** or *play with several other children,* especially those their own

TEACHING CHILDREN TO SHARE

Young children often fight over toys. Although two-year-olds may be too young to understand the concept of sharing, preschoolers can learn to share. Use the following tips to teach children about sharing.

● Use "sharing" words—such as *share, take turns, wait your turn.*

● Ask one child to show another child how a toy works.

● Help children find ways to share materials and play together. For instance, make an airplane out of chairs and create roles for everyone: pilots, flight attendants, and passengers.

● Praise the children when you see them sharing.

age. The benefits of playtime for preschoolers include taking turns and sharing with others, learning how to get along with and play with a group, and becoming more creative.

Toys for Preschoolers

As children develop, their interest in playthings gradually changes. New toys help keep pace with their natural development. Preschoolers enjoy action toys that encourage physical exercise—tricycles, climbing equipment, and balls. Toys for pretend play can include household props and occupational props—lab coats and briefcases, dress-up clothes, and non-toxic art materials.

When preschoolers play together, they learn about cooperation and sharing. What other skills do you think that these children are learning?

169

Quiet Play

Quiet play is helpful before meals, naptime, or bedtime to help children relax. Quiet play can also help to calm an upset child. Here are some suggestions for quiet play activities:

- Drawing with crayons or markers, painting, making collages from old magazines

- Playing with clay

- Making up stories, listening to books read aloud

- Listening to music

Computer software programs can open up a whole new world of learning for children. What might be some of the advantages of helping a child develop an interest in computers at an early age?

Learning Through Play

Stop to think about the favorite toys you have had over the years. Did you realize you had learned so much through playing? Through playtime and toys, infants, toddlers, and preschool children develop physically, intellectually, emotionally, socially, and morally.

LESSON THREE *Review*

Using complete sentences, answer the following questions on a separate sheet of paper.

Reviewing Terms and Facts

1. Vocabulary Define the term *attention span*. Use it in an original sentence.

2. Identify What are three developmental tasks that infants learn through play?

3. List Name three types of toys for toddlers.

4. Recall What are four ways in which play benefits preschoolers?

5. Give Examples Name three types of quiet play activities for children.

Thinking Critically

6. Contrast What is the difference between parallel play and group play?

7. Analyze Why is quiet play important for children? What might happen if a child did not have any quiet play?

Applying Concepts

8. Ask a preschooler you know what his or her favorite toys are. Share your results with your classmates and put together a "top ten" list of favorite toys for preschoolers. How does the list compare with the suggestions in this lesson?

LESSON FOUR
Child Safety

DISCOVER...
- how to keep children safe.
- how to prevent common accidents.

Children do not understand the dangers that surround them. In their eagerness to explore, they can easily hurt themselves or try to play with a dangerous object or substance. There are precautions you can take, however, to help keep children safe and prevent them from getting hurt.

Keeping Children Safe

Many families make their homes **childproof,** or *safe for children to play and explore in.* Childproofing includes putting safety latches on cabinet doors and drawers. It also includes using safety gates at the top and bottom of stairs, putting safety caps on electrical outlets, and moving cleaning supplies and other dangerous items so that they are out of children's reach. Even if a home has been childproofed, you still need to watch children to make sure that they are safe.

There are different safety concerns for children of different ages. Because babies put objects in their mouths, you need to make sure that anything that could result in harm or anything small enough to be swallowed is kept out of reach. Toddlers must be watched every minute because they move quickly, climb, and get into everything. Although preschoolers have a better idea of what they should not do, they may still get into danger-ous situations unless their behavior is monitored.

All babies put objects into their mouths. That is why toys that are safe must be too large to swallow.

Intruders

Keeping children safe involves taking care to protect the children and yourself from intruders. An **intruder** is *someone who uses force to get into a home.* Caregivers need to take the following precautions—day or night.

- Make sure that all doors and windows are locked.

- Do not open the door for any stranger.

- Call a neighbor or another trusted adult, or dial 911 (emergency center) if a stranger approaches and does not go away.

Preventing Accidents

Some common accidents are falls and injuries, fires, and poisoning. When caring for young children, you need to take special precautions to prevent accidents. To learn how to take care of basic injuries, such as a small cut or a nosebleed, you might consider taking a first-aid course or studying a book on first aid. If a child gets hurt and you do not feel capable of handling the situation, stay calm and call for help. A broken bone, lots of bleeding, a burn, or an animal bite can be dangerous. Call the child's parents, a neighbor, or dial 911 for help.

Falls and Injuries

Falls are the leading cause of accidental death at home in the United States. When caring for children, follow these guidelines to prevent falls and injuries.

- Never leave an infant alone on a changing table, sofa, or bed. The infant may roll over and fall off.

- Restrict crawling babies and toddlers to places that they can explore safely.

- Keep all young children away from electrical wires and outlets and breakable or dangerous objects.

- Make sure that toys are age appropriate and that they are smooth and free of loose parts.

- Keep plastic bags away from children to prevent suffocation.

If you care for children, you should know how to handle routine accidents. What should you do to avoid unsafe situations?

TIPS for living

PLAYGROUND SAFETY

To keep children safe on outdoor play equipment, explain that the following behavior can cause accidents.

- Standing on a swing, walking in front or in back of a moving swing, swinging empty seats, pushing other children off the swing, twisting the chains
- Climbing up the front of the slide
- Jumping off the seesaw unexpectedly
- Overloading climbing equipment
- Roughhousing on the jungle gym

Car seats are designed to prevent children from getting hurt in a car accident.

- Keep knives and breakable dishes away from children.

- Outside, always watch toddlers to prevent them from running into the street.

- In a car, children should always ride in a child car seat, no matter how short the trip is.

Fires

Fires are the second leading cause of accidental death in the United States. To prevent fires, follow these guidelines.

- Use the stove and oven properly. Turn pot and pan handles away from the edge of the stove. When cooking, avoid wearing clothes with long, full sleeves.

- Keep all matches and lighters away from children.

- Be sure that there are smoke alarms on every floor of your home. A **smoke alarm** is *a device that sets off an alarm when smoke is present.*

If you smell smoke or see a fire when you are caring for children, first get the children out safely. Then call the fire department from a neighbor's home. Do not try to put out the fire yourself or to save items from the home.

If you are trapped by smoke or fire, try not to panic. Stay close to the floor. If you can, put a wet cloth over your nose and mouth and over the children's, and crawl to safety. If you cannot get out, stay in a room—the bathroom is good if it has a window—close the door to the room, and stuff wet towels around the cracks in the door. Turn on the light, and call out the window for help.

Try **This!**

Caregivers need to teach children how to be safe. You might try one of the following ideas:
• Write a safety story and read it to the children.
• Make a safety poster for the children to color.
• Put on a puppet show.

Poisonings

Common-sense prevention is the best way to keep children away from dangerous household substances. All poisonous items should be kept in locked cabinets or stored in drawers that have safety latches on them. If that is not possible, keep the items on a high shelf, out of the children's reach.

If you suspect that a child has been poisoned, the first step to take is to call the **poison control center,** *a medical facility with staff trained to help in poisoning emergencies.* You can find the number of the nearest poison control center by looking in the telephone book or by calling directory assistance.

Be Prepared

Have you ever heard the expression, "An ounce of prevention is worth a pound of cure"? When it comes to child safety, it means that you can prevent many common accidents by being prepared. Learn basic first-aid procedures. Make sure the homes where you care for children are childproofed. Ask parents to leave you emergency numbers for their community. These simple steps may save a life.

Many common household items are poisonous and should be kept in a locked cabinet or on a high shelf away from children. What should you do while babysitting to prevent an accidental poisoning?

LESSON FOUR *Review*

Using complete sentences, answer the following questions on a separate sheet of paper.

Reviewing Terms and Facts

1. Explain What does it mean when you make a home *childproof?*

2. Describe If you smell smoke or see fire, what should you do first? Next?

3. Identify Where can you call for help if a child swallows poison?

Thinking Critically

4. Evaluate What is the single best way to keep young children safe?

5. Analyze What can happen if you rely solely on childproofing to keep children safe?

Applying Concepts

6. Check for smoke alarms in your home. They should be located on every level, especially outside bedroom areas. Test the batteries in your smoke alarms to see if they work. If your home needs more smoke alarms or the batteries are dead, ask a parent to help you install more alarms or to replace the batteries.

Caring for Children

DISCOVER...

● how to prepare for babysitting.

● how to care for infants, toddlers, and preschoolers.

Babysitting is usually the easiest kind of job for young people to find, and it provides good employment experience. However, caring for children is a big responsibility. You will be better able to handle it if you prepare in advance. Then, the more frequently you care for children, the more you will know about keeping them safe and happy.

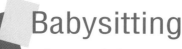 Babysitting

When you babysit, you take the place of the children's parents. You are totally responsible for the safety and well-being of the children in your care. If you do your job well, you will gain valuable experience and earn money. You will also have an opportunity to play with children and teach them new things.

Preparation

Before you begin looking for a babysitting job, you can prepare by taking a course in babysitting and first aid through a 4-H group, a local hospital, or a community center. You could also volunteer as a parent's helper—someone who cares for an infant or a young child under a parent's supervision.

Be sure to ask around to determine what the usual rate of pay is in your community. When you are starting out, you might be willing to charge a little less in order to get your first jobs.

When parents ask you to babysit, find out the following information before you accept the job:

- The number and ages of the children

- The time you will be needed

- How long the parents plan to be gone

- The rate of pay you will receive

If everything about the job is agreeable to you, check with your parents to make sure that the job meets with their approval. After you accept the job, write down the date, time, and place. Give your parents the phone number where you can be reached.

On the Job

The first time you babysit for a family, ask the parents if you can arrive a little early. That way, you will have a chance to get to know the

When you babysit for a new family, ask for a tour of the house. Why is this important?

✔ Where the parents will be and a phone number where they can be reached.

✔ The name and phone number of an adult you can call if the parents can't be reached.

✔ The phone numbers of the police and fire departments and the rescue squad.

✔ The address where you are babysitting.

✔ The location of first-aid supplies.

✔ The location of toys, diapers, and other items you may need.

✔ The children's usual routine for eating and sleeping.

✔ The time the parents will be home.

▲ **Figure 6.3**
Babysitter's Checklist

When you babysit, be sure to get this information from the parents before they leave. Is there anything else you need to know?

children while the parents are still at home. During this time, you can also ask the parents for the information shown in **Figure 6.3.**

It is a good idea to ask the parents to go over a few of the family rules—television viewing, homework time, friends' visits, snacks, and bedtime—in front of the children. Discuss rules or limits that might cause problems later, such as television viewing, homework time, friend's visits, snacks, and bedtime.

If you are friendly and caring with the children, they will feel comfortable with you in charge. Show the children that you enjoy being with them and that you are interested in what they would like to do. Try to get them involved in something enjoyable for them so that they stay happy and busy—and won't have the opportunity to behave inappropriately.

Reliable babysitters get asked back again and again and can establish a good relationship with the parents and children. Show that you are reliable by

- keeping a constant, careful watch on the children.

- keeping an accurate list of phone messages.

- leaving the house as neat as you found it.

- not allowing your friends to visit.

- not opening the door to strangers.

Television Tips

When you babysit, you should not rely on the television to keep the children busy. Ask the parents the following questions about television viewing ahead of time.

- Is it all right for the children to watch television? If so, how long may they watch?

- What programs or videotapes are OK to watch?

Caring for Children

Caring for children is a serious and important task, but it can also be enjoyable and creative. Children of different ages have different needs and require different types of care. Learning how to take care of infants, toddlers, and preschoolers will help you meet their needs and enjoy your time with them.

Caring for Infants

Infants are cute, fun to cuddle, and easy to entertain. Because they cannot do things for themselves, they rely on their caregiver for all their needs. Babies communicate their needs for sleep, food, comfortable clothing, and attention by crying.

When infants cry, first check to see if they are hungry or have dirty

One of the best ways to acquire skills for baby-sitting is to help your parents care for your younger brothers and sisters. What are some other ways to acquire these skills?

HANDLING EMERGENCIES

In a serious emergency, you will need to call for help. If you live in an area with 911 emergency service, dial 911. If not, carry an emergency card with phone numbers of the police and fire departments, rescue squad, and poison control center listed on it. Know the house number and street where you are babysitting. Here are some tips for making an emergency phone call.

- Remain calm.
- Explain that you are the babysitter and give the street address where you are.
- State the type of emergency.
- Listen to and follow any directions you are given.
- Do not hang up until you are told to do so.

When you pick up an infant, grasp the baby's entire body rather than just the arms. Hold the baby firmly and rest it against your shoulder or cradle it in your arms.

diapers. Sometimes they may be too hot or too cold, or may need to be burped. If none of these problems exist, try holding, rocking, or walking them.

The first time you take care of an infant, have the parent show you the following.

- **How to hold the baby.** Infants can't hold their heads up without help. To support an infant's head, place one hand under the head and the other hand and arm under the lower part of the baby's back. Then you can lift the baby safely to your shoulder or cradle the baby in the bend of your arm and elbow area.

- **How to change diapers.** Ask the parent to show you the diaper-changing procedure and where to put dirty diapers. When you change a diaper, assemble everything you need before you begin. Babies can roll off changing tables and beds, so never leave them unattended.

- **What to feed the baby and when.** A young baby drinks milk or formula. Cradle the baby in your arm when you give a bottle. After the baby stops drinking, hold the baby over your shoulder, and lightly pat the back until you hear a burp. It may take a minute or two for the burp to come. Be patient. Also know that babies do not always burp.

- **Where and when to put the baby to sleep.** Place the baby on the side or back, never on the stomach. Be sure to pull up the side of the crib and fasten it securely. When the baby is sleeping, check frequently to make sure that everything is all right.

Caring for Toddlers and Preschoolers

Toddlers require a lot of attention. They need help and understanding as they grow and make new discoveries. They also demand much attention because they are busy moving from one thing to another. Unless a toddler is sleeping, a caregiver must constantly keep him or her in sight.

While toddlers are beginning to enjoy showing off their budding independence, most will need special comforting when their parents leave. You may need to redirect them with a favorite toy, puzzle, or game. When you **redirect** children, you *turn their attention to something else.* They will usually get over missing their parents in a few minutes.

If the toddler has learned to use the toilet, you may have to help him or her in the bathroom. Unfasten the toddler's clothes, and help him or her get onto the toilet or potty seat.

Preschoolers are curious and often look forward to being with caregivers they like. You can share such activities as reading, coloring, and pretend play with preschoolers.

Skills IN ACTION

Treasure Chest

Children will look forward to seeing a babysitter who brings surprise activities and goodies. Here are some ideas for the treasure chest.
- A few inexpensive toys
- Colorful bandage strips
- Materials for making puppets—old clean socks, yarn, glue, tape, and scraps of fabric
- Storybooks, crayons and colored paper
- Cassette tapes or compact discs of children's songs

Toddlers enjoy playing with caregivers they like. What kinds of play activities would you enjoy with toddlers?

Babysitting can be a rewarding and valuable experience. What are some benefits of babysitting?

Toddlers need their food cut into small bites, and they may need help using a spoon or a fork. During meals and snacks, serve only foods that parents have specified and provided. Children may have allergies of which you are unaware.

When caring for toddlers and preschoolers, keep the children's normal bedtime routine. Ask parents what time each child goes to bed. Also, find out if the child always has a bedtime story.

The Rewards of Babysitting

Babysitting is not only an excellent way to develop good work habits but also an enjoyable and challenging job. As you gain more experience, you will become more confident about meeting children's needs.

LESSON FIVE *Review*

Using complete sentences, answer the following questions on a separate sheet of paper.

Reviewing Terms and Facts

1. Recall What questions should you ask before you accept a babysitting job?

2. Explain Why do toddlers require a lot of attention?

3. Vocabulary How do you *redirect* a child?

Thinking Critically

4. Recommend As a babysitter, what could you do to prevent children from objecting to family rules?

5. Describe How might you get recommended for babysitting jobs?

Applying Concepts

6. Make a list of questions to ask parents before you accept a babysitting job and when you arrive at their home. Leave space for answers as well as for names and addresses. Then look up local phone numbers for the police, fire department, ambulance, poison control center, and directory assistance. Add these phone numbers to your list.

Chapter 6 Activities

TECHNOLOGY

Software for Kids

Matthew and Nathan, four-year-old twins, crowd into a chair in front of the computer. Nathan pushes the *P* key. "P is for piano," says the computer.

Educational computer games are being created specifically for young children. These programs teach preschoolers the names and sounds of letters and numbers, and such concepts as color, shape, and size.

Try This!

If possible, try out one of the programs for preschoolers, and report to the class.

FRIENDS & FAMILY

BABYSITTING DILEMMA

Cherise and Katie wanted to start babysitting to earn extra money, but they needed a great idea to help them stand out from the competition. One day they saw a Red Cross ad saying: "Child safety and CPR class—open to parents and babysitters." *That* was what would give them an edge over other babysitters!

TRY THIS!

Why do you think that the Red Cross course will help?

A GlObal View

BRINGING UP CHILDREN

Adolescents in many cultures play an important role in caring for younger children and teaching them new skills. For example, instead of being taught directly by adults, many Native American children observe the way their older siblings perform a task. Then they practice the skill on their own and test themselves.

TRY THIS!

Why do you think that adolescents have more child-rearing responsibilities in some cultures than in others? Share your ideas with your classmates.

ART CONNECTION

Follow Up CHILDREN IN ART

Thomas Eakins. *Baby at Play.* 1876. National Gallery of Art, Washington, D.C. John Hay Whitney Collection.

1. Although Eakins's *Baby at Play* was painted over 100 years ago, it tells us that children loved to play with toys that are still popular today. Besides providing a visual record of people, times, and places, what other values does art have?

2. Bring examples of children's art to class, and discuss why young children love to paint, draw, and make things.

Chapter Summary

- Parenting is the process of caring for children and helping them grow and learn.

- Children need guidance, discipline with a positive focus, and encouragement to do tasks for themselves.

- Children progress through predictable physical, intellectual, emotional, social, and moral developmental stages. Learning about these stages helps you know what to expect from children at different ages.

- Some children have special physical, intellectual, or emotional needs. Love, understanding, and extra attention can help these children develop their abilities.

- Types of play include solitary or independent play, parallel play, cooperative play, group play, and quiet play.

- Child safety is one of a caregiver's main concerns. You should know how to prevent common accidents and what to do if an accident occurs.

- Babysitting is an important job that requires responsibility and planning. Babysitters should make sure that they have all of the information and instructions they need before the parents leave.

- Caring for infants and young children may involve changing diapers, feeding, and putting children to bed. You should know the correct procedures for these tasks.

Words to Know

Using complete sentences, answer the following questions on a separate sheet of paper.

1. What do you do when you give children *guidance?*

2. Explain what it means to be *consistent* when taking care of children.

3. Define the term *preschoolers.* What are two characteristics of preschoolers?

4. Explain what is meant by a child's *attention span.*

5. What is *group play?* At what age are most children ready for group play?

6. What is an *intruder?*

7. Why are *smoke alarms* important?

8. How could you *redirect* a child?

Review Questions

Using complete sentences, answer the following questions on a separate sheet of paper.

1. Why should a young teen learn parenting skills?

2. Give three examples of positive parenting.

3. What are the developmental tasks of infants?

4. Name four ways in which young children learn.

5. What are typical play activities for infants?

6. How does play benefit toddlers?

7. What should you do if a child becomes seriously injured while in your care?

8. How can you prevent children from getting into poisonous substances?

9. Describe a reliable babysitter.

Thinking Critically

Using complete sentences, answer the following questions on a separate sheet of paper.

1. **Compare** How are the needs of young children similar to your own needs?

2. **Analyze** Why do you think that it is important to stimulate a child's imagination?

3. **Suggest** What would you do if two toddlers wanted to play with the same toy?

4. **Explain** Why must caregivers watch children closely even if the home has been childproofed?

Cooperative Learning

1. As a class, organize a used-toy drive. Use your management skills to advertise the event and collect the toys. Be sure that all of the toys you collect are clean and safe for children. Donate the toys to the children's ward of a local hospital or to an organization that helps children with special needs.

2. Working in small groups, discuss child-care skills that a babysitter should have. Have each group member explain a skill to the group. If possible, use a doll to demonstrate the skill. Choose from this list: how to feed and burp a baby, how to hold a baby, how to change a diaper, how to bathe a baby, how to soothe a crying baby, how to play with a baby.

Family & Community

1. Check the safety of the play equipment at a nearby playground. Look for such items as missing bolts, sharp edges, and worn or shaky anchoring structures. Report anything that you think is unsafe to the playground supervisor, or write a letter to the city department in charge of the playground.

2. Find out about a babysitting or first-aid class. The local chapter of the Red Cross, the YWCA, a 4-H club, a local hospital, or community education programs may offer classes for babysitters. If possible, sign up for a class. Share what you learn with your classmates.

Building A Portfolio

1. Write down as many facts as you can remember about yourself as a young child. Who were your playmates? What were your favorite toys? Which stories did you enjoy? Put a list of facts about yourself, along with childhood photos or artwork, into your portfolio.

2. Collect cartoons and comic strips that feature young children. Share your findings with your classmates. Discuss how the cartoons and comic strips are related to information you found in this chapter. Keep your collection in your portfolio.

3 Consumer Skills and Home Management

Chapter 7:
Being a Wise Consumer

Chapter 8:
Your Home

Chapter 9:
Your Environment

7

Being a Wise Consumer

TEENS MAKING A DIFFERENCE
Clothes from Recycled Plastic

In social studies class, Rachel Davis and her friend Maria learned that most of the millions of plastic beverage bottles that are thrown out daily are never recycled. Just recently, however, the teens found clothes made from recycled plastic in a mail order catalog. The jackets were made of polyester fleece, but most of the fabric was made from recycled bottles. Rachel and Maria have decided to buy at least some clothes that are good for the environment as well as useful to them.

Try THIS!

How can you help the environment through your shopping decisions? Make a chart of items you buy regularly for which environmentally safe choices are available. Share your chart with your classmates.

189

Influences on Buying Decisions

WORDS TO KNOW

goods

services

consumer

advertisement

DISCOVER...

- what it means to be a consumer.
- how peers, habits, and advertising influence your buying decisions.

Do you remember every T-shirt, magazine, notebook, or CD you bought last year? Are you, or is one of your friends, saving money to buy something special, such as concert tickets or a new jacket? As a teen, you are a member of a group with a great deal of spending power. Many companies that make clothing, magazines, and soft drinks take teen interests very seriously. Some of these companies even specialize in products designed specifically for teens.

Teens as Consumers

On what do teens spend their money? Like all people, they buy goods and services. **Goods** are *products made for sale,* such as in-line skates, computer games, or jeans. **Services,** or *work performed by one person for others,* include the work done to repair your bike, tutor you, dry-clean your clothes, or teach you karate. Even if you don't spend a great deal of money, you can be a smarter shopper if you know what factors influence your consumer decisions. A **consumer** is *a person who buys goods and services.*

As a consumer you have many choices to make. You must decide what to buy, where to buy, and when to buy. You have to decide how to get the best value for your money. By making wise purchases, you will be a satisfied consumer.

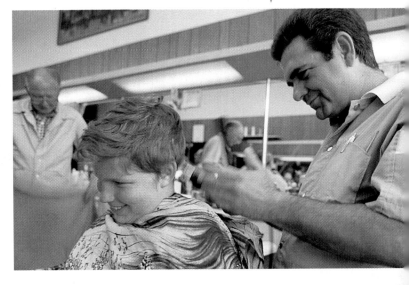

A haircut is a service. What other services do you buy?

Factors That Influence Buying Decisions

When you bought your last CD or pair of athletic shoes, what influenced your decision? Did your friends convince you that you needed the CD? Did you buy the same brand of shoes that you always buy? Maybe your decision was based on price. Perhaps you saw an advertisement that encouraged you to purchase the product. An **advertisement** is a *message to persuade consumers to buy*

Peers

Because friends are an important part of the lives of most teens, their ideas and tastes can be influential. Have you ever tried out a new shampoo because some of your friends were using it? Have you ever decided to buy a new backpack because a friend bought one?

Money Savers

Often, store brands and generic brands are made from the same ingredients or materials. The only difference may be the amount of money spent on packaging and advertising. The extra cost is passed on to consumers. Why not save some money and try the less expensive item?

Before buying goods or services, think about why you want to make the purchase. Are you being influenced by your peers?

Sometimes one or two popular students can spread a fad that was started by a movie, concert, or sports event. Other students may see them carrying a certain kind of bag or wearing a certain brand of shoes that a celebrity wears and decide to do the same. These items may even become status symbols, or signs of popularity and importance.

Teens who belong to a certain group often dress similarly. They may think that wearing a particular kind of clothes is a way of expressing who they are. For example, athletes may wear sweats and baseball caps, whereas surfers may like T-shirts and baggy shorts. Other groups may prefer preppy clothes or leather jackets.

What really matters is that you buy for yourself what is best for *you*. As you make a buying decision, ask yourself the following questions.

- Am I buying an item that is popular today but will soon be out of fashion?

- Am I getting the best value for my money?

- Am I spending a lot more money for a name-brand item?

Before you make a purchase, evaluate the product and analyze your decision. If it is not best for you, you may choose to wait or to buy something else. Do what is best for you, and be proud of your individuality.

Habit

As you have probably discovered, many of your buying decisions are influenced by your habits. If you always shop at the same store, you may be passing up good prices offered at another store. Sometimes you need to evaluate your habits to make sure that you are being a careful shopper.

Advertising

Advertising is another important influence on people's buying decisions. Advertising is everywhere you look—in newspapers and magazines, on television and radio, and on taxis and buses. It even appears on clothing and on some on-line computer services.

The major advantage of advertising is that it lets consumers know what goods and services are available. Ads introduce new products and point out their benefits. In addition, they let people know about sales. Looking at the weekly advertising circulars in the newspaper is a great way to compare prices.

Some ads deliver a public service message. They may warn people about the dangers of tobacco, alcohol, and other drugs. Other advertisements ask people to conserve natural resources or donate money to charitable organizations.

There are also disadvantages to advertising. Sometimes ads persuade people to buy items they don't need, especially if the product is endorsed by a celebrity the consumers like or admire. Advertising can be misleading. Some ads make exaggerated claims. One ad, for example, states that four out of five dentists surveyed recommend a particular brand of toothpaste. How many dentists were questioned? How were they chosen? Think carefully about such claims.

You can improve your consumer skills by learning what factors influence your buying decisions.

LESSON ONE *Review*

Using complete sentences, answer the following questions on a separate sheet of paper.

Reviewing Terms and Facts

1. Vocabulary What is the difference between *goods* and *services?*

2. List What choices do you have to make as a consumer?

3. Identify Name three factors that influence your buying decisions.

4. Recall Where might you find advertisements?

Thinking Critically

5. Interpret Why is it important to analyze your buying decisions before going along with your peer group?

6. Explain Why might it be hard to change buying decisions based on habit?

7. Analyze Do you think that the advantages of advertising outweigh its disadvantages? Explain your answer.

Applying Concepts

8. Make a list of eight or ten items that you purchased recently. Next to each item identify what most influenced your buying decision—peers, habit, or advertising. Compare your list with those of your classmates. Do you see any similarities between your buying behavior and that of your peers?

LESSON TWO
Evaluating Media Messages

WORDS TO KNOW

information ad

image ad

media

infomercial

DISCOVER...

● the messages advertisers use to convince people to buy their products.

● the types of media that carry the messages.

● how to evaluate advertising messages.

How many advertisements do you see and hear in a single day? Do the ads tempt you to try a soft drink or see a new movie? To be a wise consumer, you need to learn to evaluate, or judge, just how useful and truthful the messages in ads really are.

Why Do Companies Advertise?

Advertisements, or ads, are designed to catch the attention of consumers and convince them to buy a product or service. Ads influence consumers by presenting goods or services in an attractive way. Ads also inform consumers about new products, remind them of old products that are still available, and attract them to special sales.

Types of Advertisements

Advertisements generally fall into one of two categories: information ads and image ads. Each type of ad sends a different kind of message.

- **Information ads** are *ads that describe the features of a product or service and give facts about its price and quality.* Information ads appeal to the practical side of people. They send the message that an item gives good value for the money or that an item is a good buy because of its high quality.

- **Image ads** are *ads that connect a product or service to a lifestyle that consumers would like to have.* Image

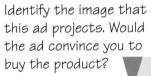

Identify the image that this ad projects. Would the ad convince you to buy the product?

You've Gotta Have It!

Try This!

Labels help you compare features of different products. Try to find labels for each of the following:

• Two brands of toothpaste that claim to fight cavities

• Two brands of quick-cooking hot cereal

• Two brands of laundry detergent

   Compare the labels of the products in each group. Is one a better value? Report your findings to the class.

ads often use actors, sports stars, or other celebrities to endorse, or recommend, a product. They send the message that consumers will be more attractive or popular, or perhaps smarter or healthier, if they use the product or service. Image ads are often used to promote fashions, cosmetics, and other items that a person may want but does not actually need.

Media Messages

Now you know about the kinds of messages advertisers use, but how do these messages reach you? *The means of communication by which advertisers send their messages* are called **media.** What types of media can you think of?

Types of Media

The three most commonly used types of media are print, electronic, and direct mail.

• **Print media** are newspapers and magazines. Food and clothing stores often place ads in newspapers to reach their local customers. Companies that sell products nationwide, such as breakfast cereal or shampoo, may take out ads in national magazines. Items that appeal to a specific audience might be advertised in specialty magazines. For example, hiking boots are likely to be advertised in magazines about hiking and climbing.

• **Electronic media** are radio, television, and the Internet. The ads that appear on radio and television are also called *commercials.* Radio commercials are generally aimed at a local audience. The ads are often designed to attract a particular group of consumers such as teens.

   Many of the ads that appear on television are aimed at people nationwide. By advertising during national shows, companies can reach millions of consumers. Sometimes advertisers use a special kind of television commercial called an infomercial. **Infomercials** are *extended-length informational commercials that appear* *on television.* These ads usually promote mail-order products and provide a toll-free number for consumers to call.

Advertising is also found on some on-line services and the Internet. When computer users are on-line, ads sometimes appear on the computer screen. In addition, consumers who are looking for a specific product or service can go to on-line "shopping malls" and look for the ads that sellers place.

- **Direct mail** includes mail-order catalogs, store circulars, and packets of ads and coupons that come in the mail. Some companies that do business nationwide use only direct mail to advertise. Catalog houses and local businesses also send ads through the mail.

Signs and displays are two other types of media that you have seen many times. Advertising signs can appear on billboards, buses, taxis, and storefronts. Advertising displays are seen in store windows and inside stores to attract buyers.

Much of what you find in your mailbox, along with letters and bills, is direct-mail advertising.

Advertising Techniques

After hearing a commercial on the radio, did you ever discover that you couldn't get the jingle out of your head? Advertisers use special techniques to get you to notice and remember their products. **Figure 7.1** on the next page shows some of the techniques they use to get their messages across.

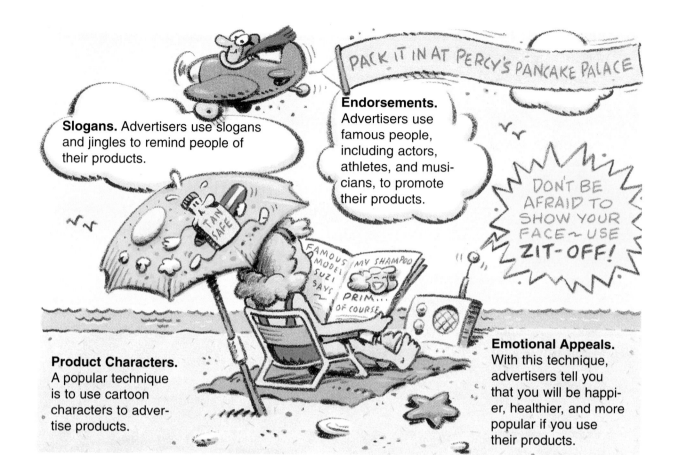

Figure 7.1
Techniques for Sending Messages
Which of these advertising techniques have you seen or heard?

How to Evaluate Messages

Before you decide to buy a service or product, be sure to analyze the advertising claims. Here are some ways.

- **Advertisements mention only the best features of a product.** Before buying, think about what you need to know about the product to decide which brand is best for you. Then look for that information in the ads.

- **Separate emotional appeals from facts.** Does the ad suggest that the product will make the buyer healthier, more attractive, or even happier than is realistic?

- **Don't trust endorsements.** Famous people appear in ads to get your attention, but they are seldom experts in nutrition, medicine, or fashion. Remember, those who look like average people are actors who are well paid to say positive things about the products.

- **Beware of slogans.** They may make certain items memorable, but they are not a guarantee of quality.

Getting More Information

Although the federal government requires advertisers to make truthful claims, companies often exaggerate how good their products are. You don't have to depend on ads for all your information about a product or service, however. Other sources of useful information are available to you.

One of the most reliable sources of information is very close to you—the people you know. Ask your family and friends what brand of a product they use, whether it works well, and if the item was worth the money they paid. Another good source is consumer magazines. Consumer organizations test products, survey the people who use them, and then report their findings. Magazines such as *Consumer Reports* publish these findings. A third source of information is the labels on the products themselves. Learning what a product is made of and how much care it needs can help you determine if it is the right one for you.

If you are trying to decide which brand of a product to purchase, ask family members and friends for recommendations. What are some other sources of information about products?

LESSON TWO *Review*

Using complete sentences, answer the following questions on a separate sheet of paper.

Reviewing Terms and Facts

1. Recall Explain why companies advertise.

2. Vocabulary Define the term *information ad.* Use it in an original sentence.

3. List What are the three most commonly used types of media?

4. Recall Name four advertising techniques.

5. Identify List four points to keep in mind when evaluating media messages.

Thinking Critically

6. Explain Why are image ads rather than information ads often used to sell products that consumers may want but don't really need?

7. Analyze What kinds of emotional appeals would work in an ad for breakfast cereals? For in-line skates?

Applying Concepts

8. Make up a product and create a television commercial for it. Find or make props and visual aids, and use music if possible. Be sure to include at least one of the advertising techniques you learned about in your ad.

LESSON THREE
Comparison Shopping

WORDS TO KNOW

impulse buying

department store

specialty store

chain store

factory outlet

discount store

warranty

DISCOVER...

● what it means to be a skillful shopper.

● how to compare items for price and quality.

● how to read product labels.

Did you ever save your money to buy something you wanted, such as a camera or video game? Then, only days after making your purchase, did you see a similar item for less money, or one that had more features or was of higher quality? By learning a few rules that skillful shoppers follow, you can often prevent this situation from happening.

The Skillful Shopper

Skillful shoppers get the best value for their money. As you develop your shopping skills, you will get greater satisfaction from the purchases you make and save a great deal of money over the years.

Now is the time to learn how to be an informed shopper. Begin by reading labels on food, clothing, and appliances. Compare prices at different stores and among different brands. Look closely at merchandise to judge its quality. Check to see whether the manufacturer will replace or repair the item if it breaks. It is possible to find out some of this information before you even walk into a store.

Gathering Information

Before you make a major purchase, it is wise to learn as much about the item as possible. Collect information about products from friends and family members, magazines, and advertisements. Gathering information before you shop will help you avoid impulse buying. **Impulse buying** means *making a sudden decision to buy.* Did you ever decide to buy candy or a magazine while you were standing in the checkout line? When people buy on impulse, they often purchase things they don't need or that are not worth the money.

Word of mouth is one of the best and easiest ways to gather information. Begin your investigation of a product by asking friends or family members who have used or owned a similar type of item. Ask them such questions as:

- Are you satisfied with the product?

- What do you like or dislike about it?

- Would you purchase the product again?

Magazines such as *Consumer Reports* compare the prices, quality, and features of several brands of the same product. They evaluate the different brands for ease of use, cost,

You can make wise purchasing decisions by gathering information about a product before you buy it. What information can you find in a newspaper advertisement?

frequency of repairs, and other such concerns. The reports also comment on how well each brand performs its function. This information helps consumers determine which brand they prefer.

Newspaper advertisements can also be helpful. Use them to find out which stores in your area carry the product you want and what price they charge for it. You can use this information to comparison shop in advance.

Selecting a Store

What types of stores are familiar to you? Different kinds of stores carry different selections of merchandise. The best store for you depends on the particular item you want to buy, the price you are willing to pay, and the service you need.

Prices for the same item often vary among stores. Suppose that you are looking for a CD player. You may go to a **department store,** *a store that carries a wide range of merchandise.* Most department stores sell clothes, shoes, household items, and electronic equipment. Department stores usually offer many services, such as customer services, delivery, and credit. You will find a moderate selection of CD players at a range of prices.

You may choose a **specialty store,** *a store that carries only a specific type of merchandise.* In a store that specializes in electronic equipment, you will probably find a very large selection of CD players. The prices in a specialty store may be higher than in a department store, unless the store is very large or part of a chain.

Chain stores are *groups of stores that bear the same name and carry the same merchandise.* There are chains of department stores as well as of specialty stores. Some specialty chains—such as clothing, shoe, and record stores—cater specifically to teens and young adults.

Another type of store is the **factory outlet,** *a store that carries only one manufacturer's products.* Outlets have a limited selection of styles, and some items may be imperfect, but you will find low prices.

Price, selection, and services may vary widely among different types of stores. What factors are most important to you?

Discount stores are *stores that carry a limited selection of items at low prices.* Some discount stores specialize in a particular kind of merchandise, such as household linens, men's or women's clothing, or athletic shoes. Others carry a wide variety of products. Few customer services are provided, but the prices are among the lowest available. Other stores that sell merchandise at discounted prices include membership warehouses and thrift shops.

Another shopping option is to buy products from catalogs. Some catalogs are associated with stores and carry merchandise that the stores cannot keep in stock. Other catalog companies do business only by phone and mail.

Electronic shopping centers are similar to catalogs, but they are found on on-line services and the Internet. Consumers can view pictures and descriptions of the merchandise offered by many different stores and manufacturers. While on-line, they can place an order that will be received instantly.

When choosing a store, you may want to consider how important it is to you to see the merchandise yourself. Also keep in mind how convenient it is to get to the store and whether it is a clean, pleasant place to shop.

Skills IN ACTION

Evaluating Clubs

Compact disc, video, and book clubs are very popular. When people join a club, they get to purchase a large number of items for a small charge— sometimes as little as one cent. Are these clubs really a bargain, though? Compare the price of the club item with the price of a similar item in a store. Don't forget to add handling and postage to the price of the club item. See if there are any hidden costs to belonging to the club. Report your findings to the class.

Before You Buy

After you have chosen a store, you will need to practice your shopping skills and consider certain factors before making your purchase. Checking quality and prices and reading labels and guarantees will help you get the best value for your money.

Checking Quality and Price

Some people think that price is an indicator of how good a product is. They think that a more expensive product must be superior. That is not always the case. You need to check both the quality and the price of an item you want to buy.

Before you purchase something, examine it closely for quality. For example, when you buy clothing, check the stitching on the seams and the width of the hem. Does the item seem well made? Is the material durable and easy to clean?

When you purchase clothing, do you know how reading the label can save you money? If clothes must be professionally dry-cleaned, you will spend extra money every time they need cleaning.

Items that are on sale may be less expensive than regular-priced items, but may not be of the same quality. Stores sometimes have sales of merchandise that they have bought at special, lower prices. The quality of these items may also be lower than that of their regular merchandise. You need to look at products on sale to see if they are, in fact, bargains.

Higher-priced items may be of good quality, but they may also contain features that you don't need. For instance, having an additional five speeds on your bike may not be a feature you consider to be worth the extra money.

Reading Labels

Labels give useful information about the features and the use and care of the product. Labels also give information required by law on products such as clothing and food.

A clothing label must contain the name of the manufacturer, country of origin, fiber content, and instructions for care. Labels on foods list ingredients, with the greatest quantity first. If a can of chili lists beans before meat, you can expect to see more beans than meat when you open the can. Food labels must also contain the name of the product, the name and address of the manufacturer, weight of the contents, and a nutrition label on all processed foods. Food labels also give information on how to prepare the food.

Checking Warranties

Many items come with a guarantee or a warranty. A **warranty** is *the manufacturer's written promise to repair or replace a product if it does not work as claimed.* Be sure to read the warranty so that you know what is promised. Some warranties apply only to certain parts of the product or only under specific conditions. For example, the frame of your bike may be covered by the warranty, but the tires may not be covered.

Try **This!**

Secondhand stores, thrift shops, flea markets, rummage sales, and garage sales can be great places to shop. Think carefully, however, before purchasing a used item. You will probably not be able to return it.

Proof of Purchase

There are several ways to pay for purchases. You can use cash, a check, a credit card, or a debit card. You will learn about these payment methods in Lesson 5 of this chapter. Regardless of the way you pay for an item, however, remember to keep the receipt as proof of your purchase. Keep the receipt and the warranty in a safe place. If you decide to return the item, you will need the receipt.

LESSON THREE *Review*

Using complete sentences, answer the following questions on a separate sheet of paper.

Reviewing Terms and Facts

1. Identify What are the benefits of being a skillful shopper?

2. Recall What factors should you consider when selecting a store?

3. Vocabulary Define the term *warranty.* Use it in an original sentence.

Thinking Critically

4. Analyze What is the relationship between price and quality? What should you consider when comparing price and quality?

5. Suggest Why would consumers choose to shop through catalogs or an electronic shopping center rather than at a store in person?

Applying Concepts

6. Look through an issue of *Consumer Reports* or a similar buying guide, and compare several brands of a similar product, such as blow dryers, tape players, or in-line skates. Compare prices, quality, and features. Explain to the class which brand and model you would purchase and why.

LESSON FOUR
Consumer Rights and Responsibilities

WORDS TO KNOW

redress

expires

shoplifting

exchange

refund

DISCOVER...

- your consumer rights.
- how to be a responsible consumer.
- how to make refunds and exchanges.

Kayla was in a hurry. She had to buy a swimsuit for a pool party that afternoon, and she didn't have much time. She grabbed two suits that she liked from the rack. She decided to try them on at home, chose one, and return the other at a more convenient time. What do you think will happen when Kayla tries to return the swimsuit? Do you know why?

Your Rights as a Consumer

Consumers have rights that protect them from false advertising and unsafe products. The law requires manufacturers to put labels on food and clothing and to make products that are safe to use. Your rights make it possible for you to voice a complaint if you are not satisfied with a product or service.

Your consumer rights may have helped you already. For example, if you returned a telephone that didn't work or a pair of shoes that didn't fit, you exercised some of your rights. Perhaps you noticed the safety warnings on your younger sister's toys. These are just a few of the ways in which consumers are protected. The following are included among your specific rights as a consumer:

- **The right to safety.** Products must be well designed and, if used properly, must not cause harm or injury.

- **The right to be informed.** Advertisements and labels give you information about products. Laws protect you from false or misleading advertisements.

- **The right to choose.** Consumers are entitled to choose from a variety of products. They have the right to select the items that fit their needs.

- **The right to be heard.** Consumers can speak out about a product if they are not satisfied with it.

- **The right to redress. Redress** is *action taken to correct a wrong.* Consumers can seek redress if they have a problem with a product.

- **The right to consumer education.** Consumers are entitled to learn about their rights.

Consumer rights protect you and help you get the best product for your money. However, along with those rights you also have responsibilities.

As a consumer, you have the right to choose from a variety of products. What are some of your other consumer rights?

Your Responsibilities as a Consumer

Do you consider yourself a responsible consumer? Being courteous, counting your change, handling merchandise carefully, and getting the information you need are all part of being a responsible consumer.

Being Courteous

Courtesy is everyday thoughtfulness that you show to other people. It means being polite and respectful to salespeople and other customers in a store. It means that you wait your turn in line. You also show courtesy when you hold the door open for other people.

When you have to return an item to the store, you do so in a polite way. Calmly explain to the salesperson what the problem is, and state how you would like to resolve it. For example, do you want your money back, or do you want to trade the item for another size or color? Remember to bring your receipt with you.

Skills IN ACTION

Identifying Quackery

Beware of quackery—the sale of worthless products and treatments by means of false claims. An example of quackery is an acne cream that is said to make pimples disappear in a few hours. Bring a "quack" ad to class, and tell why you think it isn't truthful.

Part of your responsibility as a consumer is to follow the manufacturer's instructions. What are some other ways to be a responsible consumer?

Behaving Responsibly

The manufacturer also has responsibilities—to produce a product that is good and safe and reasonably priced. As a responsible consumer, you need to read and follow the instructions. Experts, who understand the product, prepare instructions that provide for your safety and satisfaction. It is important to follow them. If, for example, the instructions say to wash a shirt by hand, do not put the shirt in the washing machine.

Another way to behave responsibly is to handle merchandise with care. This applies to more than breakable items. Clothing can also be easily damaged while you are trying it on. Remove your shoes before trying on pants. Return clothes that you have tried on in the dressing room to their hangers and leave the dressing room neat.

When you buy such items as watches and stereos, you will receive a warranty. If you get a warranty card with the product, fill it out and send it to the manufacturer. The date on the card lets the manufacturer know when the warranty **expires,** or *runs out.* Keep your warranties, sales slips, and special instructions together in one place.

Being Honest

When paying cash for your purchases, pay attention to the change you receive. If you receive too much change, return it to the salesperson. Otherwise that person may be responsible for replacing the money.

Some teens do not realize the seriousness of shoplifting. **Shoplifting,** or *taking items from a store without paying for them,* is stealing. It is a crime that costs businesses billions of dollars each year. These losses are passed on to customers as increased prices. Some teens look at shoplifting as a prank. Their friends may dare them to do it. Shoplifting, however, is a serious crime for which a person may go to jail. It is a crime that remains on that person's record.

If an item that you want to buy is marked "As Is," be sure to try it on and check it carefully for defects. Why is this important?

WRITING A COMPLAINT LETTER

What would you do if you were dissatisfied with a product you had purchased? You might decide to throw it away and forget about it. A better idea, however, would be to write a letter of complaint to the manufacturer. Here are some pointers for writing a complaint letter.

● Follow a regular business letter format. Include your name, address, phone number, and the date.

● Get the address of the company from the product label.

● State the product name, style, and model number. Include the name and address of the store where you bought the item and the date of purchase.

● Send photocopies of the receipt, bills, or warranties. Keep the originals.

● Explain why you are unhappy with the product and how you would like the problem solved.

● Keep the tone of the letter positive and courteous, and allow time for a response and action.

Knowing About Refunds and Exchanges

Like most people, you have probably purchased a product with which you were unhappy. It may not have worked properly. Perhaps it was the wrong color or size. What did you do? You may have asked for an **exchange,** *a trade of one item for another,* or a **refund,** *the return of your money in exchange for the item.* Whenever you make an exchange or ask for a refund, follow these guidelines:

● **Know the store's policy.** Every store sets its own return and exchange policy. The policy is usually posted where you pay for the item. Read the policy. If you don't understand it, ask the clerk before paying for the purchase. Never assume that you can return an item.

● **Keep proof of your purchase.** The store receipt is proof of the price, date of purchase, and store where you bought an item. Most stores require you to show your receipt in order to receive a refund.

- **Determine if you are entitled to a refund.** Some items that are defective or on sale are marked "As Is" or "All Sales Final." In these cases you are not entitled to a refund. Certain products, such as bathing suits, underwear, and pierced earrings, are usually not returnable because of health codes.

- **Be ready to process your claim.** If you are entitled to a refund, take your merchandise and sales receipt (and perhaps your warranty, if any) to the store. You may be asked to fill out a form with your name, address, and reason for returning the item. If the item is defective, be sure to provide this information so that the store can notify the manufacturer.

Knowing your rights and responsibilities as a consumer will help you now and in the future.

LESSON FOUR *Review*

Using complete sentences, answer the following questions on a separate sheet of paper.

Reviewing Terms and Facts

1. Identify List your consumer rights.

2. Give Examples What are two ways to show that you are a courteous shopper?

3. Explain How does shoplifting affect the price you pay for goods?

4. Vocabulary What is the difference between an *exchange* and a *refund*?

Thinking Critically

5. Analyze Do you think that consumers have enough rights? Explain your answer.

6. Describe What procedure would you follow when returning an item?

7. Interpret Why is it important to read instructions before using or operating a product?

Applying Concepts

8. Develop a file that organizes receipts, warranties, and special instructions to use in your home. Suggest ways to encourage family members to use the file. Discuss ideas with your classmates.

Managing Your Money

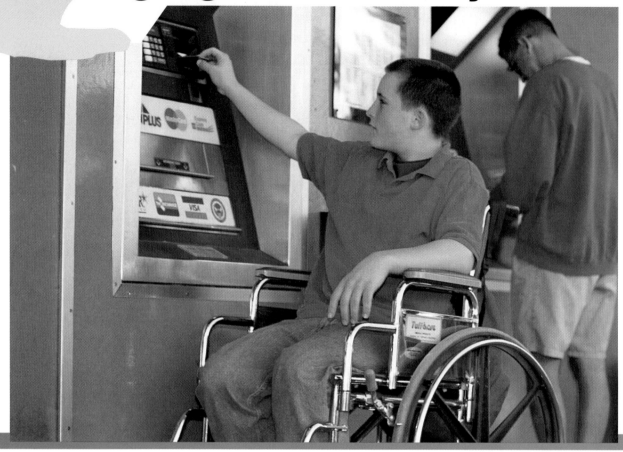

WORDS TO KNOW

income

expenses

fixed expenses

flexible expenses

budget

interest

layaway plan

debit card

credit

DISCOVER...

- your sources of income and your expenses.
- how to develop a plan for spending and saving money.
- ways to get the most from your money.

Do you ever think about how you spend your money? When you have a little extra, what do you do with it? Do you buy a new CD or go to a movie? Do you save it to buy a birthday present or your own television? The way people manage their money reflects their needs and wants. Marco likes music and is saving his money for a stereo. Nicole enjoys working with children and wants to become a teacher. She is saving part of her allowance for college. How do your needs and wants influence your spending?

How to Manage Your Money

You will be earning, spending, and saving money all of your life. Even if you have only a small amount to spend, you can stretch your buying power by learning to buy and save wisely. The key to managing your money is to remember that how much you have to spend is less important than how you spend what you have.

To manage your money wisely you will need to

- know where your money is coming from.

- determine how much money you will have.

- look at how much money you are spending.

- evaluate what you are buying.

Your Income and Expenses

Your **income** is *the amount of money you earn or receive regularly.* Your **expenses** are *the money you spend to buy goods and services.* **Figure 7.2** shows some of the many possible

Figure 7.2
Income and Expenses
There are many ways for teens to earn and spend money. What other sources of income and expenses can you think of?

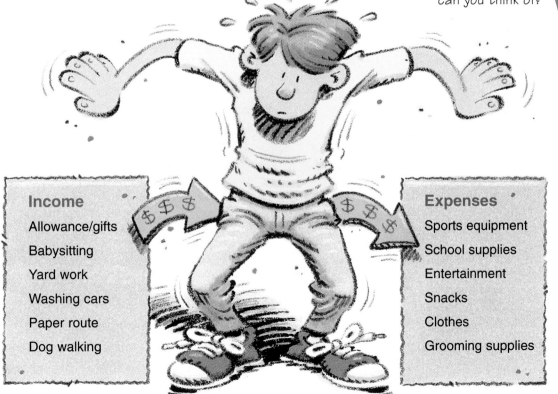

Income	Expenses
Allowance/gifts	Sports equipment
Babysitting	School supplies
Yard work	Entertainment
Washing cars	Snacks
Paper route	Clothes
Dog walking	Grooming supplies

sources of income and expenses. If you manage your money well, you will not spend more on expenses than you receive as income. What are your sources of income? What are your expenses?

Keeping Track of Your Money

You can improve your spending habits by keeping an expense record, or an organized account of what you buy and how much you spend. To keep an expense record, make a chart like the one shown on the left. Each day list the date, the items you buy, and the amount you spend that day. At the end of the week, add up each expense category. Some expenses are fixed, and some are flexible. **Fixed expenses** are *expenses that are always the same,* such as the fee for your weekly karate lesson. **Flexible expenses** are *expenses that vary,* such as the amount you spend for a concert ticket.

By looking at the totals on your expense record, you can evaluate how you spend your money. Decide if you are buying useful items or if you would like to improve your buying habits.

Keeping an expense record can help you manage your money. What items would you list on your expense record?

Setting Up a Budget

Before you set up a **budget,** or *plan for using your money,* you need to examine your personal values and goals. Do you want to save enough money for a new skateboard? Do you want to pay for singing lessons so that you can try out for the musical at school? Are you saving money to buy your parents an anniversary gift?

Once you have determined your income, have a record of your expenses, and understand your goals, you can set up a budget. Begin by setting aside enough money to cover your expenses. If your income does not cover your expenses, you will need to make some adjustments. You may choose to cut back on some of your expenses or to find new ways to add money to your weekly income.

Starting a Savings Plan

Your budget should include a savings plan. A savings plan helps you put money aside for unexpected needs and for the future. Many people find it easier to save when they set goals, such as having money for holiday activities, trips, or hobbies. Some teens begin saving for a car or a college education. Unless you plan ahead and save regularly, it might be difficult to achieve your goals.

To start a savings plan, set aside about 10 percent of your income each week. Figure out how much money you could save in a year. What could you buy with *your* savings?

It's a good idea to put the money you save in a savings account in the bank. The bank pays **interest,** or *a fee paid to use your money.* The interest is added to the money in your savings account. In this way your money grows.

Ways to Pay for Purchases

Teens generally pay for their purchases with cash. You may not always have enough cash to buy what you want, however. In that case, you may want to use a layaway plan. A **layaway plan** is *a scheduled payment plan in which you put a small amount of money down and make regular payments until you have paid for the item.* When the item has been paid for in full, you take it home.

Using a layaway plan is one way to pay for purchases. How can a layaway plan help you to be responsible with your purchases?

215

Credit allows people to purchase large, expensive items that they need and might not have enough cash on hand to buy.

Another way to pay for purchases is with a check. A check is a written order directing a bank to pay the person or business named on the check. In order to pay by check, a person must open a checking account with a bank. A checking account is a convenient way of handling larger amounts of money without keeping a lot of cash on hand.

Many people use debit cards to pay for purchases. A **debit card** is a *card that is issued by a bank and is used to withdraw money directly from a person's bank account.* For example, people can use debit cards to pay for groceries.

When you rent a video or pay back money that you borrowed, you are using credit. **Credit** is *a method of payment that lets you buy now and pay later.* Either the seller or a bank must trust in the ability of the purchaser to make payments until the item is paid for. Many families use credit to buy such expensive items as furniture, large appliances, and cars. Credit fees, or interest on the unpaid balance, are charged for the use of credit.

One way to use credit is to have a charge account with a particular store. The store issues a charge card that can be used instead of money when shopping there. Within 30 days the store sends you a bill for your purchases.

LESSON FIVE — *Review*

Using complete sentences, answer the following questions on a separate sheet of paper.

Reviewing Terms and Facts

1. List Name four things you need to know before you can begin to manage your money.

2. Explain What is the purpose of keeping an expense record?

3. Recall Why should your budget include a savings plan?

4. Vocabulary Define the term *credit*. What kind of promise are you making when you use credit to pay for a purchase?

Thinking Critically

5. Explain Why is it important to budget your money?

6. Analyze What might be some advantages and disadvantages of buying on credit?

Applying Concepts

7. Imagine that you earn $40 a week from yard work and a paper route. How much money should you put in a savings account? How much money would you have saved after a year? After two years? How would you use your savings?

Chapter 7 Activities

A Global View
"I'LL TRADE YOU..."

You are used to paying money for goods and services. Another way to get the items you need is by bartering, or trading goods and services without the use of money. You have probably bartered without even knowing it. When you and a friend swap comic books or baseball cards, you are bartering.

TRY THIS!

Arrange to barter services with a friend or parent. Report on your bartering to the class.

TECHNOLOGY
How Did They Do That?

Artists use computers to create amazing special effects for television advertising. Two techniques they use are "warping"—changing one part of a picture at a time—and "morphing"—changing one image into another image. Advertisers spend millions of dollars on these ads. They hope that the special effects will help you remember the ad—and the brand name.

Try This!

Write your own script for a special effects ad.

FRIENDS & FAMILY

THE ALLOWANCE DEBATE

Not all families agree on whether an allowance should be tied to doing chores around the house. Some parents believe that paying their children to do household tasks helps them see the connection between working and earning money. Other parents feel that children should help around the house without getting paid.

TRY THIS!

Form small groups to discuss the allowance debate. Write an allowance policy considering both the point of view of the parents and the children. Share your policy with your classmates.

MATH CONNECTION

THE $1,300 SNACK

Imagine that you spend $5 a week on soft drinks, candy bars, and pretzels. Did you know that in five years your snack habit could cost you more than $1,300?

When you put money in a savings account, the money earns **interest,** or *a fee the bank pays to use your money.* The interest is added to the **principal,** or *the money in your account.*

Follow Up

1. Imagine that instead of buying junk food you put $5 a week in a savings account that pays 6 percent interest. How much would you have after one year?

2. Many savings accounts require a minimum balance. List three ways you could earn the money.

3. Contact a bank and find out about the types of savings accounts and the rates of interest. Share your findings with your classmates.

Chapter Summary

- Goods are products made for sale. A service is work performed by one person for another.

- A consumer is someone who buys goods and services.

- Your buying decisions may be influenced by your peers, your habits, or advertising.

- Advertisements are generally considered to be either information ads or image ads.

- To get their messages across, advertisers use print media, electronic media, and direct mail.

- You can shop at a wide variety of stores, including department stores, specialty stores, discount stores, factory outlets, and membership warehouses.

- A careful shopper compares price and quality, reads labels, and checks warranties.

- Knowing your consumer rights and fulfilling your consumer responsibilities are part of responsible buying.

- As a consumer, you have the right to ask for a refund or an exchange.

- The money that you earn or receive regularly is called your income. The money that you spend on goods and services is called your expenses. There are fixed and flexible expenses.

- Keeping an expense record, setting up a budget, and starting a savings plan are smart methods of money management.

- There are several ways to pay for your purchases: cash, check, debit card, credit, or layaway plan.

Words to Know

Using complete sentences, answer the following questions on a separate sheet of paper.

1. Give examples of *goods* teens might buy.
2. What *services* could teens perform?
3. Explain the purpose of an *image ad*.
4. Give two examples of print *media*.
5. Identify a drawback of *impulse buying*.
6. Why should you read a *warranty*?
7. What is meant by right to *redress*?
8. Describe what happens when a warranty on a product *expires*.
9. What do you do when you *budget* your money?
10. How is buying on *credit* like making a promise?

Review Questions

Using complete sentences, answer the following questions on a separate sheet of paper.

1. What choices must a consumer make?
2. Besides advertising, what are two sources of product information?
3. Name three ways to get information about a product *before* you go into a store.

4. What should you do to be a skillful shopper once you are in a store?

5. Name six rights you have as a consumer.

6. How do your personal needs and wants influence your management of money? Give an example.

Thinking Critically

Using complete sentences, answer the following questions on a separate sheet of paper.

1. **Apply** Describe a situation in which a teen should resist peer influence when making a buying decision.

2. **Evaluate** Name five emotions or feelings to which advertisers appeal. Give an example of a specific ad that supports one of your answers.

3. **Analyze** Why might it be important for people to read a product label for ingredients?

4. **Explain** Why is writing a complaint letter both a consumer right and a consumer responsibility?

5. **Suggest** What advice would you give someone who has just started to use a credit card?

Cooperative Learning

1. Working in a group, create a fictitious teen. Make up facts about the teen's finances, including income and expenses. Give the information to another group. Have the group create a budget for the teen and work out any money-management problems.

2. As a class, start a consumer column in your school newspaper, or publish your own consumer newsletter for teens. Take turns writing articles. The articles could contain tips on the best places for teens to shop for goods and services in your community. You could interview classmates about their experiences with various products.

Family & Community

Ask to be involved in the next major purchase your family makes, such as a new refrigerator, a new car, or a family vacation. Help the family research different brands or models and weigh the pros and cons of each. Does advertising ever influence their preferences? If so, how?

Building A Portfolio

1. Think of a major purchase you would like to make, such as a stereo or a computer. Gather information about the product, and look for the best place to buy it. Begin to save money for your purchase. If you don't have enough income to make your goal realistic, think of ways you could earn extra money. Put a photo or drawing of the item you would like to buy in your portfolio to remind you of your goal.

2. Take an inventory of your clothes closet. Make a list of clothes you need. Ask your family to help you set a budget for clothes shopping. Watch for sale ads before you go shopping. Put the receipts from any purchases in your portfolio, along with your evaluation of how well you managed your money.

Your Home

TEENS MAKING A DIFFERENCE

Treasure Bags

Chantell Jones belongs to a youth group at her church. One Saturday the group visited a shelter for homeless women and children.

Chantell thought that the children should have some things to play with. She decided to make gift bags filled with coloring books, crayons, stickers, and small toys.

Chantell knew that she would need help to carry out her plan. She asked the women's group at her church to sew drawstring bags. Then she contacted local stores for donations.

Chantell received more than enough items to fill the bags. The director of the shelter thanked Chantell and her friends and said, "these will be like bags of treasure to the children."

Try THIS!

Try to imagine what it would be like to be homeless. What can you do to help homeless people in your community? Make a list of ideas, and compare your list with a classmate's. What new ideas did he or she suggest?

LESSON ONE
Making the Most of Your Home

DISCOVER...

- how a home provides shelter, security, and a place to express yourself.
- how to organize your living space.
- how to share space in a home.

People live in many types of homes—apartments, mobile homes, duplexes, townhomes, single-family houses, and condominiums. Homes come in all shapes, sizes, and colors, but all of them have one common feature. To the people living there, each one is called "home."

The Importance of Homes

Homes satisfy the basic need for shelter. They are built to protect people from the weather—rain, snow, wind, or extreme temperatures. Homes also provide a place for you to take care of your personal needs. In your home you can bathe, prepare meals, and sleep comfortably. You also have a place to keep your clothes and personal possessions.

You get a sense of well-being and peace of mind, or a feeling of security, in your home. It is a place to relax and be yourself. It is a place where you can enjoy leisure activities, such as listening to music, playing video games, or reading. It is a great place to spend time with family members and friends.

You can also use your home to express yourself. Take a look at your room. What do the objects in your room reveal about your interests? Does your room reflect your personality?

Special Living Areas

Most homes are divided into special living areas in order to meet people's needs and interests. Some areas, such as bedrooms, are designed for privacy. Other areas, such as living rooms, are used for gathering with family members and entertaining friends. Dividing space into special areas makes the home more convenient and easier to manage.

Try This!

When you share space with family members, it helps if everyone works together to get the chores done. One way to accomplish this goal is to organize a work schedule. Try these ideas.
• With your family, list chores that need to be done.
• Decide who will do what chores.
• Make a chore chart. Write down the list of chores that need to be done and who will do them.

Most homes are divided into special areas, such as a kitchen, a living room, a bathroom, and bedrooms. Some areas serve more than one function. What are some functions of a kitchen?

By organizing the rooms for more than one **function,** or *use,* you can make the best use of space, equipment, and furniture. For example, you probably use your bedroom not only for sleeping but also for studying, reading, relaxing, and listening to music. Besides cooking or eating meals, your family may use the kitchen for other activities, such as doing homework, paying bills, or playing games.

The way you organize your living space depends on the activities in which you and your family like to participate.

Organizing Your Living Space

To organize the space within your home, begin by thinking of the various activities of all your family members. What area would be best for each activity? For example, would exercise equipment be better located in a bedroom, the basement, or the family room? Should the family computer be set up in a bedroom or in the den?

How do you and your family use the living space now? Are there improvements that could be made? If a shelving unit or different lighting was added, could the space be expanded to serve an additional function? **Figure 8.1** shows some guidelines for arranging rooms.

Selecting Furniture

Furniture style is a matter of personal taste. You may like furniture with sleek, modern lines. Your sister may prefer country-style furniture. Try looking in magazines and books to find the furniture styles you like best.

Some furniture can serve more than one purpose. A desk that has a large surface area may be used as a computer station.

Figure 8.1 Guidelines for Room Arrangements

Here are some tips for creating a practical arrangement. Which ones can you use in your space?

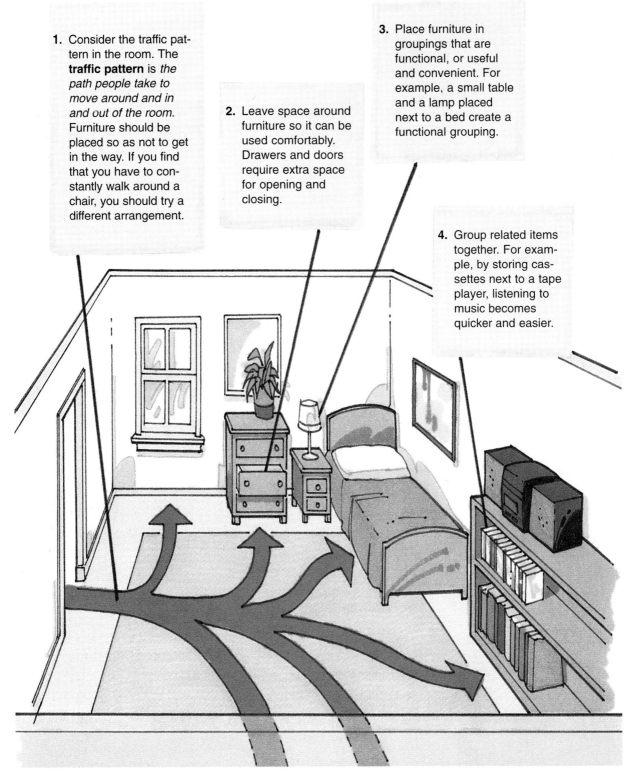

1. Consider the traffic pattern in the room. The **traffic pattern** is *the path people take to move around and in and out of the room.* Furniture should be placed so as not to get in the way. If you find that you have to constantly walk around a chair, you should try a different arrangement.

2. Leave space around furniture so it can be used comfortably. Drawers and doors require extra space for opening and closing.

3. Place furniture in groupings that are functional, or useful and convenient. For example, a small table and a lamp placed next to a bed create a functional grouping.

4. Group related items together. For example, by storing cassettes next to a tape player, listening to music becomes quicker and easier.

A small table draped with fabric could conceal an item that isn't used year-round, such as a fan.

Arranging Special Areas

Changing the placement of your furniture can make an area look quite different. Rearranging the furniture can also help you save space. Maybe your bookcase could fit on one side of the desk instead of along the wall. Arranging two single beds in an **L** shape may take up less room than placing them parallel to each other. By following a few basic rules, you will be able to arrange your furniture in the most effective way.

Furniture is available in many different styles. Which furniture styles do you like?

Storage Space

Having enough storage space is essential for a functional room. Decide what objects should be stored in a space. For example, paper, pens and pencils, and a dictionary should be stored in a study area. Items that would not be used in this area, such as videotapes, should be stored elsewhere.

TIPS
for living

CLEARING THE CLUTTER

A crowded, messy closet can be like a black hole. If you put something in there, you may never see it again. To get organized, follow these steps.

● Clean out your closet. Stack everything that you don't wear or want. Donate these items to charity, hand them down to a younger brother or sister, or sell them at a garage sale.

● Categorize your clothes. Group garments by type, season, color, or body part (top half, bottom half, or whole body). Group together similar items, such as shoes or belts. Store seasonal items in underbed boxes.

● Use double hanging rods, hooks, and clear plastic boxes to increase storage space.

The best storage places are closets, drawers, and shelves. If these spaces already seem full, look for ways to make them more useful. Start sorting your belongings. Give away or discard what you don't need.

There are many ways to make drawer space more effective. Drawer dividers, plastic trays, and shoe boxes can help.

Closets can also be made more functional. Small hooks on the closet door can hold small items. Stackable bins, see-through wire drawers, and plastic boxes help to organize storage space. What other ways can you think of?

Sharing Space

Whether you are sharing a bedroom, a bathroom, the kitchen, or a computer area, you must work with other family members to keep the space organized and clean. Sharing space will be easier if you remember the following guidelines.

With careful planning, even a small space can store a great many things. How can you modify your closet to get the most use out of it?

- **Respect other people's privacy.** If someone's door is closed, knock and wait for a response before entering. Keep your music or television turned low, or use headphones if another person wants to sleep or study. Of course, never read another person's mail or look through others' belongings without getting their permission.

- **Be considerate of others.** Show your consideration by not leaving your belongings in someone else's way. When you have finished using the kitchen or the bathroom, be sure to leave it at least as clean as you found it.

- **Cooperate with family members.** For example, is there a "morning rush hour" in your home? This can happen when several family members are trying to get ready for work or school at the same time. The morning will go more smoothly if everyone agrees on a schedule.

- **Try to compromise.** Sometimes you will need to compromise to avoid conflicts. This means that each person gives up something he or she wants in order to reach a solution that satisfies both people. For example, suppose that you like rock music, but you share a bedroom with your brother who likes country. How could you compromise? You might take turns listening to music on different days or at different times during the day.

A home is an enjoyable place to spend time with family members. What activities does your family enjoy together? ▶

LESSON ONE *Review*

Using complete sentences, answer the following questions on a separate sheet of paper.

Reviewing Terms and Facts

1. Identify What three basic needs does a home help satisfy?

2. Recall Give an example of a room that has more than one function. What are the functions of this room?

3. Vocabulary Define the term *traffic pattern*. How does traffic pattern affect furniture placement?

4. List Name three guidelines for room arrangements.

5. Identify What are four points to remember when sharing space with others?

Thinking Critically

6. Analyze Why is it important to have enough storage space?

7. Describe How can you show consideration for family members who share your home?

Applying Concepts

8. Read an article in a home-decorating magazine that gives hints on decorating and personalizing a bedroom. Summarize the article for the class. Tell which ideas you liked and which ones you didn't like and why.

LESSON TWO
Designing Your Space

DISCOVER...

● how to use design elements.

● how to give your living space a new look.

● how to add accessories to personalize your space.

Are you happy with your bedroom at home? There are many easy, inexpensive ways to turn the space you have now into a place that you can be proud of and enjoy.

WORDS TO KNOW

design

illusion

diagonal

texture

floor plan

accessories

Design in Your Room

Why do some rooms look more inviting than others? How can a room seem large, even though it is actually small? The way a room looks depends a great deal on how design was used—or not used—to create an overall effect. **Design** is *the art of combining elements in a pleasing way.* You can use design to create the type of look you want in a room.

The Elements of Design

The elements of design are space, shape, line, texture, and color. Each contributes its own special effect to the final design.

- **Space.** Space helps draw attention to objects. For example, a vase on a shelf will stand out and be seen if some space is left on either side of it. On the other hand, too much space between objects can result in a bare, empty look. You can create many illusions just by dividing space in various ways. An **illusion** is *a feeling that something is different from the way it really is.*

- **Shape.** Shape refers to the outline or form of solid objects. For example, a bed has a rectangular shape. A table may be rectangular, square, or round. Attractive designs use shape effectively. Having too many different shapes in one room makes most people feel uncomfortable.

- **Line.** Lines are very important to design. If you look around a room, you can see them in many places—the legs of a table, the frame of a door, or the stripes on a curtain. Straight lines make objects seem strong and dignified. Curved lines make objects seem softer and more graceful. Lines that are vertical go straight up and down and suggest height. They can make objects look taller. Lines that are horizontal move straight across and seem to widen objects. Lines that move at a **diagonal,** or *on an angle,* suggest action.

- **Texture. Texture** is *the way something feels or looks as if it would feel.* A rug might feel soft and fuzzy. A polished table feels hard and smooth. Texture provides visual interest in a room, and you can add more interest by using a variety of textures. Textures can also affect the mood of a room. Soft, fuzzy, and nubby surfaces make a room look cozy. Smooth, hard surfaces create a clean, modern effect.

- **Color.** Color probably has the greatest effect on the appearance of a room. A change of color can make a room look completely different. Color can also be used to create illusions. For example, white or light colors on the walls make a room look larger. Using darker colors or many different hues will make a room seem smaller.

    Colors are often described as warm or cool. Red, yellow, and orange are warm colors. If a room does not get much sunlight or is cold in winter, warm colors can make the room seem more cozy. Blue, green, and violet are cool and restful. A cool color is a good choice for a room that gets hot or has too much sunlight. You can also use cool colors to set a relaxing mood.

A color wheel shows the relationship of colors to one another. What are your favorite colors, and how might you use them to accent your room?

TIPS for living

THE PRINCIPLES OF DESIGN

The principles of design are rules that govern how artists organize the elements of design. Here is how to use them:

- **Balance.** Use elements, such as two similar shapes, to provide equal visual weight, or stability.

- **Emphasis.** Create contrast by using one element to dominate the others. Try a red pillow to provide punch.

- **Harmony.** Combine similar elements to accent their similarities by using repetition and gradual changes.

- **Variety.** Combine a number of different things of a particular kind—for example, a collection arranged on a shelf.

- **Movement.** Create the look and feeling of action by guiding the viewer's eye. Line helps guide the eye.

- **Rhythm.** Create a visual tempo, or beat, by placing elements carefully. Hang your posters to create a beat!

- **Proportion.** Keep an eye on the relationship of certain elements to the whole and to each other.

Your Own Style

Before you start planning a bedroom makeover, you need to think about the look that you want for your space. In part, that depends on what you have to start with, but it also depends on your personal taste. Of course, if you share a room you will also need to consider the taste of the other person.

The elements of design can be used in many different ways with pleasing results, but not all of them will appeal to you.

First consider what kind of mood you want to create—soft and feminine, bold and bright? What are your interests? Do you want a theme, such as sports, rock and roll, or a hobby? Do you want your space to be cool and restful or bright and lively? Are you looking for ways to make the room seem larger? Keep in mind that you will probably have to live with your changes for a long time. Be sure of your decisions before starting any work on a new look.

Creating a New Look

Once you have decided on the mood and style that you want, you can plan how to achieve that look in your room. Making a plan before you start will help everything go smoothly.

If you are thinking about creating a new look for your bedroom, you can get ideas from decorating magazines and books. Where else could you look for ideas?

Perhaps you would like a new color scheme. What parts of the room will be easiest to change? Walls can be painted a new color, and you can hang new pictures. Carpet, on the other hand, is difficult and expensive to replace. Fortunately, you can often work around the features you can't change.

If you decide to paint the walls, check with your parents first. Then choose your new color carefully. Paint a small test section on the wall to be sure that the color will create the effect you want.

Paint is great for furniture as well as walls. You can paint mismatched furniture the same or similar colors to give your room a finished look.

Fabric can add interest to a wall or turn a sturdy carton into an attractive covered table. There are books that explain how to cover chests and other pieces with cloth. You can make a simple slipcover and matching curtains, and use leftover fabric to make pillows, chair pads, lamp shades, and many other items.

Using Accessories

No room is complete without accessories. **Accessories** are *interesting items added to make a space more personal.* **Figure 8.2** shows some of the many ways that you can use accessories to give a room a personal touch.

Figure 8.2
The Personal Touch
Many different kinds of items can make your space uniquely yours. What kinds of accessories express who you are?

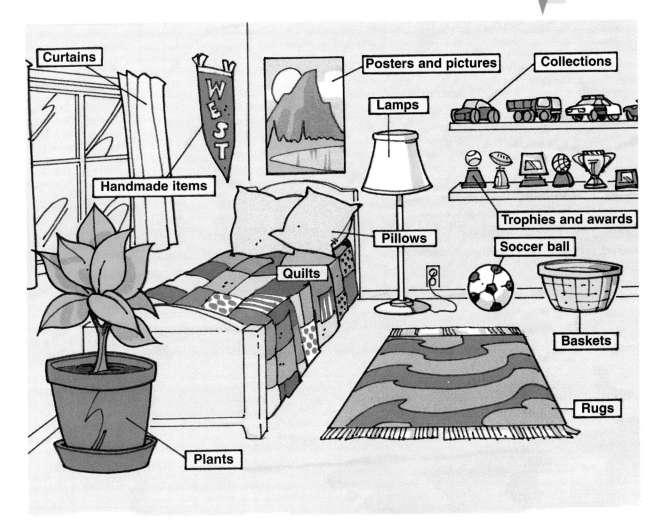

Curtains

Handmade items

Posters and pictures

Collections

Lamps

Trophies and awards

Pillows

Soccer ball

Quilts

Baskets

Plants

Rugs

TIPS for living

DRAWING A FLOOR PLAN

Have you ever worn yourself out moving furniture around to find the best arrangement? Make a **floor plan,** or *diagram of a room arrangement,* to save time and trouble. To make one, do the following.

- Measure the room and the furniture in it.

- Draw the dimensions of the room on a piece of graph paper. Have one or two squares equal each foot of space in the room.

- Show where the doors, windows, and other fixed features are. Draw a dotted line to show which way the doors open.

- On another sheet of graph paper draw each piece of furniture. Cut out and label the pieces.

- Move the pieces of furniture around on the floor plan until you get a satisfying arrangement. Allow space for walking and for drawers to open.

LESSON TWO Review

Using complete sentences, answer the following questions on a separate sheet of paper.

Reviewing Terms and Facts

1. List What are the five elements of design?

2. Vocabulary Define the term *illusion.* Use it in an original sentence.

3. Identify How does each element of design contribute to the overall effect of a room?

4. Recall Which colors are considered warm? Which ones are considered cool?

5. Vocabulary Define the term *accessories.* Give four examples of accessories.

Thinking Critically

6. Analyze Which element of design do you think is the most important? Explain your answer.

7. Describe How can texture affect the mood of a room?

8. Explain Why are accessories an important part of any room?

Applying Concepts

9. Look through magazines, and choose a picture of a room you like. Write a few paragraphs explaining how the design elements have been used to create an appealing look.

LESSON THREE
Keeping a Home Clean and Safe

DISCOVER...

- the value of keeping a home clean and safe.
- how to manage cleaning tasks.
- how to prevent accidents.

Do you feel proud of your home when it is clean and neat? Do you feel good knowing that your home is safe and secure? Keeping your home clean, neat, safe, and secure is worthwhile for many reasons.

- **It saves time and energy.** You waste time and energy when you have to search for items that you need. For example, have you ever wasted time looking for a missing notebook or shoe?

WORDS TO KNOW

sanitary

precautions

cleaning plan

- **Clothes and other possessions last longer.** If you take care of your belongings, they last longer and do not need to be replaced as often.

- **Family members stay healthier in a clean home.** A clean home is **sanitary,** or *free from germs.*

- **Most home accidents can be prevented.** By practicing safety **precautions,** or *steps to avoid danger,* family members can keep many home accidents and injuries from occurring.

- **Security measures can keep a home safe.** If a home has adequate window and door locks, it will be more difficult for intruders to break into the home.

Families may find that managing cleaning tasks is easier if they use a cleaning plan to organize the work. What items are included in a cleaning plan?

Organizing the Cleaning Tasks

Routine cleaning tasks are those that must be done every day or every week. These chores include washing dishes, emptying the dishwasher, making beds, cleaning floors, keeping rooms picked up, emptying wastebaskets, and hanging up clothes. Routine tasks keep the home clean and neat so that heavy cleaning is needed less often.

A cleaning plan can help families manage their cleaning tasks. A **cleaning plan** is *a list of daily, weekly, and occasional household jobs and of the family member or members who are responsible for each job.* To make a cleaning plan, decide with other members of the family what jobs need to be done and who will perform each task.

Cleaning Shared Space

When each person takes responsibility for keeping his or her personal space in order, much of the housekeeping gets done automatically. To get your share done with ease, you need to establish some routine habits. For example, hanging up clothes or putting them in a hamper is a habit that takes no more time than dropping clothes on the bed or in a corner. If you are cooking in the kitchen, clean up as you go along so that the cleanup at the end is easier.

Because the bathrooms and the kitchen are used by all family members, every person must help keep them in order. Rinse the bathtub and sink after each use. Hang towels and washcloths neatly in the same place after each use. Return personal grooming items to their proper place to avoid clutter.

In the kitchen leave the counter and sink clean. Wash and dry the dishes, or put them in the dishwasher. What are some other ways to keep the kitchen clean and neat?

Cleaning Up Your Room

It will be easier to keep your room clean if you take time each day to put it in order. All the tasks do not have to be done at the same time. For instance, a good plan may be to hang up your clothes and straighten the dresser and desk at night. It doesn't take long to make your bed in the morning. You can dust or empty the wastebasket in the afternoon after you finish your homework. Put away your belongings as soon as you finish using them.

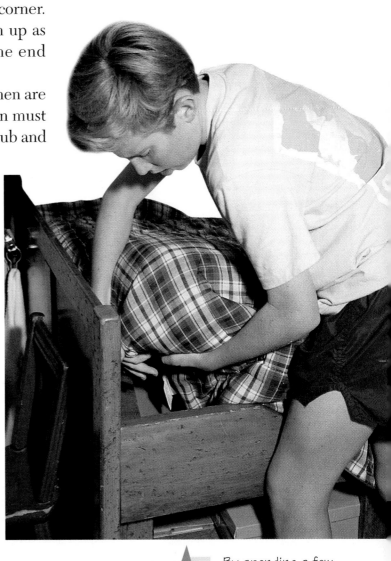

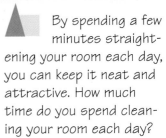
By spending a few minutes straightening your room each day, you can keep it neat and attractive. How much time do you spend cleaning your room each day?

Keeping your clothes closet organized helps you find what you need. It also helps to keep your room looking neat. Try these ideas.

- Hang up your clothes according to categories. For example, put all of your shirts or blouses, pants or skirts, and sweaters together.

- Clean soiled shoes and clothes before putting them in the closet, and keep your shoes in a shoe bag or on a shoe rack.

- Keep small articles that you use only occasionally in shoe boxes or plastic boxes. Label the outside of the boxes so that you can find the items easily.

What other closet-organizing tips can you think of?

Try This!

Use this checklist to see if your home and family are safe from intruders.

1. Is there exterior lighting over every entrance?

2. Is shrubbery trimmed near doors and windows?

3. Are there secure locks on doors and windows?

4. Are there other safety devices, such as peepholes, door chains, and motion detector lights?

5. Are doors locked at all times?

6. Are garage doors kept locked when not in use?

7. Do you avoid opening the door to strangers?

Home Safety

Many of the accidents that happen in homes could be prevented or avoided with a little care. Don't let someone in your family be hurt by carelessness. Read over the following rules, and then take the time to make your home safe.

Protect your home from fire by following these safety rules.

- Make sure that smoke alarms are installed in the home. Alarms should be installed near the kitchen, outside the bedrooms, and at the top of the stairs. Check smoke alarms once a month to be sure that they are working properly, and change the batteries routinely.

- Do not let curtains, towels, or pot holders get too close to the stove. If you are cooking, avoid wearing a shirt with loose sleeves that might easily catch fire.

- Keep the area around the stove free of grease. Grease burns easily and can spread a fire.

- Make sure that all electrical cords are in good condition. A damaged cord can cause surrounding material to catch fire.

- If you have a fireplace in your home, make sure that it is used properly. Keep flammable objects away from the fireplace, and be sure to use a screen.

- Keep a fire extinguisher in the home, and learn how to use it properly.

To protect people from falls in your home, follow these safety rules.

- Make sure that the stairs are in good repair, well lit, and free from clutter. Stairs should also have handrails.

- If something is spilled on a bare floor, wipe it up immediately.

- Place nonskid pads under small rugs so that they don't slide.

- Be sure to use nonskid strips or mats in bathtubs and showers.

If you spill something on the floor, clean it up right away so that no one slips and falls. How else can you protect people from falls in the home?

Other Safety Precautions

In addition to fires and falls, there are many other types of accidents that can happen in homes. If there are small children in the family, poisoning is a particularly serious danger. Make sure that all cleaning products and chemicals are kept out of the reach of the children. Don't forget to store lawn products carefully. Read the label on any chemical or cleaning product before using it so that you will know how to handle it correctly. If anyone in your family accidentally swallows a poisonous substance, immediately call a poison control center or a hospital.

Power tools and sharp knives can also cause injuries if they are not used with care. Learn how to handle such equipment properly. Knives and other potentially dangerous objects should be kept out of the reach of children.

Improper use of electrical appliances is another common cause of accidents. Be sure to connect and disconnect any electrical appliance with dry hands. Do not use any appliance that has a damaged cord. Do not use a hair dryer while in the bathtub or while standing on a wet spot.

Keeping your home clean and safe will benefit all members of the family. What are some of these benefits? ▶

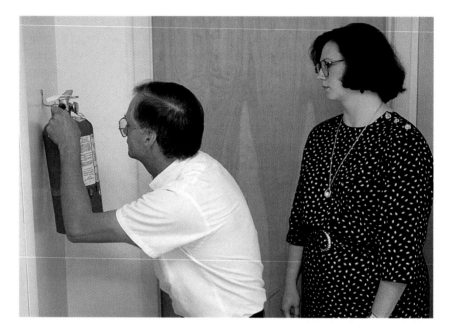

LESSON THREE *Review*

Using complete sentences, answer the following questions on a separate sheet of paper.

Reviewing Terms and Facts

1. Vocabulary Define the term *precautions.* Use it in an original sentence.

2. Recall What are routine cleaning tasks? Give four examples of these tasks.

3. List What are three tips for keeping your bedroom neat?

4. Name List four ways to protect your home from fire.

5. Identify Name four safety rules for preventing falls in the home.

Thinking Critically

6. Explain How can establishing routine cleaning habits save you time?

7. Analyze What special safety precautions should be taken if young children live in a home?

Applying Concepts

8. Make a cleaning plan for your home. First list the cleaning tasks that need to be done on a daily, weekly, and occasional basis. Then discuss with family members who can do which chores on which days. Make sure that the work is divided fairly. On the computer or by hand, create a chart that shows the cleaning tasks and each family member's assignments for a one-month period. Put your plan into effect.

Chapter 8 Activities

Consumer Focus

Fido and Fluffy

Pets can help make a home feel friendly, warm, and safe. They can also make it difficult to keep a home clean and sanitary. Many dogs and cats shed, and pets sometimes leave unpleasant stains and odors.

Fortunately, deodorizers and other products are available to help people clean up after pets.

Try This!

Consult a book on household cleaning tips for ways to remove pet stains and odors. Report to the class on your findings.

A Global View

HOME SWEET HOME

In Nigeria, Yakuba and his family reside in a mud hut with a straw roof. Chong and her parents live on a houseboat in the harbor of Singapore. Kadir and his family are nomads in Saudi Arabia. They travel across the desert and set up tents whenever they stop.

TRY THIS!

Cut out or draw pictures of different types of housing. Assemble your pictures for a classroom display. Write a paragraph about people's need for homes, and put it with your artwork.

FRIENDS & FAMILY

ACCIDENTS WAITING TO HAPPEN

Every year thousands of adults and children are seriously hurt or die as a result of home accidents.

Some accidents happen because of careless behavior. Other accidents occur as a result of unsafe conditions, such as frayed electrical cords. Most home accidents can be prevented.

TRY THIS!

Learn more about home safety hazards. Then make a home safety checklist. Use the checklist to discover potential hazards in your home. Work with your family on accident prevention.

TECHNOLOGY CONNECTION

AUTOMATION IN THE HOME

Many homes are equipped with features that help people stay safe, save energy and money, and make their lives easier.

Lights and appliances can be programmed to turn on and off at set times. Heating and cooling systems can be set to operate automatically. With a computer, modem, and fax machine, people can stay in touch with coworkers anywhere.

Follow Up

1. What role do you think that computers play in home automation?

2. What other types of automation would you like to see in homes of the future? Make a list of ideas, and exchange lists with a classmate.

3. How might home automation benefit people with physical disabilities? Write down two or three examples.

Chapter Summary

Your home not only provides the shelter you need but also reflects your personality.

- You can make your home both appealing and functional by choosing your furniture and arranging your living space with care.

- Sharing living space with others requires respect for others' privacy, consideration, cooperation, and compromise.

- The elements of design are space, shape, line, texture, and color.

- Before you change the look of your room, it is a good idea to plan how you will make the changes.

- The accessories you add to a room help define your style and give your living space a personal touch.

- There are many advantages to keeping a home clean and safe, including saving time and energy, keeping the home free of germs, and preventing accidents.

- It is much easier to keep the home clean if everyone shares the tasks and follows a cleaning plan.

- Take safety precautions to guard against accidents, fires, falls, and intruders in the home.

▶ Words to Know

Using complete sentences, answer the following questions on a separate sheet of paper.

1. Name one *function* of each of the following: a kitchen, a table, a shelf.

2. Explain what is meant by the *traffic pattern* in a room.

3. What is *design?*

4. Draw a *diagonal* line. What effect do diagonal lines suggest?

5. Name four kinds of *texture.*

6. What does *sanitary* mean?

7. Why is it important to practice safety *precautions* in the home?

8. What is listed in a *cleaning plan.*

▶ Review Questions

Using complete sentences, answer the following questions on a separate sheet of paper.

1. What does your home provide for you besides physical shelter?

2. Why are homes divided into special living areas?

3. How could a teen who shares a bedroom with a brother or sister show respect for the other person's privacy?

4. How can color be used to affect the appearance of a room?

5. Before you start a room makeover, what should you do?

6. Why should a teen maintain a clean, neat bedroom?

7. List three ways to manage your cleaning time efficiently.

8. Give two examples of ways to prevent falls in the home.

Thinking Critically

Using complete sentences, answer the following questions on a separate sheet of paper.

1. **Suggest** How might a family's values influence living space? Give examples.

2. **Analyze** What aspects of day-to-day living do you think an architect has to consider when designing a living space? Explain your answer.

3. **Recommend** How could you use the elements of design to create a room that looks large and efficient?

4. **Apply** How would you design living space to meet the needs of a family member who uses a wheelchair?

Cooperative Learning

1. Working with a partner, look in home-decorating magazines for a color picture of a room. Cut out the picture, and paste it on a piece of construction paper. Write a paragraph describing how the elements of design have been used in the room. Then exchange pictures with another pair of students. Discuss the design elements in the new picture, and see if the description the other pair wrote matches the picture.

2. Working in groups of three or four, choose a cleaning technique, such as how to wash dishes, clean glass, or clean a bathtub. Look in a

book on household hints for information on your cleaning technique. Then demonstrate your technique to the class or make a poster explaining the technique.

Family & Community

1. Discuss with your family a free or inexpensive way to improve the living space in your home. For example, you might agree on a cleaning schedule, rearrange the furniture in the living room, paint the kitchen, or make the house childproof. Make a plan and then carry it out.

2. Identify a local group that helps people safeguard their homes and be good neighbors. This may be a block club, a Neighborhood Watch program, or a community organization. Find out about the work of the group, and report your findings to the class.

Building A Portfolio

1. Plan a makeover for your personal living space. Think about how you could improve your space, and then put your plan into action. Your plan could involve redecorating, rearranging the furniture, or cleaning. Use photos or drawings to show "Before" and "After." Place the photos or drawings in your portfolio.

2. List the accessories you have in your personal living space, such as posters, collections, and knickknacks. Tell what each accessory reveals about your interests. Are your accessories similar to or different from those you kept in your living space when you were younger? Put the list in your portfolio.

9

Your Environment

TEENS MAKING A DIFFERENCE

Buddy Service

Seventeen-year-old Kevin Chang started a buddy service to help young teens in his community stay safe. Kevin's 12-year-old brother Thomas often asked Kevin to drive him home from school because Thomas felt unsafe walking home alone. Some of Thomas's friends started asking Kevin to drive them home too. That is when Kevin asked some of his friends to help him make the buddy service a business.

Kevin and his friends now take appointments and charge hourly rates for their buddy service. Parents don't mind paying for the service to ensure that their children get home safely.

Try THIS!

Do you think that a buddy service would be useful at your school? Why or why not? Write a paragraph or two explaining your answer.

LESSON ONE
Protecting Your Environment

WORDS TO KNOW

natural
    resources

pollution

conservation

insulation

energy efficient

DISCOVER...

- the natural resources that make up the environment.
- ways to conserve natural resources.
- ways to use energy wisely.

Do you like to spend time at the beach or in the mountains? Have you ever gone swimming or fishing in a lake or an ocean? Enjoying outdoor activities is one of the greatest pleasures of life. In addition, you could not survive without the elements that nature provides.

What Are Natural Resources?

Natural resources are *materials that are supplied by nature.* You might not think about them very often, and you may even take them for granted. However, your health and well-being depend on several key natural resources. These include air, water, soil, and the energy derived from coal, oil, and gas.

At one time these resources seemed almost limitless. Some, however, are nonrenewable, and if they are used up or permanently damaged, they will no longer be available. This damage is often caused by pollution. **Pollution** is *the changing of air, water, and land from clean and safe to dirty and unsafe.*

Air

Your body uses the oxygen in air to produce energy. Plants use the carbon dioxide in air to produce food and oxygen. Plants, animals, and people could not live without clean air.

Unfortunately, the air you breathe is not completely clean. It may contain dust, smoke, chemical particles, and smog.

Try This!

Every day the earth's natural resources are being polluted, misused, or damaged. Think of at least one way *you* could help to correct or prevent air pollution, water pollution, or depletion of non-renewal fuels. Share your ideas with the class.

The air that you breathe is an important natural resource. Why do you think that running would be difficult if you didn't have enough fresh, clean air to breathe?

These substances, which are all forms of air pollution, can be harmful to your health. Some causes of air pollution are

- the release of poisonous gases such as car exhaust fumes that combine with the atmosphere to create smog when fuels are burned to provide energy.

- smoke from such sources as fireplaces, barbecues, and burning leaves.

- chemicals, including those that kill insects and those used as cooling agents in air conditioners and refrigerators.

Skills IN ACTION

Using Water Wisely

Here are some ways you can conserve water.
- Run the washing machine only with a full load.
- Turn off the water when brushing your teeth.
- Take short showers instead of baths.
- Repair leaky faucets.
- Ask your family to install water-saving showerheads and toilets.

Water

Water, like air, is necessary to all living things. In fact, water is your body's most essential nutrient. It is needed for every bodily function.

You may think that there is plenty of water. After all, about 70 percent of the earth's surface is covered by water. Most of it, however, is salt water. Many plants and animals cannot use that water. They need clean, fresh water to survive.

Much of the earth's water is polluted by wastes. Common sources of water pollution are human wastes, detergents, and the chemicals used to kill insects or to fertilize crops. Polluted water can cause people to become sick or even die.

Soil

The earth's land is made up of soil, the loose material in which plants can grow. Plants get the nutrients and water they need from the soil. People, in turn, need the nutrients that plants provide in order to live.

Energy

What would happen if there wasn't any gasoline left for cars, trucks, and buses? How would we heat homes, schools, and office buildings if we ran out of oil and other kinds of fuel? You may think that this could never happen. However, many sources of energy—such as oil, natural gas, and coal—are in limited supply. Once they are used up, they cannot be replaced.

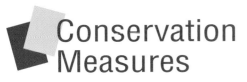

Conservation Measures

You may feel that the problems of pollution and a shrinking supply of natural resources are overwhelming and beyond your control. There are many ways, however, that you can make a difference. One important way is to practice **conservation,** *the saving of resources.* The best way to conserve a resource is to use less of it. For example, turn off the faucet to save water when you are brushing your teeth. Whenever possible, walk or use a bicycle—instead of riding in a car—to reduce smog. Reuse paper bags and return plastic bags to grocery stores.

Families can also work together to conserve natural resources. Some families have added more insulation to their homes to save fuel. **Insulation** is *a material installed in the attic or walls of a building to keep it cooler in summer and warmer in winter.* How does your family conserve resources? You will learn more about conservation in Lesson 2 of this chapter.

These teens are helping to conserve natural resources and reduce air pollution. What are some other ways to do this?

Using Energy Wisely

An important way to conserve resources is to learn to use energy wisely. Look for appliances that are **energy efficient,** or *made to use less energy.* By using energy efficiently, you not only conserve resources but also reduce pollution of the environment.

You can save energy at home in many ways. Most of the energy used at home is for heating and cooling. Depending on the season, you can reduce the heating temperature or increase the cooling temperature. The rest of the energy used in homes is for heating water, lighting the home, and running appliances. When your family members buy new appliances, they can look for the most energy-efficient ones by comparing guides that list energy costs per year. **Figure 9.1** on the next page shows other ways to be energy efficient.

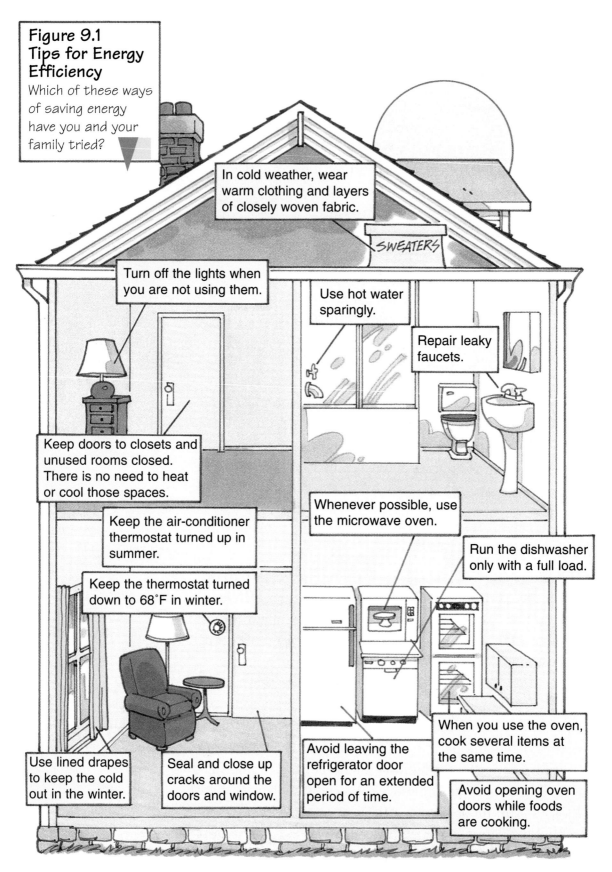

**Figure 9.1
Tips for Energy Efficiency**
Which of these ways of saving energy have you and your family tried?

In cold weather, wear warm clothing and layers of closely woven fabric.

SWEATERS

Turn off the lights when you are not using them.

Use hot water sparingly.

Repair leaky faucets.

Keep doors to closets and unused rooms closed. There is no need to heat or cool those spaces.

Keep the air-conditioner thermostat turned up in summer.

Whenever possible, use the microwave oven.

Run the dishwasher only with a full load.

Keep the thermostat turned down to 68°F in winter.

Use lined drapes to keep the cold out in the winter.

Seal and close up cracks around the doors and window.

Avoid leaving the refrigerator door open for an extended period of time.

When you use the oven, cook several items at the same time.

Avoid opening oven doors while foods are cooking.

Other Ways to Help

Protection of natural resources and the environment begins with people like you. There are plenty of ways for you to make a difference. You can use air, water, land, and energy wisely. You can make an effort to be energy efficient at home. You can be a concerned citizen who cares about the environment and works with others to keep it clean.

There are many ways for people to get involved in cleaning up their community. How might you volunteer in your area?

LESSON ONE *Review*

Using complete sentences, answer the following questions on a separate sheet of paper.

Reviewing Terms and Facts

1. Vocabulary Define the term *pollution*. List the natural resources that pollution affects.

2. List Name the major causes of air pollution.

3. Recall What is the best way to conserve a resource?

Thinking Critically

4. Analyze Why do you think that some people are not careful with natural resources?

5. Predict What might happen to our natural resources if we don't take care of them?

6. Explain Who benefits when people use energy efficiently? How do they benefit?

Applying Concepts

7. Read the label on a cleaning product at home or in a store. List the product's uses and whether it contains harmful or poisonous substances. If it does, look in a store for a substitute product that is not harmful. Share your results with the class.

Keeping Your Environment Clean

WORDS
TO KNOW

landfills

decompose

incineration

precycle

biodegradable

recycling

DISCOVER...

- where trash goes after you throw it away.
- ways to limit the amount of waste in your environment.
- what it means to reduce, reuse, precycle, and recycle.

You may think that as long as you don't litter, you are doing your part to keep your community clean. There is much more to it than that, however. Since about the middle of the 20th century we have lived in a "throwaway" society. Many items are used only once and then thrown away. As a result, we now have a serious problem because we have too much waste and not enough safe ways to get rid of it.

Where Does Waste Go?

Billions of tons of trash and garbage are disposed of every year in the United States. Where does it all go? Where *should* it all go? These questions are urgent because the mountain of waste created by Americans continues to grow.

You can work to change the situation. Even though the trash problem is a national issue, the solution depends on individual actions. Your actions can help to make a difference.

Landfills

About 80 percent of the waste in the United States is disposed of in landfills. **Landfills** are *huge pits where waste is dumped and buried between layers of earth.* Most large communities have landfills, or dumps, somewhere on their outskirts. These landfills are carefully designed to control the odors, germs, and other unpleasant or unhealthy situations that are created by piles of trash and garbage. Away from towns and carefully buried, the waste doesn't pose a threat to people's health.

Landfills do cause problems, however. They take up huge amounts of space, and no one wants to live near a landfill. Garbage buried in landfills is supposed to **decompose,** or *break down,* so that it becomes part of the soil. However, recent studies have shown that certain kinds of discarded waste, such as plastic foam, do not break down for a long time.

Incineration

Another common way to dispose of trash in the United States is by incineration. **Incineration** means *disposing of waste by burning it.* About 10 percent of the waste in the United States is incinerated. Burning trash, however, causes air pollution. When trash that is poisonous is burned, its smoke is especially dangerous. The problem is so great that many communities do not allow trash to be burned.

There are thousands of landfills like this one all across the country. Why can't we continue to rely on them as a way to dispose of all of our waste?

Limiting the Amount of Waste

Burying waste in landfills and incinerating it both have serious drawbacks. What should Americans do about the problem? The key is to reduce the amount of waste we create. All Americans can do their part by following the "three R's"— Reduce, Reuse, Recycle.

Reduce

The first step is to reduce the amount of trash created. To start reducing the amount of trash you create, you can

Check to see if the products your family uses are biodegradable. How can this help the environment?

- reduce the amount of paper you throw away by using both sides of notebook paper and by using only washable cups and plates.

- **precycle,** or *avoid buying products that use more packaging than necessary.*

- plan meals carefully so there is little waste.

- avoid buying disposable products.

- use cloth grocery bags instead of paper or plastic ones.

- buy products that are **biodegradable**—*able to degrade, or break down, and be absorbed by the environment.* Biodegradable products don't fill up landfills.

Reuse

The second of the "three R's" is *reuse.* The idea is simple: you can limit the amount of waste you create by reusing items you might otherwise throw away. If you use your imagination, you can probably think of many ways to reuse items. Here are a few ideas.

- Buy products packed in containers that can be refilled or used for something else.

- Keep boxes, bottles, and cans to use as storage containers.

With a little imagination, many items can be reused instead of thrown away. What items have you reused recently?

- Save old towels and clothes to use as rags.

- Always think twice before throwing something away. Ask yourself: "What else can I do with this?"

Reusing means being creative; it can be fun. What other ideas can you add to the list?

Recycle

You already know that Americans throw out millions of tons of trash. Have you ever wondered just what all that trash is? Is it mostly plastic bottles, discarded papers, or

TIPS for living

HOW TO RECYCLE

To make recycling a habit at home and at school, follow these steps.

- Find out where to recycle in your area. Cans, bottles, and newspapers may be picked up at your home or school, or they can be sold to a recycling center.

- Set up a recycling system at home or at school. Have separate, labeled containers for glass, cans, plastic, paper, and other recyclable items.

- Learn how to prepare items for recycling. For example, you may have to rinse out and flatten plastic containers.

- Find out the days and times for recycling in your area.

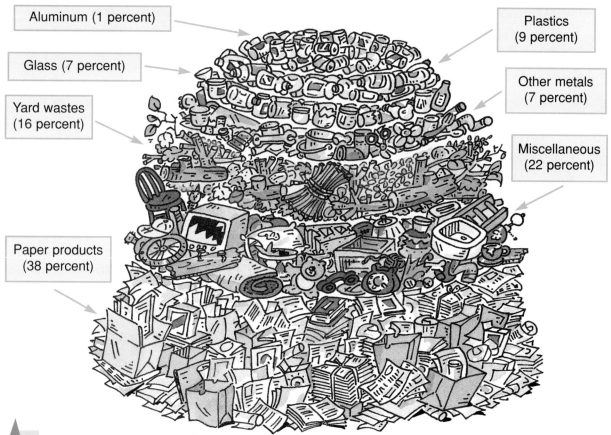

Aluminum (1 percent)

Glass (7 percent)

Yard wastes
(16 percent)

Paper products
(38 percent)

Plastics
(9 percent)

Other metals
(7 percent)

Miscellaneous
(22 percent)

Figure 9.2
Makeup of
U.S. Waste
What do you think the
most commonly thrown-
away products are made
of? Paper? Plastics?
Glass?

other material? The makeup of America's waste is shown in
Figure 9.2.

These statistics provide a clue as to how we can cut down
on waste. Many of the materials we throw away can be easily
recycled. **Recycling** is *turning waste items into products that
can be used.* For example, newspapers can be turned into pulp
to make new paper. Aluminum cans can be melted down and
turned into new cans and other products. Many plastics can
also be recycled. Because over half of the trash we create is
recyclable, a commitment to recycling can greatly reduce the
amount of waste in the country.

Other Ways to Reduce Waste

Recycling means much more than simply taking cans
and newspapers to recycling centers. When you donate
clothes, books, and other items to charities, for instance,
you are recycling them. You also recycle if you give or receive
hand-me-down clothes or trade magazines with a friend after

reading them. Can you see how holding a garage sale is also a way to recycle? All of the actions suggested in this lesson may seem small, but every one helps to limit the amount of waste. By applying the "three R's" to your own life, you will do your share to make our environment a much better place.

Instead of throwing away furniture and buying new items, try repainting, refinishing, reupholstering, or using slipcovers. Besides reducing the amount of waste, what are some other benefits of this approach?

LESSON TWO *Review*

Using complete sentences, answer the following questions on a separate sheet of paper.

Reviewing Terms and Facts

1. Vocabulary Define the terms *landfill* and *incineration*. What do they have in common?

2. Explain How can *biodegradable* products help the environment?

3. Identify List three ways to reduce the amount of trash discarded in the United States.

4. List Name four ways to reuse items.

Thinking Critically

5. Explain Why are current methods of waste disposal inadequate?

6. Suggest Think of something you threw away recently. Describe two ways that you could have reused it.

7. Predict Do you think that reducing the amount of waste produced will be enough to solve the waste-disposal problem? Why or why not?

Applying Concepts

8. Write a letter to the editor of your local newspaper encouraging the people in your community to reduce, reuse, and recycle. Identify ways to encourage people to follow the plan. Then post your letter on the bulletin board.

LESSON THREE
Your Personal Safety and Violence Prevention

WORDS TO KNOW

risk

hazard

pedestrian

violence

DISCOVER...

- how the accident chain works.
- how to avoid unnecessary risks.
- how to prevent violence.

Are there any small children in your family who are not yet steady on their feet? Do you or any members of your family enjoy sports or hobbies that might be dangerous? Have you or your friends ever been bothered by a bully at school? For safety and peace of mind, it is important for everyone to take precautions that prevent accidents or injuries.

Acting Safely

Have you ever been annoyed at yourself for behaving carelessly so that you were bruised or scratched, or a favorite article was broken or torn? Knowing how to work or play in the right way or the safe way is not always enough. When people act unsafely out of habit or laziness, they **risk** or *take a dangerous chance of hurting themselves or others.*

Accidents are the leading cause of death among teens. Sadly, most accidents could have been prevented. Avoidable accidents often happen when people take unnecessary risks. These accidents frequently follow a pattern called the *accident chain*. The accident chain has five steps.

- **Step 1: an unsafe situation.** For example, while wearing in-line skates, Jake wants to cross a four-lane road to skate at a park on the other side.

- **Step 2: an unsafe habit.** To get to where he wants to go, Jake often skates on busy streets instead of walking.

- **Step 3: an unsafe act.** Still on skates, Jake begins to cross the road.

- **Step 4: an accident.** Realizing that he doesn't have enough time to get to the other side of the road before the light changes, Jake doubles back to the median strip and falls.

- **Step 5: the result.** Jake twists his ankle and scrapes his arm.

Fortunately, such accidents can be avoided. That does mean, though, that a person has to take the time to think of a safer way of doing or getting what he or she wants. Any of the

By following the rules and avoiding unnecessary risks, you can prevent most accidents from happening. How are these teens acting safely?

Many activities involve some risk. If you stay within the limits of your abilities and take safety precautions, however, you will greatly reduce your risk of accident or injury.

first three steps of the accident chain can be changed to achieve one's goal safely.

- **The situation can be changed.** Jake could have looked for a safer route to the park.

- **The unsafe habit can be changed.** Jake should skate only in areas without traffic.

- **The unsafe action can be changed.** Jake could have changed into shoes and walked to the park. He probably wouldn't have expected to get all the way across the road at a slower pace and wouldn't have had to double back.

There are steps you can take to change risky situations, habits, or actions. First, know the limits of your abilities, and stay within those limits. Second, think before you take action. Is the situation safe? Are there any risks involved? Third, don't let other people pressure you into doing what you know—or even sense—is not a good idea.

At Home

Every home has some **hazards,** or *dangers.* Some hazards are unavoidable in the course of everyday life. For instance, wet bathtubs and showers are slippery, but people need to bathe or shower regularly. Likewise, detergents are poisonous, but clothes need to be washed.

On the Road

Whether you travel on foot, on skates or a bike, or in a car, the most important way to keep safe is to know and follow the rules of the road. As a **pedestrian,** or *a person who travels on foot,* you must stay aware of what drivers and other pedestrians are doing. Always cross at crosswalks or intersections, and look out for vehicles turning right on a red light. In a car, make sure that you wear a seat belt—both the lap belt and the shoulder harness—and never distract the driver.

Outdoors

Have you ever been sunburned from being outdoors without sunscreen or gotten blisters from walking too long in new shoes? Outdoor safety requires common sense—just like safety at home and on the road. Whether you enjoy water sports or hiking or winter sports, you need to take precautions to make the most of your outing.

- **Water activities.** The most important precaution when participating in water sports is knowing how to swim very well. If you plan to swim, make sure that you go with a buddy and that there is a lifeguard on duty. If you go boating, wear a life jacket, and be sure that you know how to handle the boat properly.

- **Hiking and camping.** When hiking or camping, make sure that you wear the right clothing for the weather. You should also be careful to use marked trails and designated campsites. Tell someone where you are going and when you expect to return.

- **Winter sports.** When you think of winter sports, you might imagine boots, gloves, and heavy sweaters. Wearing appropriate clothing and dressing in many layers are necessary precautions for enjoying the outdoors in winter. You also have to check to see that the conditions are good for the sport you have in mind. For instance, check ahead of time to be sure that the ice is thick enough for safe skating.

No matter what activity you choose or where it takes place—beach, mountain, or field—there are certain precautions you should always take.

- Know how much you are really capable of doing. Pushing yourself beyond your training and ability is taking unnecessary risks.

- Use the correct equipment for the sport or activity.

Skills IN ACTION

Bicycle and Skating Safety

Bicycling and in-line skating can be great fun when you follow safety rules.

For information on safety workshops in your community, contact your local police department or parks and recreation department. Demonstrate safe bicycling and skating for younger children in your neighborhood.

When you take part in winter sports, it is important to protect your hands and feet by wearing gloves, boots, and extra socks.

- Know the safety rules for your activity and follow them.

- Remember to warm up before and cool down after an activity to avoid injury.

- Practice the buddy system. When people pair up during activities, they can look after each other and help each other in an emergency.

- Use sunscreen to protect your skin from ultraviolet rays.

- Check the weather conditions where you plan to go. Avoid being out in extreme temperatures and electrical storms.

In Your Community

Have you ever been startled by a loud noise as you sat on your porch lost in thought? Have you ever felt uneasy when you walked home from a friend's house at dusk?

You—just like anyone else—want to feel safe in your own neighborhood. There are steps you can take to protect yourself. You and your family can join or help set up a Neighborhood Watch group in which neighbors look after one another and one another's homes. Members of such groups are trained by the police to identify and report suspicious activities. When you walk down the street, keep alert—especially at night. Pay attention to the people around you and to what they are doing.

TIPS
for living

STRANGER DANGER

Although most people you meet in stores and on the streets are kind and helpful, you still need to be careful around people you don't know. Follow these tips to stay safe.

- Don't get too close to a car if a stranger calls out for directions. It's easy for a stranger to pull you into a car.

- Beware of strangers who offer you gifts or money or ask you to help find a lost dog or cat.

- If a stranger follows or grabs you, run away, scream, and make lots of noise.

- Always let your family know where you will be.

- Tell your parents or other trusted adults if someone makes you feel uncomfortable.

Stay away from dangerous areas and poorly lighted streets. Avoid taking any unnecessary risks.

What Is Violence?

Violence is *the use of physical force to harm someone.* Violence often takes place between people who know each other, but some violent acts are directed at complete strangers.

Why Violence Occurs

Why do some conflicts turn violent? You have probably seen teens argue over a boyfriend or a girlfriend or get angry at what someone else said about them behind their backs. If arguments get heated or anger gets out of control, fights can break out. Here are some reasons why violence occurs:

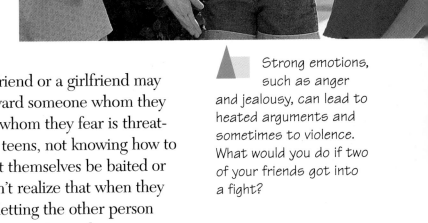

Strong emotions, such as anger and jealousy, can lead to heated arguments and sometimes to violence. What would you do if two of your friends got into a fight?

- **Strong emotions.** People who lack healthy ways of handling strong emotions may break into violence when they are upset. *Jealousy* over a boyfriend or a girlfriend may cause teens to act violently toward someone whom they are dating or toward someone whom they fear is threatening their relationship. Some teens, not knowing how to handle a confrontation, may let themselves be baited or taunted into fighting. They don't realize that when they take the bait they are actually letting the other person control them. The desire for *revenge* is another strong emotion that leads to teen violence. If Kristen is the subject of unpleasant rumors or Marc is made to look foolish in an argument, the desire to get even may lead to a fight.

- **Drugs and alcohol.** Violent acts are often committed by people who are under the influence of drugs and alcohol. These substances prevent people from thinking clearly and may even make them act violently.

- **Peer pressure.** Teens sometimes pressure their peers to look and act like the rest of the group. Sometimes teens feel that they have to prove their loyalty to a group by conforming to the group's standards, even when it means going against their personal values.

- **Prejudice.** When a person forms an opinion about another person without factual knowledge of that individual, hostile feelings can develop and may lead to acts of violence.

Preventing Violence

There are many precautions you can take to keep yourself safe and help prevent violence in your school and community.

- Carry yourself with confidence to avoid looking like a potential victim.

- Travel with friends, and stay out of unfamiliar areas.

- Don't give in to baiting and taunting. Remember that the baiter is trying to get a reaction out of you.

- Try to resolve conflicts peacefully.

- Tell a parent, a counselor, or another responsible adult if you feel threatened.

Traveling with a friend is a good way to keep yourself safe from violence. What are some other ways?

LESSON THREE *Review*

Using complete sentences, answer the following questions on a separate sheet of paper.

Reviewing Terms and Facts

1. Recall List the five steps of the accident chain.

2. Vocabulary Define the term *hazard.* Use it in an original sentence.

3. List When participating in outdoor activities, what are four precautions you should always take?

4. Identify Name four reasons why violence occurs.

Thinking Critically

5. Explain Why is the person who takes the bait and fights when taunted letting the baiter control him or her?

Applying Concepts

6. Take a personal safety inventory. Think about the safety precautions mentioned in this lesson. Do you follow these rules and avoid risks in all situations? Prepare two lists: one of precautions that you already take and one of ways in which you could act more safely.

FRIENDS & FAMILY

SAVING A CREEK

Twelve-year-old Jordan Taylor noticed that a creek near her home was littered with waste. Jordan organized family members and friends to help with the cleanup.

TRY THIS!

Identify an area in your community that is in need of repair. Make a list of ways that you can help. Then put your plan into action.

A Global View

LONG-DISTANCE POLLUTION

Damage to the environment in one part of the world affects other parts of the world as well. The sulfur in drifting smoke mixes with moisture and falls as acid rain. Scientists believe that chemicals released into the atmosphere have created holes in the ozone layer. The burning of rain forests adds to global warming.

TRY THIS!

What can you do at a local level that will help the environment worldwide? Write down some ideas and share them with your classmates.

TECHNOLOGY

Homes 2000

Early science fiction writers described homes in the year 2000 as looking like the interior of a spaceship. People would roar around wearing jet packs, and dinner would consist of a power-packed capsule. These predictions aren't likely to come true, but you can be sure that housing will become more environmentally sound.

Try This!

Look in home-decorating magazines for examples of conservation of resources in home building and remodeling. Share your examples with the class.

SCIENCE CONNECTION

ALTERNATIVE SOURCES OF ENERGY

Scientists have many ideas for new energy sources. Alternative energy sources must be renewable, nonpolluting, practical to obtain, and affordable. Natural resources can provide alternative sources of energy. For example, some possible sources come from geothermal energy, hydropower, tidal power, wind, and solar power.

Follow Up

1. As a class, conduct an energy conference. In groups of three or four, research one alternative source of energy per group. Find out how the energy is produced and its advantages and disadvantages. Each group should report its findings to the class.

2. How might you use your human energy as an alternative energy source? What are the advantages and disadvantages of human energy?

Chapter Summary

- Natural resources include air, water, land, coal, oil, and gas. Some natural resources are in limited supply, and if they are used up they will no longer be available.

- Ways to conserve natural resources include using less of them and using energy efficiently.

- Americans create an enormous amount of waste. Disposing of waste each year has become a national problem.

- You can help solve the waste crisis by reducing the amount of trash you create, reusing items instead of throwing them away, precycling, and recycling.

- Your environment includes the natural environment and the people, events, and conditions around you. Your home and your community are part of your total environment.

- You can help keep your environment safe by avoiding unnecessary risks and by taking precautions.

- Violence among teens is a growing problem. Jealousy and anger, drugs and alcohol, peer pressure, and prejudice are some of the reasons why teens fight.

Words to Know

Using complete sentences, answer the following questions on a separate sheet of paper.

1. Explain the effect of *pollution* on natural resources.

2. What is the purpose of *conservation?*

3. What does an *energy-efficient* appliance do?

4. Describe a *landfill.*

5. What is a *biodegradable* product?

6. Give an example of a *hazard* in the home.

7. Define the term *violence.*

Review Questions

Using complete sentences, answer the following questions on a separate piece of paper.

1. Why do we need to conserve our natural resources?

2. List ways in which you can contribute to solving the larger problems associated with pollution and waste disposal.

3. Why can't Americans depend on landfills for disposal of waste?

4. Why is incineration not a good answer to the waste problem?

5. What are two methods of recycling?

6. What are some precautions you can take to avoid a sports injury?

7. What are some precautions you can take to keep yourself safe in your school and your community?

Thinking Critically

Using complete sentences, answer the following questions on a separate sheet of paper.

1. **Suggest** What effect do you think that a dirty environment has on people?

2. **Explain** Why do you think that people had less trash to throw out 50 years ago than people do today?

3. **Analyze** Why do you think that many teens take risks?

Cooperative Learning

1. Working in a group of five, form an "accident chain." Have one person think of an unsafe situation, the next person an unsafe habit, and so on. Present your chain to the class, and discuss ways the accident could be avoided.

2. As a class, decide on a project to improve your school's environment. For example, you could plant a tree, conduct an antilitter campaign, or make safety posters. You might conduct an "energy audit" of your school and recommend ways for the school to conserve energy. Use your management skills to carry out the project.

Family & Community

1. Talk to family members about ways to become more energy efficient at home. Have each family member name one change he or she will make. For example, your sister may offer to turn off her radio when she is not listening to it. After two weeks, ask family members whether or not the change was easy to make.

2. Join a clean-up campaign in your neighborhood or start one of your own. You might adopt a certain block, a bus shelter, or a walking trail and pick up litter on a regular basis.

Building A Portfolio

1. Make a list of the trash you throw away during a week. Every time you throw out an item, add it to the list. At the end of the week, look over your list. Put a circle around each item you could have used again, a square around each item you could have recycled, and a star next to each item you probably didn't need in the first place. Keep the list in your portfolio as a reminder to follow the "three R's."

2. Enroll in a class or workshop in your school or community that teaches safety to teens. You might choose a class on boating safety, a Red Cross lifesaving course, a workshop on violence prevention, or a demonstration of self-defense. When you finish the class, put your certificate of attendance in your portfolio.

Foods and Nutrition

CHAPTER

10 Nutrition and You

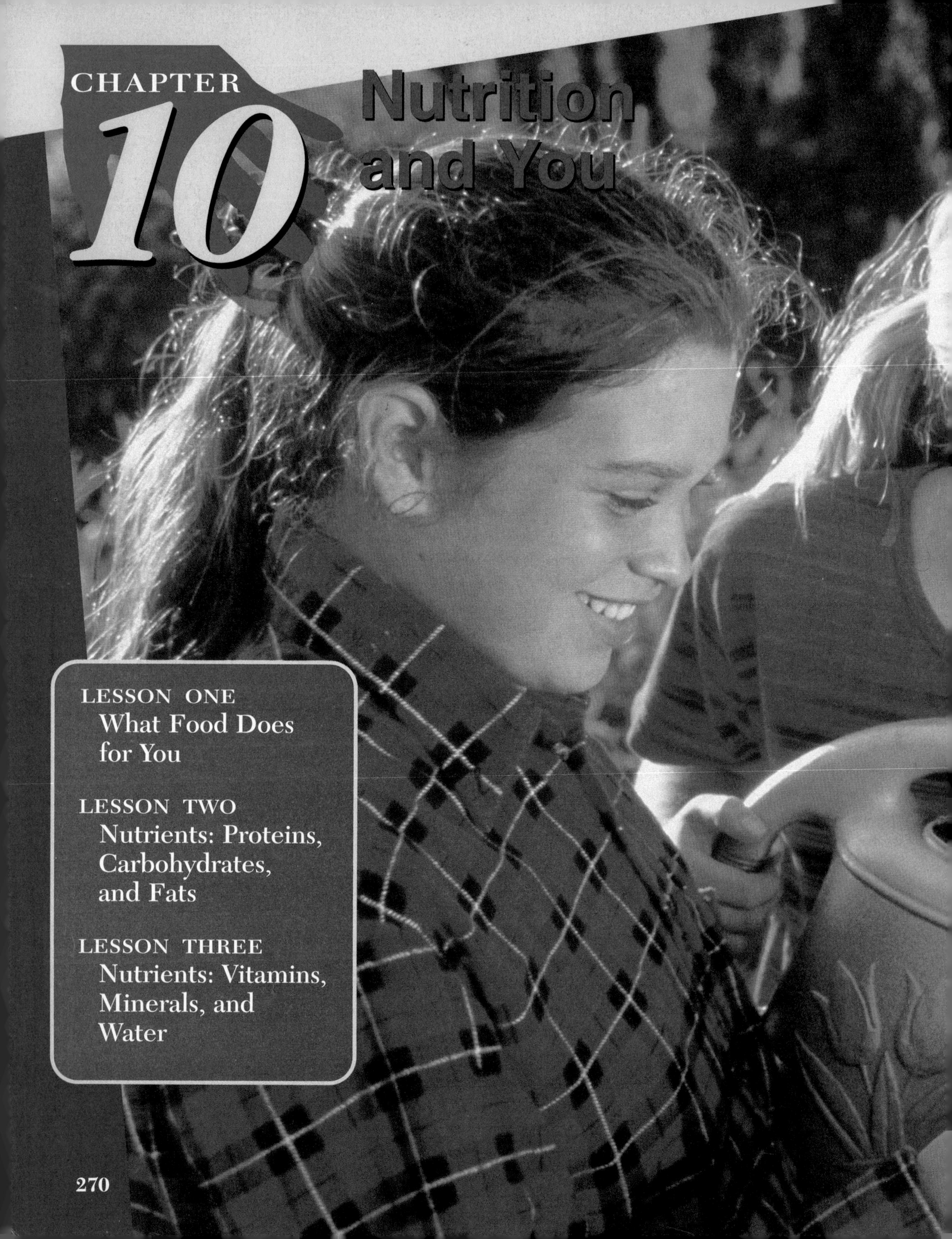

TEENS MAKING A DIFFERENCE

Community Service Club

One Saturday, when Jillian Thompson was helping out at her family's restaurant, she noticed how much leftover food got thrown away. Jillian wondered if there was a way for that food to be used to feed hungry people. Jillian's father suggested that she call a local soup kitchen to see if they could use the food.

Jillian then asked her social studies teacher to help her set up a community service club at school. Many students volunteered to help, and their parents agreed to take turns doing the driving. Now good, nutritious food serves to keep people healthy instead of going to waste.

Try THIS!

Talk to your teachers, guidance counselor, or librarian to learn about programs in your community that help feed people in need. Find out what you can do to help.

What Food Does for You

WORDS TO KNOW

nutrients

diet

hunger

appetite

calorie

nutrition

digestion

DISCOVER...

- how food affects the way you look and feel.
- the difference between hunger and appetite.
- factors that influence food choices.

Carly's favorite foods are pizza, salads, and yogurt. Even though these foods are healthful, Carly knows that she needs to eat a variety of foods to supply her body with the nutrients it needs. **Nutrients** (NOO-tree-ents) are *substances in food that are important for the body's growth and maintenance.* Carly still eats her favorite foods, but she balances her diet by including many different choices. **Diet** means *everything you regularly eat and drink.*

Looking Good

Your diet affects the way you look. Eating healthful foods can help you look your best. Exercise, adequate rest, and personal hygiene also contribute to your appearance. Most healthy young teens have these physical characteristics:

- Normal growth
- Average weight
- Sparkling eyes
- Good posture
- Healthy teeth
- Shiny hair

Skin problems are common among teens, but they usually go away as people get older. Contrary to popular belief, eating such foods as chocolate or potato chips does not cause skin problems. However, eating a nutritious diet, washing your face every day, and getting enough rest will help keep your skin healthy.

Eating nutritious foods helps keep up your energy level. What activities might be more fun if you had more energy?

Feeling Good

Have you ever noticed how young children get cranky when they are hungry? Along with exercise and rest, food affects how you feel, no matter what your age. Feeling good and being healthy go hand in hand. A healthy person is

- energetic and not easily tired.
- mentally alert.
- calm, not stressed.
- rarely sick.

Food is your source of energy for physical and mental activities. You need energy to perform well in school, in sports, and in all your other activities. Without adequate food and nutrients, you may tire easily and feel less alert.

A healthful diet protects you from illness. By getting the nutrients you need, your body is better able to fight infections, heal wounds, and recover quickly if you do get sick.

The sight and smell of some foods can cause people to develop an appetite even when they are not hungry.

Satisfying Your Hunger

When your stomach growls or feels empty, you are experiencing signs of hunger. **Hunger** is *the physical need to eat.* Once you eat, that empty feeling goes away. Hunger tells you that your body needs food, but it does not tell you what to eat. You must learn to select healthful foods. You must also learn how much to eat.

Appetite is different from hunger. **Appetite** is *the desire to eat.* When you smell fresh strawberries or see a chocolate layer cake, you might develop an appetite without really being hungry.

When hunger is satisfied, it may be time to stop eating. Some people still have an appetite, however, so they continue to eat. If they eat too much food, or food that is too high in calories, they may gain excess weight. A **calorie** is *a unit of heat that measures the energy available in food.* Food provides energy for your daily activities. If you eat food that has more calories than your body uses, however, the extra energy is stored as fat.

What Influences Your Food Choices?

Like most people, you eat for many reasons. Food helps keep you healthy. Some foods may be part of family traditions. For example, you may have a favorite menu for a particular holiday meal. Some people eat because they are bored or depressed. Food is usually part of social gatherings. You have probably eaten snacks or cake and ice cream at a birthday party.

Have you ever thought about why you choose to eat the foods you do? Of course, you have likes and dislikes, but other factors also influence your food choices:

- **Family.** Your family has taught you about food. Over the years, you have learned to eat and enjoy foods that are part of your family's habits, lifestyle, and traditions.

- **Cultural background.** You may like foods that are part of your culture. Foods from many cultures are popular in the United States.

- **Religion.** Some religious teachings forbid certain foods. For example, Hindus don't eat beef. Many Jewish people and Muslims don't eat pork.

- **Friends.** As you get older, your friends may introduce you to new food experiences.

Skills IN ACTION

Creative Breakfasts

Try the following nutritious breakfast ideas for a change of pace:

- Plain yogurt with fruit and granola
- A breakfast burrito—an egg scrambled with ham and rolled in a warm tortilla
- Hot or cold sandwiches, such as grilled cheese, tuna, or turkey

Your family influences your food choices. What could you do to influence their choices?

Try **This!**

How healthful is your diet? Rate your eating habits by answering the following questions.
• Do you eat breakfast every morning?
• Do you eat meals at regular intervals?
• Do you eat a varied diet?
If you answered no to some of these questions, make a plan to improve your diet.

• **Convenience.** People who have little time to cook may choose foods that are easy to prepare.

• **Cost.** To get more for their money, many people choose less expensive foods.

• **Area where you live.** You may eat foods that are popular and easily available in your part of the country. For example, fish is common in the coastal areas.

• **Advertising.** You may be persuaded to buy and eat certain foods because of television, radio, and magazine advertisements.

• **Health.** When you know about food and nutrition, you can choose foods that promote your health.

Eating nutritious foods is essential to keep your body running smoothly. This snack is satisfying and healthy.

Nutrients for Health

When you make food choices, the factor that should influence you most is your health. Nutrients in food keep you healthy, help you grow, and give you energy. Eating a variety of foods will provide you with good nutrition. **Nutrition** (noo-TRI-shuhn) is *the study of nutrients and how they are used by the body.*

There are six kinds of nutrients: proteins, carbohydrates, fats, vitamins, minerals, and water. Each one has an important function.

• **Proteins** help build, repair, and maintain body cells and tissues.

• **Carbohydrates** provide energy and fiber.

• **Fats** provide energy and supply essential fatty acids for normal growth and healthy skin.

• **Vitamins, minerals, and water** help regulate the work of the body's systems.

Nutrients are released from food during digestion. **Digestion** is *the process of breaking down food into a form the body can use.* Nutrients are absorbed into the bloodstream and carried to cells to do their work.

The food choices that you make will affect your health now and for years to come. How can you be sure that you are making the right choices?

Nutrients affect all your body processes, such as your heartbeat, blood flow, and breathing. These processes, in turn, affect the way you feel and how much energy you have. They also affect how you look—the quality of your skin, hair, and nails.

Your body, like everything else that belongs to you, requires good care. To keep your body functioning properly, you must choose foods that supply enough of each nutrient. Lack of nutrients can cause health problems now or in the future.

LESSON ONE *Review*

Using complete sentences, answer the following questions on a separate sheet of paper.

Reviewing Terms and Facts

1. List Name five characteristics of a healthy person.

2. Explain How does diet affect your energy level?

3. Vocabulary Define the term *nutrition.* Use it in an original sentence.

4. Recall List the six nutrients and their functions.

Thinking Critically

5. Explain Why is it so important to get the necessary nutrients from your diet?

6. Contrast What is the difference between hunger and appetite?

7. Analyze Identify five factors that affect your food choices. Which one most strongly influences your diet? Explain your answer.

Applying Concepts

8. Identify your personal eating habits. Are you a picky eater? Do you eat only a limited number of foods? Do you eat fruits and vegetables only when forced to? Write a paragraph or two describing your eating habits. Do you need to make changes in your diet? Have your eating habits changed since you were younger?

Nutrients: Proteins, Carbohydrates, and Fats

WORDS TO KNOW

proteins

amino acids

carbohydrates

fiber

whole grains

saturated fats

unsaturated fats

cholesterol

DISCOVER...

- the functions of proteins, carbohydrates, and fats in the human body.
- the types of foods that are good sources of proteins, carbohydrates, and fats.

Tyler has learned a lot about nutrients while training for the track team. He knows that he needs to eat plenty of foods that contain proteins, carbohydrates, and fats. These nutrients provide calories and energy. The body needs large amounts of them to stay healthy.

Proteins

Proteins are *nutrients that are needed to build, repair, and maintain body cells and tissues.* All of your body tissues—including your skin, hair, blood, muscles, and vital organs—are made of proteins. During the teen years, you need proteins to help your body grow and develop to its adult size. Even after you stop growing, you still need proteins to help your body repair itself. Billions of worn-out body cells are replaced every day, and proteins are used to make those new cells.

Each protein is a different combination of amino acids. **Amino** (uh-MEE-noh) **acids** are *chains of building blocks that make up proteins.* Your body can manufacture some amino acids. Others, called essential amino acids, can't be made by your body. They must come from the food you eat.

Some foods contain all the essential amino acids. These foods, called *complete proteins,* come from animals. Meat, fish, poultry, milk, cheese, and eggs are examples of complete proteins. Other foods are good sources of protein, but they lack one or more of the essential amino acids. These foods, called *incomplete proteins,* come from plants. Dry beans, nuts, and grains are examples of incomplete proteins.

Combining Proteins

You can combine incomplete protein sources to make complete proteins. These combinations provide all the amino acids needed for the body to grow and repair itself. Proteins from dry beans and nuts lack some amino acids. Grain proteins lack other amino acids. By combining these types of foods, however, you can get all the essential amino acids. Such combinations include

- bread and peanut butter.

- cereal with nuts.

- rice and beans.

By combining proteins from grains with proteins from dry beans and nuts, you can get all the essential amino acids that your body needs. Twelve to fifteen percent of daily calorie intake should come from protein.

TIPS
for living

UNDERSTANDING FOOD TERMS

Have you ever compared food labels and wondered what the difference was between *lite* and *low-calorie* or *low-fat* and *fat-free* foods? Understanding the terms used on food labels has become much easier, because the government has standardized the meanings of these terms. The following definitions refer to a single serving.

- **Light or lite:** one-third fewer calories or 50 percent less fat than the traditional version of the product
- **Low-calorie:** 40 calories or fewer
- **Low-fat:** 3 grams of fat or less
- **Fat-free:** less than 0.5 gram of fat
- **Reduced sugar:** 25 percent less sugar than the typical product
- **Sugar free:** less than 0.5 gram of sugar
- **Low sodium:** 140 milligrams of sodium or less
- **High fiber:** 5 grams of fiber or more

Carbohydrates

Carbohydrates are *the starches and sugars that give the body most of its energy.* Almost all carbohydrates come from plant sources, which also provide fiber.

Starches and Sugars

Starches and sugars are excellent energy sources. Starches are found in grains, such as oats, rice, and wheat. Foods made from grain—including bread, tortillas, pasta, and cereals—also provide starch. Potatoes, corn, dry beans, and nuts are additional sources of starch.

Natural sugars are found in fruits and milk. These foods are good sugar sources because they are also high in other nutrients. Foods such as candy, cake frosting, and soft drinks also contain sugar, but they are not beneficial sources of it. These prepared foods are high in calories but low in other nutrients, so they should be eaten sparingly.

Fruit is a good source of natural sugars. Why are natural sugars an important part of your diet?

Fiber

Fiber is *the tough, stringy part of raw fruits, vegetables, and grains that your body cannot digest.* Although fiber is not a nutrient, eating the right amount of fiber-rich foods helps the body function normally. Fiber provides bulk, which helps move food through your digestive system. It also helps your body eliminate wastes.

Eating foods that contain fiber is important for digestion. Without enough fiber, digestion can slow down. This may cause constipation, or infrequent bowel movements. In addition, a diet rich in high-fiber foods can reduce the risk for certain diseases, including colon cancer.

Good sources of fiber include foods made from whole grains. **Whole grains** are *foods that contain all of the edible grain, including the outer layer, the bran, and the germ.* Whole-wheat breads, whole-wheat cereals, and popcorn are whole-grain foods. Fruits and vegetables—especially those with edible skins, stems, and seeds—also contain fiber.

Fats

Like carbohydrates, fats are an important source of energy. Fats contain twice as many calories, ounce for ounce, as carbohydrates. Your body relies on fat cells to store energy and to help regulate body temperature. Your skin needs fats to stay

Skills IN ACTION

Finding the Sugar in Foods

Because sugar comes in so many forms, you may not realize how much of it is added to the foods you eat. Here are some snack foods and the amount of sugar per serving:

- Cola—9 teaspoons
- Sweetened cereal— 8 teaspoons
- Yogurt with sweetened fruit— 7 teaspoons
- Popcorn— 0 teaspoons

What are your favorite snacks? Check the labels to see how much sugar has been added.

Figure 10.1
Tips for Reducing Fat
By following these guidelines, you can reduce the amount of fat in your diet but still eat delicious food.

1. Start your day with breakfast.
Choose a healthful breakfast to start your day. Did you know that a doughnut and a glass of whole milk have a total of 22.1 grams of fat? Instead, try a bagel with nonfat cream cheese and a glass of skim milk, which have a total of only 1.5 grams of fat.

2. Choose a healthful lunch.
What is your favorite lunch food? If you enjoy a tuna sandwich, keep in mind that tuna packed in oil and served on white bread contains a total of 11.4 grams of fat. A healthier choice is tuna packed in water and served on whole-wheat bread, which contains a total of only 3.8 grams of fat.

4. Make wise choices for dinner.
The way in which food is prepared makes a big difference in the food's fat content. A dinner of fried chicken and french fries, for example, contains a total of 18.7 grams of fat. By choosing grilled chicken and a baked potato instead, you can still eat the foods you like but with a total of only 3.3 grams of fat.

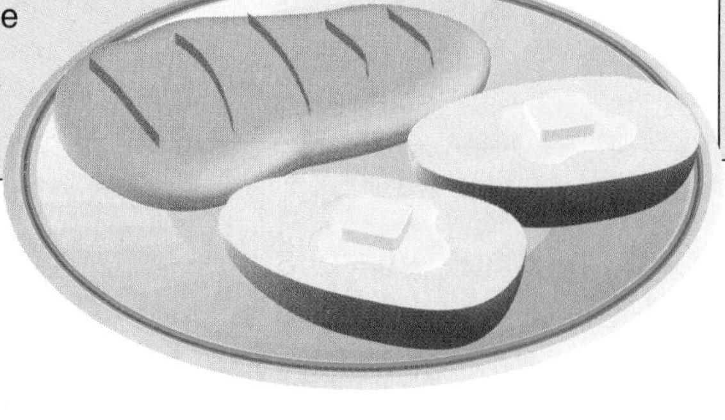

3. Snack smart.
Some snack foods are loaded with fats. Potato chips have 39.8 grams of fat; chocolate chip cookies, 30.1 grams; and premium ice cream, 16.1 grams. For a snack that is lower in fat, try nonfat frozen yogurt, with 0 grams of fat; an apple, with .6 grams; or pretzels, with 4.5 grams.

smooth, and your nervous system needs them to work properly. Fats also carry several vitamins needed by the body, such as vitamin A.

Fats come from both animal and plant sources of food. **Saturated fats** are *fats found in food from animal sources.* Meats, egg yolks, cheese, and butter contain saturated fats. Eating too much saturated fat can cause health problems, including an increased risk of heart disease. **Unsaturated fats** are *fats that come from plants.* They are generally liquid at room temperature and are found mainly in vegetable oils, such as olive, corn, or canola oil. No more than 30 percent of the calories you consume should come from fat, preferably unsaturated fats. **Figure 10.1** gives some tips for reducing the amount of fat in your diet.

Saturated fats contain **cholesterol** (kuh-LES-tuh-rawl), *a waxlike substance our bodies produce and need in small amounts.* Since your body produces all the cholesterol it needs, you don't need cholesterol in your diet. In fact, diets high in cholesterol have been linked to an increased risk of heart disease.

Eating a diet with enough of the proper nutrients will give your body the energy it needs. Which foods might you eat before a race?

LESSON TWO — *Review*

Using complete sentences, answer the following questions on a separate sheet of paper.

Reviewing Terms and Facts

1. Recall What do proteins do for the body?

2. Describe What are complete proteins? Name three foods that provide complete proteins.

3. List What foods are good sources of carbohydrates?

4. Vocabulary Define the term *saturated fats.* List three foods that contain saturated fats.

Thinking Critically

5. Suggest How can you make sure that you are eating foods that contain all the essential amino acids?

6. Contrast What are the advantages of eating foods that contain natural sugars over eating foods with sugar added?

7. Explain Why is fiber important? List three foods you eat that are good sources of fiber.

Applying Concepts

8. Create a poster about proteins, carbohydrates, and fats. Cut out or draw pictures of various foods that contain these nutrients. Group them according to the nutrients found in them. Then, below each group of foods, list the functions in the human body for that nutrient.

Nutrients: Vitamins, Minerals, and Water

WORDS TO KNOW

vitamins

enriched

minerals

calcium

osteoporosis

iron

DISCOVER...

- the functions of vitamins, minerals, and water in the human body.
- the types of food that are good sources of vitamins, minerals, and water.

Brittany loves to eat junk food—potato chips, cookies, and candy. She rarely eats fruits and vegetables, and she doesn't like the taste of milk. Brittany doesn't worry about her health, however, because she is careful to take a multiple vitamin once or twice a week. Lately, though, Brittany has been feeling tired all the time. She seems to get colds often, too. Do you think that Brittany's problems may be related to her diet? What could she do to improve her health?

The Need for Vitamins

Vitamins are *substances needed in small quantities to help regulate body functions*. Vitamins are important for many reasons. They help your body use other nutrients, store and use energy, and fight infection. **Figure 10.2** on pages 286–287 shows what some vitamins and minerals do for your body.

There are many types of essential vitamins, including the following: A, B-complex, C, D, and E. Because your body can't make most vitamins, you must get them from the foods you eat. These nutrients can easily be obtained from a variety of delicious foods, such as those listed in Figure 10.2.

Vitamin A

Have you ever walked into a dark room after being in the bright sunlight? Did you notice that your eyes had to adjust to less light before you could see again? Vitamin A enables your eyes to adjust to the dark. It also helps keep your skin healthy and helps your body resist infection. Dark green, leafy vegetables, deep yellow vegetables, and dairy products are good sources of vitamin A.

B-Complex Vitamins

The B-complex vitamins—riboflavin, thiamine, and niacin—give you energy by helping your body use calories from carbohydrates, fats, and proteins. Riboflavin also helps keep your eyes and skin healthy. Thiamine and niacin promote a healthy nervous system.

B-complex vitamins come from many different foods. Dairy products are the best sources of riboflavin. Thiamine and niacin are found in meat, dry beans, and some grain products. When selecting grain products, such as flour and bread, choose whole-grain or enriched foods. When wheat and other whole grains are turned into flour, nutritious parts of the grain are often lost. If these foods have been **enriched,** *the lost nutrients have been replaced in the same quantity or in greater quantity than the unprocessed food originally contained.*

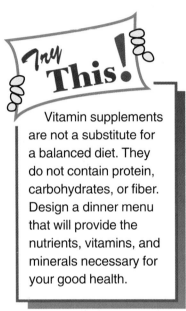

Try This!

Vitamin supplements are not a substitute for a balanced diet. They do not contain protein, carbohydrates, or fiber. Design a dinner menu that will provide the nutrients, vitamins, and minerals necessary for your good health.

Figure 10.2 Benefits and Food Sources of Vitamins and Minerals

Vitamins and minerals are essential for good health. What are some benefits of vitamin B? Which foods are good sources of iron?

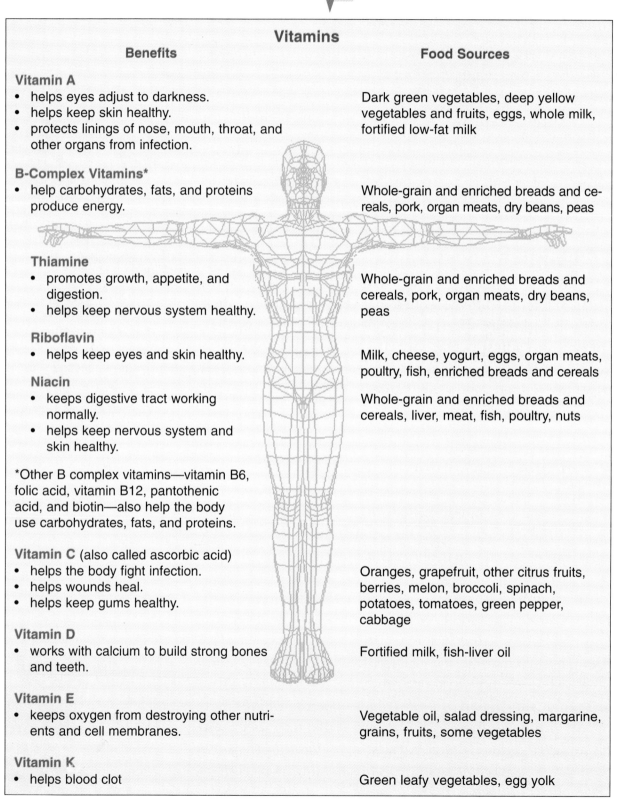

Vitamins

Benefits	Food Sources

Vitamin A
- helps eyes adjust to darkness.
- helps keep skin healthy.
- protects linings of nose, mouth, throat, and other organs from infection.

Dark green vegetables, deep yellow vegetables and fruits, eggs, whole milk, fortified low-fat milk

B-Complex Vitamins*
- help carbohydrates, fats, and proteins produce energy.

Whole-grain and enriched breads and cereals, pork, organ meats, dry beans, peas

Thiamine
- promotes growth, appetite, and digestion.
- helps keep nervous system healthy.

Whole-grain and enriched breads and cereals, pork, organ meats, dry beans, peas

Riboflavin
- helps keep eyes and skin healthy.

Milk, cheese, yogurt, eggs, organ meats, poultry, fish, enriched breads and cereals

Niacin
- keeps digestive tract working normally.
- helps keep nervous system and skin healthy.

Whole-grain and enriched breads and cereals, liver, meat, fish, poultry, nuts

*Other B complex vitamins—vitamin B6, folic acid, vitamin B12, pantothenic acid, and biotin—also help the body use carbohydrates, fats, and proteins.

Vitamin C (also called ascorbic acid)
- helps the body fight infection.
- helps wounds heal.
- helps keep gums healthy.

Oranges, grapefruit, other citrus fruits, berries, melon, broccoli, spinach, potatoes, tomatoes, green pepper, cabbage

Vitamin D
- works with calcium to build strong bones and teeth.

Fortified milk, fish-liver oil

Vitamin E
- keeps oxygen from destroying other nutrients and cell membranes.

Vegetable oil, salad dressing, margarine, grains, fruits, some vegetables

Vitamin K
- helps blood clot

Green leafy vegetables, egg yolk

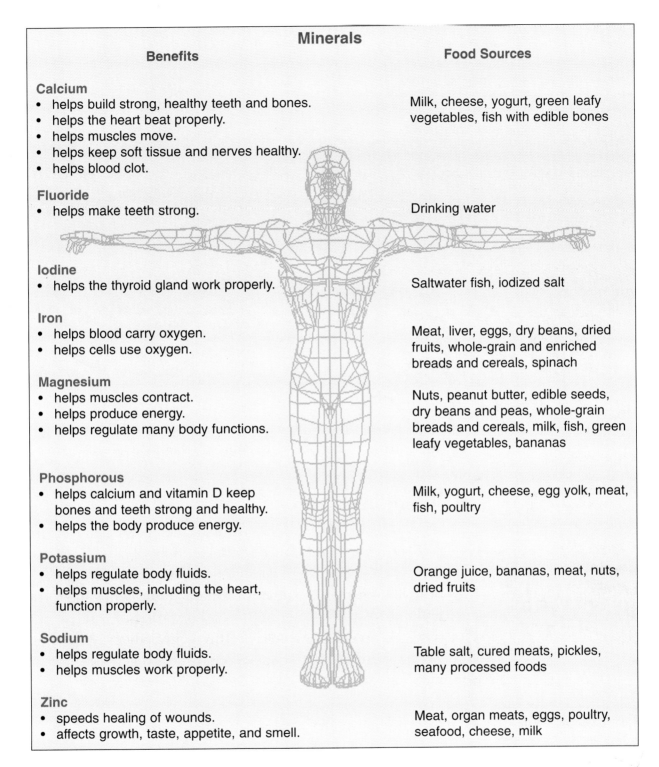

Minerals

Benefits

Food Sources

Calcium
- helps build strong, healthy teeth and bones.
- helps the heart beat properly.
- helps muscles move.
- helps keep soft tissue and nerves healthy.
- helps blood clot.

Milk, cheese, yogurt, green leafy vegetables, fish with edible bones

Fluoride
- helps make teeth strong.

Drinking water

Iodine
- helps the thyroid gland work properly.

Saltwater fish, iodized salt

Iron
- helps blood carry oxygen.
- helps cells use oxygen.

Meat, liver, eggs, dry beans, dried fruits, whole-grain and enriched breads and cereals, spinach

Magnesium
- helps muscles contract.
- helps produce energy.
- helps regulate many body functions.

Nuts, peanut butter, edible seeds, dry beans and peas, whole-grain breads and cereals, milk, fish, green leafy vegetables, bananas

Phosphorous
- helps calcium and vitamin D keep bones and teeth strong and healthy.
- helps the body produce energy.

Milk, yogurt, cheese, egg yolk, meat, fish, poultry

Potassium
- helps regulate body fluids.
- helps muscles, including the heart, function properly.

Orange juice, bananas, meat, nuts, dried fruits

Sodium
- helps regulate body fluids.
- helps muscles work properly.

Table salt, cured meats, pickles, many processed foods

Zinc
- speeds healing of wounds.
- affects growth, taste, appetite, and smell.

Meat, organ meats, eggs, poultry, seafood, cheese, milk

Vitamin C

Vitamin C helps keep you well. When you cut or bruise yourself, for example, vitamin C helps the wound heal. It keeps your gums healthy and helps your body fight infection. Good sources of vitamin C include such fruits as oranges, melons,

Vitamin C helps your body heal wounds and keep them from becoming infected. Which foods contain vitamin C?

and berries. Some dark green, leafy vegetables—such as spinach and broccoli—also contain vitamin C.

Vitamins D and E

Vitamin D helps your body use minerals, such as calcium and phosphorus. It is also essential for normal bone and tooth development. If you get enough sunlight, your body makes its own vitamin D. Foods that provide vitamin D include fortified milk, fish oils, beef, butter, and egg yolks.

To keep red blood cells healthy, your body needs vitamin E. You can find it in vegetable oils, yellow vegetables, grains, nuts, and green leafy vegetables.

The Function of Minerals

When you hear the word *minerals,* you may think of the minerals found in rocks and soil. Food also contains many **minerals,** which are *elements needed in small amounts for sturdy bones and teeth, healthy blood, and regular elimination of body wastes.* Like vitamins, minerals are essential to good health.

Try This!

Not all foods labeled *low-fat,* or *sugar-free* are necessarily healthful. For instance, cereals made with whole grains may also be high in fat.

The next time you are at the market, compare several brands of an item to see which one is really healthiest.

Each one has a special job to perform. Look again at Figure 10.2, which shows some of the many functions of minerals.

Every day your body uses small amounts of minerals. Some, such as calcium, phosphorus, and magnesium, are needed in greater amounts than others. Trace elements, such as iron, zinc, and iodine, are needed only in tiny amounts. The minerals your body needs can be found in various types of food, many of which are listed in Figure 10.2.

Calcium

You need calcium to grow and to stay healthy. **Calcium** is a *mineral that helps build bones and teeth and ensures normal growth.* Young people need to get enough calcium to develop strong teeth and bones. Calcium is necessary throughout life, particularly for women, to reduce the risk of **osteoporosis,** *a condition in which bones gradually lose their mineral content and become weak and brittle.* Calcium also has other functions, including helping your muscles move and your heart beat. When you bleed, calcium aids vitamin K in helping the blood to clot. Calcium also helps to keep your nerves and soft tissues healthy. The best sources of calcium are dairy products.

Iron

Like calcium, iron is one of the most important nutrients. **Iron** is *an essential component of blood.* It helps carry the oxygen you breathe to your brain, your muscles, and all of your body's cells. Oxygen helps your body produce energy to keep body processes going and for physical activity. Females need about twice as much iron as males, because they lose blood during menstruation.

The best sources of iron are meat, poultry, dry beans, dried fruits, and dark green, leafy vegetables.

Water

Although you may not think of water as a nutrient, you can't live without it. Water helps regulate body functions and

Your body needs calcium to build strong bones and teeth. What foods are good sources of calcium?

When you exercise, it is important to replace the fluids you lose through sweat. How can you do that? ▶

carries nutrients to body cells. It aids in digestion, removes wastes, and helps control your body temperature.

Because water is lost through perspiration, urine, and breath, you must replace it. You should drink between six and eight glasses of water each day in addition to other beverages. When you play basketball, tennis, or other active sports, your body perspires a great deal, and you need additional water.

LESSON THREE *Review*

Using complete sentences, answer the following questions on a separate sheet of paper.

Reviewing Terms and Facts

1. Vocabulary Define the term *enriched.* Use it in an original sentence.

2. Recall How does vitamin C keep you healthy?

3. Explain What is the purpose of iron in your body?

4. List Name two functions of water in your body.

Thinking Critically

5. Describe Why are vitamins and minerals called regulators?

6. Explain Why is it especially important for young people to get enough calcium in their diets?

7. Analyze The body can survive without food for longer than it can survive without water. What might be the reason for this?

Applying Concepts

8. Make a list of all the foods you ate and beverages you drank yesterday. Next to each item, write down the vitamins and minerals supplied by that food. (Refer to Figure 10.2 for help.) Are there any vitamins or minerals lacking in your diet? What foods could you eat to improve your nutrition?

Chapter 10 Activities

A Global View — ETHNIC CUISINE

Have you ever eaten Italian, Mexican, or Chinese food? Has your family ever been to a Japanese, Greek, or Indian restaurant? Many popular ethnic foods have been brought to the United States from other countries.

TRY THIS!

Test your knowledge of ethnic cuisine by taking the quiz below. Match the foods on the left with the country or culture on the right.

1.	burrito	a.	North Africa
2.	croissant	b.	Japan
3.	grits	c.	Greece
4.	wonton soup	d.	Middle East
5.	fettuccine Alfredo	e.	India
6.	pita	f.	France
7.	couscous	g.	China
8.	curry	h.	United States
9.	baklava	i.	Mexico
10.	sushi	j.	Italy

Answers: 1. i; 2. f; 3. h; 4. g; 5. j; 6. d; 7. a; 8. e; 9. c; 10. b

Consumer Focus

The Vitamin Diet

You have probably seen advertisements for vitamin pills. Some ads suggest that vitamins alone can keep you healthy and energetic. Some even claim that certain diseases can be cured simply by taking vitamins. In reality, however, vitamin supplements are not a substitute for a nutritious diet.

Try This!

Draw a magazine ad for a nutrient-dense food. Think of a catchy logo to promote your product.

SOCIAL STUDIES CONNECTION

FOODS AROUND THE WORLD

Many factors influence the kinds of foods that people eat. One major factor is where people live. Climate, soil conditions, and availability of water determine which foods can be grown. Certain regions have typical dishes. Rice is eaten with different varieties of beans in parts of Latin America, and Italy is famous for its pasta dishes. Many Indian curry dishes are flavored with a mixture of herbs and spices called *masala*.

Follow Up

1. What are the favorite ethnic or cultural foods among people in your class? As a class, make a chart or map showing how many parts of the world influence your diet.

2. In small groups, discuss cultural food traditions in your families. What foods have been passed down by grandparents that have become family favorites? Have some families continued to eat more of these traditional foods than others?

Chapter Summary

- Eating nutritious foods can help you look and feel your best.

- Food provides you with energy for physical and mental activity. A healthful diet also protects you from illness.

- Hunger is the physical need to eat, whereas appetite is the desire to eat. You can have an appetite without being hungry.

- Your food choices are influenced by many factors, including family, cultural background, religion, and friends.

- To stay healthy, your body needs six kinds of nutrients: proteins, carbohydrates, fats, vitamins, minerals, and water.

- Proteins are needed to build, maintain, and repair your body.

- Carbohydrates, or starches and sugars, provide energy. Fiber is not a nutrient, but it helps move food through the digestive system and eliminate wastes.

- Fats provide energy, help keep your skin smooth, help your nervous system work, and carry several vitamins. Unsaturated fats are more healthful than saturated fats.

- Vitamins are substances your body needs in small quantities to regulate its functions.

- Minerals help your body work properly. The minerals your body needs, including calcium and iron, are found in a variety of foods.

- Water is essential for life. It carries nutrients to body cells and aids in digestion, temperature control, and removal of wastes.

▶ Words to Know

Using complete sentences, answer the following questions on a separate sheet of paper.

1. Explain what a person's *diet* consists of.

2. What is a *calorie?*

3. Define the term *digestion*.

4. Where can you find *amino acids?*

5. Which foods contain *fiber?*

6. Why are *whole grains* good fiber sources?

7. Explain why you need *calcium* to stay healthy.

8. Why does your body need *iron?*

▶ Review Questions

Using complete sentences, answer the following questions on a separate sheet of paper.

1. Name four factors that affect the way you look and feel.

2. What happens if you eat food that has more calories than your body needs?

3. Explain how each of the following factors influences your food likes and dislikes: family, advertising, and health.

4. What foods contain carbohydrates?

5. Explain what might happen if a person's diet has too little fiber.

6. Why do you need to drink water every day?

Thinking Critically

Using complete sentences, answer the following questions on a separate sheet of paper.

1. **Explain** Do you think that a person can be healthy if he or she doesn't eat meat? Why or why not?

2. **Analyze** Why do you think that some people overeat?

3. **Contrast** What is the difference between a complete protein and an incomplete protein?

4. **Apply** Why should you avoid foods that contain added sugar?

5. **Suggest** How can you get enough calcium in your diet if you don't like milk?

Cooperative Learning

1. Bring in a food advertisement. In groups of three or four, evaluate the advertisements by answering the following questions: How does the advertisement try to influence your food choices? Is it successful? Would you buy the food? Why or why not?

2. In groups of four or five, research a nutrient. Write an analysis that includes the benefits of the nutrient, the problems that result from a lack of it, and the foods that contain it. Find two recipes that use a food

or foods rich in that nutrient. Share your group's findings with the class.

Family & Community

1. Examine two or three convenience foods that you and your family eat regularly for dinner. Read the labels to determine which nutrients can be found in these foods. Do they contain saturated or unsaturated fats? Discuss with family members whether those convenience foods are healthful choices for your family.

2. Take a survey of ten friends and family members to find out what factors most influence their food choices. Ask each person to name his or her three favorite foods and explain why they are favorites. Which factor influenced the most people? What conclusions can you draw from your survey?

Building A Portfolio

1. Write down everything you eat for one day. You can use this textbook and information from labels or a computer program to categorize the foods as proteins, carbohydrates, or fats. Then break each item down further as complete protein, incomplete protein, starch, sugar, fiber, saturated fat, or unsaturated fat. Is your diet varied? Are you getting too much or too little of any food category? Write a paragraph summarizing your results, and put it in your portfolio.

2. Write a paragraph about a family food tradition. Explain how the tradition has been passed down from generation to generation. Put your paragraph in your portfolio.

Developing Healthy Habits

TEENS MAKING A DIFFERENCE

The School Store

The student council at Kennedy Middle School operates a student store. The store sells pencils, notebook paper, school caps and T-shirts—and candy bars.

After learning about good nutrition in class, a majority of the council members voted to stop selling candy bars. The council decided to sell apples, oranges, and small cans of fruit juice instead.

At first, some students grumbled about not being able to buy candy at school. However, many more students said that they liked the tasty red apples and the sweet, juicy oranges. The fruit juice, they said, really hit the spot.

Try THIS!

Consider how good nutrition is promoted in your school. Think of changes you could suggest that would improve students' nutrition.

LESSON ONE
The Food Guide Pyramid

WORDS TO KNOW

Food Guide Pyramid

food group

serving

vegetarian

DISCOVER...

- the Food Guide Pyramid.
- the foods that make up the five food groups.
- how to use the Food Guide Pyramid to plan healthful meals.

Knowing which nutrients your body needs is a first step toward a healthful diet, but how do you know which foods you should eat to get those nutrients? How much of each kind of food should you eat? That is where the Food Guide Pyramid comes in handy.

What Is the Food Guide Pyramid?

The **Food Guide Pyramid** is *a set of guidelines to help you choose what and how much to eat to get the nutrients you need.* It is easy to plan healthful meals if you follow the Food Guide Pyramid. You can use it to choose foods that suit your tastes and lifestyle as well as to meet your nutritional needs.

The Food Groups

Look carefully at the Food Guide Pyramid in **Figure 11.1.** Notice that it is divided into six sections. Each section lists foods from a general category. Each *category of foods on the Food Guide Pyramid* is called a **food group.** Notice also that the sections are not all the same size. As you move up from the base of the Pyramid, the sections get smaller. This

Try This!

You can learn to "eyeball" correct serving sizes.
- An ounce of cheese is about the size of a walnut.
- One-half cup of rice or pasta is about the size of a tennis ball.
- A three-ounce serving of meat or fish is about the size of a deck of cards.

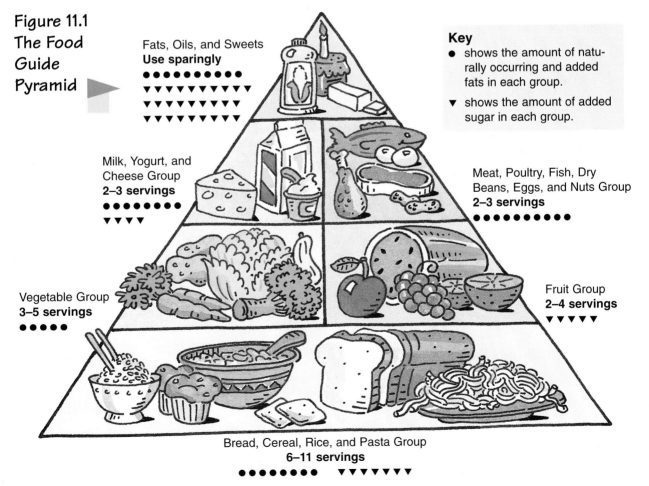

Figure 11.1
The Food Guide Pyramid ▶

Fats, Oils, and Sweets
Use sparingly

Milk, Yogurt, and Cheese Group
2–3 servings

Meat, Poultry, Fish, Dry Beans, Eggs, and Nuts Group
2–3 servings

Vegetable Group
3–5 servings

Fruit Group
2–4 servings

Bread, Cereal, Rice, and Pasta Group
6–11 servings

Key
- ● shows the amount of naturally occurring and added fats in each group.
- ▼ shows the amount of added sugar in each group.

tells you at a glance which groups of food should be more plentiful in your diet and which should make up a smaller part of it. The larger the section of the Pyramid a food group occupies, the more servings of that group you need to eat. **A serving** is *a portion of food that a person would be likely to eat at one time* (such as one apple or one slice of bread).

The five lower sections of the Pyramid show the five food groups. Each group provides you with some of the nutrients necessary for good health. The five food groups include the

- Bread, Cereal, Rice, and Pasta Group.

- Vegetable Group.

- Fruit Group.

- Milk, Yogurt, and Cheese Group.

- Meat, Poultry, Fish, Dry Beans, Eggs, and Nuts Group.

The tip, or smallest section, of the Pyramid includes fats, oils, and sweets—items that you should eat only in small amounts. **Figure 11.2** on pages 300 and 301 provides more information about the five food groups.

Making wise food choices is easy if you use the Food Guide Pyramid to plan meals.

Using the Food Guide Pyramid

Kimberly has invited two of her friends to sleep over on Friday night. This afternoon Kimberly and her mother are planning the meals. Kimberly's mom suggests that Kimberly plan to serve a snack on Friday night as well as dinner because the girls will probably stay up later than usual. That means that Kimberly has to decide what foods to eat for three meals, and she wants to make each one different and interesting. Saturday's breakfast will be easy. Everyone likes fresh fruit and cereal or bagels. What about dinner, though? Where can Kimberly get some ideas?

Planning Meals

The Food Guide Pyramid is a great source of ideas. It tells you which foods fit into which group and how many servings of each group you should eat in a day.

Kimberly and her mom decide to plan a dinner that will require very little last-minute preparation. After looking over the Food Guide Pyramid, they build the meals from the base up and make sure that they include all five food groups. They choose chicken sandwiches on whole-wheat bread and a platter of raw vegetables for dinner. Because Kimberly wants to serve brownies for dessert, she decides to have fruit and yogurt shakes as a nutritious late-night snack.

As you look over the Food Guide Pyramid, you will notice that there is a range of recommended servings for each of the five food groups. A range is given because different people have different nutritional needs. People who are physically active, for example, need to eat more than less active people. The important point to remember is that you need to eat enough servings of all five food groups to get the nutrients you need.

Another fact to keep in mind is that many dishes are made up of foods from more than one food group. For example, spaghetti with meatballs and tomato sauce includes foods from the bread group (pasta), the meat group (meatballs), and the vegetable group (tomatoes).

People who follow special diets may wonder if the Food Guide Pyramid can help them plan meals. For example, a **vegetarian** is *a person who eats mainly fruits, vegetables, and grains.* Some vegetarians eat fish and dairy products. Others do not eat any animal products, not even dairy foods. A person who follows such a diet must be especially careful to get all of the vitamins, minerals, and protein needed for good health.

By trading off, you can eat foods with small amounts of fat and sugar while still getting the nutrients you need. What trade-offs might you make in your food choices?

Making Trade-offs

Remember how Kimberly served fruit and yogurt shakes as a snack so that she could have brownies for dessert? She made a trade-off, or chose a food that is lower in sugar at snack time so that she could serve one that is high in sugar at dinner.

Figure 11.2
The Five Food Groups

For a healthful diet, choose foods from each of the five food groups. What is an example of a single serving from the Bread, Cereal, Rice, and Pasta Group?

The Bread, Cereal, Rice, and Pasta Group

Nutrients
Carbohydrates, iron, B-complex vitamins

Servings Per Day
6–11

Sample Serving Sizes
1 slice bread
½ bagel or ½ English muffin
½ cup (125 mL) cooked cereal, rice, or pasta
1 ounce (28 g) ready-to-eat cereal

The Vegetable Group

Nutrients
Vitamins A and C, iron, and fiber

Servings Per Day
3–5

Sample Serving Sizes
½ cup (125 mL) chopped raw or cooked vegetables
1 cup (250 mL) raw, leafy vegetables

The Fruit Group

Nutrients
Vitamins A and C, carbohydrates, and fiber

Servings Per Day
2–4

Sample Serving Sizes
1 medium apple, banana,
  or orange
¾ cup (175 mL) fruit juice
½ cup (125 mL) canned fruit
¼ cup (50 mL) dried fruit

The Milk, Yogurt, and Cheese Group

Nutrients
Calcium, phosphorus, riboflavin, vitamins A and D

Servings Per Day
2–3

Sample Serving Sizes
1 cup (250 mL) milk or yogurt
1½–2 ounces (42–56 g) cheese

The Meat, Poultry, Fish, Dry Beans, Eggs, and Nuts Group

Nutrients
Protein, iron, B vitamins

Servings Per Day
2–3

Sample Serving Sizes
2–3 ounces (56–84 g) cooked lean
  meat, poultry, or fish

Foods that count as 1 ounce (28 g) of meat
½ cup (125 mL) cooked dry beans
1 egg
2 tablespoons (30 mL) peanut butter
⅓ cup (75 mL) nuts

Trading off allows you to have small amounts of the foods at the tip of the Food Guide Pyramid while still eating a nutritious diet.

Checking Food Labels

An easy way to figure out what foods can be traded off is to check the nutrition labels on food packages. These labels tell you the amount of each essential nutrient as well as the amount of fat, sugar, and sodium (salt) in each serving of a particular food. In addition, the labels list the number of calories per serving. You will learn more about nutrition labels in Chapter 13, Lesson 2.

◀ Developing healthy eating habits now will contribute to good health throughout your life.

LESSON ONE *Review*

Using complete sentences, answer the following questions on a separate sheet of paper.

Reviewing Terms and Facts

1. Recall What is the Food Guide Pyramid?

2. Vocabulary Define the term *food group*. List the five food groups.

3. Identify What nutrients are provided by the milk, yogurt, and cheese group?

4. Explain Why is a range of servings given in the Food Guide Pyramid?

Thinking Critically

5. Analyze Explain why it is useful to plan a meal by starting at the bottom of the Food Guide Pyramid and going up.

6. Apply Give an example of a meal that includes foods from all five food groups. Explain your choices.

7. Interpret Why could a person who follows a special diet be at risk of not getting the proper nutrients?

Applying Concepts

8. Write down all the foods you ate yesterday. Next to each item, note the amount you ate. Compare your diet with the Food Guide Pyramid. Add up the number of servings you had from each food group and check against the suggested number. How well did your diet follow the guidelines? Write down some possible ways of improving your diet.

LESSON TWO
Following Healthy Guidelines

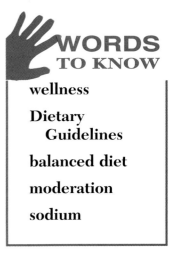

DISCOVER...

- how the Dietary Guidelines can be used to promote health.
- ways to cut down on fat, sugar, and salt in the diet.

Andrew's health is especially important to him. He wants to be a major league pitcher some day. Andrew knows that to be at his best he needs to feel good physically and mentally. You could say that Andrew works for wellness. **Wellness** is *a high level of overall health.* The foods you eat play an essential role in determining your level of wellness.

WORDS TO KNOW

wellness

Dietary Guidelines

balanced diet

moderation

sodium

The Dietary Guidelines

How can you make sure that your diet contributes to your wellness? First, you can use the Food Guide Pyramid. It shows you visually how to follow the Dietary Guidelines for Americans.

The **Dietary Guidelines** are *advice on what Americans should eat to stay healthy.* These guidelines were developed by the U.S. Department of Agriculture (USDA) and the U.S. Department of Health and Human Services using recommendations by nutrition authorities. The guidelines take into account the important effect diet has on health. By following them, you can ensure that you are eating the right types of foods. You can also reduce your chances of developing certain health problems, such as heart disease and high blood pressure.

Of course, food alone can't make you healthy. Good health also depends on your heredity and environment. Your lifestyle—for example, your exercise habits—is also important to your health. However, a diet based on these guidelines can help keep you healthy, perhaps even help improve your health. **Figure 11.3** shows the Dietary Guidelines for Americans.

Figure 11.3
Dietary Guidelines for Americans
Give your health the green light by following these guidelines.

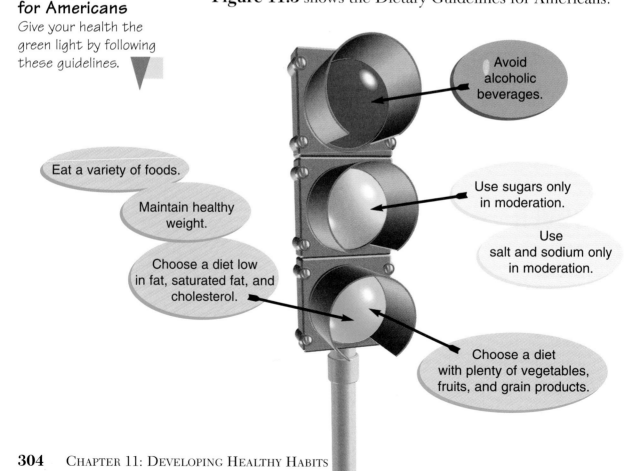

- Avoid alcoholic beverages.
- Eat a variety of foods.
- Maintain healthy weight.
- Choose a diet low in fat, saturated fat, and cholesterol.
- Use sugars only in moderation.
- Use salt and sodium only in moderation.
- Choose a diet with plenty of vegetables, fruits, and grain products.

Eat a Variety of Foods

How many different foods do you eat during a typical day? The first guideline says that variety is the key to good nutrition and good health. You need more than 40 different nutrients for good health. No single food or food group can supply all of these nutrients in the amounts you need. To get the nutrients you need, you must balance your food choices. A **balanced diet** is *a diet that is made up of a variety of foods with nutrients in the recommended amounts.*

One way to be assured of a balanced diet is to choose foods each day from all five food groups. Remember that these include grain products, vegetables, fruits, milk and milk products, and meats and meat alternatives. Refer back to pages 300 and 301 for information on recommended servings per day and serving sizes.

Maintain Healthy Weight

A person who is at a healthy weight is not too fat or too thin. Being too fat is linked with many illnesses, including high blood pressure, heart disease, stroke, diabetes, certain cancers, and others. Although being too thin is less common, it is also linked with disease and a greater risk of early death.

How can you know if your weight is "healthy"? You can't compare your weight with that of your friends. There are differences among people of the same age. For example, people with a large body frame usually weigh more than people of the same height with a smaller body frame. At this time in your life, growing and gaining weight are normal.

To determine if your weight is right for you, consult your doctor. He or she can consider all the factors that contribute to a healthy weight for you.

You can't compare your own best weight with that of your friends. There are differences among people of the same age. Do you know what those differences are?

Choose a Diet Low in Fats and Cholesterol

Fat is an important nutrient that provides energy. If you are like many Americans, however, your diet is too high in fat. Health experts recommend a diet that is low in fat and cholesterol.

Why is eating too much fat harmful? A diet high in fat leads to such health problems as obesity and certain types of cancer. A diet high in saturated fat and cholesterol is linked to an increased risk of heart disease.

You can reduce the fats in your diet by using nonstick pans and baking or broiling foods. Why isn't frying a recommended way of cooking food?

The amount of fat in your diet depends on what you eat over several days, not on one meal or type of food. For example, if you like a small amount of butter on your baked potato, you will not be getting too much fat as long as you limit the amount of other fats you eat.

Some foods that contain fats and cholesterol—meats, milk, cheese, and eggs—also contain high-quality protein and important vitamins and minerals. To reduce fats and cholesterol, choose low-fat versions of these foods such as nonfat milk and cheese.

Eat Plenty of Vegetables, Fruits, and Grains

Vegetables, fruits, and grain products are an essential part of a varied and healthful diet. They contain complex carbohydrates, fiber, and other nutrients that contribute to good health. In addition, these foods are usually low in fats. If you eat the suggested amounts of them, you are also likely to decrease the fat in your diet and get more fiber.

Complex carbohydrates, such as starches, are essential to good nutrition. Starches give you long-lasting energy as well as

Beware of foods whose labels list sugar by its other names: glucose, fructose, maltose, lactose, corn sweetener, high-fructose corn syrup, molasses. Where can you look to find out if products contain sugars?

vitamins and minerals. Starch is found in breads, cereals, pasta, rice, dry beans, peas, potatoes, and corn.

Fiber helps to keep your digestive system healthy. Fiber is found naturally in whole-grain breads and cereals, dry beans and peas, vegetables, and fruits.

Use Sugars Only in Moderation

Sugar is a type of carbohydrate that is found in many foods. Sugar provides calories, and most people like the way it tastes. Fruit contains natural sugar. Many processed foods, such as cookies and soft drinks, contain refined sugar.

This guideline calls for **moderation**—*avoiding extremes* in diet. That means that although eating too much sugar may not be healthful, it isn't necessary to eliminate sugar from your diet entirely. To cut down on the sugar in your diet, you can

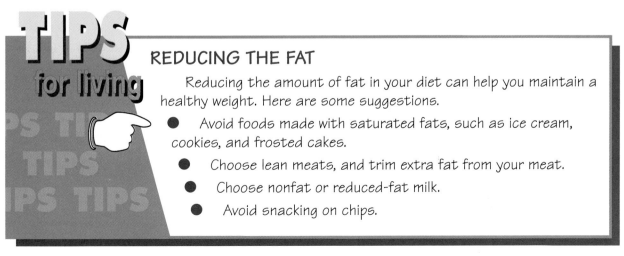

TIPS
for living

REDUCING THE FAT

Reducing the amount of fat in your diet can help you maintain a healthy weight. Here are some suggestions.

- Avoid foods made with saturated fats, such as ice cream, cookies, and frosted cakes.
- Choose lean meats, and trim extra fat from your meat.
- Choose nonfat or reduced-fat milk.
- Avoid snacking on chips.

One way to reduce the amount of sodium in your diet is to cook with and eat fresh ingredients.

- eat fresh fruit instead of desserts with added sugars.

- eat less of all foods with added sugars.

- keep nutritious snacks on hand.

Use Salt and Sodium Only in Moderation

Salt contains **sodium,** *a mineral that helps regulate the amount of fluid in our bodies.* You need some sodium to stay healthy. However, most Americans eat more sodium than they need.

For some people, too much sodium can lead to high blood pressure. High blood pressure makes the heart work too hard. Cutting back on sodium can benefit everyone. To cut down on sodium, you can

- use very little salt, if any, in cooking and at the table.

- limit the amount of salted foods you eat, such as chips, pretzels, and nuts.

- eat less processed food, such as packaged sandwich meat, canned soup, and cheeses.

Avoid Alcoholic Beverages

The last guideline concerns the use of alcohol. Drinking alcoholic beverages is illegal for young people. Even for adults, it is not recommended. Although alcohol supplies calories, it has no other nutritional value.

Drinking alcohol does not benefit your health—in fact, it is linked with many health problems. People who drink before driving increase their risk of having accidents. A pregnant woman who drinks alcohol may damage her unborn baby's health.

Balancing Your Diet

Following the Dietary Guidelines can help you choose a diet that contributes to wellness. The first two guidelines form the foundation of a balanced diet: *Eat a variety of foods* for the nutrients you need and in the right amounts to *maintain a healthy weight.* The other guidelines offer advice on which types of foods to eat and which types of foods to limit to ensure that your diet is healthful.

About 75 percent of the sodium in your diet comes from canned and packaged foods. One way to reduce the sodium in your diet is to read food labels and buy brands with less added sodium chloride (salt), mono-sodium glutamate, disodium phosphate; sodium alginate, benzoate, sulfite, hydroxide, propionate; or brine.

What are some other ways of reducing the salt in your diet?

LESSON TWO Review

Using complete sentences, answer the following questions on a separate sheet of paper.

Reviewing Terms and Facts

1. Vocabulary What are the *Dietary Guidelines?*

2. Recall How can you be sure that your diet is well balanced?

3. Explain Why are complex carbohydrates essential to good nutrition?

4. List Name three ways to cut down on added sugars in your diet.

Thinking Critically

5. Analyze Why should you follow the Dietary Guidelines?

6. Explain Why can too much fat and cholesterol be harmful?

7. Apply How can you determine which processed foods are high in sodium?

Applying Concepts

8. Read the section of a nutrition, biology, or life sciences textbook that describes how the body uses fat and cholesterol and what happens to the body when you eat too much. In your own words, write a few paragraphs to explain the process.

LESSON THREE
Snacking and Eating Out

 **WORDS**
TO KNOW

snacks

nutrient-dense foods

empty-calorie foods

menu

DISCOVER...

● what makes a healthful snack.

● how to choose a restaurant.

● how to order from a restaurant menu.

How often do you grab a bite to eat on the go? Do you think about the nutritional value of the food, or do you just look for something to keep you going until the next meal? When you are at a restaurant, do you pay attention to the nutrient content of the foods you order, or are you likely just to choose something that seems tasty? Both snacking and eating out can be healthful. Just remember to follow the Food Guide Pyramid and the Dietary Guidelines when you eat between meals and away from home.

Eating Snacks

Tanya plays softball and runs in the off-season to stay in shape. Even though she is active and gets very hungry by mealtime, she finds that the recommended servings from the bread group are more than she can eat in just three meals. Tanya now carries a bagel and fresh fruit as morning and afternoon snacks. **Snacks** are *foods eaten between meals.*

The key to healthy snacking is to treat snacks as part of your regular diet. To do so, follow these guidelines.

- Count the calories in snacks as part of your total calories for the day.

- Choose foods that help you get the number of servings your body needs from each of the food groups.

- Time your snacks so that you don't eat too close to lunch or dinner.

Choosing Nutrient-Dense Snacks

What are your favorite snacks? Do you choose **nutrient-dense foods**—*foods that are rich in the nutrients your body needs to stay healthy?* These foods supply proteins, carbohydrates, vitamins, minerals, and water. For nutrient-dense snacks, choose from the five food groups, as Tanya did. Select whole-grain items from the bread group. A wide variety of nutrient-dense snacks can be found in the fruit and vegetable groups.

Try This!

"Snack attacks" occur quite often during the school day. Working in small groups, create a list of healthy snacks. All items should be high in nutrients and low in calories. Share your list with other groups.

By choosing nutrient-dense snacks, you will help your body stay healthy. What are some examples of nutrient-dense snacks?

Avoiding Empty-Calorie Snacks

Empty-calorie foods are *foods that are high in calories but low in nutrients.* The foods we usually think of as "junk food"—such as potato chips, candy, and soft drinks—are empty-calorie foods. Many of these foods are found at the tip of the Food Guide Pyramid. They often contain large amounts of sugar, salt, and fat, all of which should be eaten sparingly. A candy bar, for example, provides lots of calories in the form of sugar and fat, but little nutrition.

Eating Out

Do you enjoy eating out? Maybe you like getting together with friends over a meal. Perhaps your family enjoys eating at a restaurant to try new foods. When you eat out, remember to choose your meals with the same eye to nutrition as when you eat at home.

Selecting a Restaurant

The food choices, types of service, and price ranges vary greatly from one restaurant to another. At what types of restaurants have you eaten?

What types of restaurants do you like? You are probably familiar with fast-food restaurants. They give quick service, are

fairly inexpensive, and serve popular foods, such as hot sandwiches, french fries, salads, and shakes.

A second type of restaurant is a cafeteria, similar to your school cafeteria. Customers take a tray and choose foods while going through a serving line. Cafeterias are also fairly inexpensive, charging separately for each item. Many selections are offered in each food category.

Some restaurants offer meals at a fixed price. Customers pay a set price and are entitled to eat whatever foods are offered. In many cases, these restaurants feature all-you-can-eat buffets and salad bars.

Another common type of restaurant is one that provides table service. After you are seated at a table, a waiter or waitress takes your order and brings your food.

Restaurants also vary widely in the kinds of foods they offer. Some specialize in certain types of dishes, such as seafood, steaks, or pancakes. Ethnic restaurants specialize in the food of a particular country or region.

Choosing Wisely from the Menu

What exactly is a menu? A **menu** is *a list of all the dishes a restaurant serves, organized by category.* The categories might include appetizers, salads, main dishes, side dishes, desserts, and beverages. Menus also generally list the price for each dish. Some menus feature low-fat choices.

Many restaurants post their menus outside the door. How might that be helpful to customers?

As you look at a menu, the most important point to remember is to choose foods from all five food groups—just as you would do if you were planning a meal at home. Here are some tips for ordering when you eat out.

- Select dishes that are low in fat, sugar, salt, and calories. Baked potatoes have much less fat than french fries.

- Choose nutrient-dense dishes. At Italian restaurants, have whole-wheat or vegetable pasta. Instead of soft drinks or milk shakes, have juice or milk.

- Limit the number of treats you allow yourself. If you really want dessert, make a trade-off. If you can't resist the fried ice cream at a Mexican restaurant, have simmered beans instead of refried beans, and avoid the tortilla chips.

- Remember that sauces and salad dressings add calories. When eating Italian foods, choose red sauces, made with tomatoes, rather than white sauces made with butter and cream.

- Most portion sizes are larger than a serving. Bring leftovers home in a box.

- Eat only until you feel satisfied.

Take-out Food

A popular alternative to eating at a restaurant is getting food "to go." Take-out food includes food that you pick up, have delivered, or get at a drive-through window. Pizza, tacos, and Chinese food are popular take-out items. When ordering take-out food, try to include foods from all five food groups.

Making Healthy Food Choices

Snacking and eating out can be both enjoyable and nutritious. Remember, however, that the food choices you make when snacking or eating out are part of your overall diet. By following the Food Guide Pyramid, choosing nutrient-dense foods, and avoiding empty-calorie foods, you will help keep your body healthy.

If you choose wisely, take-out food can be nutritious.

LESSON THREE *Review*

Using complete sentences, answer the following questions on a separate sheet of paper.

Reviewing Terms and Facts

1. Identify What are *nutrient-dense* foods?

2. Contrast What is the difference between a cafeteria and a restaurant with table service?

3. Vocabulary Define the term *menu*. What categories are usually found on a menu?

4. List Name four guidelines for selecting foods at a restaurant.

Thinking Critically

5. Analyze Why do you think that some people gain weight from eating snacks? How could this problem be avoided?

6. Interpret Why is it a good idea to look over an entire restaurant menu before ordering?

Applying Concepts

7. Create a simple menu for a new fast-food restaurant. Offer healthy choices from the five food groups, and be sure to include beverages and desserts. Exchange menus with a classmate.

LESSON FOUR
Exercise and Weight Control

WORDS TO KNOW

fitness

stamina

obesity

aerobic exercise

fad diet

DISCOVER...

- why fitness is important.
- how exercise can help you stay fit.
- what you can do to maintain a healthy weight.

Aaron has a lot of responsibilities. Schoolwork takes up much of his time. He has chores to do at home, and he delivers flyers for some local restaurants. Aaron spends time with friends too. Even though Aaron is busy, he still finds time to exercise and to eat well. He stays fit by riding his bike, skating, and swimming at the community pool.

The Importance of Fitness and Physical Activity

When you are physically fit, you look and feel your best. **Fitness** is *the ability to handle day-to-day events in a healthy way.* Fitness means that you

- have enough energy to do your schoolwork, have fun, and handle problems.

- can keep your weight at the right level for you.

- can deal with stress and the ups and downs of life.

- are confident about your abilities.

- make exercise and activity a part of your life every day.

Exercise and Fitness

You cannot be fit unless you exercise. By exercising regularly, as long as you also eat well, you will enjoy all the benefits of fitness.

- You will feel positively about yourself. Knowing you're taking care of your body is good for your self-esteem.

- You will look your best. Exercise helps control weight and gives you a healthy glow.

- Day-to-day tasks will seem easy because you will have the energy you need.

- You will be able to relax and sleep easily.

- You will have physical and mental stamina. **Stamina** is *the ability to focus on a single activity for a long time.* For example, you will be able to

Exercise can be a way for teens to have fun together. What activities do you enjoy with your friends?

317

dance without getting very tired, and you can pay attention in class and learn easily.

- You will be able to deal with stress.

There are plenty of enjoyable, inexpensive ways to exercise. What's important is that you make exercise a regular part of your life. For example, Jennifer walks to school instead of taking the bus. Although walking takes longer, she enjoys that time alone. Her friend Nick prefers organized exercise. He plays on a softball team and enjoys getting together with friends to play volleyball on weekends.

Your Healthy Body Weight

Are you happy with your weight? Do you think that you're too heavy or too thin? People who maintain a healthy body weight are neither overweight nor underweight.

Being overweight can lead to obesity, one of our country's leading problems. **Obesity** is *a condition in which a person's weight is 20 percent or more above his or her healthy weight.* Obese people are at greater risk for such illnesses as heart disease and diabetes.

TIPS
for living

CALORIES FOR FITNESS

Fitness involves more than just exercising regularly. It also includes avoiding empty-calorie foods and eating foods that are rich in nutrients. Follow these eating tips for physical fitness.

- Avoid high-calorie foods, such as french fries, pastries, and candy, and cake with frosting.

- Turn down second helpings, except for low-calorie vegetables and fruits.

- Eat regular meals with average-size portions.

- Have a nutrient-dense snack between meals to keep your energy level up.

- Enjoy fresh fruit instead of sweet desserts.

- Eat slowly. You will be less likely to overeat because it takes 20 minutes for your brain to signal that you have eaten enough.

Being underweight is unhealthy too. People who are underweight often aren't eating enough, or aren't eating properly. This means that they aren't getting the nutrients they need. For instance, Tina thinks that being thin is all that matters. She eats very little so that she won't gain weight. What she doesn't realize is that the foods she eats are usually "fast" foods, such as french fries, that are high in fat and calories and low in nutrients. If she ate a well-balanced diet with lots of fruits and vegetables, she would be healthier and still able to control her weight.

What is your healthy body weight? That depends on you—your height, your frame size, your gender. Each person has a weight that is best for him or her. By looking in the mirror, you can probably see how well your weight suits you. If you're unsure, consult a doctor or a school nurse who can help you evaluate your weight.

Controlling Your Weight

Many teens are concerned about their weight. They want to look their best, and they often think that this means losing or gaining weight. They may believe that they have to give up certain foods or skip specific meals to control their weight. For example, Kenny has tried several times to lose 10 pounds. The problem is that he can never seem to go for more than one week eating prepackaged diet foods. He thinks that skipping breakfast will help him cut down on calories, but that doesn't work either. Kenny needs to learn the basics about eating and exercising to control weight.

You can control your weight and still eat your favorite foods as long as you balance the calories you eat with the amount of exercise you get.

A Balancing Act

Think of controlling your weight as a balancing act: you have to balance the calories you get from the foods you eat with the calories you use for energy. To maintain your weight, you must make sure that the calories you eat equal those you burn as energy. If you take in more calories than your body uses, you gain weight. If your body uses more calories than it takes in, you lose weight.

To control your weight, you need to eat a balanced diet from the five food groups. Include foods you enjoy, but limit the number of servings you eat of fats, oils, and sweets. To lose weight, eat fewer calories than your body uses. The healthiest way to lose fat is to take in fewer calories and exercise more. That helps you burn the calories you take in while also burning body fat.

The Benefits of Exercise

Exercise is necessary if you want to reach and maintain a healthy body weight. Whether you want to lose weight, gain weight, or maintain your weight, exercise has many benefits.

- **Exercise burns calories.** The harder and longer you exercise, the more calories you burn. **Figure 11.4** shows how many calories you can burn doing different types of exercise.

- **Exercise helps your heart and lungs work better.** Aerobic exercise is the best kind for this purpose. **Aerobic exercise** is *nonstop, repetitive, vigorous exercise that increases breathing and heartbeat rates.* Bicycling, swimming, dancing, and jogging are all examples of aerobic exercise.

- **Exercise tones your muscles.** This improves the shape of your body.

- **Exercise helps you control your appetite.** It also relieves tension that could lead to overeating or loss of appetite.

Avoiding Fad Diets

Achieving fitness and a healthy body weight through a well-balanced diet and exercise takes time. If you are overweight or obese, you might be tempted to lose weight quickly

Skills IN ACTION

Starting a Fitness Program

Use your knowledge of exercise and a balanced diet to get started on a personal fitness program. Follow these steps.
1. Choose an activity you enjoy.
2. Set your own personal goals, but be realistic.
3. Be sure to warm up and cool down every time you exercise.

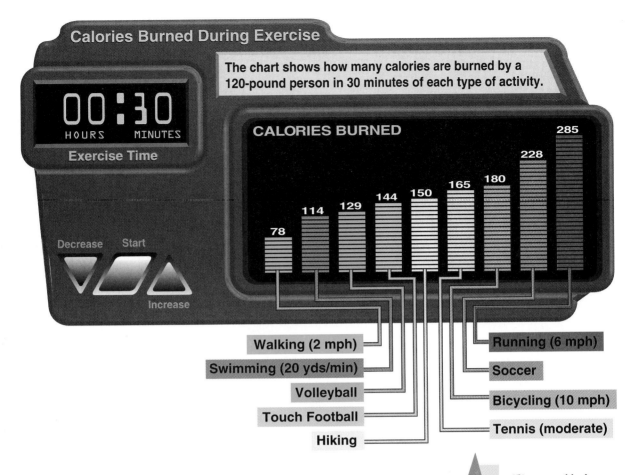

Calories Burned During Exercise

00:30
HOURS MINUTES
Exercise Time

Decrease Start Increase

The chart shows how many calories are burned by a 120-pound person in 30 minutes of each type of activity.

CALORIES BURNED

Activity	Calories
Walking (2 mph)	78
Swimming (20 yds/min)	114
Volleyball	129
Touch Football	144
Hiking	150
Tennis (moderate)	165
Bicycling (10 mph)	180
Soccer	228
Running (6 mph)	285

Figure 11.4 Calories Burned During Exercise

The chart shows how many calories are burned by a 120-pound person in 30 minutes of each type of activity.

by going on a fad diet. A **fad diet** is *a diet that promises quick weight loss through unusual means.*

Fad diets are rarely successful in controlling weight. It is hard to stay on fad diets because they cut out certain foods, lack variety, and don't usually satisfy people's appetites. Most people who lose weight on a fad diet gain the weight back—and sometimes more. For example, Gretchen tried a fad diet in which she drank a milk shake for breakfast and lunch but ate a sensible meal for dinner. She stuck with it for two days. Then she started snacking in the afternoon and evening because she craved food. By the fifth day, Gretchen gave up and found herself eating more than before. When she weighed herself on the seventh day, she discovered that she had gained a pound!

A more serious problem is that fad diets are unbalanced—so they don't provide the nutrients you need to be healthy and fit. Some may even cause physical harm, especially to people who don't follow them under the guidance of a physician.

You need to make exercise a part of your lifestyle to be physically fit and healthy. Which types of exercise do you enjoy the most?

A more sensible approach to controlling your weight is to combine a good diet with exercise. If you plan a diet with foods you like from the five food groups, you will probably stick with it. In the long run, you will maintain your health while losing weight. You'll be more likely to keep the weight off too.

LESSON FOUR *Review*

Using complete sentences, answer the following questions on a separate sheet of paper.

Reviewing Terms and Facts

1. List What are three benefits of fitness?

2. Explain Why is being underweight unhealthy?

3. Identify What do you have to balance to control your weight?

4. Vocabulary What is a *fad diet*? Why are fad diets rarely successful?

Thinking Critically

5. Relate How are calories related to your diet and the amount of exercise you get?

6. Contrast What is the difference between weight control and weight loss?

Applying Concepts

7. Make a two-column chart entitled "The Benefits of Fitness and Exercise." In one column list the physical benefits. In the second column list the mental benefits. Then write a letter to yourself to convince yourself to exercise regularly.

TECHNOLOGY

Consumer FOCUS

CASCADE RECYCLED LEGAL PAD

Choosing Snacks

How many times have you seen carrot or celery sticks advertised as snack foods on television? Probably never. On the other hand, you have seen countless ads for cookies, chips, and soft drinks. Advertisers know how to create a desire for sweet, salty, and greasy snacks.

Try This!

Look for a TV ad for an empty-calorie snack. Take notes on the methods the advertiser uses to sell the product. Discuss the ad with your classmates.

Having Your Cake and Eating It Too

Imagine being able to eat a scoop of rich ice cream without worrying about the fat and calories! Simplesse, developed in 1982, was one of the earliest fat substitutes. Made from milk and egg protein, it greatly reduces the fat content of frozen desserts when substituted for cream or other fats. For example, 4 ounces of ice cream normally contains 15 grams of fat. When made with Simplesse, it has less than 1 gram of fat.

Try This!

Find out more about fat substitutes. Summarize your findings in a brief report.

FRIENDS & FAMILY

EXERCISING THE FAMILY

Teens have found that it's easier to begin an exercise program if other family members are involved. You can start by discussing your plan with parents. Tell them what your goals are and how you would like to reach them. For example, you may want to start exercising four times a week.

TRY THIS!

Talk to family members about types of exercises you could do together. Then plan a weekly schedule of specific exercise sessions.

MATH CONNECTION

Follow Up

GETTING ACTIVE

Several factors influence the number of calories you burn during physical activity. One factor is the type of activity. Aerobic exercise—such as jogging, bicycling, and swimming—gives your heart and lungs a workout and burns the most calories per minute. Another factor is your weight. The heavier you are, the more calories you will burn.

1. Choose a sports activity from the chart on page 321. Plan to spend 30 minutes at that activity three times a week. Approximately how many calories will you burn in a week?

2. Sports and regular exercise routines are two ways to get active. What are some other ways you can add physical activity to your daily life at home and at school?

Chapter Summary

- The Food Guide Pyramid shows you how to plan a healthful diet for each day. It suggests a number of daily servings for each category of food.

- The five food groups are grains; vegetables; fruits; milk products; and meat, poultry, fish, eggs, dry beans, and nuts. Each category of food contains different nutrients.

- Following the Dietary Guidelines will help you stay healthy: Eat a variety of foods; maintain healthy weight; choose a diet low in fat—especially saturated fat—and cholesterol; eat plenty of vegetables, fruits, and grains; use sugar, salt, and sodium only in moderation; avoid alcoholic beverages.

- A balanced diet is necessary to provide your body with the nutrients it needs.

- Eating healthful snacks can be part of your daily meal plan. You should eat snacks that are nutrient-dense and avoid empty-calorie snacks.

- By choosing wisely, you can eat nutritious meals in restaurants.

- Physical fitness brings many benefits, such as feeling healthy and having stamina.

- The key to controlling your weight is to balance the number of calories you get from the foods you eat with the amount of energy you use.

- Exercise is necessary to reach and maintain a healthy body weight.

▶ Words to Know

Using complete sentences, answer the following questions on a separate sheet of paper.

1. Select a *food group* and name five foods that are in that group.

2. What is a *vegetarian?*

3. Describe *wellness.*

4. If you do something in *moderation,* what do you do?

5. What are *nutrient-dense foods?* Give two examples of nutrient-dense snacks.

6. Why are candy, chips, cola, and sweet desserts called *empty-calorie foods?*

7. What does it mean when you have *stamina?*

8. What is *aerobic exercise?* Give an example.

▶ Review Questions

Using complete sentences, answer the following questions on a separate sheet of paper.

1. How does the shape of the Food Guide Pyramid help you remember what to eat each day?

2. How do you know how many servings to eat from each food group?

3. Why is it important to eat a variety of foods?

4. List the Dietary Guidelines for Americans.

5. What guidelines should everyone follow when choosing snacks?

6. How can you select healthy foods when eating out?

7. How does exercise help you control your weight?

8. Why are fad diets generally unsuccessful in helping people control their weight?

Thinking Critically

Using complete sentences, answer the following questions on a separate sheet of paper.

1. **Analyze** Why do you think that many teens have poor eating habits?

2. **Explain** Why do manufacturers of food products aim a large portion of their advertising at children and teens?

3. **Evaluate** Do you think that the American lifestyle contributes to physical fitness? Why or why not?

Cooperative Learning

1. Working in groups of four or five, plan menus for your school's lunch program. Have each group member write a menu for one day of the week. Base your menus on the Food Guide Pyramid and the Dietary Guidelines for Americans. Exchange weekly menu plans with another group and evaluate each other's ideas.

2. Working with a partner, invent a sweet, salty, or greasy food product. Design the packaging for your product. Include a warning label that lists the health hazards of eating the food. Display your design on the class bulletin board.

Family & Community

1. Plan some family fitness fun. Organize backyard games, such as volleyball or badminton, or get your family to go bowling together on a Saturday afternoon. Think of other ways to encourage your family to be physically active.

2. Find out about organized exercise programs and sports activities for young teens in your community. These programs may be sponsored by schools, community centers, parks, or youth groups. If you are not already participating in a program, make plans to join one.

Building A Portfolio

1. Make two changes in your behavior each day that reflect healthful choices. They can be small changes, such as eating an apple instead of a candy bar or walking up a flight of stairs instead of taking an elevator. Record these healthful choices in a daily diary. Keep your diary in your portfolio.

2. Plan a meal based on the Food Guide Pyramid and Dietary Guidelines. Prepare the meal for your family. Then write a report on how the meal turned out. Place your report and your menu in your portfolio.

326

TEENS MAKING A DIFFERENCE

Meals on Wheels

Every Saturday, Eric goes to work in a church kitchen where he helps prepare 200 meals. He is a volunteer for Meals on Wheels, a national program that prepares and delivers meals to elderly shut-ins. Whether he's peeling potatoes or mixing muffins, Eric's help is always needed.

Once prepared, the meals are delivered by Eric and other volunteers. It's clear to Eric that for most of the people he serves, his smiling face and cheery hello are the high point of their day. The feeling that he's making a difference is all that Eric needs to keep up the hard work—and to give up his Saturdays.

Try THIS!

Learn more about the Meals on Wheels program in your community. How can you volunteer? Do you think that it's something you would like to do?

LESSON ONE
Food Safety and Sanitation

WORDS TO KNOW

contamination

salmonella

perishable

DISCOVER...

- the sources of food contamination.
- how to handle food safely.
- ways to keep the kitchen clean.

When Samantha gets home from school, she washes her hands in warm, soapy water and looks for a snack. She finds some leftover chicken in the refrigerator, but because it smells funny, she throws it out. She uses a clean spoon to dish out a bowl of applesauce. Before she takes the bowl to the kitchen table, she puts the jar of applesauce back in the refrigerator. Why do you think Samantha is so careful with food?

Keeping Food Safe

Samantha knows that eating unsafe food can make people very sick. Her eating habits and cleanliness help to prevent **contamination,** or *becoming infected with bacteria.*

You may think that food contamination is not a serious problem. In mild cases of food poisoning, people may experience headaches, stomach cramps, and fever. In more severe cases, however, medical attention may be necessary. The good news is that you have the power to reduce the risk of food contamination by understanding what causes it. Then you can follow some simple procedures when handling and preparing food to protect yourself from food poisoning.

A few types of bacteria cause most food poisoning. One of the most serious forms of food poisoning is caused by **salmonella** (SAL-muh-NELL-uh), or *bacteria that are often found in raw or undercooked foods, such as meat, eggs, fish, and poultry.* Salmonella grow quickly at room temperature and can be spread by hands and cooking utensils. For this reason, you must thoroughly cook all meat, poultry, fish, and eggs. You should also wash your hands, knife, and cutting board with soap and hot water whenever you cut raw meat, fish, or poultry.

Another way to reduce the risk of food poisoning is to handle perishable foods carefully. Foods that are **perishable** are *likely to spoil quickly.* Common perishable foods include meat, poultry, fish, eggs, and dairy products. Bacteria grow quickly at temperatures between 60°F and 125°F (16°C and 52°C). Therefore hot foods, such as hamburgers, should be kept hot, and cold foods, such as yogurt, should be kept cold until they are eaten. Keep hot foods at 140°F (60°C) or above and cold foods at 40°F (4°C) or below.

Foods that have been cooked should not stand at room temperature for more than two hours. If you are packing food for a school lunch or a picnic, use cold packs and a cooler to keep the cold foods cold.

Try This!

To make sure that you are washing dishes as safely and efficiently as possible, soak cooked-on food in pots and pans while you are eating so that they are easier to wash later. To avoid injury, wash knives and other sharp objects separately. Wash dishes in hot, soapy water, and rinse them with plenty of hot water.

Why is it important to wash a cutting board with soap and hot water?

How to Store Leftovers

Figure 12.1

Figure 12.1
Preventing Food Contamination
For your health and the health of others, it is important to handle foods safely and to keep the kitchen clean. ▼

To keep leftovers from spoiling, refrigerate or freeze them immediately after the meal. Put leftovers in a tightly covered shallow container, and store them in the refrigerator. Many leftovers can also be frozen for use at a later date. When freezing leftovers, pack them in an airtight container, and label them with the name of the food and the date. Freezing foods keeps bacteria from growing until the food is thawed out. Most foods can be stored in the freezer for several months. **Figure 12.1** shows other ways to prevent food contamination.

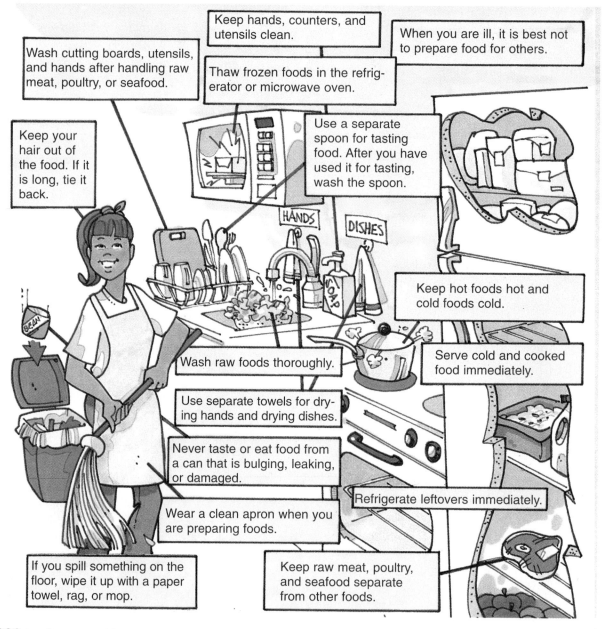

Keep hands, counters, and utensils clean.

When you are ill, it is best not to prepare food for others.

Wash cutting boards, utensils, and hands after handling raw meat, poultry, or seafood.

Thaw frozen foods in the refrigerator or microwave oven.

Keep your hair out of the food. If it is long, tie it back.

Use a separate spoon for tasting food. After you have used it for tasting, wash the spoon.

HANDS

DISHES

SOAP

Keep hot foods hot and cold foods cold.

Wash raw foods thoroughly.

Serve cold and cooked food immediately.

Use separate towels for drying hands and drying dishes.

Never taste or eat food from a can that is bulging, leaking, or damaged.

Refrigerate leftovers immediately.

Wear a clean apron when you are preparing foods.

If you spill something on the floor, wipe it up with a paper towel, rag, or mop.

Keep raw meat, poultry, and seafood separate from other foods.

Keeping the Kitchen Clean

Jeff and his dad always clean up the kitchen as they cook. They wipe up spills immediately and clean off the countertops. As they finish using pots, pans, and cooking utensils, they wash them in hot, soapy water. By keeping the kitchen clean, Jeff and his dad make it a more healthful and pleasant place to work.

A Safe, Clean Kitchen

The best defense against food poisoning in the kitchen is to work actively to prevent it. That means following the procedures suggested in this lesson. Put these ideas into practice to keep food safe and to keep the kitchen clean.

▲ Properly stored leftovers will be safe for later use. Why should you write the date on these leftovers?

LESSON ONE *Review*

Using complete sentences, answer the following questions on a separate sheet of paper.

Reviewing Terms and Facts

1. Describe What are the symptoms of mild food poisoning?

2. Recall What causes food poisoning?

3. Vocabulary Define the term *perishable*. Give two examples of perishable foods.

4. Identify What should you do to keep leftovers from spoiling?

Thinking Critically

5. Apply What could you do in your kitchen to prevent food from becoming contaminated?

6. Explain Why is a dirty kitchen unhealthy and unpleasant?

Applying Concepts

7. Write two food safety slogans you might find helpful. If possible, display them in the kitchen at home or at school.

8. Imagine that your class is having a dinner party for parents. Your job is to make sure that the food served is safe to eat. Write down ten procedures you would follow to make the food safe as well as delicious.

Kitchen Safety

WORDS TO KNOW

flammable

conduct

DISCOVER...

- the causes of common kitchen accidents.
- ways to prevent common accidents from occurring in the kitchen.

When Michael realizes that he has only 20 minutes before he has to leave for practice, he grabs a dining room chair, stands on it, and starts looking through a high cabinet for a snack. As he reaches for the crackers on the top shelf, the chair wobbles, and Michael falls to the kitchen floor. He picks up most of the crackers that spilled out and throws them away. Then he pours himself a glass of milk and takes his food into the dining room.

Preventing Accidents

Michael's fall is a typical kitchen accident. The most common accidents that occur in the kitchen include

- falls.
- burns.
- cuts.
- electric shocks.

These types of accidents and injuries are usually preventable if people develop good, safe work habits.

Falls

The same day that Michael fell, Michael's sister Marcie ran into the kitchen, slipped on cracker crumbs, and also fell. Because Michael was rushing to practice, he hadn't done a good job of cleaning up the mess he had made. Although neither Michael nor Marcie was badly hurt, one or both of them might have been. To prevent falls, Michael and Marcie now follow these guidelines.

- Keep cupboard doors and drawers closed when not in use.
- Stand on a short stepladder or a sturdy step stool with a waist-high hand bar to get at high or hard-to-reach items.
- Turn pot and pan handles toward the center of the stove or counter so that the pots or pans won't get knocked over.
- Clean up spilled foods or liquids immediately.

Burns

Jenny was cooking french fries on the stove when the phone rang. She left the kitchen to answer it. After a few minutes, Jenny heard the smoke alarm go off. She ran into the kitchen and found that the pan was smoking and popping. Jenny hadn't realized how quickly a grease fire can start.

If you need to reach for something on a high shelf, use a small stepladder or step stool. What else can you do to prevent falls from occurring in the kitchen?

Skills
IN ACTION

How to Use a Fire Extinguisher

Every kitchen should be equipped with a fire extinguisher. To learn how to use one, study the following steps.

1. Pull the ring.
2. Stand back several feet from the fire, point the nozzle at the base of the flames, and squeeze the handle.
3. Spray the foam back and forth across the base of the fire.

You can prevent most fires and burns in the kitchen if you follow these safety precautions.

- Avoid leaving the kitchen if you have food cooking. Fires can spread in seconds.

- Use medium or low temperatures for cooking greasy foods, such as french fries or fried chicken. If a grease fire starts, turn off the heat and smother the fire with a tight-fitting lid. Never use water—it will make a grease fire spread.

- Keep all flammable objects away from the stove. **Flammable** means *capable of burning easily.* Be especially careful with paper bags, pot holders, kitchen towels, curtains, and plastic containers.

- Use dry pot holders when cooking hot foods and liquids or removing them from the stove, oven, or microwave.

- When cooking, remove pan lids by tilting them away from you. This allows steam to escape safely at the back of the pot, away from your hands and face.

- Don't wear clothing with long, loose-fitting sleeves when cooking. The sleeves can easily catch fire.

- If your hair is long, tie it back.

- Keep a fire extinguisher in or near the kitchen where you can reach it quickly and safely. Be sure that you know how to use it properly.

If you cook, you should know how to use a fire extinguisher. Where should it be kept?

Cuts

Belinda wanted to make a salad for lunch. Since she couldn't find the cutting board, she decided to peel and chop the vegetables over the sink. The good knives were all dirty, so she found an old knife in the back of the drawer. As she was slicing a tomato, she cut her finger. Belinda probably could have avoided cutting herself if she had followed a few safety precautions. To prevent kitchen cuts, observe the following safety rules.

To prevent cuts, use a cutting board when you chop food. In which direction should you cut food?

- Keep knives sharp. Sharp knives are safer than dull ones.

- Cut food away from your body. Use a cutting board for all cutting jobs—even if it's only a single apple.

- Wash knives and sharp objects separately from other utensils.

- Store knives in a special compartment in the drawer or in a knife holder. Put them away immediately after cleaning them.

- Never pick up broken glass with bare hands. Sweep it into a dustpan immediately. Then wipe the floor with several thicknesses of damp paper towel, put broken pieces into a bag, and place the bag in a trash can.

Electric Shocks

Emilio was making breakfast when his bagel got stuck in the toaster. Emilio's mother told him to unplug the toaster and then use a fork or tongs to get the bagel out.

Electrical appliances make kitchen tasks easier, but they can also cause electric shocks. To prevent shocks, take the following precautions.

- Always unplug a toaster before trying to pry food from it. Forks, knives, or other metal utensils can **conduct,** or *carry electricity,* and cause an electrical shock.

- Avoid using any appliance that has a frayed or worn cord.

- Dry your hands thoroughly before touching electrical equipment.

- Disconnect appliances by pulling out the plug, not by tugging on the cord.

- Keep portable appliances unplugged when not in use.

To avoid electric shocks, you need to be careful when using kitchen appliances. What is this teen doing to prevent a shock?

Safety in the Kitchen

Family members tend to spend a lot of time in the kitchen. Many of the accidents that occur in the kitchen can be prevented. By following the rules outlined in this lesson, you can make the kitchen a safe place to work and eat.

LESSON TWO *Review*

Using complete sentences, answer the following questions on a separate sheet of paper.

Reviewing Terms and Facts

1. Recall What are the four most common types of kitchen accidents?

2. List Name five ways to prevent kitchen falls.

3. Vocabulary Define the term *flammable.* Give two examples of objects that are flammable.

4. Describe Explain the safest way to pick up broken glass.

Thinking Critically

5. Explain Why is it necessary to develop good, safe work habits in the kitchen?

6. Apply How can you improve your work habits in the kitchen to make them safer?

7. Predict What might happen if you plugged in a blender with wet hands? Explain your answer.

Applying Concepts

8. Read about first-aid procedures in a health textbook. Find out how to treat a minor burn, or cut. Write a paragraph explaining the proper procedure and listing the supplies you would need.

Kitchen Tools and Equipment

DISCOVER...

- how to use basic kitchen tools.
- the purposes of small kitchen equipment.
- the types of major appliances used in a kitchen.

Molly decided to bake a cake for her mother's birthday, so she bought a cake mix and vanilla icing. Because Molly had never baked a cake before, she asked her friend Chelsea to help. Chelsea said that she would bring some cookware and kitchen tools that would make their job easy. What do you think that Chelsea brought? Do you know the basic kitchen tools, cookware, and appliances to use to make your cooking tasks easier?

WORDS TO KNOW

utensils

small appliances

major appliances

microwave oven

Which Tool?

Test your kitchen know-how by naming the right tool for each of the following jobs:

- Turning hamburgers on the grill
- Mixing dry ingredients for a cake
- Shredding cheese to put on a pizza
- Draining the water from cooked pasta

Small Equipment

Not all kitchen tools and cookware are essential. For example, you don't have to have a vegetable peeler to peel a carrot. You can do the job with a small knife. However, a kitchen equipped with the basic tools and cookware makes food preparation much easier.

A variety of **utensils,** or *kitchen tools,* and cookware is available. The most commonly used utensils include those for cooking, mixing, and slicing or cutting. The best cookware to use depends on the type of food you are cooking and where you are cooking it. For instance, you could use a metal cake pan to bake cookie bars in a conventional oven but not in a microwave oven. **Figure 12.2** on pages 339–341 describes some of the most basic kitchen tools and cookware.

Small Appliances

When Molly made the cake, she used a hand mixer to beat the batter. A hand mixer is a **small appliance,** or *small, electrically powered kitchen equipment.* Commonly used small appliances include toasters, food processors, and blenders.

Large Appliances

Molly needed to use one major appliance to bake her cake. **Major appliances,** or *large kitchen equipment,* include the stove, oven, refrigerator, dishwasher, and microwave oven. A **microwave oven** is *an appliance that cooks by vibrating the molecules in food.* Some major appliances, such as a stove and a refrigerator, are needed in every kitchen. Others, such as a microwave oven and a dishwasher, make food preparation easier but are not essential.

The cost of major appliances varies, depending on the extra features that are included. Each family must decide which features would be most useful to them. For example:

- Stoves usually come with conventional ovens. Some stoves also include microwave ovens, while others include convection ovens. (Continued on page 342.)

Many people use food processors to save time when chopping such foods as vegetables. Which small appliances have you used?

COOKING TOOLS

**Figure 12.2
Kitchen Tools
and Cookware**
Which kitchen tools and
cookware do you think
are essential?

TONGS
Used for lifting and
turning hot foods.

COLANDER
Used for drain-
ing liquids from
cooked food or
for rinsing fruits
and vegetables.

ROTARY BEATER
Used for beating
light mixtures or
adding air to eggs.

**RUBBER
SCRAPER**
Used for cleaning
foods completely
from sides of bowl.

SPATULA
Used for lifting and
turning foods such
as pancakes and
hamburgers.

LARGE SPOON
Used for stirring
and spooning
ingredients.

KITCHEN FORK
Used for lifting
and turning food.

MIXING BOWLS
Used for mixing
ingredients. Usually
come in different
sizes.

MIXING TOOLS

WIRE WHISK
Used for beating and blending. Especially good for beating egg-white mixtures and stirring sauces.

PEELER
Used for peeling fruits and vegetables.

SIFTER
Used for removing lumps and adding air to flour before measuring. Can also combine dry ingredients.

CHEF'S KNIFE
Used for cutting, mincing, slicing, and dicing food.

SLICING AND CUTTING TOOLS

PARING KNIFE
Small knife used for peeling and cutting fruits and vegetables.

CUTTING BOARD
Used to protect the counter when cutting.

GRATER
Used for grating, shredding, or slicing vegetables and cheese.

SLICING KNIFE
Used for slicing meat and poultry.

COOKWARE

COOKIE SHEET
Used for baking cookies or pizza.

MUFFIN TIN
Used for baking muffins, cupcakes, and rolls.

ROASTING PAN WITH RACK
Used for roasting meat and poultry.

PIE PAN
Used for baking pies and quiches.

LOAF PAN
Used for baking bread and meat loaf.

DOUBLE BOILER
Used for foods that burn easily, such as milk and sauces.

CAKE PANS
Used for baking cakes and bar cookies. Available in square, round, rectangular, and tube.

CASSEROLES
Ovenproof dishes, which come in a variety of sizes.

SAUCEPANS
Used for top-of-the-stove cooking. Have one long handle and a lid. Available in different sizes.

A convection oven uses a high-speed fan to circulate hot air throughout the oven, which speeds up the cooking. Conventional ovens may be self-cleaning or continuous cleaning. An automatic timer that can turn the oven on or off is another possible feature.

- Microwave ovens are fast, convenient, and easy to use. They come in a variety of sizes and have a range of power settings. You will learn more about microwave ovens in Lesson 4 of this chapter.

- Refrigerators may have the freezer on the top, on the bottom, or on the side. Some are self-defrosting and have extra freezer space, ice makers, or ice cube and water dispensers.

Major appliances come in a variety of sizes, colors, and brands and may have many different features. What features would you like in a new refrigerator?

Cooking with Ease

You can cook just about anything if you have the most basic kitchen utensils, cookware, and appliances and know how to use them. Preparing food will be easier, more enjoyable, and safer when you select the right tools for the job.

LESSON THREE *Review*

Using complete sentences, answer the following questions on a separate sheet of paper.

Reviewing Terms and Facts

1. Recall What is a colander used for?

2. List Identify five kitchen tools you would use to mix ingredients.

3. Identify Name one type of cookware you would use on the stove top and one type you would use in the oven.

4. Vocabulary Define the term *microwave oven*. What are the advantages of using a microwave oven?

Thinking Critically

5. Analyze If you could have only four pieces of cookware, which ones would you choose? Explain your answer.

6. Describe How do the small appliances in your kitchen make cooking easier?

7. Apply If you were buying a refrigerator, what features would be most important to you? What features would be least important?

Applying Concepts

8. Suppose that you do not have one of the utensils you need. Describe how you could prepare the food without that utensil. Explain how the utensil would have made your work easier.

Microwave Cooking

DISCOVER...

- how a microwave oven works.
- how to use a microwave oven.
- ways to prepare foods for microwave cooking.

WORDS
TO KNOW

defrosting

arcing

rotating

variables

Gino's family rarely eats dinner together on weekdays. His mom and older brother fix dinner and eat before they go to work at the hospital. When Gino's dad gets home from work, he and Gino reheat the food in the microwave oven. The microwave doesn't dry out the food, and it is fast and easy to use.

Many people use microwave ovens for jobs that, in the past, could be done only by stoves and conventional ovens. In fact, microwave ovens have features that make them more versatile than many other kitchen appliances. It is no wonder that they are changing the way people cook.

How a Microwave Oven Works

Although microwave ovens vary in size, power, and features, they all operate the same way. They produce microwaves, or energy waves that penetrate food and agitate its molecules. This process results in heat that cooks the food. Unlike conventional ovens, microwave ovens heat only the food—the container usually does not get hot.

Microwave ovens are a fast and convenient way to cook. Foods cook up to 75 percent faster than in a conventional oven. You can reheat leftover food, cook food, or defrost frozen food. **Defrosting** means *thawing or unfreezing frozen food.*

Because microwave ovens cook food so quickly, they use less electricity than other methods of cooking. The nutrients in food are better preserved because of this quick cooking time and because such foods as vegetables require little or no added water.

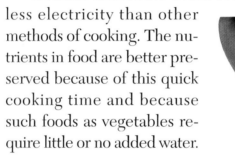

Because vegetables take less time to cook in a microwave, they taste better than those cooked on a stove. What guidelines do you use when cooking vegetables in a microwave?

Using a Microwave Oven

The amount of power that an appliance uses is measured in watts. Most household microwave ovens use a maximum of 500 to 700 watts. The higher the wattage, the faster most foods will cook. If you are unsure of the wattage, you can look it up in the instruction manual or on the label attached to the oven.

Although you cannot control the wattage, you can control the amount of power with which you cook. The power control on the microwave oven may be a control panel or a single dial. Some control panels are numbered from 1 to 10, so that "1" means 10 percent of the available power and "10" means 100 percent. Other control panels simply have settings for low, medium, and high.

To determine which power setting to use and how long to cook a particular food, consult a recipe or the instruction manual. Some control panels list common foods with specific power settings and cooking times.

The control panels vary among different microwave ovens. What are some of the more common power settings you have seen?

Choosing Cookware

Kendra thought that it was all right to use any plastic, glass, or ceramic container in the microwave oven. Then one day, while she was reheating leftovers in a plastic container, the plastic started to melt. Since then, she has learned to make sure that containers are labeled "microwave safe" before using them in the microwave oven. These containers will not get too hot, melt, crack, or shatter from the heat produced in the oven. Round containers allow more even heating and cooking than square or rectangular ones.

Because the microwaves that heat the food cannot pass through metal, metal containers should never be used in a microwave oven, and aluminum foil should not be used as a cover.

Metal can also cause **arcing,** or *electrical sparks that can damage a microwave oven and start a fire.* Brown paper bags and other products made from recycled paper should also be avoided because they can catch fire.

Cooking Preparation

Because microwave ovens cook food differently from conventional ovens, you need to follow specific guidelines when preparing food for cooking.

- Choose a container that will fit into the microwave oven without touching the sides or the top. To keep liquids from boiling over, use a container that has extra space in it.

- Arrange the food so that it can heat up or cook evenly. Cut foods into pieces of the same size so that they will cook at the same rate. Place the thickest pieces toward the outside of the container, where they will receive the most energy.

- Use a fork or knife to pierce foods that are encased in a skin, such as whole potatoes and hot dogs. This will ensure that the steam does not build up and cause them to burst.

- Cover foods so that they hold in their moisture and do not spatter. You can use paper towels, waxed paper, plastic wrap, or covers that come with microwavable containers. Cover the food *loosely,* or make a vent by turning back a corner of the plastic wrap to let the steam escape.

The Cooking Process

You will often need to use special techniques when cooking foods in a microwave oven.

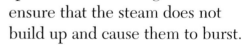

Before you cook food in a microwave oven, you may need to use special techniques to prepare it. What technique is this teen using?

- **Stirring.** To help some foods, such as soups and stews, to cook evenly, stir them after they are partly cooked. Since the outside cooks first, stir from the outer edge of the container toward the center.

- **Rearranging.** Some foods, such as baking potatoes, might have to be rearranged or turned over after a few minutes. Move pieces that have been on the outer edges of the container into the center so that they can heat up, defrost, or cook evenly.

- **Rotating.** Some foods need to be rotated. **Rotating** means *turning the dish a quarter-turn or a half-turn in the oven.* This allows the microwaves to enter the food on all sides. The package directions or the recipe you are following will usually specify how often to rotate the food. Most newer microwave ovens have a turntable that automatically rotates whenever the oven is in use.

- **Standing time.** Microwave recipes tell you to let the food stand after the power shuts off. It can stand on the counter if you need to put another dish into the oven. This standing time is required to let the temperatures equalize. In fact, standing time is almost as important as cooking time for the food to turn out just right.

TIPS for living

MICROWAVE TRICKS

Here are some quick microwave tricks to try.

- Soften hard ice cream by microwaving a half gallon for 45 to 60 seconds at the defrost setting.

- Freshen soggy pretzels, crackers, or popcorn by microwaving 2 cups for 45 seconds at high power and then letting it stand for 1 minute.

- Make your own microwave dinners by freezing leftovers in divided plates. Then reheat them at a later date.

- Microwave juice oranges or lemons for 30 seconds each at high power before squeezing. They will be easier to squeeze, and you will get more juice.

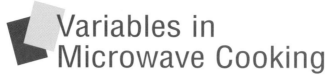

Variables in Microwave Cooking

When you use a microwave oven, you need to follow different procedures to cook different types or sizes of food. That is because of variables in microwave cooking. **Variables** are *conditions that determine how long a food needs to be cooked and at what power level.* Variables include the following:

- **Density.** The denser the food, the longer it takes to cook. The heavier a food feels for its size, the denser it is. For example, a slice of meat is denser than a slice of bread of the same size.

- **Volume of food.** The amount, or number of servings, determines how much power and time are needed. Generally, the smaller the amount of food, the faster it cooks.

- **Shape of food.** Round foods, such as pancakes, cook more evenly than foods that have corners, such as lasagna. This is because the corners can overcook. Thin pieces cook more quickly than thick pieces.

- **Temperature of food.** If food is at room temperature, it will heat faster than food taken directly from the refrigerator or freezer.

Converting Conventional-Oven Recipes

If your time is limited and you need to bake a dish in a hurry, you can often convert a recipe meant for a conventional oven to a microwave recipe. Here are some general guidelines to follow.

- Reduce liquid ingredients by 1 or 2 tablespoons per cup.
- Reduce cooking time by about 50 to 75 percent.
- Add very little salt to meats and vegetables—it dries out foods during microwave cooking.

Safe Use of Microwave Ovens

Cooking in a microwave oven can be easy and safe as long as you take a few basic precautions.

- To avoid fires and other accidents, use dishes labeled "microwave safe."

- Remove covers slowly after food is cooked, tilting the cover or removing the plastic wrap so that steam escapes away from you.

- Do not microwave foods in containers that are completely sealed. When pressure from steam builds up, the container can burst.

- Do not use an extension cord with a microwave oven or plug it into the same electrical outlet as other large electrical appliances.

- If the oven door does not close tightly or if you hear unusual sounds coming from the oven, tell an adult.

- If there are sparks inside the oven or if there is a fire, turn off the oven or unplug it immediately and get help.

Although some people are concerned that it is unsafe to stand in front of a microwave oven while the oven is on, it is generally safe to do so.

Because steam builds up in a covered container, you need to remove the cover carefully. What are some other safety rules to keep in mind when using a microwave oven? ▶

Review

Using complete sentences, answer the following questions on a separate sheet of paper.

Reviewing Terms and Facts

1. Vocabulary Define the term *arcing*. How can arcing be avoided?

2. Recall Why is it important to rotate foods while they are cooking?

3. Identify What are the four variables to consider when you cook foods in a microwave oven?

4. List Name six safety precautions to take when using a microwave oven.

Thinking Critically

5. Evaluate Do you think that there are any disadvantages to cooking food in a microwave oven? If so, what are they?

6. Analyze Why would an egg crack if it were cooked with the shell on in a microwave oven?

7. Predict Which food would cook faster in a microwave oven—a slice of steak or a slice of meat loaf the same size? Explain your answer.

Applying Concepts

8. Find a recipe with directions for cooking a dish you like in the microwave oven. Make a list of all the techniques used, such as piercing and rotating, that make the recipe suitable for use in a microwave oven.

The School Foods Lab

WORDS TO KNOW

work plan

dovetailing

DISCOVER...

- how to work as a team member in the school foods lab.
- how to make and follow a work plan.

Once a week, Adam plans, shops for, and prepares one meal for his family. When he plans the meal, he takes into account the nutrition principles he learned in the school foods lab. When he prepares the meal, he uses cooking techniques that he learned in class.

Cooking in your kitchen at home is not the same as cooking in a foods class. At school, you have to work closely with your classmates. At home, you may be alone or you may be working with only one other person. With these differences in mind, how can you make the best use of the school foods lab?

Cooking Teams

A school foods lab session needs to be carefully planned, organized, and managed. Typically, the class is divided into cooking teams of three to six members each. Just as in any successful team, every member has specific responsibilities, or duties to perform. In addition, all team members must be able to

- get along with other team members.

- read and follow directions.

- handle food safely and follow safety precautions.

- help other team members. For example, if you have finished stir-frying the vegetables for your team, you can help the student who is slicing bread.

Creating a Work Plan

Before each team can begin to work, team members must create a work plan for the group. A **work plan** is *a list of the jobs that need to be done and the name of the person who will do each job.* For instance, a work plan might list a task such as "Chop two small onions," with Dave's name printed beside it. Plans also list the equipment and the ingredients the team needs and give step-by-step directions on how to combine the ingredients.

The following tasks are a part of each team's work plan:

- **Pre-preparation.** Team members need to put out all the supplies, equipment, and ingredients; wash food if necessary; and measure ingredients, using the correct measuring utensils. For example, to measure two teaspoons of vanilla, you need a measuring teaspoon, not a regular spoon.

When team members work together to complete tasks in the school foods lab, the whole group benefits. In what other situations is teamwork helpful?

- **Mixing and preparation.** Team members must combine ingredients and prepare food. For instance, in making baked apples, you need to combine sugar and cinnamon, fill the apple centers with the mixture, and then bake the apples.

- **Table setting and serving the food.** Team members must set the table and serve the food correctly.

- **Cleaning up.** Team members should clean up as they go along so that they don't have to rush to clean up at the last minute.

In a well-run foods lab, the tasks are divided so that they can be dovetailed. **Dovetailing** means *fitting different tasks together smoothly and efficiently.* For example, Jesse may wash the lettuce while Allison makes the salad dressing. Each time a new work plan is made, these tasks are moved from one person to another. That way, Jesse can learn to measure and combine ingredients the next time while Allison learns how to prepare vegetables.

How to Follow the Work Plan

A work plan is easy to follow when all team members understand the tasks to be done, who is to do each task, and how to do their own tasks correctly. Any questions should be resolved before each team begins cooking.

TIPS for living

SAVING TIME IN THE KITCHEN

Make the most of your time by following these timesaving tips.

- **Plan ahead.** Read the entire recipe, make sure that you understand each instruction, and plan each step before you begin.

- **Get organized.** Assemble all the necessary ingredients and equipment.

- **Share the work.** Divide tasks among lab partners or family members, and help others when your job is done.

- **Dovetail tasks.** When possible, overlap the jobs you are doing. For example, prepare salad while the pasta cooks.

- **Clean as you go.** Keep the counters wiped clean, and soak dirty dishes in a sink filled with hot, soapy water.

Following a work plan, team members should check off steps as they are completed. Why is this important?

Following a work plan will help you stay on schedule. After each member completes a step, he or she should check it off. That way, the steps will be completed in the correct order.

Does the Plan Work?

When the work is completed, team members need to evaluate, or judge, their work plan, so that they understand what they did correctly, what could be improved, and whether they reached their goal. For example, when team members evaluate their oven-baked french fries, they may decide that the potatoes would not have burned if two team members had checked the baking time.

As you continue to complete projects in the school foods lab, you will gain experience and learn from your team's evaluations. In time, you can take on more difficult tasks. For example, your first project may be to make grilled cheese sandwiches, but in a short time you may find yourself helping to prepare full meals.

A Successful Lab Team

Being a good team member in the foods lab is the same as being a good member of any team. If team members have a

Skills IN ACTION

Rating the Team's Success

Take this quiz to rate the success of your foods lab team.

- Was the work schedule followed?
- Did team members work together willingly and help each other?
- Was each step of the recipe followed properly?
- Did the food look and taste good?
- Was kitchen cleanup completed on time?

If you answered no to any of the questions, think about how you can do better next time.

When team members carefully detail, organize, and carry out their work plan, they can enjoy a successful meal.

plan, follow it, perform their assigned tasks, and work together cooperatively, cooking projects will be easier and more enjoyable for everyone involved.

LESSON FIVE — *Review*

Using complete sentences, answer the following questions on a separate sheet of paper.

Reviewing Terms and Facts

1. Recall List the duties that all team members should be able to perform.

2. Vocabulary What is a *work plan?* Identify the four tasks that are part of the work plan.

3. Explain Why are foods-lab tasks moved from one person to another?

4. Identify How do team members ensure that steps are performed in the correct order?

Thinking Critically

5. Analyze Which tasks do you think would be the most difficult when working with a team? Which do you think would be the easiest? Explain your answers.

6. Apply Make a list of other activities, besides cooking, in which dovetailing would be helpful.

7. Explain Why is it important to evaluate the work plan? What might happen if team members fail to evaluate it?

Applying Concepts

8. Choose a recipe you would like your team to use in the foods lab. Be sure to determine that your team has the skills, budget, and time to prepare the dish you choose. Then create a work plan with job assignments.

Chapter *12* Activities

Consumer Focus

Buying Wisely

Check these before you buy:
- **The expiration date.** This is the date by which the product should be eaten.
- **Signs of spoilage.** Cans should not have dents or bulges.
- **Signs of tampering.** Make sure that the safety seal is unbroken.

Try This!

Find out the meanings of the following types of dates found on product labels: pull date, sell by, and pack date. Share your findings with your class.

TECHNOLOGY

Computers in the Kitchen

Some kitchen appliances use computer technology. For example, there are computer cookbooks. Can't think of anything to fix for dinner? Type in a list of foods you have on hand, and with special software, your computer will print out recipes you can make with those ingredients.

Try This!

Visit a store that sells software. Find out what programs are available to help you shop for, prepare, or cook food. Make a list of the titles and their prices.

A Global View

FROM EARTH OVENS TO MICROWAVES

People all over the world have been using ovens for thousands of years, yet the way ovens work has changed very little. Microwave ovens, which were invented in the 1940s, introduced the first real change in oven technology in thousands of years.

TRY THIS!

Bake one potato in a microwave oven and another potato in a conventional oven. Compare cooking times and the texture of the potatoes. Which potato do you prefer? Write a paragraph on the results.

SCIENCE CONNECTION

FRICTION PRODUCES HEAT

In a conventional oven, food is heated mainly by the radiation of heat waves from the hot oven walls. The food heats by conduction—the transfer of heat through the exchange of energy.

The waves produced by a microwave oven penetrate the food, where they quickly pull the food particles back and forth. The movement creates friction, and the friction, in turn, produces heat.

Follow Up

1. Explain why quickly rubbing your hands together is similar to the operation of a microwave oven. Try it, and see if your hands feel warmer.

2. Electromagnetic waves are attracted to water, fat, and sugar. How might that affect the rates at which different foods cook in a microwave oven?

Chapter Summary

- Food contamination is a serious health hazard. Handling, preparing, and storing food safely can prevent food contamination.

- Perishable foods—such as eggs, meat, and milk—must be kept at the proper temperature to avoid spoiling. Keep hot foods hot and cold foods cold.

- When handling food, wash your hands frequently to prevent the spread of germs. Wash cutting boards and countertops after using them.

- Common types of accidents in the kitchen are falls, burns, cuts, and electric shocks.

- Most kitchen accidents can be prevented by developing safe work habits.

- There are many types of kitchen tools and equipment. Knowing how to use them properly will make cooking tasks much easier.

- Microwave ovens cook food quickly and preserve the nutrients in food.

- When using a microwave oven, you need to use microwave-safe cookware, follow specific guidelines for preparing food, and use special cooking techniques.

- Variables to consider when using a microwave oven include the density, volume, shape, and temperature of food.

- Teamwork is essential in the foods lab. Each member of the group has specific responsibilities.

- When members of the foods lab team follow a work plan, complete their tasks, and cooperate, success is almost guaranteed.

▶ Words to Know

Using complete sentences, answer the following questions on a separate sheet of paper.

1. Define the term *contamination*. What can happen to a person as a result of food contamination?

2. Give two examples of *perishable* foods.

3. Define the word *flammable*.

4. Give two examples of *utensils*.

5. What is *arcing*, and how is it caused?

6. What is a *work plan*, and when do you need to make one?

7. Define the term *dovetailing*.

▶ Review Questions

Using complete sentences, answer the following questions on a separate sheet of paper.

1. Why is kitchen cleanliness necessary for food safety?

2. Explain why it is important to keep hot foods hot and cold foods cold.

3. Give two examples of each of the following: cooking tools, mixing tools, slicing and cutting tools.

4. Why is it important to use microwave-safe containers when cooking food in a microwave oven?

5. Why is standing time necessary after food is cooked in a microwave oven?

6. List the four types of tasks each team must complete in the school foods lab.

7. What is the final step of the foods lab?

Thinking Critically

Using complete sentences, answer the following questions on a separate sheet of paper.

1. Explain If you were taking food to a picnic on a hot summer day, how could you make sure that it stayed safe to eat?

2. Suggest List some small appliances that might have more than one purpose and describe each purpose.

3. Interpret Why do many people own both a microwave oven and a conventional oven?

4. Analyze What kinds of cooperative behavior, besides those mentioned in the text, do you think would help the school foods lab run more smoothly?

Cooperative Learning

1. In small groups, choose one illness caused by improperly cooked or handled food. Research the illness to find out how it is caused, its symptoms, and ways to prevent it. Present your findings in class.

2. In teams of three or four, choose a dish to prepare. Then create a work plan for your team, including all the steps outlined in Lesson 5 of this chapter. If possible, prepare your dish in the foods lab.

Family & Community

1. Choose a restaurant to visit, and evaluate it for cleanliness and safety. Rate the restaurant on a scale of 1 to 10, with 1 meaning *unacceptable* and 10 meaning *excellent*. Make a list of reasons why you chose the rating you did, and discuss them in class.

2. Go through your kitchen with a parent or another older relative. Have that person explain or demonstrate how to use any tools or equipment with which you are not familiar. Based on what you learned in this chapter, discuss items you would recommend purchasing for the kitchen.

Building A Portfolio

1. Evaluate your safety consciousness and cleanliness when working in the kitchen at home. Do you handle, prepare, and cook food as discussed in the text? How do you store leftovers? Do you have safe work habits? Write down your answers to these questions and suggest improvements. Put your assessment in your portfolio.

2. Think of a situation in your life in which you work as part of a team. Evaluate your behavior as a team member. Are you cooperative? Do you contribute as much to the group effort as others do? Are you responsible, prompt, and good at following directions? Write a summary of your strengths and weaknesses, and keep it in your portfolio.

CHAPTER

13 Preparing to Cook

LESSON ONE
Planning a Menu

LESSON TWO
Food Shopping and Storage

LESSON THREE
Following Recipes and Directions

LESSON FOUR
Measuring Ingredients

TEENS MAKING A DIFFERENCE

Community Food Drive

Boy Scout Troop 196 decided to sponsor a food drive to benefit a food pantry for needy families. First the Scouts persuaded a supermarket to donate grocery bags. Then they wrote a letter about the food drive, saying that donations should be nutritious, nonperishable, and easy to store.

The Scouts stapled a copy of the letter to every grocery bag and delivered a bag to each house in the community. Residents were asked to fill the bag and leave it on their doorsteps the next week. When the Scouts returned, they collected 1,200 pounds of groceries for the pantry!

Try THIS!

Make a list of food products that would be good donations for this type of drive. Then work with your classmates to compile a master list to use for your school's next food drive.

Planning a Menu

WORDS TO KNOW

appetizer

meal pattern

texture

garnish

time schedule

DISCOVER...

- how to plan balanced meals that fit your lifestyle.
- the importance of variety in meal planning.
- how to evaluate your available resources.

Whether you are throwing a birthday party for a friend or cooking a meal for your family, it is best to start by making a plan. Serving tasty, attractive, and nutritious meals requires more than just being a good cook. It takes management skills.

The first step in creating a meal is planning ahead. It is best to plan all your meals for an entire day. This way, you can be sure that you are getting the right number of calories and enough servings from each food group.

The Planning Stage

As you plan your menu, think of meals that are simple and nutritious. Include a variety of foods, and consider your skills, time, and money. Plan your meals around the Food Guide Pyramid and your own eating patterns.

Meals are more enjoyable if the table is attractive and properly set. What guidelines do you follow when setting your table?

Using the Food Guide Pyramid

You learned in Chapter 11, Lesson 1, that the Food Guide Pyramid divides foods into five basic groups. For good nutrition, you should plan meals that include foods from each group.

- **The Bread, Cereal, Rice, and Pasta Group.** You need 6 to 11 servings every day. Some foods in this group, such as pasta, can be used as the basis of a main dish. Others, such as rice and bread, are usually served as side dishes.

TIPS for living

SETTING THE TABLE

Setting the table is an important part of meal preparation. Follow these guidelines to set a formal table.

- If you use a tablecloth, spread it over the table evenly and smoothly.
- If you use place mats, position them near the edge of the table.
- Center the plates on the place mats or at each place on the tablecloth.
- Place a knife to the right of each plate and a fork to the left of each plate. The cutting edge of the knife should be turned toward the plate.
- Place a spoon to the right of each knife.
- Set a water or beverage glass near the tip of each knife.
- Place a napkin beside each fork.
- If using a salad or bread-and-butter plate place it near the tip of each fork.

Practicing Good Table Manners

The next time you sit down to a meal with your family or friends, you can show good manners by following these rules.

- Avoid putting your elbows on the table.
- Lift the food to your mouth instead of lowering your head.
- Don't talk with your mouth full.
- Ask someone to pass food that is out of your reach.
- Lay your knife and fork across the center of your plate when you finish eating.
- Lay your napkin neatly beside your plate when the meal is over.

- **The Vegetable Group.** Three to five servings are needed every day. Raw vegetables can be eaten as a salad, a snack, or an **appetizer**—*a dish served before the meal.* Raw or cooked vegetables can be served as a side dish.

- **The Fruit Group.** From this group, you need two to four servings every day. These may include fresh, frozen, dried, and canned fruit as well as fruit juice. Fruit can be part of any meal.

- **The Milk, Yogurt, and Cheese Group.** As a growing teen, you need three servings every day. Foods from this group can accompany any meal.

- **The Meat, Poultry, Fish, Dry Beans, Eggs, and Nuts Group.** Two to three servings are needed every day. Foods from this group are usually served as the main dish in a meal.

Analyzing Your Meal Pattern

Most people follow a **meal pattern,** or *habit that determines when and what they eat each day.* They may eat a main meal at noon or in the evening. They usually select similar types of foods each day for breakfast, lunch, dinner, and snacks. For example, your meal pattern for the day might be as follows:

- **Breakfast:** cereal with fruit and nuts, juice, milk

- **Lunch:** sandwich, fruit or vegetable, dessert, milk

- **Dinner:** meat or poultry, vegetable, rice or pasta, milk

- **Snack:** fruit

If you are aware of your meal pattern and use the Food Guide Pyramid, menu planning is easy. Simply choose a combination of foods from the five food groups that fit the meal pattern. To plan a lunch for the meal pattern above, you might choose a tuna salad sandwich, carrot sticks, oatmeal cookies, and milk. Meal patterns should be flexible. Your schedule may change, you may be trying to gain or lose weight, or you may be invited to eat at a friend's home.

Meal Appeal

Including a variety of foods in your meals makes eating more interesting. Meals planned with variety in mind can look and taste better. Eating many different foods also makes it easier to get all the nutrients you need. One way to add variety is to vary the way foods are prepared. Another way is to choose foods that provide different textures, colors, sizes and shapes, flavors, and temperatures.

- **Texture.** Foods with different textures add more variety. **Texture** means *the way food feels when it is eaten.* Rolls may be crusty, raw vegetables are crisp, and pudding is smooth. One way to vary the textures of foods is by preparing them in different ways. For example, think of the difference in texture between raw carrots and cooked carrots.

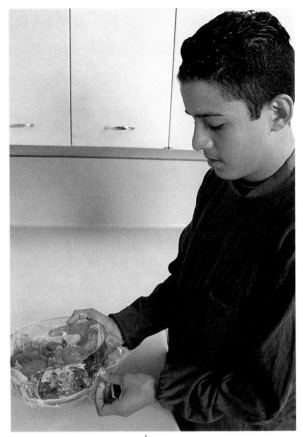

If you plan wisely, you can prepare some foods ahead of time. How would this help you?

- **Color.** Choosing foods of different colors will make the meal look more interesting. For instance, salad with green lettuce, red tomatoes, and orange carrots will add color to your meal. Adding a **garnish,** *a small amount of a food or seasoning to decorate the food,* is another way to provide more color. Parsley, lemon wedges, and orange slices are garnishes.

- **Size and Shape.** Varying the sizes and shapes of foods will give you a much more appealing meal. For example, a dinner of fish sticks, zucchini sticks, and french fries would seem dull. How would you change this menu?

- **Flavor.** Combine flavors that vary and complement each other. Turkey and mashed potatoes, steak and onions, and broccoli and cheese are some flavors that go well together.

- **Temperature.** Vary the temperatures of food in a meal. Plan some hot and some cold food.

Planning Ahead

As you plan your menus, take time to read through the recipes carefully and make sure that you have all of the resources you will need.

- **Skills.** If you are a beginning cook, you may want to avoid complicated recipes. Could you choose convenience foods for part of the meal? For instance, you might make a dessert from a mix rather than cook it from scratch.

- **Equipment.** Some recipes call for a specific utensil. Make sure that you have all of the necessary tools and equipment.

- **Ingredients.** Do you have all the ingredients the recipe calls for? If you don't, think of substitutions that could be made.

- **Money.** Do the ingredients fit your food budget? Can you save money with coupons or use foods that are less expensive because they are in season?

- **Time.** If you know that you will be working within a time frame, such as having only one hour in which to cook dinner, you must choose foods that can be prepared within the time allowed.

Using a Time Schedule

An important part of planning a meal is making a time schedule. A **time schedule** is *a plan to make sure that all foods are ready to serve at the right time.* Some dishes take longer than others to prepare, and some foods take longer than others to cook. For this reason, you must know what to do first and when to do it. A sample time schedule is shown in **Figure 13.1.**

Managing Meals

Taking time to plan ahead helps you create nutritious, attractive meals that fit your lifestyle, skills, and budget. With a little practice, the planning will become so natural that you will hardly even have to think about it.

Figure 13.1 Sample Time Schedule

Using a time schedule helps you make sure that all foods are ready at the right time.

First list the job that will take longest to do. Then list in order the other jobs to be done until you have listed them all.

Some foods take longer to cook than others, so you must plan what to do first and when to do it.

Besides cooking time, consider that some dishes take longer to prepare than others.

Don't forget to allow time for setting the table, serving the food, and cleaning up.

Plan a time schedule backward, from the end to the beginning. First decide at what time you will serve the meal. Then figure out how much time you will need to prepare each of the different foods.

It is easier to follow a time schedule if the preparation jobs are listed in the order in which they are to be done.

4:30 Start preparing chicken.
4:45 Turn on oven.
5:00 Place chicken in oven.
5:15 Wash and chop broccoli.
5:30 Begin cooking rice.
5:40 Set table.
5:50 Steam broccoli in microwave.
5:55 Remove broccoli, rice, and chicken.
6:00 Serve the meal.
6:45 Wash dishes and clean up kitchen.

LESSON ONE *Review*

Using complete sentences, answer the following questions on a separate sheet of paper.

Reviewing Terms and Facts

1. Recall Why should meal patterns be flexible?

2. List Name five ways to add variety to meals.

3. Vocabulary Define the term *texture*. Describe the textures of three different foods.

4. Name List five resources that you should consider before preparing a meal.

Thinking Critically

5. Explain What is the advantage of planning meals for a whole day?

6. Analyze Why is it important to include variety when planning meals?

Applying Concepts

7. Write down your typical meal pattern. Then plan a daily menu that follows the recommendations of the Food Guide Pyramid and fits your meal pattern.

Food Shopping and Storage

![hand icon] WORDS TO KNOW

staples

national-brand products

store-brand products

generic products

grade labeling

unit pricing

open dating

DISCOVER...

- why it is helpful to plan before you shop for food.
- how to make wise food purchases.
- how to store foods safely.

Have you ever helped with the family grocery shopping? You probably know how many different brands and food items there are to choose from. Learning good shopping skills can help you make wise food choices. You can learn how to buy foods that provide nutrition and flavor and still get the most for your money.

Before You Shop

Before you head for the store, make a list of everything you need for the meals you have planned. Review the recipes, and don't forget to check your staple foods. **Staples** are *foods that you are likely to use often.* Examples of staples include milk, eggs, salt, and pepper.

You can save money by adjusting your menus to take advantage of weekly specials. Check supermarket advertisements in your local newspaper to find out what items are on sale.

Smart Shopping

Learning how to find the best buys is an important part of being a smart shopper. Some brands are better buys than others. Store brands and generic products, for example, are usually less expensive than national brands.

- **National-brand products** are *those products that you see advertised on television or in newspapers or magazines.* These products often cost more than others because the manufacturer spends a great deal of money on advertising. This advertising cost is added to the price of the product.

- **Store-brand products** are *foods and household items that have the store's name or another name used only by that store on the label.* They usually cost less because there is little or no advertising cost. They often have the same ingredients and nutrients as national brands.

- **Generic products** are *products with labels listing only the product name and nutritional information.* These cost even less than store-brand products.

Clipping coupons is one way to make the most of your family's food dollars. What are some other ways?

The next time you go to the supermarket, remember these rules of shopping etiquette.

- Handle food items with care, especially fruits and vegetables.
- Don't open a container until you have paid for the item.
- If you decide that you don't want an item, put it back where you got it.
- Return shopping carts to their appropriate place. What can you add to this list?

It takes practice to find which brands give you the most for your money. You will want to compare national-brand, store-brand, and generic products to see which ones you prefer.

Understanding Grade Labeling

Understanding and using grade labeling can also help you when you shop. **Grade labeling** is *a measurement of food quality using standards set by the government.* Many food items—including eggs, poultry, and meat—are graded. The highest grade is the highest in quality. For example, Grade AA eggs are of higher quality than Grade A eggs.

Reading Food Labels

Food labels also give you valuable shopping information. By law, food labels must provide the following:

- The name of the food
- The name and address of the product's manufacturer
- The nutritional content, including serving size, calories, and nutrient amounts per serving
- A list of ingredients in order of amount (so that a dry cereal might list oat flour first, then sugar, followed by

Higher grades of meat may have a better flavor than lower grades, but they are more expensive.

other ingredients, to show that oat flour is the main ingredient, then sugar, and so on)

- The total weight

Labels give other helpful information as well. **Figure 13.2** shows a sample label and the kinds of information provided.

You can use the weight and volume information on the label to compare quantities and find the best buy. For

Figure 13.2 Nutrition Facts

A great deal of important information is provided on the Nutrition Facts label. How much fat does one serving of this product contain?

1. Serving size is an important reference because calorie and nutrient content are based on this amount. Foods that are similar, such as breakfast cereals, will have similar serving sizes.

2. Knowing the number of calories from fat can help you meet Dietary Guidelines. These guidelines state that 30 percent or less of your daily calories should come from fat.

Nutrition Facts
Serving Size 1 cup (228g)
Servings Per Container 2

Amount Per Serving

Calories 250   Calories from Fat 110

	% of Daily Value
Total Fat 12g	18%
Saturated Fat 3g	15%
Cholesterol 30mg	10%
Sodium 470mg	20%
Total Carbohydrate 31g	10%
Dietary Fiber 0g	0%
Sugars 5g	
Protein 5g	

Vitamin A 4%	•	Vitamin C	2%
Calcium 20%	•	Iron	4%

Percent Daily Values are based on a 2000 calorie diet. Your daily values may be higher or lower depending on your calorie needs.

	Calories	2,000	2,500
Total Fat	Less than	65g	80g
Sat Fat	Less than	20g	25g
Cholesterol	Less than	300mg	300mg
Sodium	Less than	2,400mg	2400mg
Total Carbohydrate		300g	375g
Dietary Fiber		25g	30g

Calories per gram:
Fat 9 • Carbohydrate 4 • Protein 4

3. Percent Daily Values are based on a diet of 2,000 calories a day. You can adjust the Percent Daily Values to your own diet and calorie intake.

4. Nutrient content is provided in metric amounts (grams or milligrams) and by Percent Daily Values. This information is useful for comparing foods.

5. Information about certain nutrients is required on the label. These nutrients are total fat, saturated fat, cholesterol, sodium, total carbohydrate, dietary fiber, sugars, protein, vitamins A and C, calcium, and iron.

6. A reference chart provides information for both 2,000- and 2,500-calorie diets. The chart shows the highest amount of total fat, saturated fat, cholesterol, and sodium that a person should consume. It also shows the ideal intake for total carbohydrate and dietary fiber.

7. Some labels show the number of calories supplied by one gram of fat, carbohydrate, and protein.

example, which is a better value—a 1-pound (500-gram) bag of tortilla chips for $1.99 or an 11-ounce (300-gram) bag for $1.49?

Unit pricing makes these kinds of price comparisons simpler. **Unit pricing** means *showing the cost of the product per unit.* Examples of units include ounce, pound, gram, liter, and gallon. Look for the unit pricing label on the front of the store shelf. It will give you the product name, the size, and the price per unit. You can easily decide which size is the best buy.

Checking for Freshness

Products that are packaged fresh—such as bread, milk, yogurt, and meat—also have a date on their labels. **Open dating** is *the display of a freshness date on packaged food.* The date shown is generally the last day a food may be sold as fresh.

Before purchasing dairy products, check the open dating to be sure that the food is fresh. What happens to the food after that date?

Shopping for Quality

There is more to smart shopping then just reading the labels. You need to know how to judge food quality and safety, too. Here are some tips to remember.

- Buy meat, poultry, and fish that is wrapped in fresh, undamaged packaging material.

- Buy fresh fruits and vegetables in season that are firm and do not have spots.

- Never buy dented or bulging cans. The food may be spoiled.

- Pick up frozen and refrigerated foods last.

Food Storage

When you get home from the supermarket, you will need to store the food you bought. Heat, light, time, and moisture destroy vitamins. They can also affect the flavor and spoil foods. Storing foods properly helps them keep their freshness, flavor, and nutrients.

Refrigerated and Frozen Foods

The first foods you should put away are frozen foods. Put them in the freezer so that they won't thaw out. Place perishable foods in the refrigerator immediately too. Perishable foods are those that spoil quickly without refrigeration. Milk, meat, poultry, and fish should be stored in the back of the refrigerator—the coldest part.

If fresh meat is to be frozen, remove the store wrapping and wrap the meat in special freezer paper. You can also put meat in a plastic bag made for freezing or wrap it in heavy aluminum foil. Eggs should be kept in the egg carton.

Fresh Fruits and Vegetables

Most fruits need to be stored in the refrigerator. Salad vegetables, such as lettuce and celery, should be stored in plastic wrap, bags, or containers in the refrigerator. Before storing root vegetables—carrots and radishes, for instance—remove any tops. Certain vegetables, such as potatoes and whole onions, can be stored in a vegetable bin in a cool, dry place. Wash all fruits and vegetables well before cooking or eating them.

Nonperishable Foods

Nonperishable foods are usually packaged in cans, bottles, or boxes. They may include soup, tuna, bottled beverages, pasta, and cake mix. These foods should be stored in a cabinet where they will stay cool and dry. As you unpack groceries, move the older nonperishable items to the front of the shelf and place the newest items at the back. This helps keep your food supply fresh by making sure that the older items get used first.

Once they are opened, many nonperishable items become perishable. Mayonnaise, salad dressing, and spaghetti sauce can be stored in a cool cabinet only until they are opened. After that, they should be kept tightly covered in the refrigerator. Refrigerate bottles of juice, jams and jellies, ketchup, and mustard after they are opened as well.

Use these tips to get the most from your family's food budget. Don't shop when you are hungry. If you do, you may buy items that you don't need. Use coupons. Some stores double the face value of manufacturers' coupons. Take advantage of sales.

When storing nonperishable foods, rotate the oldest items to the front of the shelf. Why is this important? ▶

A Well-Stocked Kitchen

Knowing how to shop wisely and store food correctly will make meal preparation easier. You will have the ingredients you need, ready to use, when you begin cooking. You can serve tasty and nutritious meals while also making the most of your food dollars.

LESSON TWO *Review*

Using complete sentences, answer the following questions on a separate sheet of paper.

Reviewing Terms and Facts

1. Vocabulary Define the term *staples*. Give three examples of staples.

2. Contrast What is the difference between a store brand and a generic product?

3. List Name four types of information that are provided on a food label.

4. Identify List four tips for judging food quality and safety.

5. Recall When unpacking groceries, what foods should you store first? Explain your answer.

Thinking Critically

6. Explain How can you use unit pricing to save money?

7. Analyze Do you think that all food labels should contain open dating? Why or why not?

Applying Concepts

8. Ask two or three adults for tips on judging freshness, quality, and value when food shopping. Compare your findings with those of your classmates. Then compile a master list of the most popular tips.

Following Recipes and Directions

DISCOVER...

- how to follow different recipe formats.
- the meanings of abbreviations and preparation terms.
- how to prepare convenience foods.

Just about everyone knows how to cook something. Maybe you're a whiz at scrambled eggs or pancakes. Perhaps you are already in charge of preparing entire meals once in a while. Whatever level of experience you have in the kitchen, this lesson will help you improve your cooking skills.

WORDS TO KNOW

recipe

yield

standard format

narrative format

convenience foods

The Importance of Recipes

Almost all good cooks use recipes. A **recipe** is *a list of ingredients and directions for preparing a specific food.* If you

You can find recipes in cookbooks or magazines, or by asking friends and relatives. Start a recipe file or notebook in which to keep your favorites.

know how to read and follow recipes, you will greatly increase your chances of success in the kitchen.

Not all recipes are written in the same way. Some are easier to follow than others. While you are learning to cook, look for simple, easy-to-read recipes that

- list the necessary ingredients.
- state the amount of each ingredient.
- provide step-by-step instructions on how to combine the ingredients.
- mention the sizes of pans that will be needed.
- specify the cooking time and temperature.
- estimate the **yield,** or *the number of servings.*

Look at the recipes on page 375. Which would be easier for you to follow? Can you find each of the parts of a recipe mentioned above in the one you chose?

Recipe Formats

The type of recipe you will see most often is the standard format. A recipe in a **standard format** is *a list of all the ingredients in order of use and step-by-step directions for preparing the food.* **Figure 13.3** shows a recipe in this format.

Figure 13.3 shows the same recipe in a **narrative format,** or *a paragraph description of the steps and ingredients in order of use.* This format is sometimes used in newspapers and magazines because it takes up less space.

Whatever the recipe format, the procedure for following the recipe remains the same. Here are some general guidelines for using recipes. Read through the entire recipe. Make sure that you understand all the terms and abbreviations. Then, assemble all the ingredients and equipment before you start. Next, do any necessary preparation, such as turning on the oven or greasing the pan.

The Language of Recipes

Recipes have their own special language. To be able to follow them, you need to know some common cooking terms and abbreviations.

Preparation and Cooking Terms

You probably already know the meaning of some of the words used in recipes. *Boil* and *bake* are cooking terms that are easy to understand. However, can you explain the

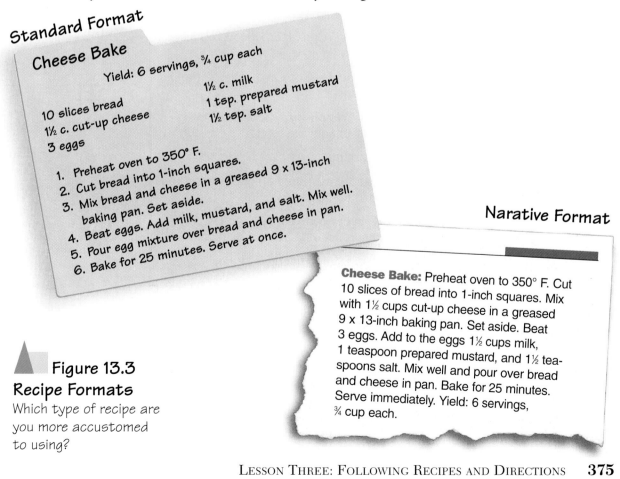

Standard Format

Cheese Bake

Yield: 6 servings, ¾ cup each

10 slices bread
1½ c. cut-up cheese
3 eggs

1½ c. milk
1 tsp. prepared mustard
1½ tsp. salt

1. Preheat oven to 350° F.
2. Cut bread into 1-inch squares.
3. Mix bread and cheese in a greased 9 x 13-inch baking pan. Set aside.
4. Beat eggs. Add milk, mustard, and salt. Mix well.
5. Pour egg mixture over bread and cheese in pan.
6. Bake for 25 minutes. Serve at once.

Narative Format

Cheese Bake: Preheat oven to 350° F. Cut 10 slices of bread into 1-inch squares. Mix with 1½ cups cut-up cheese in a greased 9 x 13-inch baking pan. Set aside. Beat 3 eggs. Add to the eggs 1½ cups milk, 1 teaspoon prepared mustard, and 1½ teaspoons salt. Mix well and pour over bread and cheese in pan. Bake for 25 minutes. Serve immediately. Yield: 6 servings, ¾ cup each.

Figure 13.3
Recipe Formats
Which type of recipe are you more accustomed to using?

Figure 13.4
Common
Cooking Terms

There are many ways to cook foods. Which is your favorite method for cooking chicken? Meat? Vegetables?

difference between *simmering* and *steaming?* **Figure 13.4** illustrates many commonly used cooking terms.

It is equally important to understand preparation terms. For example, do you know how to *shred* cabbage? Can you describe how *chopping* differs from *mincing?* **Figure 13.5** explains the meaning of common preparation terms.

Bake—Cook in the oven in dry heat without a cover. Usually refers to cakes, pies, and breads.

Boil—Cook in liquid hot enough to bubble rapidly.

Braise—Simmer gently in a small amount of liquid in a covered pan. Meat may be browned first.

Broil—Cook under direct heat.

Brown—Cook in a small amount of fat over high heat to brown the surface.

Chill—Put in the refrigerator until cold.

Cook—Prepare food by dry heat, moist heat, or direct heat.

Cook by dry heat—Cook food uncovered without adding any liquid.

Cook by moist heat—Cook in a covered pan with added liquid.

Deep-fat-fry or French-fry—Cook in fat deep enough to cover or float the food.

Fry—Cook in hot fat.

Preheat—Heat the oven to the right temperature before putting in the food.

Roast—Cook in the oven in dry heat. Usually refers to meat.

Sauté—Fry in a small amount of fat until done.

Scald—Heat milk until it steams and just begins to bubble around the edge of the pan.

Simmer—Cook to just below the boiling point. The liquid will just barely bubble.

Steam—Cook by steam over boiling water.

Stew—Cook slowly in liquid.

Stir fry—Cook quickly in a small amount of fat at high heat.

Figure 13.5
Common Preparation Terms

Which of these preparation methods have you used?

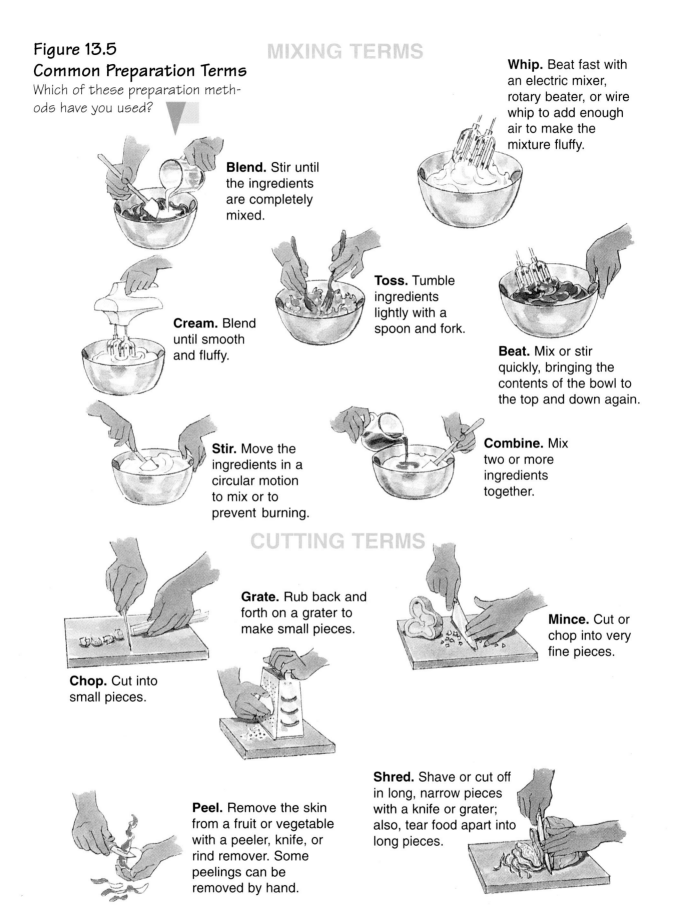

Blend. Stir until the ingredients are completely mixed.

Whip. Beat fast with an electric mixer, rotary beater, or wire whip to add enough air to make the mixture fluffy.

Cream. Blend until smooth and fluffy.

Toss. Tumble ingredients lightly with a spoon and fork.

Beat. Mix or stir quickly, bringing the contents of the bowl to the top and down again.

Stir. Move the ingredients in a circular motion to mix or to prevent burning.

Combine. Mix two or more ingredients together.

CUTTING TERMS

Grate. Rub back and forth on a grater to make small pieces.

Mince. Cut or chop into very fine pieces.

Chop. Cut into small pieces.

Shred. Shave or cut off in long, narrow pieces with a knife or grater; also, tear food apart into long pieces.

Peel. Remove the skin from a fruit or vegetable with a peeler, knife, or rind remover. Some peelings can be removed by hand.

CUSTOMARY

teaspoon . . . . tsp. (or t.)

tablespoon . . . . Tbsp. (or T.)

cup . . . . c. (or C.)

pint . . . . pt.

quart . . . . qt.

gallon . . . . gal.

ounce . . . . oz.

pound . . . . lb.

degrees Fahrenheit . . . . °F

METRIC

milliliter . . . . mL

liter L

gram . . . . g

degrees Celsius . . . . °C

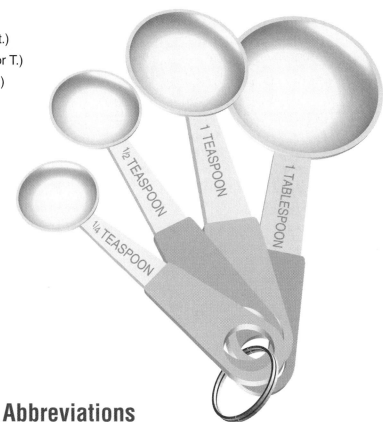

Figure 13.6

Common Abbreviations

Why is it important to understand these common abbreviations?

Abbreviations

Recipes often show measurements in shortened form to save space. To follow the recipe, it is essential to understand what the abbreviations mean. **Figure 13.6** explains the customary and metric abbreviations most often used. Abbreviations for "teaspoon" and "tablespoon" can be confusing, so be sure that you know the difference. Can you imagine how your vegetable soup would taste if you added one tablespoon of salt instead of one teaspoon?

The Basic Ingredients

Now that you know how to read a recipe, you are ready to begin combining the ingredients. Remember that the success of your dish depends in part on following step-by-step instructions. As you learn to cook, you will notice that a few common ingredients are found in most recipes. These basic ingredients are flour, sugar, shortening (fats such as butter, oil, or margarine), milk, eggs, and spices. Each ingredient in a recipe is used for a specific purpose. Leaving one out could ruin the dish.

Using Packaged Foods

Sometimes you may want to use convenience foods when you cook. **Convenience foods** are *foods that are already partly prepared to save you time.* For instance, you might buy a bag of tossed salad instead of purchasing all the ingredients and cutting them up yourself. One common type of convenience food is a mix. Many people use cake and muffin mixes instead of baking from scratch. Using instant pudding mix is quicker than cooking pudding.

Following Package Directions

When you use convenience foods, you should follow the directions given on the package, just the way you would any other recipe. Make sure that you have all the ingredients and utensils you will need and that you understand all the instructions.

If you are using a general-purpose baking mix, use only the recipes provided on the box. Don't try to substitute the mix for ingredients in another recipe.

Convenience foods can cut preparation time. Why is it important to read and follow the package directions?

LESSON THREE *Review*

Using complete sentences, answer the following questions on a separate sheet of paper.

Reviewing Terms and Facts

1. List Name five pieces of information that a good recipe should give you.

2. Vocabulary What are the two types of *recipe formats?*

3. Identify Give the meaning of the following abbreviations: *tsp., Tbsp., mL, L.*

4. Recall Define the word *yield,* and use it in an original sentence.

Thinking Critically

5. Analyze What problems might result if you didn't read through an entire recipe before starting to cook?

6. Compare Explain the differences among chopping, grating, and shredding.

7. Evaluate What are some advantages of using convenience foods? What might be some disadvantages?

Applying Concepts

8. Create a cookbook of your family's recipes. Can you find out exactly what makes Grandpa's spaghetti sauce so good, or why the French toast always tastes better when your sister makes it? Write down your family's special recipes in a notebook. Decorate the cover with a drawing or a family snapshot.

Measuring Ingredients

WORDS TO KNOW

metric measurement

customary measurement

graduated measuring cups

leavening agent

DISCOVER...

- customary and metric units of measure.
- the best measuring tool for each job.
- techniques for measuring dry and liquid ingredients.

Recipes your great-grandparents might have used were not always precise in their measurements. Long ago, recipes often called for "butter the size of a walnut," a "scant cup of sugar," or "two handfuls of flour." These measurements worked all right for experienced cooks, but they must have been pretty difficult for beginners! Fortunately, modern recipes are much more precise. They tell us the exact amount of each ingredient to use.

Measure Up

By measuring accurately, using the proper measuring tools, and following directions, you will ensure that your recipes turn out the same every time you use them. You will also gain the confidence to try new dishes.

Types of Measurement

You have probably studied metric measurement in math and used it in your science classes. **Metric measurement** is *a system of measurements based on multiples of ten.* Some metric units used in cooking are liters and milliliters for volume and grams and kilograms for weight. When you cook, you will probably use *traditional units of measure,* or **customary measurement.** Examples of customary units used in cooking are fluid ounces and cups for volume, and ounces and pounds for weight. **Figure 13.7** shows equivalent measurements in the two systems.

Figure 13.7 Equivalent Measurements
You may use any of these three different types of measurements when you cook. What types of recipes may use metric measurements?

Customary	Customary Equiv.	Approximate Metric Equiv.
1 teaspoon	⅓ tablespoon	5 milliliters
1 tablespoon	3 teaspoons	15 milliliters
½ cup	8 tablespoons	125 milliliters
1 cup	16 tablespoons 8 fluid ounces	250 milliliters
2 cups	1 pint	500 milliliters
4 cups	1 quart	1000 milliliters or 1 liter
1 pound	16 ounces	500 grams

Try This!

Adding seasonings will make almost any food taste better. Try one of the following in your own cooking: Fresh mint, ginger, basil, sage, or thyme.

You might even try growing your own herbs.

Some recipes show ingredients in both metric and customary amounts. You can use either system, as long as you have the right measuring utensils.

Measuring Equipment

The right kinds of measuring equipment make cooking easier. Here are several items you will want to have handy.

- **Graduated measuring cups** are *sets of measuring cups in commonly used sizes.* They are also called dry measuring cups because they are usually used to measure dry ingredients, such as flour, sugar, and oats. Customary measuring cups usually come in sets of four: ¼ cup, ⅓ cup, ½ cup, and 1 cup. A set of metric dry measures usually includes 50 mL, 125 mL, and 250 mL sizes.

- **Liquid measuring cups** are used to measure such ingredients as milk, water, and oil. These cups are usually made of glass or clear plastic so that you can accurately see the amount of liquid. They have a handle, a pouring spout, and space beyond the top measuring line to allow for a full measure without danger of spilling. Liquid measuring cups are marked on the side with specific graduated amounts.

- **Measuring spoons** are used to measure smaller amounts of all types of ingredients. A typical set of customary measuring spoons includes ¼ teaspoon, ½ teaspoon, 1 teaspoon, and 1 tablespoon. Metric measuring spoons include 1 mL, 5 mL, 15 mL, and 25 mL.

Using the right measuring utensil will make cooking easier. Which of these tools are used to measure dry ingredients? Liquid ingredients?

Measuring Techniques

The reason you need many tools is that different ingredients require different measuring techniques. Knowing the proper technique to use is just as important as having the right equipment. **Figure 13.8** shows how to measure some common ingredients.

Figure 13.8 Measuring Basics

Learning how to measure different types of ingredients will help you prepare successful meals. Which of these measuring techniques have you used?

Butter and margarine. The wrappers on a stick of butter or margarine are marked in tablespoons. Just cut off the amount you need.

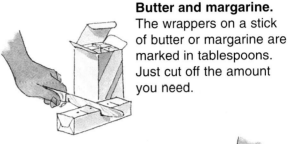

Flour. Presifted and whole-wheat flour must be stirred with a fork before measuring. Regular flour may have tiny lumps and must be sifted first. In all cases carefully spoon the flour into the dry measuring cup. Level off with a metal spatula or the back of a knife. Avoid tapping a cup to level flour because that packs it again.

Granulated sugar. Fill the dry measuring cup to overflowing, and level off with a metal spatula or knife.

Shortening. To measure shortening, press it into a dry measuring cup, making sure there are no air pockets. Level with a metal spatula. Remove shortening with a rubber spatula.

Brown sugar. Pack brown sugar in a dry measuring cup until the sugar holds its shape. Level the top with a knife or metal spatula. Do not use hard lumps. You can soften hard lumps by heating them for a short time in the oven or a microwave.

Liquids. Place the liquid measuring cup on a flat surface, pour to the marker line, and check it at eye level. For smaller amounts, dip the measuring spoon into the liquid.

Leavening agents and spices. Baking powder and baking soda are two types of **leavening agents,** which are *ingredients that make baked foods rise.* Baking powder, baking soda, and spices must be stirred first to remove any lumps. Dip in the measuring spoon, and then level.

Confectioner's sugar. Sift the sugar before measuring. Spoon it into a dry measuring cup, and level off.

Accuracy in Measuring

While you are still a beginner, it is best to measure all ingredients exactly. As you become more experienced, you will discover where and when it is safe to be less precise.

Some foods—such as cakes, cookies, and other baked goods—require accurate measurements for good results. If ingredients are not measured accurately, the cake may not rise or the cookies may spread and burn. With other foods—such as soups, stews, and casseroles—it is not necessary to be quite so careful. In these cases you can more easily experiment and add leftovers. For example, if you are making beef vegetable soup, you can add small amounts of leftover vegetables in addition to the ingredients the recipe calls for.

When you want to be sure that your recipe will come out just right, it is always best to be accurate. That means using the right tools and the right techniques. Then you can be sure of getting the right result—a successful product.

Measuring accurately is essential to success in the kitchen. What might happen if this teen did not measure accurately?

LESSON FOUR *Review*

Using complete sentences, answer the following questions on a separate sheet of paper.

Reviewing Terms and Facts

1. Vocabulary What is the difference between *metric measurement* and *customary measurement?*

2. Recall What units are used to measure weight, volume, and temperature in the metric measuring system?

3. List Name three common types of measuring equipment.

4. Give Examples Name three ingredients that could be measured in a liquid measuring cup.

Thinking Critically

5. Compare Explain the differences between dry and liquid measuring cups.

6. Explain What types of food require the most accurate measurements? Why?

Applying Concepts

7. With a partner, take turns demonstrating the proper measuring technique for two of the ingredients mentioned in this lesson. Ask your partner to assess your technique based on the instructions in the text.

TECHNOLOGY
High-tech Packages

New high-tech food packaging will not only protect and identify products but also may have an effect on the food it contains. For example, when a package of potato nuggets is placed in a microwave oven, special sensors inside the package will heat up to make the nuggets brown and crispy.

Try This!

Imagine that you could improve a food package in any way that you choose. Explain what you would change.

A Global View CHOOSING FOOD

Do you know anyone who goes to a market or grocery store every day? It's most likely that you don't. In some cultures, however, it is common for people to shop for food every day. Often they may not even have access to refrigerators or freezers to store their food.

TRY THIS!

Research a culture and plan a menu for a nutritious main meal in that culture's ethnic tradition.

Consumer Focus

Food Shopping Lures

Some food-store managers give out free samples of snack foods as well as coupons for those products. Impulse items, such as candy and magazines, are displayed in checkout lanes. These techniques can lure shoppers into buying items they may not want or need.

Try This!

What can you do to resist impulse buying? First, make a shopping list before you go to the store. Once you're in the store, stick to your list.

MATH CONNECTION

RECIPE CONVERSIONS

Recipes are written to yield a certain number of servings. You can make more or less of a dish by converting, or changing, the amount of each ingredient. This is called recipe conversion. To increase the number of servings, multiply all the ingredients by the same number. To decrease, divide all the ingredients by the same number.

Follow Up

1. Look at the Cheese Bake recipe on page 375. Convert the recipe so that it yields twice as many servings.

2. Find a recipe that yields an average number of servings (for example, six or eight). Convert the recipe so that it yields twice as many servings. Then convert the recipe so that it yields half as many servings. Exchange recipes with your classmates for more practice in recipe conversion.

Chapter Summary

- It is best to plan meals ahead of time. Remember to follow the Food Guide Pyramid and try to keep your meal patterns flexible.

- For variety in your meals, choose foods that have different textures, colors, sizes and shapes, flavors, and temperatures.

- Good shopping skills include planning before you shop and choosing the best buys. Smart shopping makes meal preparation easier and saves money.

- Storing foods properly helps prevent spoiling.

- A recipe is a list of ingredients and directions for preparing a specific food.

Recipes are written in either standard or narrative format.

- To follow a recipe, you must understand common abbreviations and cooking terms.

- If you use convenience foods, the work of preparation has been partially done to save you time. You need to follow the package directions, just as you would follow a recipe.

- There are several basic types of measuring tools: graduated, or dry, measuring cups; liquid measuring cups; and measuring spoons.

- There are different ways to measure different types of ingredients. It is important to learn how to measure accurately.

▶ Words to Know

Using complete sentences, answer the following questions on a separate sheet of paper.

1. Explain what is meant by the *texture* of food. Give two examples.

2. Why might you add a *garnish* to food?

3. Describe what a *time schedule* for meal preparation should include.

4. What are *staples?* Give an example.

5. Explain the purpose of *grade labeling*.

6. What is meant by *open dating* on food products?

7. What does *yield* mean on a recipe?

8. How is a recipe in *standard format* different from a recipe in *narrative format?*

▶ Review Questions

Using complete sentences, answer the following questions on a separate sheet of paper.

1. What are three ways to use management skills in meal preparation?

2. Why is it important to include variety in meals?

3. What are three ways to save money when shopping for groceries?

4. Explain how you would store each of the following foods: an unopened jar of spaghetti

sauce, a head of lettuce, a carton of ice cream, an opened jar of mayonnaise, and eggs.

5. List five preparation terms and five cooking terms you might see in a recipe.

6. What technique is recommended for measuring dry ingredients?

▶ Thinking Critically

Using complete sentences, answer the following questions on a separate sheet of paper.

1. **Analyze** Think about the ways to ensure variety in meals—texture, color, size and shape, flavor, and temperature. Which of these do you think is most important to vary for an appealing meal? Which do you think is least important to vary? Explain your answers.

2. **Suggest** When might lower-grade food products be preferable to higher-grade food products?

3. **Explain** Why are sets of dry measuring cups called *graduated* cups? Why don't dry measuring cups have extra space for overflow?

▶ Cooperative Learning

1. Working in a small group, conduct a nutrient review. Have each group member bring a Nutrition Facts label to class. Then have each person select a nutrient from the label and tell the group about food sources of the nutrient, its benefits to health, and the effects of eating too much or too little of it.

2. Make a class cookbook. Have everyone contribute a favorite recipe. Write all the recipes in standard format, and use correct abbreviations.

Make sure that directions are clear and complete. Divide the responsibilities for compiling and distributing the cookbook.

Family & Community

1. With a parent or another adult in your family, make a weekly meal plan for your household. Work together to make a shopping list, and shop for the food items you need. Use the information on product labels and unit pricing to help you select items. Be sure to store the groceries properly when you return from the supermarket. Write a summary of your planning session and shopping trip.

2. Make a directory of neighborhood food stores that could be helpful to someone new to your community. Include wholesale grocery stores, large supermarkets, convenience stores, specialty stores, and farmers' markets. Explain the advantages and disadvantages of each type of store.

Building A Portfolio

1. Write a story about your favorite childhood memory of food. You might describe the first time you tried to cook something by yourself, or you could tell about learning to cook with a family member. What did you cook? Exchange and discuss stories with a classmate. Then put your story in your portfolio.

2. Start a file of menu ideas. Be sure that each menu includes a variety of foods, textures, colors, sizes and shapes, flavors, and temperatures. Keep your file in your portfolio.

Let's Cook

TEENS MAKING A DIFFERENCE

School Bake Sale

Last fall the students at Lincoln Middle School planned several events to raise money for the school's computer lab. Angela Martinez and her friends volunteered to put on a bake sale. They arranged to hold the sale at a shopping mall near their school. Then they sent flyers home with the students, asking families to donate baked goods.

On the morning of the sale, the teens set up card tables for the baked goods and made price tags. By early afternoon, the bake sale had sold out with profits of more than $500. Just a few more bake sales, thought Angela, and the school could buy a new computer!

Try THIS!

Locate four recipes for baked goods that you feel would be popular and appropriate to make for a bake sale. Compare recipes with your classmates.

LESSON ONE
Fruits

WORDS TO KNOW

produce

seasonal

processed

DISCOVER...

● how to choose fruit.

● ways to cook fruit.

● how to serve fruit.

Every June, Lauren and her father go to the local straw-berry fields and fill buckets with freshly picked strawberries. In addition to eating some of the strawberries plain, they make their own strawberry jam and pies, use some berries in fruit salad, and freeze some for later use. Of all the fresh fruit Lauren eats in the summer, strawberries are her favorite.

Fruit—From Appetizers to Desserts

Besides tasting great, fruit provides important vitamins and minerals, carbohydrates, and fiber. It's easy to get the recommended number of daily servings because fruit goes well with any meal or snack. Vanessa likes to eat dried fruit on her breakfast cereal. Luke enjoys an apple or orange with his lunch.

Choosing Fruit

You can buy fruit in many different forms. Most supermarkets carry frozen, canned, and dried fruit in addition to the fresh fruit found in the produce section. **Produce** means *fresh fruits and vegetables.* When selecting produce, be sure that it is truly fresh and in good condition. Damaged fruit loses nutrients and will not keep well. **Figure 14.1** explains how to choose fruit.

**Figure 14.1
Buying Fresh Fruit**
The next time you select fresh fruit, follow these guidelines.

- ☞ **Test a fruit by pressing it gently. Choose fruit that feels firm but not hard.**

- ☞ **Avoid fruits that look dry or withered, or that feel especially soft or hard.**

- ☞ **Look for fruit that has a good color. Avoid fruits that have spots or bruises.**

- ☞ **Look at the shape of the fruit. If it appears misshapen, it may not taste good.**

- ☞ **Smell fruits that have a hard rind, such as cantaloupe. Ripe fruits usually have a pleasant smell.**

- ☞ **Check the heaviness of fruit. If it feels heavy, it is usually juicy.**

Some produce, like Lauren's strawberries, is **seasonal,** or *more plentiful, more readily available, and less expensive at certain times of the year.* When you buy produce in season, you get the best possible quality while also saving money. Produce that is available out of season may be more expensive and less nutritious because it is often artificially ripened or shipped a long distance.

If fresh fruits are not available or if you want the fruit in another form, you might choose processed fruits. **Processed** means that a food is *changed from its raw form before being sold.* Fruits that are frozen, canned, or dried are considered processed, as are fruit juices.

Improvements in storage, transportation, and packaging make it possible to enjoy a variety of fresh fruits from around the world.

Cooking Fruit

Ben's grandmother likes to bake fruit for dessert. Her favorites are baked apples and baked pears. She used to bake them in a conventional oven, but now she prefers to use the microwave oven. There is no change in the color or flavor from the fresh fruit, and she knows that fewer nutrients are lost during microwave cooking as well.

Sabrina likes to cook fruit on the stove. She adds a little bit of water to her favorite fresh fruit and covers the pan with a lid. To reduce the amount of nutrients lost in cooking, she uses a heavy-bottomed pan and cooks the fruit at a low, even temperature. She refrigerates the fruit after it cools and adds it to plain yogurt for an afternoon snack.

Fruits taste and look best when they're cooked properly. During cooking, small amounts of some vitamins—B vitamins and vitamin C—are lost. Some dissolve in water, and some are destroyed by heat and air. To minimize nutrient loss, use low heat and as little water as possible.

Serving Fruit

The ways in which you can serve fruit are limited only by your taste and imagination. You can leave the edible skins or peels on many fresh fruits. They provide fiber as well as nutrients. Just be sure to wash fruit thoroughly under cold running water to remove dirt, bacteria, and pesticides.

You may prefer to peel your fruit before eating it. Some fruits—such as apples, bananas, pears, and peaches—darken in color if they are peeled and not eaten right away. You can prevent this discoloration by sprinkling the cut surfaces with lemon juice and wrapping the fruit in plastic or another airtight covering. You can also dip them in a bowl of water with lemon juice added.

A Healthful Treat

Fruits are an important part of a well-balanced diet. They are available in a variety of forms and are a healthful addition to any meal or snack. To get the most nutrients from the fruits you eat, be sure that they are in good condition, and prepare them properly.

When cooking fruit, use as little water as possible, and cover the pan with a lid. Why is this important?

LESSON ONE *Review*

Using complete sentences, answer the following questions on a separate sheet of paper.

Reviewing Terms and Facts

1. Recall What should you look for when selecting fresh fruits?

2. Vocabulary What is meant by the term *seasonal*? Give an example of a seasonal fruit.

3. List Name the types of processed fruits.

4. Identify When cooking fruit on the stove, how can you limit the amount of nutrient loss?

5. Explain How can you prevent fruits from darkening in color after you peel them?

Thinking Critically

6. Compare and Contrast How are fresh, frozen, canned, and dried fruits similar? How are they different?

7. Explain Why is it important to cook fruits properly?

Applying Concepts

8. Survey your friends and relatives to find out which fruits they like best. Do they have any favorite recipes? As a class, compile a list of the top five favorites. If possible, prepare one dish in class.

Vegetables

WORDS TO KNOW

casserole

salad

dressing

broth

dehydrated

DISCOVER...

- how to prepare, serve, and cook vegetables.
- how to make salads.
- ways to use vegetables in soups.

Dylan didn't like to eat vegetables until other family members started trying new and interesting ways to prepare them. Now they add vegetables to spaghetti sauce, stir-fry them with chicken and sweet-and-sour sauce, and add them to soups and muffins. Dylan likes several vegetable dishes so much that he even prepares them himself.

Vegetables—Good Anytime

Vegetables are a delicious part of a well-balanced diet. They are also valuable sources of carbohydrates, fiber, and many important vitamins and minerals. New varieties are developed every year, including miniature versions of such old favorites as squash and eggplant.

Selecting and Preparing Vegetables

Like fruits, vegetables are most nutritious when they are fresh. Although vegetables are seasonal, most are available year-round. If you prefer processed vegetables, you can usually buy them frozen, canned, or dried.

Fresh vegetables need to be refrigerated until you are ready to use them. For best results, they should be used within a few days after you buy them. Before serving fresh vegetables, wash them carefully under cold running water. If you plan to eat them raw, you may want to peel them and blot them dry. To keep raw vegetables crisp, do not wash them too far in advance of serving them.

To retain nutrients in vegetables, cook them in a microwave oven so that they need little or no water. What are some other healthful ways to cook vegetables?

Cooking Vegetables

Vegetables can retain their nutrients and keep their shape, texture, flavor, and color if they are cooked properly. To prevent vitamin and mineral loss during cooking, add as little water as possible, use a lid to speed cooking time, and avoid overcooking. Cook vegetables until they are tender and crisp, not soft, so that they keep their flavor and color.

To determine whether vegetables are overcooked, look for color changes. Vegetables that are cooked properly have a somewhat brighter color than raw ones. Green beans are bright green when they are done and olive green when they have cooked too long.

To avoid overcooking vegetables, pay attention to their color. Vegetables should be bright when they are cooked properly. Cook them just until they are tender-crisp. ▶

Try This!

New studies show that eating carrots may help to prevent certain kinds of cancer. Find out more about this link between carrots and cancer prevention, or find a magazine or newspaper article about a study related to other vegetables and the prevention of diseases. Prepare a brief written report.

Vegetables can be cooked and served as a side dish or added to other ingredients to make a main dish, such as a casserole. A **casserole** is *a combination of ingredients cooked and served in a baking dish.* There are many different ways to cook vegetables. The most common are listed below:

- **Steaming.** To steam vegetables, place them in a steamer over simmering water in a covered pan. They should not touch the water.

- **Simmering.** To simmer, cook vegetables in a small amount of liquid, just below the boiling point. Cover the pan with a tight-fitting lid. If large puffs of steam come from the pan, the water is boiling and the heat needs to be turned down.

- **Baking.** Some vegetables, such as potatoes, are baked with their skins on. Before placing them in the oven, be sure to pierce the skins several times to prevent them from bursting.

- **Frying.** Some vegetables, such as potatoes and zucchini squash, can be cooked in fat. This cooking method is not as healthful as others, however.

- **Stir-frying.** To stir-fry, cook vegetables quickly over high heat while stirring them in only a small amount of oil.

- **Microwave cooking.** You may need to cut vegetables in pieces, place them in an appropriate container, and cover them while cooking. Refer back to Chapter 12, Lesson 4, for microwave cooking techniques.

Making Delicious Salads

One popular way to eat vegetables is in salads. A **salad** is *a food or a combination of foods, usually served cold with a dressing.* A **dressing** is *a sauce that adds flavor to a dish.* Dressings may be made with oil and vinegar, yogurt, tomato sauce, or mayonnaise. Many types of ready-made salad dressings—such as ranch-style, French, and Italian—are sold in supermarkets.

Tips for Good Salads

To make fresh and delicious salads, handle the ingredients with care. Follow these guidelines:

- Keep ingredients cold until you are ready to prepare them.

- Remove discolored or bruised sections of vegetables or fruits.

- Tear tender salad greens, such as lettuce, instead of cutting them.

- Cut vegetable pieces large enough to identify but small enough so that they are bite-sized.

- Wait until just before serving the salad to add dressing, which can wilt leafy greens if added too soon.

Making Soups

How can you fit foods from all five food groups into one bowl? The answer is by

Salads are a delicious way to eat vegetables. What ingredients do you like in your salad?

making soup. Soup is a nutritious way to combine ingredients from any or all of the food groups. Soup can be hot or cold, hearty or light, and creamy or clear.

- For a main dish, try hot vegetable soup, corn chowder, or bean-and-ham soup.

- Creamy soups are hearty. Usually they contain milk and are thickened with flour. Soups of this kind should be cooked over low heat and stirred often to avoid lumping and burning.

- For a side dish, you might use beef or chicken broth. **Broth** is *the liquid left when meat, poultry, fish, or vegetables have been cooked in water.* You can add vegetables, meat, or noodles to broth to make a main dish.

Many people do not have the time to make soups from scratch. Instead, they may enjoy using convenience soups because they can simply follow the directions on the label. Soups that are **dehydrated,** or *dried so that all or most of the liquid has been taken out,* come in packets. They must have water added to them before they are heated.

LESSON TWO *Review*

Using complete sentences, answer the following questions on a separate sheet of paper.

Reviewing Terms and Facts

1. Explain How can you prevent vegetables from losing vitamins and minerals during cooking?

2. List Name six common ways to cook vegetables.

3. Identify Give three tips for making good salads.

Thinking Critically

4. Compare and Contrast Think of two methods of cooking vegetables. What are the advantages and disadvantages of each method?

5. Recommend List the different ways of preparing soup. Which would you recommend to a friend who is looking for convenience? Which would you recommend to a friend who is looking for the best flavor? Explain your choices.

Applying Concepts

6. Create your own salad recipe. Be creative and try to think of unusual combinations. Write down your recipe, labeling each ingredient by its food group. Explain what part of a meal your salad would be and what you might serve with it.

LESSON THREE
Breads, Cereals, Rice, and Pasta

DISCOVER...

- how to make and use breads.
- how to prepare sandwiches.
- what you need to know to cook pasta and rice.

Lori is planning a menu for the class picnic. She wants to serve something besides the usual hamburgers, chips, and brownies. She thinks that she may include crusty rolls and breads and several kinds of cheeses and meats. She also has a favorite pasta salad recipe that she thinks everyone would like. For dessert, she might serve apple-granola crisps. What other foods would you suggest?

WORDS TO KNOW

dough

sandwich

pasta

Bread is a popular part of most meals. What are your favorite breads to eat for breakfast, lunch, and dinner?

Preparing Breads

How many foods did Lori think of that were breads? People serve breads at many meals—from toast at breakfast to buns and rolls at picnics. Breads are made from the flour of many grains. Some of the most common flours are wheat, rye, white, and corn. Other ingredients are added to give each type of bread its particular flavor, texture, and appearance.

Making Quick Breads

Kenny likes to bake quick breads—such as muffins, biscuits, and coffee cakes—because they are fast and easy to make. He simply mixes the ingredients together to make a **dough,** *a thick mixture of flour, liquid, and other ingredients.* Then he places the dough in a pan and bakes it.

Air bubbles, which form during baking, make quick breads light and fluffy. Two ingredients used in quick bread—baking powder and baking soda—cause the air bubbles to form, making the dough rise quickly as it bakes.

When preparing quick breads, it is important to mix the dough just long enough to blend the ingredients. Too much mixing makes quick breads flat and heavy.

Making Yeast Breads

Yeast breads are another type of bread. They take longer to prepare than quick breads. Yeast breads are also made with dough, but with this type of bread, it is yeast that makes the bread rise. Most store-bought sandwich bread, French and Italian bread, and hamburger buns are yeast breads.

A dough made with yeast must rise twice. First, you must let it rise in a warm place outside the oven for an hour or more. Then you punch it down, shape it, and let it rise in the pan before baking. If you want to take a short cut, you can buy frozen dough. Then all you have to do is let the dough warm to room temperature and rise until it is ready to be baked.

When you bake quick breads such as muffins, baking soda or baking powder causes the bread to rise quickly. What are some other examples of quick breads?

Serving Bread

There are many ways to serve bread for meals. To make garlic bread, you can slice French bread, spread it with butter to which you have added minced garlic, wrap the bread in foil, and heat it in the oven.

Another way to use bread, even if it is several days old, is to make French toast. Soak one slice at a time in a mixture of milk and beaten eggs. Then brown the slices in a skillet with a little butter or margarine. You can top them with fresh fruit.

Making Basic Sandwiches

One of the most popular ways to eat bread is as part of a sandwich. A **sandwich** is usually *two pieces of bread*

Skills IN ACTION

Brown-bagging It

A packed lunch can be nutritious and delicious. Here are some ideas:

- Include a hearty food, such as a sandwich or hard-cooked eggs.
- Pack fresh fruit or raw vegetables.
- Put milk or juice in a reusable container.
- Nutritious cookies, such as oatmeal or peanut butter, are a good dessert choice.

surrounding a filling, such as meat or cheese. Although there are many kinds of sandwiches, all good sandwiches include

- bread that is fresh.

- butter, margarine, mayonnaise, or another spread to keep the bread moist.

- a filling, such as chicken salad, spread to the corners of the bread, or slices of meat or cheese.

- ingredients for extra flavor and texture, such as lettuce or tomato.

You can make sandwiches with any type of bread, including whole wheat, enriched white, rye, pumpernickel, seven-grain, and oatmeal. Pita bread, croissants (krah-SAHNZ), and French bread are also good choices. A variety of sandwich fillings will help you fulfill your daily nutritional requirements.

When choosing breads and other grains, remember that whole-grain products are higher in nutrients and fiber than breads made from refined flour, such as white bread.

Making Special Sandwiches

Do you ever feel as if your sandwiches are getting a little dull? If so, you may want to try something different. Sandwiches don't have to be cold. For variety, you can make a tuna melt by putting tuna and cheese on a bagel or bread and melting the cheese in the oven or broiler. Peanut butter with banana slices on oatmeal bread provides foods from three food groups.

Grains

Some foods made from grains must be cooked before you eat them. These include some breakfast cereals, rice, and pasta. Since they all contain starch, some of the cooking techniques are similar for each one.

How to Make Cooked Cereals

When you think of cereal, do you think about the kind you pour out of the box and eat cold with milk? Many people also enjoy eating cooked cereals, such as oatmeal, grits, and cream of wheat.

Like other grains that are cooked, cereals expand to two or three times their original volume. They can be cooked with water or milk on the stove or in the microwave oven.

How to Cook Rice

One type of grain that must be cooked is rice. Rice should be simmered in water, not boiled. When cooked properly, rice is light and fluffy, never heavy or gummy. When you cook rice, follow these tips:

- Don't rinse rice, because rinsing removes some nutrients.

- Use a little oil in the cooking water to help keep the grains separate and to prevent foaming.

- Don't remove the lid while the rice is cooking.

- Because all of the water is absorbed during cooking, rice does not need to be drained.

- Fluff the rice with a fork before serving.

Before you cook rice, read the directions on the package. Different kinds of rice require different amounts of water and lengths of cooking time.

There are many ways to serve rice. For example, rice can be rolled in a flour tortilla with cooked chicken and beans. It is also an important ingredient in chicken-rice soup and rice pudding. What other ways do you like to eat rice?

When you cook rice, be sure to follow the package directions. Why is this important?

Figure 14.2 Cooking Pasta

Follow these guidelines when cooking pasta. What texture should pasta have when it is cooked properly?

How to Cook Pasta

If you have eaten spaghetti, macaroni, or noodles, then you have eaten pasta. **Pasta** is *a food made from flour and water and formed into shapes,* including noodles, spirals, shells, and many others.

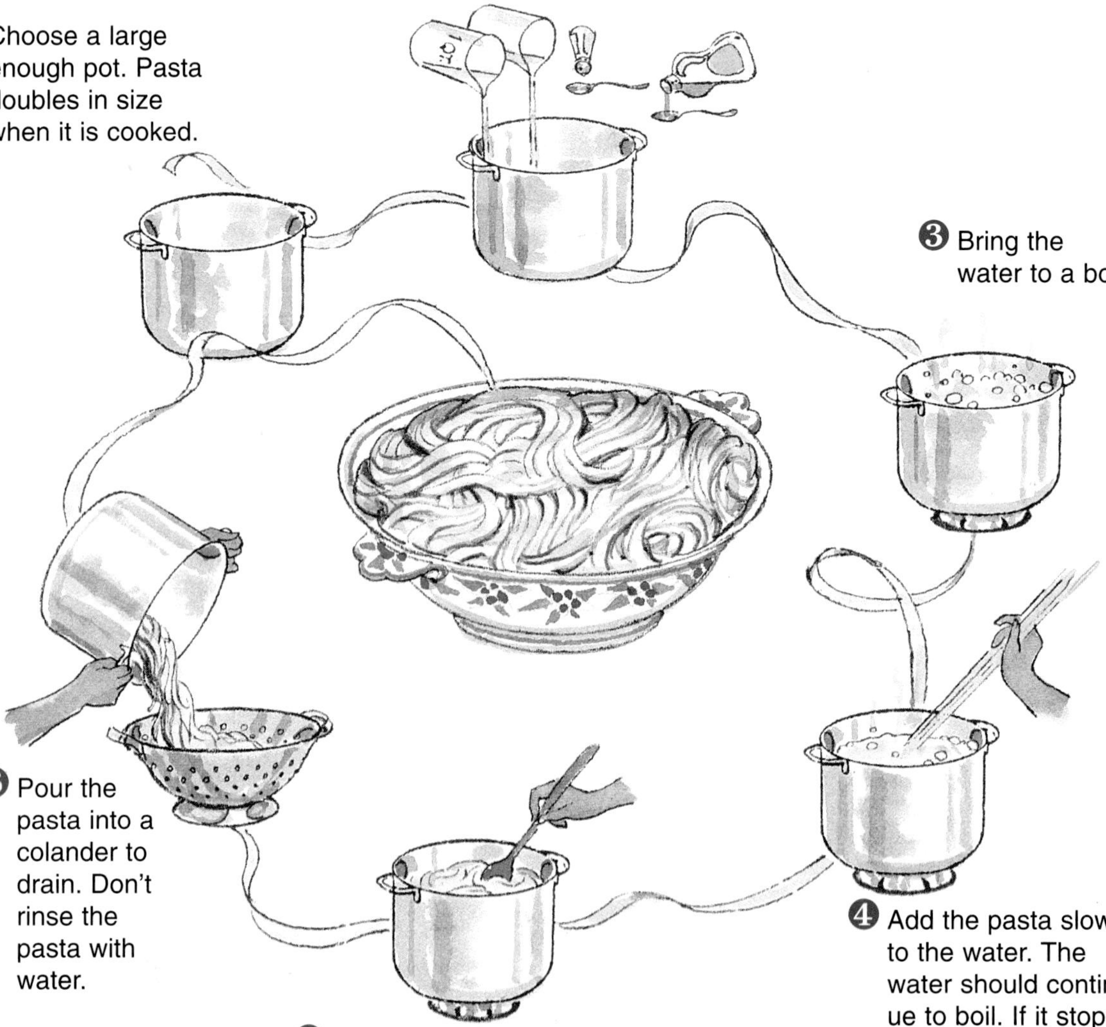

❷ Measure water and salt into a large pot. You'll need 2 quarts (2 L) water and an optional 1 teaspoon (5 mL) salt for every 8 ounces (224 g) pasta. Add one teaspoon (5 mL) cooking oil to the water. This helps to keep the water from boiling over. It also helps keep the pasta from sticking together.

❶ Choose a large enough pot. Pasta doubles in size when it is cooked.

❸ Bring the water to a boil.

❻ Pour the pasta into a colander to drain. Don't rinse the pasta with water.

❺ Stir the pasta from time to time. This also helps keep it from sticking. Cook the pasta only until it's tender. The package directions tell you how long.

❹ Add the pasta slowly to the water. The water should continue to boil. If it stops, the pasta might stick together.

Pasta is usually dried. It becomes soft enough to eat when it is cooked. Properly cooked pasta is slightly firm, not soft, limp, or mushy. **Figure 14.2** describes how to cook pasta.

Healthy Grain Choices

Breads, cooked cereals, rice, and pasta provide you with important nutrients: iron, B vitamins, carbohydrates, and fiber. Once you know how to cook and prepare grains, you will see that there are many ways to include them in your diet every day.

Pasta should keep its shape and stay firm even after it has been cooked.

LESSON THREE *Review*

Using complete sentences, answer the following questions on a separate sheet of paper.

Reviewing Terms and Facts

1. Recall What is the purpose of using baking soda and baking powder in quick breads?

2. Recall Describe the appearance of rice that has been cooked properly.

3. Vocabulary What is *pasta?* Give three examples of types of pasta.

Thinking Critically

4. Apply Imagine that you are going on a picnic. Give examples of three types of sandwiches that would need to be kept in a cooler and two types of sandwiches that could be packed in a brown bag.

5. Explain How do you know how much liquid to use when cooking a grain? Why is it important to cook it properly?

6. Compare and Contrast What are the similarities and differences between cooking rice and cooking pasta?

Applying Concepts

7. Write seven menus for one week of dinners, using breads, rice, and pasta. For example, one dish might be lamb curry over rice; another might be pita pockets with chicken salad, tomato, cucumber, and onion. Remember to vary your menus as much as possible.

LESSON FOUR
Milk, Yogurt, and Cheese

WORDS TO KNOW

dairy foods

scald

curdles

DISCOVER...

- how to add milk to your diet.
- the many ways you can use dairy products.
- how to prepare dairy foods.

When Emily gets home from softball practice, she grabs a tall glass and pours herself some milk. She finds milk refreshing and thirst-quenching. Her brother Rob opens the freezer and takes out a strawberry frozen yogurt bar. He enjoys having something sweet and creamy for an afternoon snack.

Milk and other dairy foods provide you with calcium and other nutrients, including vitamins A, B, and D. **Dairy foods** are *foods made from milk.* For good health, you need to include dairy foods in your diet every day. Which dairy foods do you like best?

406   CHAPTER 14: LET'S COOK

The Many Uses of Milk

People of all ages drink milk at mealtimes and with snacks. In addition, milk is used in many recipes. What foods can you think of that are made with milk?

Cooking with Milk and Cream

Have you ever cooked foods whose ingredients included milk, buttermilk, or cream? For example, you might use milk or cream to make creamy soups, sauces, puddings, and custards. Milk and buttermilk are often used in cakes, breads, and muffins.

When cooking with dairy foods, it is important to be especially careful. Milk products burn, or scorch, easily if the temperature is too high or if they are cooked too long. To cook milk you need to **scald** it, or *bring the food slowly to a temperature just below the boiling point.* Never let milk boil. Heat only until little bubbles begin to appear around the edge.

If you do not handle milk properly, it may curdle. When milk **curdles,** it *separates into little particles (curds).* Adding anything acidic—such as fruit, tomato, or fruit juices—to milk may cause curdling. To avoid this, add these foods very slowly and stir the milk constantly.

Thick, creamy sauces add flavor to many dishes. For example, a basic white sauce made with milk can be served over vegetables or noodles. For extra flavor, add cheese or herbs to the sauce.

Preparing Milk Drinks

For a delicious cold drink, blend milk with fruit, juice, ice cream, or yogurt in a blender or food processor. You can also mash the fruit, combine all the

To keep milk from burning when you cook it, use a double boiler or a heavy pan. What else should you do to prevent milk from burning?

Milk comes in many forms—nonfat, low-fat, whole milk, half-and-half, cream, whipping cream, evaporated milk, sweetened condensed milk, nonfat dry milk, and buttermilk! Bring samples of these products to class. Taste and compare. Discuss the characteristics of each.

Hot chocolate is an alternative to plain milk. What other beverages supply you with calcium?

ingredients in a covered container, and shake it well. Try some of these combinations:

- **Orange shake:** 1 cup (250 mL) buttermilk, 3 tablespoons (45 mL) orange juice concentrate, and 1 teaspoon (5 mL) honey

- **Banana milk:** ¾ cup (175 mL) milk, 1 mashed banana, 5 crushed ice cubes, and 1 teaspoon (5 mL) sugar

- **Lemon-strawberry yogurt smoothie:** ½ cup (125 mL) lemon yogurt, ½ cup (125 mL) milk, ¼ cup (50 mL) sliced strawberries, and 1 teaspoon (5 mL) sugar

- **Coffee shake:** ½ cup (125 mL) coffee ice cream and ½ cup (125 mL) milk

Yogurt—Plain or Fancy

Yogurt is a dairy product that contains most of the same nutrients as milk. Because yogurt is easier to digest than milk, many people who cannot drink milk can still eat yogurt. From

Yogurt is a versatile food. You can eat it plain, add toppings, and even cook with it. Have you ever tried yogurt instead of sour cream on a baked potato?

plain or vanilla to kiwi or papaya, yogurt comes in a wide variety of flavors. It is also available in several forms, including regular, low-fat, and nonfat. In addition, yogurt can be used instead of sour cream or mayonnaise in some recipes.

Cheese—Many Variations

Can you imagine what some of your favorite foods would taste like without cheese? Pizza and lasagna just wouldn't be the same. What other foods do you eat that would lack flavor and appeal if the cheese were left out?

Cooking with Cheese

Cheese is an important ingredient in many recipes. For the best results, though, it must be cooked carefully. If you cook cheese too long or at high temperatures, it may burn or become rubbery or stringy. When cooking with cheese, follow these tips:

- Use low to medium heat, and avoid overcooking.

- Grate or shred hard cheeses, such as cheddar, before adding them to other ingredients. The cheese will blend faster and more evenly.

- Add cheese to sauces or casseroles at the end of the cooking time, if possible, so that the cheese won't become overcooked.

Cheese comes in many varieties: soft, semisoft, hard, or processed. Cheeses range in flavor from mild to tangy, sharp, and strong. Which types of cheese do you like?

Enjoying Cold Cheeses

Besides cooking with cheese, you can also enjoy cheese cold, either by itself or added to a variety of foods. For example, try sprinkling grated cheese on soups, chili, baked potatoes, spaghetti, and burritos. For an easy snack, eat cheese with crackers, crusty bread, or fresh fruit. Firm cheeses that can be sliced, such as cheddar and Swiss cheese, taste best at room temperature. Take them out of the refrigerator about an hour before they will be eaten.

Desserts Made with Dairy Foods

Besides tasting good, many desserts made with dairy foods are also nutritious. Have you ever made custard or pudding for dessert? Maybe you enjoy eating ice cream or frozen yogurt as an after-dinner treat.

Custards and Puddings

Custards are made with milk, eggs, and flavorings. The eggs are used to thicken the custard. Some custards are baked in the oven, while others are cooked in a saucepan on the stove. Either way, custards should be cooked at low temperatures, and not for too long. After custard cools, it should be chilled in the refrigerator.

Another dairy dessert that may be cooked is pudding. The thickening agent in pudding is flour or another starch, rather than eggs. Pudding is made by blending flour with milk and then adding other ingredients. Cook pudding over low heat, and stir it often. Puddings are also usually chilled before serving. An easier way to make custards and puddings is to use packaged mixes.

Pudding is a nutritious dairy dessert that can be cooked or made from an instant mix. How would you prefer to make pudding?

Dairy Treats

When people think about getting enough calcium each day, they usually think about drinking milk. However, there are many other ways to add dairy foods to your diet. You can cook with milk or cheese, add cold cheese to other foods, and enjoy dairy desserts. When choosing a frozen

▲ Pizza is a popular food that provides calcium because it is topped with cheese. What other popular foods are made with dairy products?

dessert, check the nutrition labels carefully. Many low-fat and nonfat products taste delicious and contain far less fat and fewer calories than regular ice cream or frozen yogurt.

LESSON FOUR *Review*

Using complete sentences, answer the following questions on a separate sheet of paper.

Reviewing Terms and Facts

1. Vocabulary Define *dairy foods.* Give two examples of dairy foods.

2. Recall How can you prevent milk from curdling?

3. Describe What would happen to cheese if you cooked it too long?

4. Identify Name two cooked dairy desserts. What ingredients are used to thicken them?

Thinking Critically

5. Summarize What are three problems you might have when cooking with milk and cheese? How can you avoid these problems?

6. Analyze Why do you think that yogurt has become so popular?

7. Recommend Make a list of cheeses that you like to eat. Then suggest some foods to which you could add these cheeses to increase the amount of dairy foods in your diet.

Applying Concepts

8. For three days, keep a record of all the dairy foods you eat and drink. Then compare your intake with the number of servings recommended in the Food Guide Pyramid. Do you eat and drink enough dairy foods? If not, how could you increase the amount in your diet?

Meat, Poultry, Fish, Dry Beans, Eggs, and Nuts

DISCOVER...

- how to prepare meat, poultry, fish, dry beans, and eggs.
- ways to include lower-cost protein in your diet.
- how to make a small amount of meat go farther.

Carrie and Chris volunteered to plan and prepare dinner for their parents' anniversary on Saturday. They decided that they needed to choose a main dish first. They narrowed down their choices to meat loaf, grilled chicken, or salmon steaks.

WORDS TO KNOW

moist-heat
cooking

dry-heat
cooking

hard-cooked
eggs

meat extenders

Preparing Meat, Poultry, and Fish

When Carrie and Chris chose a few main dishes they could cook, they selected foods made with meat, poultry, and fish. These protein-rich foods are popular main dishes, partly because of their versatility. They are not only cut and sold in a variety of ways but can also be prepared in countless ways.

The dish Carrie and Chris chose to make was meat loaf. Because ground meat has no bones, it yields more servings per pound. You can find many types of ground meat at the supermarket—beef, chicken, turkey, veal, and pork. You can use your favorite or vary the meats you use in such dishes as hamburgers, chili, lasagna, taco filling, and spaghetti sauce.

When you prepare meat, poultry, or fish, the two basic cooking methods you will use are moist heat and dry heat. The method you choose depends on the recipe you are following and the tenderness of the meat or poultry. **Figure 14.3** shows some common methods used for cooking with moist heat and dry heat.

When you prepare stew, you can add a variety of ingredients to make your own special recipe. What foods or seasonings would you add?

Figure 14.3
Methods for Cooking Meats

Meat, poultry, and fish can be cooked in a variety of ways. Which of these cooking methods do you prefer?

Roasting and Baking. Place the meat, poultry, or fish on a rack in a shallow pan, uncovered, in the oven.

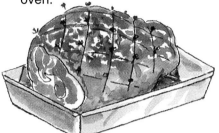

Braising. To braise food, such as a pot roast, brown the meat. Then put the food in a covered pan with a small amount of liquid. Cook it slowly until tender.

Stewing. Cut meat into small pieces. Cover with liquid and cook slowly according to recipe directions.

Frying. Meat, poultry, or fish can be fried in oil, butter, or margarine. Thin slices of meat, poultry, or fish can be stir-fried, which means that they are cooked quickly in a small amount of fat at a high temperature.

Microwave Cooking. Meat, poultry, and fish can be cooked in a microwave oven. They won't brown much, however.

Deep-fat Frying. Chicken and fish are sometimes fried in a lot of oil. The oil must be hot, but not too hot. Chicken and fish are usually coated with a batter before deep-fat frying.

Broiling. Place the meat, fish, or poultry on a broiler pan under the oven broiler. High heat from the broiler cooks food from the top. Turn the food over so that it cooks on both sides.

Cooking With or Without Liquid

Have you ever eaten pot roast or beef stew? If so, then you have tasted meat cooked with moist heat. **Moist-heat cooking** is *cooking in liquid.* It involves cooking food slowly in a covered container, usually with water, broth, or a sauce.

Moist-heat cooking methods are good to use with less expensive, tougher cuts of meat and poultry. When you cook them slowly in liquid, they become more tender and flavorful.

Do you enjoy eating roast turkey, broiled steak, or baked fish? Each of these foods is cooked with dry heat. **Dry-heat cooking** is *cooking without liquid.* It is best to use dry heat when cooking tender cuts of meat and poultry. Fish is often cooked with dry heat too. **Figure 14.4** shows which cuts of meat and poultry to cook with moist heat and which to cook with dry heat.

Some meats can be cooked to different levels of doneness. The three levels are *rare, medium,* and *well-done.* Rare meat is pink on the inside. Well-done meat is thoroughly cooked inside and out. Medium is in between rare and well-done. Beef can be cooked to any of these levels. Pork, poultry, and fish, on

Figure 14.4
Cuts of Meat and Poultry

How does cooking with moist heat improve less tender cuts of meat and poultry?

Tender Meat and Poultry
(Use dry heat.)

Beef rib roast
Sirloin steak
Ground beef, pork, turkey
Pork chops
Ham
Pork sausage
Leg of lamb
Frying chicken

Less Tender Meat and Poultry
(Use moist heat.)

Stew meat
Pot roast
Round steak
Chuck roast
Corned beef
Spareribs
Pork blade steak
Stewing chicken

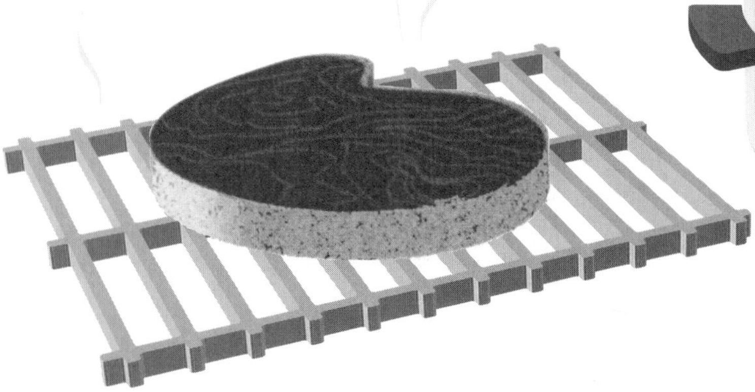

RARE, MEDIUM, OR WELL-DONE?

When you cook meat, you may not be able to tell how well-done it is simply by looking at it. Here's what to do:

● Use an instant-read meat thermometer to measure the internal temperature of meat that you're broiling or roasting. Beef that is rare will register 140°F; medium will register 160°F; well-done will register 170°F. Pork, poultry, and fish should all be cooked until they are well-done!

● If you don't have a thermometer, prick the meat with a cooking fork. If the juice runs red, the meat is rare; pink, medium rare; colorless, well-done.

the other hand, must be cooked until they are well-done. Otherwise, they are not safe to eat.

Meat Substitutes

Other high-protein foods can be used as a main dish instead of meat, poultry, or fish. Beans and eggs are good substitutes. Not only are they high in protein, vitamins, and minerals, but they are also low in cost. In fact, they are two of the most versatile and nutritious foods you can cook.

Cooking with Dry Legumes

Dry beans and peas come in a variety of tastes and textures. Have you ever seen or tried cooking with red kidney beans, black beans, white beans, lentils, lima beans, split peas, or black-eyed peas? These and other legumes offer healthful alternatives to more familiar main dishes.

When you buy dry beans, they will be hard. To soften them, soak them in water for several hours. Then they can be prepared in many ways. For example, you can make baked beans or use beans in burritos, rolled in tortillas with rice and cheese. To save time, you can buy most types of beans in cans.

Although dry beans are a good source of protein, they are not quite as good a source as eggs, meat, or cheese.

Beans are a good meat substitute. They are inexpensive, are easy to cook with, and come in many varieties. With what foods can beans be combined to make complete proteins?

Skills IN ACTION

Meat Extenders

Find a recipe for one or more of the following ways to extend meat. Share your recipe with the class. If possible, try out the recipe on your family.

- Rice combined with meat in a casserole
- Bread crumbs or oatmeal mixed with ground meat to make meat loaf or meatballs
- Pasta combined with fish or chicken to make a cold salad

You can, however, make beans a complete protein by combining them with other ingredients, such as grain products or nuts. Examples of nutritious, high-protein combinations include

- rice and beans in Mexican meals.

- peanut butter on bread (peanuts are actually a kind of legume, not a nut).

- kidney beans on a corn tortilla.

Cooking Eggs

What is your favorite way to cook eggs? No matter how you like them, there are two basic rules to follow.

- Keep the temperature low so that the eggs don't get tough.

- Cook eggs thoroughly so that the whites and yolks are firm. Harmful bacteria in raw or undercooked eggs can make you sick.

When you cook eggs in the shell, cover the eggs with cold water and gradually bring the water to a boil. Let the eggs stand in the hot water, covered, after they have reached the boiling point. **Hard-cooked eggs** are *eggs that are left in hot water, covered, for 15 to 18 minutes.* That allows both the whites and the yolks to become hard. After cooking, immediately run cold water over the eggs to stop the cooking process.

Fried eggs are usually cooked in fat—butter, margarine, or oil. To fry an egg, crack the shell gently, and slip the white and the unbroken yolk into a greased frying pan. Eggs can also be cooked without fat in a nonstick pan.

To make scrambled eggs, beat the whites and yolks together. Then pour the eggs into a little hot fat in a frying pan, or use a nonstick pan or spray. Cook eggs slowly over low heat, stirring them gently and frequently so that they cook evenly. You can also make scrambled eggs in a microwave oven.

Eggs can also be used in more elaborate dishes, such as quiches and omelets. A quiche is a main-dish pie filled with eggs, cream, cheese, and such other ingredients as ham, spinach, and mushrooms. An omelet is a well-beaten egg that is first cooked in a frying pan without stirring. Then it is topped with other ingredients—such as mushrooms, peppers, and cheese—and folded over. Quiches and omelets are convenient because they can be filled with almost anything you might have on hand.

Stretching Meat

How can you make your grocery dollars stretch farther when planning main dishes made with meat? The answer is to use meat extenders. **Meat extenders** are *foods added to meat to make a small amount of meat go farther.* Dry beans, nuts, and grain products are meat extenders. For example, by adding rice and beans to a chicken dish, you can double the number of servings. A small amount of ground beef will feed more people if you combine it with pasta, tomato sauce, and cheese.

Although you may think of eggs as a breakfast dish, there are many ways to prepare them for dinner. What fillings do you like in an omelet?

Your family probably uses meat extenders often without realizing it. Which meat extenders were used in this dish?

Review

Using complete sentences, answer the following questions on a separate sheet of paper.

Reviewing Terms and Facts

1. Identify Name five moist-heat or dry-heat methods of cooking. Describe two of them.

2. Explain Why are beans and eggs good alternatives to meats as main dishes?

3. Recall What are the two basic rules to follow when you prepare eggs?

4. Vocabulary Define the term *meat extender*. Give an example of a main dish that includes meat extenders.

Thinking Critically

5. Contrast What are the differences between cooking with moist heat and cooking with dry heat? Which types of meats are best for each? Why?

6. Recommend Describe the method you would use to cook each of the following foods: pork chops, meatballs, stew meat, flounder.

7. Explain What is the difference between a meat substitute and a meat extender?

Applying Concepts

8. List the main dishes you ate this week. Next to each item, note which cooking method was used, which cut of meat was used, or if meat substitutes or meat extenders were used.

FRIENDS & FAMILY

PERSONALIZED RECIPES

Some people name recipes after family members or friends. For example, a recipe might be called "Aunt Helen's Chicken Soup," or "Grandma's Spice Bars." Personalized recipes not only tell you how to cook something good to eat but also remind you of special people in your life.

TRY THIS!

Think of an entrée, salad, soup, sandwich, or dessert that could be named for you. Write the recipe on a card, including your name, and give it to a friend.

A Global View

TROPICAL FRUIT BASKET

People who live in the United States are familiar with bananas, pineapples, and coconuts. Until recently, other tropical fruits—including carambolas, pomelos, kiwi fruit, mangoes, papayas, and passion fruit—were less familiar to many Americans.

TRY THIS!

Find out more about one tropical fruit that is new to you. In what countries is the fruit grown? What does it look like? Share your findings with the class.

TECHNOLOGY

Grocery Shopping by Computer

Years ago, many people shopped for groceries from home by making a shopping list and telephoning the store. Store employees filled the order and delivered it.

Home shopping for groceries is making a comeback—this time via computers and modems. The only charge customers pay is for home delivery.

Try This!

What are the advantages and disadvantages of shopping for groceries by computer? Compare your answers with those of your classmates.

TECHNOLOGY CONNECTION

GENETICALLY ENGINEERED FOOD

Imagine eating bananas that stay yellow for weeks or grain with more protein. Genetic engineering is making these foods a reality. In 1994 scientists identified the gene in tomatoes that promotes rotting, copied it, and put it back in—but backward. As a result, "Flavr Savr" tomatoes became the first genetically altered food.

Follow Up

1. How might genetically engineered fruits and vegetables that stay fresh longer affect the job of a produce manager in a supermarket?

2. Learn more about genetically engineered food. Then have a class debate on its pros and cons.

3. Find out how genetic engineering is different from traditional animal or plant crossbreeding. Write a brief explanation.

Chapter Summary

- Fruits are a nutritious addition to any meal. They are available fresh, frozen, canned, dried, or as juices.

- Fruits should be served fresh or cooked carefully to retain vitamins A, B, C, D, and E and potassium.

- Vegetables can be served as appetizers, salads, or part of soups and main dishes.

- A salad is a food or a combination of foods served cold, usually with a dressing.

- Soups are nutritious because they can be made with ingredients from any or all of the five food groups.

- Quick breads and yeast breads complement any meal and contain fiber and nutrients. Baking powder and baking soda cause quick-bread dough to rise quickly while baking. Yeast breads take longer to prepare than quick breads.

- Rice and pasta are high-energy grain products that must be cooked.

- Drinking milk or beverages made with milk, cooking with milk, eating yogurt, and adding cheeses to foods are some ways to include dairy foods in your diet.

- Meat, poultry, and fish are usually cooked with moist heat or dry heat and are often served as main dishes.

- Meat substitutes, such as beans and eggs, can serve as main dishes.

- Meat extenders make a small amount of meat go farther and help stretch your grocery dollars.

Words to Know

Using complete sentences, answer the following questions on a separate sheet of paper.

1. What would you find in the *produce* section of the supermarket?
2. What is a *casserole?*
3. What is the main ingredient in bread *dough?*
4. What is *pasta?*
5. Name three *dairy foods.*
6. Explain the difference between a *meat extender* and a meat substitute.

Review Questions

Using complete sentences, answer the following questions on a separate sheet of paper.

1. Why is it important to cook fruits properly?
2. List four ways to cook vegetables, and briefly describe each one.
3. What is the difference between a creamy soup and broth?
4. Explain how sandwiches can be nutritious.
5. Give three tips for cooking with cheese.
6. Give four examples of desserts made with dairy foods.

7. How would you determine the appropriate cooking method for a particular cut of meat?

8. What is the difference between stir-frying and deep-fat frying?

Thinking Critically

Using complete sentences, answer the following questions on a separate sheet of paper.

1. **Interpret** Why is fresh fruit more nutritious than processed fruit?

2. **Analyze** Why do you think that the cooking directions for frozen vegetables call for only ¼ to ½ cup of water?

3. **Apply** The package directions for quick bread said to mix the dough for two minutes. Jenna thought that she would do an extra-good job and mix the dough for five minutes. When she took the bread out of the oven, it was flat and heavy. Why didn't the bread rise?

4. **Explain** Why would plain yogurt with fresh raspberries be more nutritious than raspberry yogurt?

Cooperative Learning

1. Divide into five groups, each group choosing one of the five food groups. Brainstorm ways to encourage teens to eat nutritious foods from your group. Share your ideas with the class.

2. In groups of four or five, choose a single food, such as eggs, potatoes, or hamburger. Each student in the group should find one low-fat recipe containing that food.

Compare the preparation steps and cooking methods used in the recipes.

Family & Community

1. Encourage your family to try a new fruit or vegetable. Make a list of suggestions, and be sure that you know where to buy the fruit or vegetable. Volunteer to try out a recipe using the family's selection.

2. Ask friends and neighbors about cooking methods, special foods, and recipes from their cultural heritage. Share what you learn with the class, and discuss similarities in cooking traditions. Your class might sponsor an ethnic cooking fair.

Building A Portfolio

1. Compile all the techniques you have learned for cooking various foods into a *How to Cook...*cookbook. For example, include directions for cooking pasta, rice, and vegetables. Keep the cookbook in your portfolio for reference.

2. Visit food stores in your neighborhood, and look for "point-of-purchase" information. This is information provided at the particular place in the store where you would purchase a specific food. You might find directions for cooking various cuts of meat in the meat department or recipes for using cheese in the dairy department. Compare your findings with the information in this chapter. Add your point-of-purchase information to your portfolio.

5 Clothing and Textiles

Chapter 15:
Looking Good

Chapter 16:
Planning Your Wardrobe

Chapter 17:
Preparing to Sew

Chapter 18:
Sewing Skills

CHAPTER 15

Looking Good

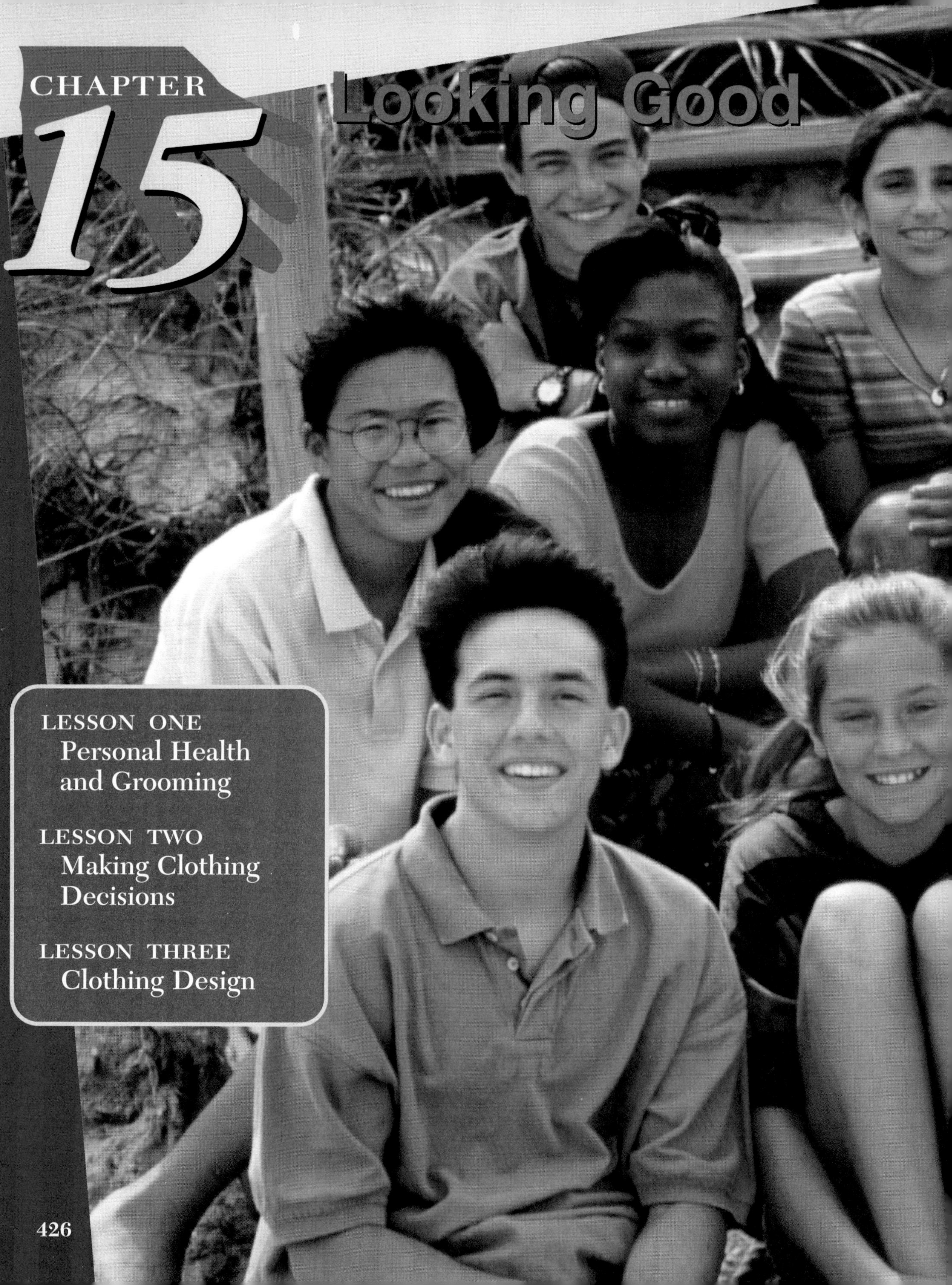

LESSON ONE
Personal Health and Grooming

LESSON TWO
Making Clothing Decisions

LESSON THREE
Clothing Design

TEENS MAKING A DIFFERENCE

Recycling Clothes for Charity

When the Clothing Exchange opened last year, its owner, 14-year-old Samantha Rider, became the youngest person in her town to operate a store. At Samantha's store, all the profits are donated to charity.

Samantha has always been interested in fashion. She decided to volunteer at a clothing-resale shop operated by a charity, but she couldn't find such a shop in her community. Samantha then decided to open her own clothing-resale shop.

Samantha started the shop in her basement, selling clothes donated by friends and relatives. Now the Clothing Exchange has expanded to two rooms in a church basement. Adult volunteers help Samantha run the store on Wednesdays and Saturdays.

Try THIS!

The community benefited from Samantha's volunteer work. What do you think that Samantha gained from volunteering in her community? Share your ideas with classmates.

LESSON ONE
Personal Health and Grooming

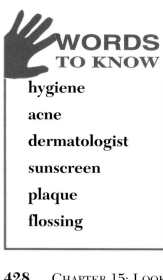

WORDS TO KNOW

hygiene

acne

dermatologist

sunscreen

plaque

flossing

DISCOVER...

- how good health and good grooming help you look and feel your best.
- how to care for your skin, hands, feet, nails, hair, and teeth.

Bonnie takes care of herself because she knows that when she looks her best, she feels good. Friends often ask her what her secret is—she has such attractive skin, hair, and teeth. She tells them that there's no secret, but that she makes good grooming and healthful habits a part of her everyday routine.

The Importance of Good Health

Health affects your appearance in many ways. People who are in good health

- are full of energy.

- maintain a healthy weight.

- have good posture.

- have healthy skin, nails, hair, and teeth.

Eating healthful foods is the first step to good health. You learned in Chapter 10 that your body needs the nutrients in food to stay in good condition. Nutrients protect your body and help it look and feel better too.

Regular exercise not only helps you maintain a healthful weight but also improves your posture, the health of your skin, and your circulation. Rest is also essential to good health. On the average, you need about eight hours of sleep a night. Sleep gives your body a chance to grow and re-pair skin tissues.

Practicing good posture is another health-ful habit to develop. Your posture is the way you hold your body. When you have good posture, you stand or sit erect with your head held high. You can improve your posture by sitting straight in your chair, standing with equal weight on both feet, and walking with your head upright.

Your posture is a reflection of your health and your attitude. Which teen has better posture?

Building Good Grooming Habits

How many magazine and television advertise-ments have you seen about grooming aids for teens? These ads may lead you to believe that it takes time, money, and certain products to look good. The fact is that you can look your best by following a basic hygiene routine every day. **Hygiene** involves *practices that promote health.*

Your Skin

Many teens are concerned about their skin. During the teen years, the oil glands in your skin begin to work harder. The extra oil can clog pores and cause skin problems. Many teens get **acne,** *a skin condition caused by overly active oil glands.* Acne is usually mild enough to take care of at home. Teens who have more severe acne may need to consult a **dermatologist,** *a doctor who treats skin disorders.*

It is important to keep your skin healthy and protect it from the wind and sun. Use a moisturizer and a **sunscreen,** *a lotion that guards the skin against harmful rays of the sun.* **Figure 15.1** explains how to care for your skin.

To take care of your skin properly, you should know what type of skin you have. The most common types are dry skin, oily skin, and sensitive skin. Which type of skin do you have?

- Amy has dry skin that looks rough and flaky. She may have underactive oil glands, or her diet may lack essential nutrients, including water. Amy needs to be sure to drink

Figure 15.1
Caring for Your Skin
You can keep your skin healthy by following these guidelines. ▼

- Eat a balanced diet.
- Get enough rest and exercise.
- Drink six to eight glasses of water each day.
- Wash your face and neck with mild soap and water at least twice a day.
- Use over-the-counter medications if blemishes are a problem. Do not pick at or squeeze pimples.
- Choose grooming products that will not irritate your skin. Look for products that are labeled "mild" or "hypoallergenic."
- Protect your skin from the sun. Use a sunscreen with a sun protection factor (SPF) of at least 15, and reapply the sunscreen if you go swimming.

at least eight glasses of water daily. She should wash with a mild soap and apply a moisturizer afterward.

- Julio has oily skin that is usually shiny and feels greasy. He has overactive oil glands, a common condition during the teen years. Julio should wash frequently and gently to remove excess oil and dirt. After washing, he can apply an astringent to help control the oil.

- Rachel has sensitive skin that develops rough patches and rashes and is easily irritated by weather or by certain ingredients found in grooming products. To find products that won't irritate her skin, she should look for labels that read "mild" or "hypoallergenic," found on cosmetics that have little likelihood of causing an allergic response.

Your Hands, Feet, and Nails

Good hygiene includes care of your hands, feet, and nails. To look their best, your hands, feet, and nails should always be kept clean and neat. Wash hands often using plenty of mild soapsuds to wash away dirt, dead skin, and germs. Feet should be washed every day to prevent foot odor. After washing, be sure to dry your feet thoroughly.

Caring for nails means washing them regularly and giving them special care once a week. To trim and shape them, first clip them with a nail clipper. Then shape and smooth them with a file or emery board. Toenails, which need to be trimmed occasionally, should be cut straight across and kept short.

Why is it important to wash your hands often?

Your Hair

For many teens, hair is a means of self-expression. Regardless of the hairstyle you prefer, your hair is most attractive when it is clean and healthy. To keep it that way, wash and brush it regularly. Brushing your hair helps to distribute the natural oils, keeps hair from becoming dry.

TAKING CARE OF YOUR EYES

Many people have a hard time imagining a life without eyesight, yet they don't often think about taking care of their eyes. Here are some suggestions.

● Protect your eyes from the sun with a good pair of sunglasses.

● Avoid eyestrain by using plenty of light for close work.

● Prevent eye injuries by wearing eye-safety gear for sports and other dangerous activities.

● Detect and treat vision problems and eye disease by getting regular eye exams—every year if you wear glasses or contact lenses, every other year if you don't wear them.

When you buy shampoo, check the labels to find one that matches your type of hair. Why do you think that this is important?

Choose a shampoo made for your type of hair—normal, dry, or oily. Shampoo your hair gently, using your fingertips (not your fingernails) to work the lather through your hair. Be sure to rinse hair thoroughly. If you use a conditioner after shampooing, follow the directions on the bottle.

The high heat of blow dryers, curling irons, or hot rollers can damage hair. If possible, let your hair dry by itself, or lower the temperature setting on your blow dryer.

Your Teeth

Your teeth affect not only your appearance but also your health. Your teeth help you chew food and shape your mouth and your smile. Taking care of your teeth will help prevent cavities and gum diseases. The best way to avoid these problems is to keep your teeth clean. Teeth start to decay when plaque is left on them too long. **Plaque** (PLAK) is *a soft, sticky film created by the bacteria that live in your mouth.*

Keeping your teeth clean and your gums healthy begins with brushing and flossing regularly. Choose a brush with soft bristles, and use a toothpaste that contains fluoride. To brush, use gentle up-and-down strokes to clean between the teeth and massage the gums. Brush all tooth surfaces and your tongue at least twice a day.

Flossing should be a part of your hygiene routine once a day. **Flossing** means *pulling dental floss back and forth between your teeth at the gum line to remove food particles.* Ask your dentist or dental hygienist to show you the proper technique.

Good dental care also includes eating nutritious foods and avoiding sweet and sticky foods. Regular dental checkups are also important.

Brushing regularly will help you keep your teeth and gums healthy. What else should you do to take care of your teeth?

Your Appearance and Grooming

Good grooming contributes to your overall appearance and helps you feel positively about yourself. You don't have to spend a lot of time or money on personal hygiene products. All you need to do is follow a few daily routines to get the benefits of good grooming and hygiene.

LESSON ONE *Review*

Using complete sentences, answer the following questions on a separate sheet of paper.

Reviewing Terms and Facts

1. List What are the four signs of good health?

2. Vocabulary What causes *acne?*

3. Identify Name three common skin types.

4. Recall How can you keep your teeth clean and healthy?

Thinking Critically

5. Analyze Why do you think that advertisers try to make people believe they need certain grooming products to look and feel good?

6. Suggest Why do you think that hairstyles are important to teens?

7. Apply Make a list of the basic grooming products you should have on hand to complete your hygiene routine every day.

Applying Concepts

8. Working in groups, evaluate three different brands of the same product. Compare labels and prices. Determine which is the best buy, and report your findings to the class.

LESSON TWO
Making Clothing Decisions

WORDS TO KNOW

status

logos

modesty

style

fashions

fads

classic styles

DISCOVER...

● the factors that influence your clothing choices.

● the different meanings of styles, fashions, and fads.

● how clothing affects the impression you make on other people.

Danielle and Brianna are sisters, but you would never know it by the clothes they wear. Danielle likes clothing in bold, flashy colors. She wears the same styles that her friends wear. Brianna likes clothes that are comfortable. She wears jeans and T-shirts most of the time. She is not influenced by what other people wear. Why does each sister choose the type of clothing she does? What made you choose the clothes you are wearing now? Do you like your clothing choices? What would you change if you could?

The Purpose of Clothing

People first wore clothing to protect themselves against the wind, snow, rain, cold, and heat. That first clothing was made from animal skins. As time went on, people decorated their clothes with stains and powders made from natural materials, such as earth and clay. Seeds, stones, and shell beads were sometimes added to clothing to show a person's **status,** or *level of importance.*

Today, clothing choices are much more varied than they used to be, but the purpose of clothing has not changed. Learning why you wear the clothes you do and what influences your clothing decisions will help you choose the clothes that are best for you. **Figure 15.2** describes the reasons why people select specific types of outfits.

Figure 15.2 Reasons for Clothing Choices
People wear clothes for many reasons. What other reasons can you think of?

Decoration. Clothes, such as caps and vests, are used as decoration.

Modesty. The way you wear your clothes and the type of clothing you wear suggests your personal sense of **modesty,** or *what people feel is the proper way for clothing to cover the body.*

Protection. Clothing keeps you comfortable and protects you from the weather and climate.

Status. Some garments are worn to reflect a person's status. Jeans with designer labels and sneakers with company **logos,** or *identification symbols,* can give a person a feeling of importance.

Identification. Clothes tell as much about you as what you say. For example, uniforms may signify that you work at a particular restaurant, play in a school band, or are part of an athletic team.

Making Clothing Decisions

When Danielle and Brianna buy clothes, they choose different styles. A **style** is *the design of a garment.* For example, a *bomber* jacket, a *straight* skirt, and *baggy* pants are all styles.

Not all styles of clothing are considered fashions. **Fashions** are *styles of clothing that are accepted as popular at a particular time.* Fashions change frequently. Some practical clothing, such as jeans, are popular season after season. Only a few changes in the style are made to give them a fresh, new look. Fashions may include changes in skirt length, jacket length, collar shape, or width of pant legs. At any one time, however, you can find some new fashions coming in, some going out, and other styles that continue to remain popular.

Some fashions become popular very quickly but then lose their appeal. *Fashions that are very popular for a short time* are called **fads.** Fad clothing may be fun to wear, especially if your friends are wearing it. Because a fad does not last very long, however, it is not a good idea to spend a lot of money on fad items. Instead, you can choose **classic styles,** which are *styles that remain in fashion for a long time.* Classics include a blazer, crew neck shirt, and cardigan sweater. To update your look, you can buy trendy accessories, such as belts, hats, and jewelry.

The Right Clothes for the Occasion

The occasion or activity for which you are dressing helps to determine your clothing choices. For instance, you would wear different clothes to a basketball game than to a formal dance. For some events, such as having lunch with friends at the mall or going to a movie, casual clothing is acceptable. Other occasions, such as going to a fancy restaurant or a wedding, require dressier clothes.

Clothing—The Message It Sends

Even clothing that is comfortable or casual tells others something about you. People often use clothing as a way to

Try This!

Clothing and other gear can protect you not only from the weather but also from injury. For example, cyclists wear helmets to protect their heads, and firefighters wear insulated suits that are flameproof to protect themselves from burns.

With a group of classmates, brainstorm other examples of clothing or gear that helps protect people from injury.

Fad clothing does not remain popular for very long. Do you know when this type of clothing was popular?

Skills
IN ACTION

Dressing Appropriately

If you want to dress for success, remember these tips:

- For job interviews, select clothes that are neat, businesslike, and conservative.
- At school, wear clothes that are appropriate for learning.
- For outdoor activities, consider the weather when you dress so that you will not be too cold or too hot.

express themselves. How do you express yourself through your clothing choices?

Self-Expression

Your clothing can tell others a lot about your personality. If you are an outgoing person, you may prefer bold colors and patterns. Your best friend, who is quiet, may prefer to wear clothes that are simple and subdued.

Your moods can also affect your clothing choices. When you are feeling happy, you may choose to wear bright colors. On days when you're feeling thoughtful and quiet, you may

People's clothing needs differ depending on their interests. What purpose do uniforms serve?

select pale or dark colors. Some people use clothes to help change their moods. For example, Stephanie always wears a bright red shirt when she's feeling a little down, because it lifts her spirits.

First Impressions

The clothes you wear contribute to the impression you make on other people. People will form an impression of you the first time they meet you. That impression is partly influenced by what you are wearing.

Have you ever decided you wanted to meet someone because of his or her appearance? Perhaps what you liked most was the way that person was dressed. People make the same judgments about you. Their ideas about you are based on your personality and your appearance. If a person met you now, would he or she want to get to know you better?

Choosing Clothing Wisely

You make clothing decisions for a variety of reasons. Even though there are many different styles of clothing available, you can learn to choose clothes that flatter you. Keep in mind that no matter what you wear, it reflects your personality and sends out messages to other people.

If you understand basic styles and fashions, you can make wise clothing decisions. How can you improve the choices you make?

LESSON TWO *Review*

Using complete sentences, answer the following questions on a separate sheet of paper.

Reviewing Terms and Facts

1. List Name five reasons why people wear clothes.

2. Explain Why is it best not to spend a lot of money on fad clothing?

3. Give Examples Name two situations in which you might wear dressy clothing.

4. Identify Give an example to show how clothing could be used to express someone's personality.

Thinking Critically

5. Relate What are some examples of clothes that people wear purely for status?

Do you think that these clothes are worth the price? Why or why not?

6. Compare and Contrast What are the similarities and differences among styles, fashions, and fads?

7. Analyze Do you think that it is fair to judge a person by his or her clothing? Why or why not?

Applying Concepts

8. Make a list of fad clothing that is currently popular. Survey ten friends or classmates to determine how many wear these fad items. Which items are the most popular? Why? Discuss results with your classmates.

LESSON THREE
Clothing Design

WORDS TO KNOW

hues

value

intensity

color wheel

neutral color

shape

texture

DISCOVER...

- how color, line, and texture of clothing affect your appearance.
- how to combine design elements when selecting clothes.

Tim's favorite outfit is a baseball jersey and navy blue sweatpants. He feels comfortable in it. Tim doesn't pay much attention to how clothing affects his appearance. He just wears clothes he likes. Tamara is quite different. Her favorite is a jeans outfit with boots. She likes the way the color and styles flatter her appearance, and people always compliment her when she wears this outfit.

These teens are wearing their favorite outfits. They may like these clothes best because of the colors, types of fabric, or the way they look in them. What do you like best about your favorite outfit?

How Color Affects Appearance

Why do some colors look better on you than others? If you become familiar with the relationships among colors, you will understand how colors affect your appearance and the way clothes look on you.

To understand the basic principles of color, you need to know *the names of the colors*, or the **hues.** The three basic hues are red, yellow, and blue. They are called the *primary* colors because all other colors can be made from them. The *secondary* hues are orange, green, and violet. Orange is made by combining equal amounts of red and yellow. Equal amounts of blue and yellow make green, and violet is made by combining red and blue.

Another basic element to consider is the **value,** or *the lightness and darkness of color.* For instance, blue can vary in value from very light blue to navy blue. A light value of a hue is called a *tint.* A dark value of a hue is called a *shade. The* *brightness or dullness of a color* is called its **intensity.** Bright red is a high-intensity color. Pale pink is a low-intensity color.

Colors are considered either warm or cool. Red, yellow, and orange are warm colors. They give a sense of brightness and cheerfulness. Blue, green, and violet (purple) are cool colors. They give a sense of calm.

When you put clothes together, you can create either single-color outfits or outfits that combine colors. By following specific guidelines, you can learn to combine colors successfully. These guidelines are based on the color wheel. A **color wheel** is *an arrangement of colors that shows the relationships of colors to each other.* **Figure 15.3** shows a color wheel. **Figure 15.4** shows different ways to create color schemes for a flattering look.

**Figure 15.3
Color Wheel**
The color wheel shows how colors are related to one another. Why is it important to learn about the color wheel?

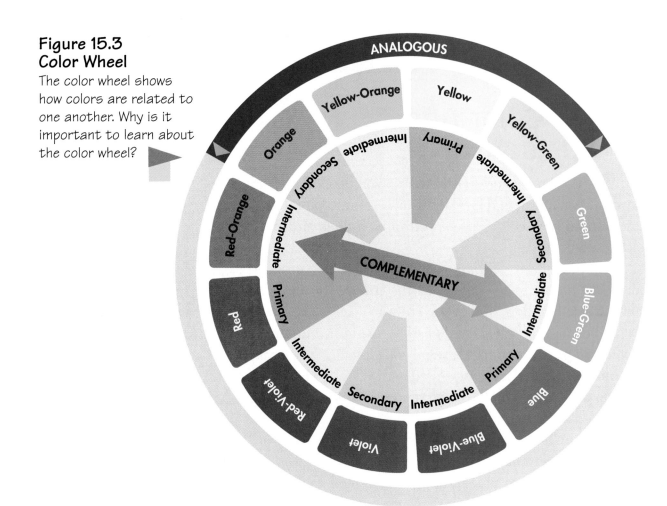

**Figure 15.4
Color Schemes**
Which of these types
of color schemes have
you tried?

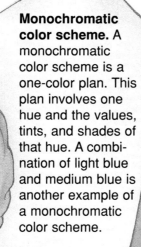

Monochromatic color scheme. A monochromatic color scheme is a one-color plan. This plan involves one hue and the values, tints, and shades of that hue. A combination of light blue and medium blue is another example of a monochromatic color scheme.

Analogous color scheme. An analogous color scheme is made up of hues found next to each other on the color wheel. The colors have one common hue. A combination of red-violet, violet, and blue-violet is another analogous color scheme.

Complementary color scheme. Complementary colors are those opposite each other on the color wheel. This type of color scheme gives great contrast.

Accented neutral color scheme. A *neutral color* is *black, white, beige, or gray.* An accented neutral color scheme uses one of the neutral colors plus another color as the accent. A combination of black and red is an example of an accented neutral color scheme.

The Right Lines for You

You can change your appearance by changing the lines of your clothes. Follow these guidelines:

- Clothes with vertical lines make you look taller and thinner.
- Clothes with horizontal lines make you look shorter and wider.
- Clothes with diagonal lines can make you look taller and thinner or shorter and wider, depending on the length and angle of the lines.

Selecting Colors

When you try different colors and color combinations, you will discover that some look better on you than others. Becoming colors make your complexion look healthy and show off your hair and eyes.

Colors affect your appearance in other ways too. They can accent or play down certain areas of your body. Light, warm, and bright colors can make you look larger. Dark, cool, and dull colors can make you look smaller. Carl wears one-color outfits so that he will look taller, whereas Judy selects contrasting colors so that she appears shorter.

Lines in Clothing

The way a garment looks on you is also affected by its lines. Lines form the outer **shape,** or *outline,* of a garment, as you can see by comparing tapered, straight-leg, and flared pants. Sometimes lines are formed by features of the garment's construction, such as seam lines and waistlines. Other lines can be part of the fabric's design, such as stripes or plaids.

The lines of a garment can affect your appearance. How do lines affect the way these teens look?

SHAPING UP

Few people are completely satisfied with their bodies. However, you can change the appearance of your proportions by choosing the right clothing styles.

For example, if you want to make your waist look narrower, you can

- choose single-breasted or V-neck jackets.
- wear darker colors on top.
- avoid contrasting belts at the waist.
- wear long vests and tunics.

If you want to make your hips look smaller, you can

- wear tops with shoulder pads.
- wear shirts, sweaters, and jackets that fall below the widest part of the hips.
- avoid clothing that is too tight.

Lines can be either straight or curved. Curved lines soften a garment's appearance. Straight lines can look severe and strong. Straight lines can be

- vertical—lines that go up and down.

- horizontal—lines that go across.

- diagonal—lines that go at an angle.

When you shop for clothes, learn to look for lines. Try to see vertical lines instead of just a row of buttons or a zipper down the front. Look for horizontal lines instead of seeing only belts, waistlines, or hemlines. See diagonal or curved lines instead of necklines and collars.

Lines can be used to make you look taller or shorter, larger or smaller. See the "Skills in Action" feature on the opposite page for some tips.

Clothing comes in a variety of interesting textures. How can you use texture to change the way you look? ▶

The Texture of Clothing

When you choose clothing, you need to consider its **texture,** *the way something feels or looks as if it would feel.* Texture is created by using different yarns and weaves in making fabric. For instance, a wool sweater has a coarse texture that is created in the knitting process. A fabric may be dull or shiny, nubby or smooth. What textures do you prefer?

You can use textures to change the way you look. Dull textures make you look smaller. Nubby or shiny textures make you seem larger. A tall person can wear a coarse texture, but the same fabric may overpower a small person. To see which textures look best on you, try on clothing with different types of textures.

By understanding the effects of color, lines, and texture, you can choose clothes that will help you look your best. What do you usually consider when you make clothing choices?

Making Fashionable Combinations

When you buy clothing, consider the effect of color, line, and texture to make selections that will help you look your best. You can use your knowledge of these design elements to emphasize your best features.

LESSON THREE

Review

Using complete sentences, answer the following questions on a separate sheet of paper.

Reviewing Terms and Facts

1. List Name the three primary colors. Why are these colors important?

2. Vocabulary What is a *color wheel?* What can you learn from it?

3. Name What are the three main directions of lines in fashions?

4. Describe How is texture created? Name three types of textures.

Thinking Critically

5. Contrast What is the difference between value and intensity?

6. Apply If you wanted to look taller and thinner, what types of prints, textures, or patterned fabrics would you choose?

Applying Concepts

7. In a catalog or magazine, find a picture of an outfit that you think would look good on you. Using what you have learned about color, line, and texture, describe the outfit, and explain why you chose it.

Chapter 15 Activities

TECHNOLOGY
Plastic Hair

Hairstyling products—such as sprays, gels, and mousses—work well because they contain polymers and resins—compounds found in plastics—that attach firmly to hair to hold it in place. However, regular shampoos can't wash them out completely.

Try This!

Read labels on some hair-care products at home or at the store. Find a "clarifying" shampoo that would help prevent or remove residue buildup. Share your findings with the class.

Consumer Focus

Label Lowdown

The manufacturers of personal care products sometimes make claims that are vague or misleading. Acne medications don't always "get rid of zits," for example, and "dermatologist-tested" beauty products aren't necessarily safer than other kinds.

Try This!

Do ads for makeup and grooming products in magazines make claims that sound too good to be true? What sources could you consult to find out whether they are true or not?

FRIENDS & FAMILY

CLOTHES COMMUNICATION

Regina and her parents sometimes disagree on the clothes she chooses for school. Her parents think that she should dress in a way that will make a good impression on her teachers. Regina wants to dress only to please herself.

TRY THIS!

Ask three or four of your teachers what kind of clothes they think students should wear to school. Report the findings of your survey to the class.

TECHNOLOGY CONNECTION

RECYCLED PLASTIC

Can you imagine wearing a fleece pullover made from empty milk jugs?

Recycled-plastic fibers have been used in carpets for years. However, it has been difficult to produce fibers soft enough for clothing—until now. You can't tell the difference between the recycled-plastic clothing and any other clothing made from synthetic materials.

Follow Up

1. Why are plastic-recycling efforts, such as making clothing from plastic soft drink bottles, as important as sorting waste materials in the first place?

2. The fibers, which are spun from used plastic bottles and other plastic products, look and feel like polyester. The finished products also cost about the same as regular clothing. Would you wear clothing made from recycled plastic? Why or why not?

Chapter Summary

- Health affects your appearance in many ways. Good health can result from eating healthful foods, exercising regularly, getting enough rest, and practicing good posture.

- You can look your best by following a basic hygiene routine every day.

- Good grooming habits include the way you care for your skin, nails, hair, and teeth.

- People wear clothing for a variety of reasons, including protection, decoration, modesty, status, and identification.

- A style is the design of a garment. A fashion is a style of clothing that is popular at a particular time. A fad is a fashion that is very popular for a short time. A classic is popular for a long time.

- Your clothing choices are influenced by the occasion and by the type of activity in which you will be participating.

- Your clothes express your unique personality and influence the impression you make on people.

- You can combine colors to create various kinds of color schemes. Monochromatic, analogous, complementary, and accented neutral are examples of color schemes.

- Colors, lines, and textures affect your appearance and how clothes look on you.

Words to Know

Using complete sentences, answer the following questions on a separate sheet of paper.

1. Why might someone need to see a *dermatologist?*

2. How does *sunscreen* protect your skin?

3. What is *plaque?* When does it become a problem?

4. How does *modesty* influence clothing choices?

5. How long do *fads* usually last?

6. What are *hues?*

7. Give an example of a *neutral color.*

Review Questions

Using complete sentences, answer the following questions on a separate sheet of paper.

1. List three guidelines for caring for your skin.

2. Why is it important to brush your hair?

3. Describe the best way to brush your teeth. How often should you brush?

4. Why are classic styles good clothing choices?

5. How can clothing be used to help you make a positive first impression?

6. Name and describe the four basic color schemes.

7. How can you use line and texture in clothing to improve your appearance?

Thinking Critically

Using complete sentences, answer the following questions on a separate sheet of paper.

1. **Analyze** Many teens have problems with acne. How might this problem affect a person's self-concept and self-esteem? Do you think that it should?

2. **Relate** Give two examples, other than those discussed in the text, of situations in which appropriate dress is important. Explain your choices.

3. **Apply** In terms of color, line, and texture, how would you describe your clothing choices? How do these factors affect your appearance?

Cooperative Learning

1. Working in groups of three or four, compare prices of designer items of clothing with non-designer items. Have each person in the group choose one type of garment. Group members should find out the price of the garment with a designer label and the price of a similar garment without a designer label. Then have group members compare findings and discuss whether designer items are worth the difference in price.

2. With a partner, research the clothing most often worn by people in another country. Find out how the clothing reflects the climate and culture of the country. Discuss the similarities and differences between clothing in that country and clothing worn in the United States. Present your findings to the class.

Family & Community

1. Ask your parents or grandparents to tell you about clothing styles that were popular when they were in their teens. Have them compare what they wore to certain places or events, such as school and parties, to what today's teens wear. What fads were there? Were there particular colors, lines, or textures that most teens wore? Share your findings with the class.

2. Write a one-page article about someone you know who dresses well. Describe the types of clothing the person wears and what the clothing says about the person. What could you learn from this person?

Building A Portfolio

1. For two days, keep track of your grooming habits. Write down each time you care for your skin, nails, hair, or teeth. At the end of the two days, compare your habits with those described in the chapter. Are there habits you need to change? If so, what should you do differently? Write a plan for improving your habits, and place it in your portfolio. Review it periodically.

2. Make a list of your five favorite garments or outfits. Analyze each one to determine what looks best on you in terms of style, color, line, and texture. Based on your analysis, write a conclusion about which types of clothing help you look your best. Keep the analysis in your portfolio, and refer to it the next time you shop for clothes.

CHAPTER 16

Planning Your Wardrobe

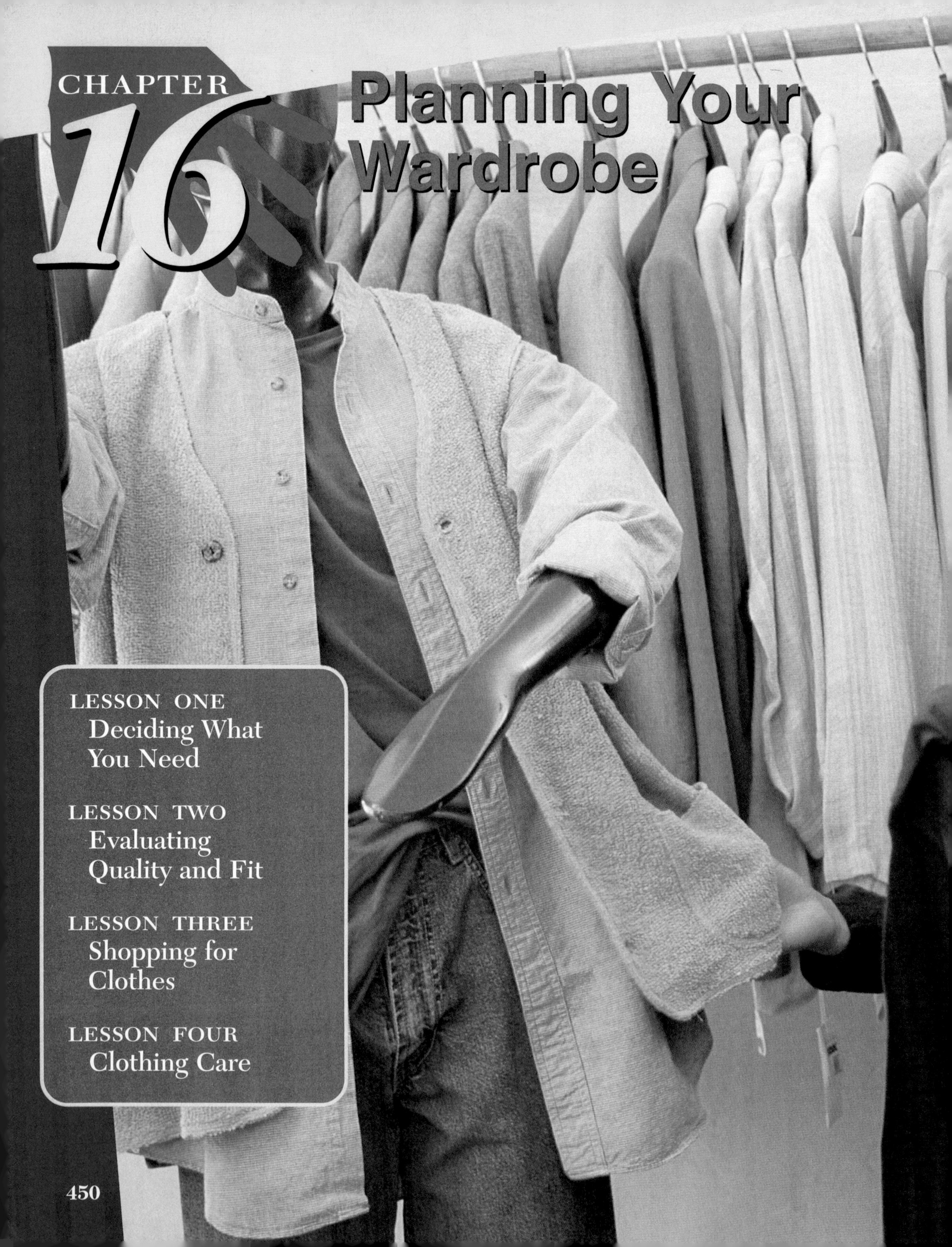

LESSON ONE
Deciding What You Need

LESSON TWO
Evaluating Quality and Fit

LESSON THREE
Shopping for Clothes

LESSON FOUR
Clothing Care

TEENS MAKING A DIFFERENCE

The Boutique Look

Janine Bryant noticed that a few of her sweat-shirts looked a bit drab from too many washings. Janine decided to try reviving the shirts by adding fabric paint, beads, and glitter. When she wore one of her "new" shirts to school, several people asked Janine where they could buy a shirt like the one she had made.

Janine started taking orders for her decorated shirts, but she soon had more work than she could handle. Now Janine pays a few of her artistic friends to help her.

Try THIS!

Make a list of the clothes in your closet that need repair or a new look. Next to each item, write down one or two ways in which you could improve the garment's appearance. Then follow through on one of your ideas.

LESSON ONE
Deciding What You Need

WORDS TO KNOW

accessories

personal style

versatile

wardrobe inventory

focal point

DISCOVER...

- how to assess your wardrobe needs.
- how to take a wardrobe inventory.
- ways to extend your wardrobe with accessories and smart clothing choices.

When you look in your closet, what do you see? Do you like most of your clothes and get a lot of use from them? Do you have enough casual clothes and enough dressy clothes? By thinking about what you need and what you like, and by making smart clothing choices, you can have a wardrobe that works for you without spending a lot of money.

Looking at Your Wardrobe

A good way to begin is by taking a look at the clothes you have now. The best planning involves thinking about your entire wardrobe, not just about individual outfits. Keep in mind, too, that **accessories,** *such items as shoes, belts, scarves, hats, socks, ties, and jewelry,* are part of your wardrobe. Think about your total wardrobe needs—the different types of clothes you need for all the places you go and the activities in which you participate.

Your Wardrobe Needs

The first step in deciding what kind of clothes you need is to think about what kind of clothes you wear. Think about your various activities: you need clothes for school, casual clothes for spending time with friends, dressier clothes for special occasions, and clothes for special activities, such as sports or Scouts.

You also need to evaluate your **personal style,** *the kind of clothes you like best.* For example, do you wear a lot of tailored, buttoned shirts, or do you feel more comfortable in T-shirts?

The most practical clothes are **versatile,** or *able to be worn for many occasions.* The same sweater might be fine to wear with jeans and running shoes when you go to the mall, or with pants or a skirt and dressier shoes when you go to a restaurant with your family. A few items in neutral colors—such as white, beige, black, or gray—can be coordinated with many other items in your wardrobe.

Outer garments are part of your wardrobe, too. Because these items are often more expensive than others, it is especially important that coats and jackets be versatile. If it gets cold where you live, you will need at least one heavy jacket or coat.

Try This!

Rather than let old clothes take up space in your closet, you can donate them to a charitable organization. Get your clothing ready by making sure that everything is clean and in good repair.

Taking a Wardrobe Inventory

Now that you have a good sense of your wardrobe needs, take a look at what you already have. This would be a good

Figure 16.1
Wardrobe Inventory
What do you think are the
benefits of taking a
wardrobe inventory?

Wardrobe Inventory	School	Casual	Sports	Dressy	Special Activities
Slacks					
Shirts/ Blouses					
Skirts					
Dresses					
Jackets					
Accessories					

time to clean out your closet and drawers. Draw a chart like the one shown in **Figure 16.1.** This is called a **wardrobe inventory,** *a list of all the clothes, shoes, and accessories that you have.*

As you take your inventory, sort your clothing into the following four categories:

- **Clothes that you like and wear regularly.** Include these in your wardrobe inventory. Also, use them to help you evaluate your personal clothing style. What do you like about these clothes—style, color, fabric, texture?

- **Clothes that you no longer wear.** These might be clothes that no longer fit or that you just don't like anymore. There is no point in keeping these clothes in your inventory or in your closet. Before you set them aside, however, think about how they might still be used. If the sleeves on a shirt are too short, could they be cut off and re-hemmed to make a short-sleeved shirt instead? Clothes that you're sure you don't want can be given to friends or family members or donated to charity.

- **Clothes that you like but never seem to wear.** Make a note of these clothes. You may be able to add items to your wardrobe that will make them more useful.

- **Clothes in need of repair.** Set these to one side and see if they can be fixed. Schedule time to mend them and replace missing buttons. You will learn about repairing clothing in Chapter 18, Lesson 5.

As you make your wardrobe inventory, set aside clothes that you no longer wear, and donate them to charity. Where can you donate used clothing in your community?

When you have finished your wardrobe inventory, review it to see if you have enough clothing to meet all your needs. Notice which clothes can be used for more than one purpose. Be creative. Could you belt a short dress to wear as a tunic over leggings? Check to be sure that you have enough items in each category. Perhaps you have plenty of casual clothes but need to add to your dressy wardrobe.

Window shopping is one way to view the current styles. What are some other ways?

After you have identified gaps in your wardrobe, consider what clothing items you need to fill them. Perhaps adding a basic garment, such as black pants or a white shirt, would allow for more clothing combinations. Think about what items would coordinate with clothes you already own.

Extending Your Wardrobe

You now have a good idea of what clothes you need. Before you buy anything new, think about what is in style. Look at magazines, advertisements, and clothing-store displays. Observe what your friends and classmates are wearing. Study clothing combinations and ways to change the look of an outfit by adding accessories. Decide which of these current styles fit your personal style and your clothing needs.

While you are thinking about which styles you like, you should also start to note the price of the clothes and accessories that you want to buy. Another important consideration is the care these items would require. Do some of them need to be washed by hand, ironed, or dry-cleaned?

Building from the Basics

A basic wardrobe will ensure that your clothing is well planned and versatile. A good way to expand your wardrobe is by combining separates, or single pieces of clothing that mix and match. **Figure 16.2** on the next page provides some tips on planning a mix-and-match wardrobe.

Figure 16.2
Mix and Match

Follow these suggestions when planning a basic mix-and-match wardrobe. Can you think of any other tips?

Inexpensive accessories can easily change the mood of an outfit from casual to dressy. Look through your favorite fashion magazines for new ideas.

When you go shopping, wear the clothes that you want to match.

Think again about the items that you already own. For example, a favorite shirt could be worn as a lightweight jacket. A scarf might look great as a belt.

Purchase clothes in the colors and fabrics that look good on you and fit your particular lifestyle.

Plan your wardrobe around a few favorite and flattering colors.

Combine a casual article of clothing with something more dressy. For instance, wear a silk shirt with a pair of jeans.

Adding Accessories

A wardrobe is not complete without accessories. Accessories can be essentials—such as shoes and belts—or such nonessentials as ties, scarves, hats, and jewelry.

Well-chosen accessories can stretch your wardrobe by giving the same outfit an entirely different look. You can also use accessories to draw attention to your best features and away from less attractive ones. For instance, a wide belt can emphasize a slim waistline. A distinctive watchband or bracelet can draw attention to strong or graceful hands.

When using accessories, it is best to choose one *center of interest,* or **focal point.** Choose a wide belt with a big buckle, for example. Any other accessories should be less noticeable and blend in with the outfit. Too many eye-catching accessories will create a cluttered look.

A Successful Wardrobe

By building from what you have and planning what you need, you can create a versatile, coordinated wardrobe. Adding the right accessories will help you achieve different looks and give every outfit a finishing touch.

LESSON ONE *Review*

Using complete sentences, answer the following questions on a separate sheet of paper.

Reviewing Terms and Facts

1. Vocabulary Define the term *accessories.* Give two examples each of essential and nonessential accessories.

2. Give Examples Name some clothing items that could be used for more than one purpose.

3. Recall How can you turn a few clothing items into a large wardrobe?

Thinking Critically

4. Explain What is the purpose of a wardrobe inventory?

5. Describe Give an example of how accessories could be used to change the look of an outfit.

Applying Concepts

6. Look through a clothing catalog and select six basic separates from which to make a mix-and-match wardrobe. Using these separates, how many outfits can you suggest? What would the total cost be? Make a poster showing your basic wardrobe. Display your poster in class.

Evaluating Quality and Fit

WORDS TO KNOW

fibers

synthetic fibers

woven fabrics

knit fabrics

grain

ease

DISCOVER...

● how to judge quality in clothing.

● how to find the best style and the right fit for you.

Have you ever bought a shirt that got a hole in it after only one or two washings? Perhaps you have a sweater that you never wear because it makes you feel itchy. You can avoid these problems in the future if you learn how to judge clothing quality. Quality in an item of clothing means that it is well made, durable, and comfortable to wear. To judge clothing quality, you need to look at the fabric, the construction, and the fit.

Recognizing Quality Fabrics

The best way to learn about fabrics is to handle and compare them for yourself. Make a trip to a fabric store. Check the labels to see the fiber content, or what the fabrics are made of. Look at the prices and compare fabrics in different price ranges. Feel various fabrics to see how they handle. When stretched or crushed, quality fabric will spring back. A basic understanding of fabrics can help you make better clothing choices.

Fibers and Fabrics

Most fabrics are made from fibers. **Fibers** are *the tiny strands that make up yarns.* Originally, all fibers came from natural sources. Some natural fibers commonly used in clothing are cotton, linen, silk, and wool. Do you know from which natural sources these fibers come?

- **Cotton**—the seed pod of the cotton plant

- **Linen**—the flax plant

- **Silk**—spun by a silkworm

- **Wool**—the hair of sheep

More recently, scientists have developed a wide variety of **synthetic fibers,** *fibers made partially or entirely from chemicals.* Polyester and nylon are two types of synthetic fibers.

Skills IN ACTION

Identifying Fabrics

Being able to identify different types of fabrics will help you select clothes that are well made and comfortable. Gather as many different fabric swatches (small pieces of material) as you can. Identify and label the various types of fiber (natural, synthetic, blend) and weave (woven, knit). Mount your fabrics and display your poster in class.

All clothing must have a label that gives the fiber content of the fabric and instructions for its care and a hangtag that gives additional information.

Fabrics can be made all of one fiber or by combining two or more fibers. The clothing label must tell you what percentage of each type of fiber makes up the fabric. For example, a shirt might be 100 percent cotton, or it might be a blend, such as 65 percent cotton and 35 percent polyester. A sweater might be labeled 70 percent lambs wool, 20 percent angora, and 10 percent nylon.

Fibers are made into fabrics by two main methods: weaving and knitting. The way a fabric is made affects its appearance and performance.

- **Woven fabrics** are *fabrics made on a loom by interlacing lengthwise and crosswise threads at right angles.* Several methods of interlacing are used to achieve special effects. The most durable weaves are plain and twill. The fabrics used in bedsheets and men's dress shirts are examples of plain weave. Denim used for jeans is one example of a twill weave.

- **Knit fabrics** are *fabrics made by looping threads together.* Depending on the knitting method, different fabrics can be made. Not all knits are heavy like sweaters. Cotton T-shirts are also made of knit fabric. Most knit fabrics can be stretched easily. This stretching makes them comfortable and wrinkle resistant.

Fabric Grain

Grain in fabric is *the direction in which the threads run.* Both knit and woven fabrics have a grain. The grain runs up and down and across the fabric, forming a true right angle. Well-constructed clothes should be cut on grain, with the threads running straight up and down and straight across.

Threads may sometimes be pulled off grain when the fabric goes through the finishing process. This makes the grain slant. If the fabric is off grain, the garment will appear to sag to one side, especially after a few washings.

You can test the fabric grain of a shirt by making sure that the grain is straight across the back from one underarm seam to the other. Test pants and skirts at the back of the hipline. The grain should be the same on both sides. If not, the garment probably won't look right when you wear it.

Fabric Finishes

Manufacturers sometimes add various finishes to improve the quality or durability of fabrics. Some finishes add body or bulk. Some set or hold the threads in place so that the fabric will wear well and will not pull out at the seams. Other finishes add softness, luster, strength, crispness, or shrinkage control. Finishes can also make caring for fabrics easier.

Clothing labels often tell you what finishes have been added. For instance, a fabric may be treated to be stain- or water-repellent. Washable clothes may have a drip-dry or permanent-press finish, which means that the garment requires little or no ironing.

Grain in a garment should run straight up and down and across the fabric. How might a garment look if it were off grain?

Recognizing Quality Construction

No matter from what type of fabric clothing is made, a quality garment also requires quality construction. Poor construction can ruin the appearance or durability of an otherwise attractive style. When evaluating clothing construction, use the information provided in **Figure 16.3** on the next page.

- All the top stitching is evenly spaced and straight.

- The seams are straight and made with short, evenly spaced stitches.

- The seams' ends are securely finished.

- The seam lines on the outer side of the garment are smooth. They should not be puckered or crooked.

- Plaids and stripes match at the seams.

- Seams on collars and facings are flat, not bulky.

- Darts taper to a sharp point.

- Gathering is evenly distributed.

- Buttonholes have enough stitches to hold the edges securely.

- Buttons are securely sewn.

- Cuffs and sleeve plackets are neatly finished.

- Pockets are secure, smooth, and flat.

- Zippers move easily without catching threads and fabric.

- Fasteners are neatly applied.

- Sleeves are evenly gathered or eased and smooth along the seam line.

- The garment fits smoothly and hangs well.

**Figure 16.3
Signs of Quality Construction**
Why is it important to check for quality construction when buying clothes?

Comfortable Clothes

To enjoy wearing your clothes, you must be comfortable in them. First, the clothes need to fit correctly. The fabric from which a garment is made and the style of the garment also affect comfort. Knowing how to evaluate these three factors will help you select clothes that you will feel comfortable wearing.

Finding the Best Fit

Clothing is sold in a variety of size categories. Each is designed for a particular body size and shape. Clothing for females comes in different sizes from clothing for males.

Female clothing is sold in girls', juniors', misses', women's, and plus sizes. Girls' sizes go up to 14 or 16 and are roughly equivalent to the age of the wearer. Juniors' sizes (such as 3, 5, 7, 9, 11, and 13) are designed for a developing figure but are usually smaller and shorter-waisted than misses sizes (such as 6, 8, 10, 12, 14, and 16). Juniors' clothes are generally styled for teens, while misses' and women's clothes cater more to adult tastes. Within each size category, petite sizes are shorter in length, while tall sizes are longer.

For males there are three basic size groups: boys', teen boys', and men's. Boys' sizes are designed for small, undeveloped bodies. Teens' sizes are for slim teens and young men. Men's sizes are designed for adult figures. Men's pants are sized by the waist measurement and the inside leg measurement, or inseam. For example, jeans with a 28-inch waist and a 30-inch inseam would be labeled "Size 28/30." Dress shirts also list two measurements—the collar size and the sleeve length—such as 15/34. Sports jackets are sold by chest measurement and length, such as 38 Short or 38 Long.

For both females and males, some clothing may be sized simply as Small, Medium, Large, or Extra-large. Examples of this type of clothing include T-shirts, sweatshirts, and sweaters.

Try on and compare the fit of various brands and styles until you find one that feels comfortable to you. Check the fit by looking at yourself in a full-length mirror. Be sure also to test the fit by sitting, bending, walking, and reaching. **Figure 16.4** provides guidelines for judging the fit of garments.

Figure 16.4 Judging Fit in Garments

For a comfortable fit in clothing, be sure to check these features. What might happen if you didn't check them before buying a garment?

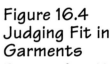

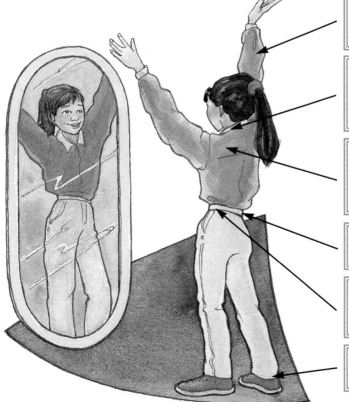

SLEEVES Do long sleeves cover your wrist-bone? Can you lift your arms over your head with ease?

NECK OPENING Is the neck opening comfortable? If it is too large, the front of the garment falls forward and sags. If it is too small, the neck binds and the front rides up.

SHOULDER SEAMS Do the shoulder seams hit you at the shoulder? They should not go over your shoulder unless the garment is designed that way.

FASTENERS Do buttonholes, zippers, and other closures lie smoothly?

WAISTBAND AND HIPS Does the waistband feel comfortable and fasten easily? Can you sit comfortably in pants or jeans?

HEMLINE Is the hemline even around the bottom? Is the length right for you?

CHOOSING SHOES

Shoes are an important part of your wardrobe. You want to buy shoes that are both comfortable and durable. Here are some tips.

- Shop early in the day to get a more accurate fit.
- Get your feet measured so that you are sure of your size.
- Try on shoes with the type of socks or stockings that you would normally wear.
- Look for shoes that are not too tight or too loose. Be sure that you have room to wiggle your toes.
- Try on both left and right shoes, and walk around the store in them.
- If you are trying to find shoes to go with a certain outfit, wear the outfit or bring a sample of the fabric.

The Way Fabrics Feel

The fabric from which a garment is made can affect its comfort in many ways. Fabrics made of natural fibers absorb perspiration and generally feel cooler than fabrics made of synthetic fibers. Synthetic fibers usually dry faster, however, and may be more comfortable in bathing suits, for example. The fiber content of each garment must be listed on its label. Knowing the characteristics of different fibers will help you choose the most comfortable fabric.

Which fabrics do you think feel pleasant to the touch? Some people dislike the feel of slippery or clingy fabrics. Others find woolen knits rough and scratchy. You will want to buy clothes that suit your own preferences. When you buy clothes, be sure to check the feel of the fabric carefully.

If you don't like the way a fabric feels, you probably won't enjoy wearing it. From what fabrics are your favorite clothes made?

Comfort and Style

Clothing style also affects its comfort. For example, a full skirt or pants with pleats may provide for more **ease,** or *ability to move freely*, in a garment. A scoop neckline or an open collar may feel less restrictive than a turtleneck sweater.

Some styles may suit your body shape better than others. Trying on a garment is the best way to decide whether a particular style is comfortable for you. A style that feels comfortable will often look flattering as well.

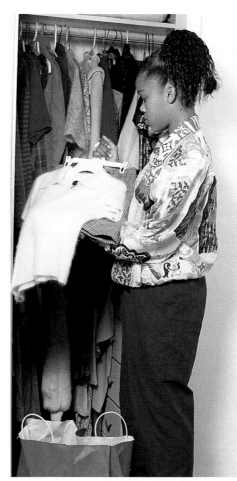

Understanding how to evaluate the quality and fit of garments will help you to make wise clothing choices. How might this save you money? ▶

LESSON TWO *Review*

Using complete sentences, answer the following questions on a separate sheet of paper.

Reviewing Terms and Facts

1. Identify Name four natural fibers and identify the source of each.

2. Vocabulary How does a *woven fabric* differ from a *knit fabric?*

3. List Give four reasons why a finish might be added to a fabric.

4. Recall Name three factors that affect the comfort of clothes.

Thinking Critically

5. Explain How would you check the fabric grain on a shirt?

6. Apply What measurements would you need to know if you were buying a dress shirt for your father?

7. Compare and Contrast What is the difference between style and fit? How are they related?

Applying Concepts

8. Imagine that you are a clothing designer. Describe one garment that you would design and the fabric you would use to make it. Explain how the characteristics of this fabric would enhance the garment's design. Draw a sketch of your creation.

9. Working with a small group, look through a clothing catalog. Find as many terms as you can that describe the style of one type of garment, such as shirts. Make a list of these style terms, and try to define or describe the characteristics of each one.

LESSON THREE
Shopping for Clothes

WORDS TO KNOW

shopping plan

status symbols

cost per
    wearing

DISCOVER...

- how to develop a shopping plan.
- what clothing labels tell you.
- how to get the most for your clothing dollars.

How do you feel about shopping for clothes? Maybe you love to shop, whereas your best friend would rather do almost anything than look for new clothes. No matter how you feel about shopping, you can be a smarter shopper by following a few simple guidelines. By planning your clothing needs and looking for the best value, you can save both time and money.

Your Shopping Plan

In Lesson 1 of this chapter, you learned how to plan a wardrobe. The final step was to make a list of the clothes you needed. That list is the first step in developing a shopping plan. A **shopping plan** is *a strategy for spending the money you have available to purchase the clothing you need or want.* Before you develop a shopping plan, you should talk over your wardrobe ideas with your parents. They can help you determine how much money is available to buy the clothes you need, as well as how much of that amount you can use for other items you want.

In addition to your list of clothing needs, your shopping plan should consider these three factors:

- **Your clothing budget.** It is a good idea to set up a monthly or seasonal spending plan for your clothes. Go over your spending plan with your parents and decide how you can make your money go farther. For example, can you wait until the jacket goes on sale? Can you replace the missing buttons on your shirt instead of buying a new one?

- **How you will pay for the purchase.** You learned about several payment methods, including cash, check, credit card, and debit card, in Chapter 7, Lesson 5. Can you recall some of the advantages and disadvantages of each? For major purchases, such as a formal dress or suit, running shoes, or a winter coat, you may need to save your money. Another alternative for more expensive items is to use a layaway plan. Unlike buying on credit, layaway means that you can't take the item home until it is paid for in full.

- **Where you will shop.** In most areas, there are several stores from which to choose. Specialty stores, discount stores, and department stores are some options.

Another choice is to shop for clothes by mail order. Although you can't try on the clothes before you order them, you may prefer the convenience of shopping in your own home. Clothes that do not suit you can usually be returned.

Before you shop, you need to plan your clothing budget. Why is this important?

What the Label Tells You

You can find a great deal of helpful information by reading clothing labels. Taking time to check the label and the hangtag before you buy can help you determine the quality, durability, and care of garments.

Care Labels

Every item of clothing must carry a label describing its fiber content and how to care for it. This information may be on the same label or on two different labels. Look for these labels inside the collar or waist. Sometimes you will find the care label sewn into a side seam instead.

The care required depends on the fibers and finishes used in making the fabric. Check garment tags for special information about finishes, such as "little or no ironing," "wrinkle-resistant," or "water-repellent." The care label will give you specific cleaning and care instructions. **Figure 16.5** provides information about care labels.

Figure 16.5 Understanding Labels

Checking care labels before you buy clothing can save you time and money. For example, you may decide not to purchase clothing that needs to be washed by hand or dry-cleaned because the item is more difficult or expensive to care for.

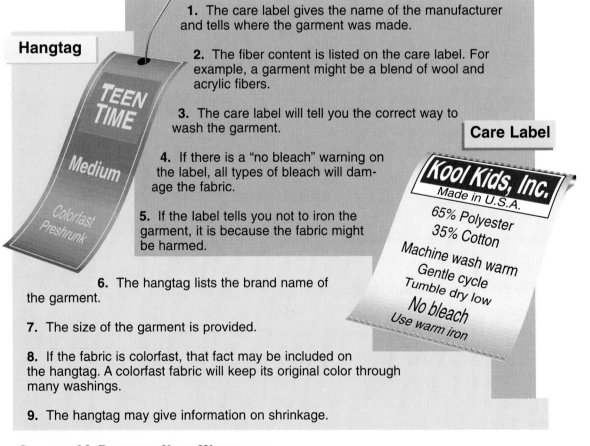

Hangtag

TEEN TIME

Medium

Colorfast Preshrunk

Care Label

Kool Kids, Inc.
Made in U.S.A.
65% Polyester
35% Cotton
Machine wash warm
Gentle cycle
Tumble dry low
No bleach
Use warm iron

1. The care label gives the name of the manufacturer and tells where the garment was made.

2. The fiber content is listed on the care label. For example, a garment might be a blend of wool and acrylic fibers.

3. The care label will tell you the correct way to wash the garment.

4. If there is a "no bleach" warning on the label, all types of bleach will damage the fabric.

5. If the label tells you not to iron the garment, it is because the fabric might be harmed.

6. The hangtag lists the brand name of the garment.

7. The size of the garment is provided.

8. If the fabric is colorfast, that fact may be included on the hangtag. A colorfast fabric will keep its original color through many washings.

9. The hangtag may give information on shrinkage.

Brand Name Clothing

A brand name is a trademark used by a manufacturer to identify its products. Sometimes stores have their own brand names. In addition, clothing labels may identify the designer, which is another kind of brand name. Some people use brand names as a guide in selecting clothing. Some brands may have better styles than others, and some may have better quality. Brand names and designer labels are not always signs of quality, however. They can be just **status symbols,** or *clothes or other items that give the owner a special feeling of importance.*

Through experience in wearing and comparing various articles of clothing, you will discover which brands are well made and fit well. Brand name items are usually more expensive than those with less well known names. You will have to decide if brand name clothing is worth the extra cost.

Shopping for Value

When you made your shopping plan, you had to calculate your clothing budget—how much money you had to spend. You can make that money go farther by understanding and following some simple guidelines.

TIPS for living

THE HIDDEN COSTS

When you shop for clothes, keep in mind that a garment may end up costing more than the price tag indicates. Beware of these hidden wastes of time and money:

- Fabrics that can't be washed in the washing machine. Dry cleaning can be expensive. Hand washing takes extra time.

- Fabrics that ball up (pill) on the surface or that snag easily. If the fabric needs to be repaired each time you wear it, you won't want to wear it much.

- Fabrics that must be ironed.

- Special features that may increase the cost of dry cleaning. For example, dry cleaners often charge extra to clean leather or to press pleats.

Stretching Your Clothing Budget

You don't have to spend a great deal of money to have a wardrobe that fulfills your needs. To reduce your clothing costs, follow these tips:

- **Start with two or three basic outfits.** Add coordinated pieces to build your wardrobe around a few basic colors. You can create many different clothing combinations that way.

- **Make the best use of what you have.** Try different uses, combinations, and accessories with clothes you already own.

- **Compare cost and quality.** Keep in mind that it may not always be smart to buy the best quality. Why pay more for durability in a fad item that won't be in fashion next year?

- **Take advantage of sales.** Planning ahead and shopping during seasonal sales can be a good way to get more for your money.

- **Take good care of your clothes.** By following the directions on the care label, you can make clothes last longer.

- **Learn to sew.** Making simple repairs and simple clothing items yourself can be a way to save money and express your personality.

Shopping during sales is a good way to get more for your clothing dollars. What are some other ways?

Understanding Cost per Wearing

An easy way to find out how much value you are getting for the money you spend is to calculate the cost per wearing. **Cost per wearing** is the *amount of money spent for each time you wear an article of clothing.* To determine cost per wearing, first estimate how many times you will wear a particular garment. Then add up the cost of the garment and the cost of cleaning it. Divide the total cost by the number of times you will wear the garment. This will give you an estimated cost per wearing.

Cost per wearing can help you decide where your clothing dollars will best be spent. For example, do you really want to buy an expensive ski jacket that will be worn for only one ski trip? Can you afford the better-quality leather if the same pair of shoes can be worn for school, casual wear, and dress-up occasions? A little simple math will help you develop a sound shopping plan.

A more expensive item can be a better value if it will outlast the cheaper alternative. How can cost per wearing help you decide which item to purchase? ▶

LESSON THREE *Review*

Using complete sentences, answer the following questions on a separate sheet of paper.

Reviewing Terms and Facts

1. List What three factors should you consider when developing a shopping plan?

2. Identify Name two types of information you can find on a care label.

3. Vocabulary Define the term *status symbol*. Give an example of a status symbol.

4. Recall What are four ways to stretch your clothing budget?

Thinking Critically

5. Compare and Contrast How is using a layaway plan to make a purchase similar to using a credit card? How are the two payment methods different?

6. Evaluate Do brand names always determine quality? Why or why not?

7. Apply Determine the cost per wearing for a pair of jeans that cost $50, do not require dry cleaning, and will be worn 80 times.

Applying Concepts

8. Check the fabric content and care labels of clothing you own. What generalizations can you make about how fiber content is related to care? Make a chart of typical care instructions and the types of garments to which they usually apply.

LESSON FOUR
Clothing Care

DISCOVER...

- how to remove spots and stains from clothing.
- techniques for washing, drying, and ironing clothes.
- how to store clothes properly.

Griffin had to get dressed quickly or he would miss the bus for school. He pulled his favorite shirt out of the closet, only to find a stain on the front. He reached for another shirt, but that one was missing a button. Finally, Griffin opened his dresser drawer to look for a T-shirt. The drawer was so over-stuffed that all of the shirts were badly wrinkled. Griffin threw one on anyway and ran for the bus.

Have you ever been frustrated by not having your clothes ready to wear when you were ready to go?

Taking Care of Your Clothes

Keeping your clothes in ready-to-wear condition is partly just a matter of common sense. Follow these simple guidelines to take proper care of your clothes:

- Wear appropriate clothing for the activity. When doing yard work or cleaning out the garage, for example, wear old clothes so that it doesn't matter if they get very dirty.

- Dress and undress carefully to avoid snagging, ripping, or stretching garments.

- Inspect your clothes carefully after each wearing. **Mend,** or *repair,* any tears or holes before they get bigger. If you find spots or stains, remove them immediately and wash the garment as soon as possible. A **stain** is a *soiled or discolored area.*

If you protect your clothes, they will look better and last longer. Besides wearing an apron, what are some other ways to protect your clothes?

Keeping Your Clothes Clean

Cleaning clothes properly requires a basic knowledge of fabrics and simple cleaning techniques. Handling the laundry isn't hard if you follow the instructions on clothing care labels and on laundry products and appliances.

Removing Spots and Stains

If you get a spot on your favorite shirt, it doesn't have to mean the end of the shirt. You will have the best chance of getting the spot out if you treat it as soon as possible, however. There are two basic types of stains: water based and oil based. Water-based stains include those from some foods, perspiration, grass, and washable inks. Oil-based stains come from oils, makeup, ballpoint ink, and oil-based paints. **Figure 16.6** on the next page shows how to remove common stains.

Washing Clothes

Learning the right way to launder clothes will help you keep your clothes looking newer longer. Follow these guidelines when washing your clothes:

- **Pretreat stains and dirty areas.** Besides spots and stains, sleeve cuffs and the fold line on collars often need to be pretreated. **Pretreat** means *to apply a liquid detergent or stain remover on the spots before laundering.*

Figure 16.6 How to Remove Stains

Why is it important to remove spots and stains right away?

Chewing gum. Rub with an ice cube to harden the gum. With a dull knife scrape it off.

Blood. Soak in cold water and detergent. Use bleach if safe for fabric.

Chocolate. Soak in cool water. Rub with detergent and wash.

Grease. Use a prewash stain remover, then wash. If the stain is still visible, sponge with cleaning fluid and rinse.

Ink. Spray with hair spray or sponge with rubbing alcohol. Rinse. Then rub any remaining spots with detergent and wash.

Soft drinks. Sponge with cold water. Wash using bleach if safe for fabric.

Paint. Rub detergent into stain and wash. If some of the stain remains, sponge with mineral spirits and turpentine and rinse.

Grass. Rub detergent into stain and wash.

- **Sort clothes.** Check care labels on clothes carefully. Then separate each pile by color: whites and light-colored fabrics, medium-colored fabrics, and dark fabrics.

- **Select the correct water temperature.** Wash your clothes in the water temperature recommended on the care label. Unless otherwise specified, most clothing can be washed in warm water and rinsed in cold.

- **Choose the correct load size.** If you are washing only a few clothes, choose a small-load setting to save water and energy. Never overload the washing machine. Clothes won't get clean if they are packed in too tightly.

- **Add detergent.** Check the detergent bottle or box for the correct amount to use. Remember to adjust for the load setting you selected.

- **If static is a problem, use a fabric softener.** Fabric softeners can be added in the washer or in the dryer. Read product labels carefully to determine which type you are using and how and when it should be added.

Drying Clothes

Clothes can generally be either line-dried or machine-dried. Line drying saves energy and money but takes longer. Line-dried clothes may feel stiff and often need to be pressed. Machine drying is quick and convenient, but it uses energy and therefore costs more.

As soon as the clothes are dry, remove them from the dryer. This will help prevent wrinkling. Hang up items such as shirts, pants, and dresses as soon as you take them out of the dryer. Then fold and sort the other items.

Ironing Clothes

Some fabrics require ironing after each wash. Even permanent-press items sometimes require touch-up pressing with a steam iron. The care label gives the proper temperature setting for the fabric. Always match the temperature setting on the iron with the fiber listed on the label. Synthetic fabrics may melt if the iron is too hot.

Skills IN ACTION

Hand Washing Clothes

Washing machines can damage certain fabrics. Hosiery, silk or nylon dresses and blouses, and woolen sweaters, mittens, and scarves usually need to be washed by hand. Always check labels for washing instructions. If hand washing is required, use a gentle soap. Wash the garment in cool or warm water. Rinse twice to make sure that all the soap is out. Lay the garment flat on a towel to dry.

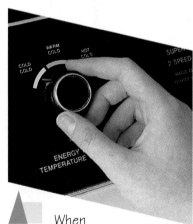

▲ When washing clothes, adjust the settings on the washing machine to match the care labels on the garments. Why should you not overload the washing machine?

Start by ironing small areas of a garment, such as the collar, yoke, and sleeves. Then press the larger areas. This way, you avoid wrinkling areas you have already ironed.

Storing Clothes

An important, but sometimes overlooked, part of caring for clothes is storing them properly. When you hang up your clothes, take the time to close zippers and fasten buttons so that the garment will hang straight. Do not overcrowd closets and drawers, or your clothes may wrinkle.

Seasonal clothes—those that are worn only for a few months each year—or clothes that are worn only for special occasions should be given extra storage attention. Check to be sure that pockets are empty and that garments are clean and mended before putting them away. When soiled clothes are stored for a long time, stains become permanent.

It is important to learn the proper techniques for ironing clothes. How do you know what temperature setting to use when ironing?

Looking Your Best

You will always be well dressed if you keep your clothes fresh and neat. By learning to launder and store clothes properly, you can keep your wardrobe in good condition.

LESSON FOUR *Review*

Using complete sentences, answer the following questions on a separate sheet of paper.

Reviewing Terms and Facts

1. Identify What are three guidelines for keeping your clothes in ready-to-wear condition?

2. Vocabulary Define the term *stain*. Name two oil-based stains and two water-based stains.

3. List Identify the steps to take when machine-washing clothes.

4. Explain Why is proper storage especially important for seasonal clothes?

Thinking Critically

5. Explain How can carelessness damage your clothes?

6. Compare and Contrast What are the advantages and disadvantages of line-drying clothes? Of machine-drying?

Applying Concepts

7. Ask family members about home-remedy stain removers. Write a paragraph or two describing the advantages and disadvantages of using home remedies.

Consumer Focus

Fun-House Mirrors

Have you ever felt surprised at your reflection in the mirror of a dressing room? It's a fact that store mirrors can reflect an inaccurate, even unflattering, image. If a mirror does not hang flat against the wall, it can change the way your body looks.

Try This!

Ask your parents or other family members for tips about trying on and purchasing clothes. Discuss their advice with your classmates.

A Global View NATURAL FIBERS

Different plant fibers thrive in different climates. Flax, for example, grows best in cool and rainy climates. Cotton needs warm and sunny weather. Wool is processed all over the world. In ancient times, the Chinese learned how to raise silkworms, and China is still the world's leading producer of silk.

TRY THIS!

Find out the characteristics of one of these fibers. Share your findings with the class.

TECHNOLOGY

Electronic Clothes Shopping

Home-shopping channels are becoming increasingly popular. Television's selling power can be tremendous. For example, a designer recently appeared on a shopping channel and sold more than 12,000 silk blouses in less than 20 minutes.

Try This!

What do you think are the advantages and disadvantages of clothes shopping via television? Discuss your answers with a classmate.

SOCIAL STUDIES CONNECTION

CLOTHING AND CLIMATE

The main principle of clothing design in cold climates is *tailoring*—clothing follows body lines and fits snugly at the wrists and ankles to hold in body warmth.

In hot, dry areas, the first rule of clothing design is *draping*—clothes hang loosely, allowing air to flow around the body and cool it.

Follow Up

1. Find pictures that illustrate the tailored principle and the draped principle of clothing design. Discuss your pictures with the class.

2. Choose five garments from your wardrobe. Write a brief description of how each garment keeps you warm or cool.

CHAPTER 16 REVIEW

Chapter Summary

- A wardrobe plan consisting of mix-and-match outfits and versatile clothing will make your wardrobe seem larger than it is.

- Accessories—such as shoes, hats, and jewelry—can update and enhance your wardrobe.

- Fabrics and fibers have different characteristics that can affect durability, style, and comfort.

- Clothing fit depends on more than choosing the correct size. When trying on garments, check the neck opening, sleeves, fasteners, waistband, shoulder seams, and hemline.

- A shopping plan will help you shop wisely and stretch your clothing budget.

- Clothing care labels help you choose clothes and care for them properly.

- Stains can be either water based or oil based. Most stains can be removed if they are taken care of immediately.

- Caring for clothes requires you to read and follow directions on clothing care labels and on laundry products and appliances.

- Proper storage helps keep clothes looking their best.

Words to Know

Using complete sentences, answer the following questions on a separate sheet of paper.

1. Give an example of an *accessory* used as an outfit's *focal point*.
2. Explain why *versatile* clothing is a good wardrobe choice.
3. What does it mean to take a *wardrobe inventory?*
4. Describe how a *woven fabric* is made.
5. Define the term *grain* as it applies to clothing.
6. Why is *ease* important in evaluating fit and style?
7. What is a *shopping plan?*
8. What is another word for *mend?*
9. Explain how to *pretreat* a stain.

Review Questions

Using complete sentences, answer the following questions on a separate sheet of paper.

1. Explain how mix-and-match dressing can stretch your wardrobe.
2. What are three ways to learn about current styles and fashions?
3. Why should you check the fabric grain when purchasing clothing?
4. Name four areas you should examine to judge the fit of a garment.

5. What three factors affect how comfortable your clothes are?

6. Describe two ways clothing labels can be useful.

7. What could be some consequences of improper laundering?

▶ Thinking Critically

Using complete sentences, answer the following questions on a separate sheet of paper.

1. Apply What can you learn from each category of clothing in your wardrobe inventory?

2. Contrast What are the differences between woven and knit fabrics?

3. Evaluate What are some advantages and disadvantages of shopping by mail?

4. Recommend Suppose that a friend wants to buy an expensive new dress for a special party. What advice would you give her about deciding on her purchase? About paying for it?

▶ Cooperative Learning

1. As a class, organize a used-clothing drive. Encourage students in your school to clean out their closets and to contribute clean items in good condition. Make minor repairs if needed. Donate the clothing to charity, or plan a one-day thrift sale.

2. Working in small groups, select five styles that are currently in fashion at your school. Evaluate each for comfort, versatility, and whether or not you would classify it as a fad. Display your evaluations in the form of

a chart, and have each group present a brief report to the class.

Family & Community

1. Take a survey of the clothing stores in your community. How many fall into each category: specialty store, department store, discount store, thrift shop? How far do you have to travel to get to each? Write a one-page evaluation of your community's shopping resources.

2. Interview one or two family members or friends whose wardrobes you admire. Which types of fabrics do they prefer? What do they look for when judging clothing construction? Do they have any special tips or techniques for washing, ironing, or storing clothes? Share your findings with the class.

Building A Portfolio

1. Make an inventory of your wardrobe. List five items you need to buy. Using catalogs and sales circulars, estimate how much money it would cost to purchase these items. Then determine which garments in your wardrobe can be repaired, updated, or accessorized instead of being replaced. How much money would you save? Keep your list in your portfolio.

2. Find magazine and newspaper articles with home advice tips. Collect clippings of tips and techniques for removing specific kinds of stains. Make a folder to organize the tips for easy reference, and add the folder to your portfolio.

CHAPTER 17
Preparing to Sew

LESSON ONE
The Sewing Lab and Equipment

LESSON TWO
Choosing a Sewing Project

LESSON THREE
Choosing Fabrics and Notions

TEENS MAKING A DIFFERENCE

Clothes for Children

Andrea's friend Kristen came to her for help in organizing a clothing drive for children in a local shelter. Kristen said that the children needed general clothing as well as specific items, such as pants, sweatshirts, and pajamas.

Andrea offered to sew some items for the children. First, she contacted the shelter to get a list of the sizes and items the children required.

The clothing drive was a huge success. Kristen collected more clothes than were needed. Andrea had fun and felt proud that she could use her sewing skills to make a difference.

Try THIS!

With a group of classmates, think of ways to use your sewing skills to help others. For example, you could make simple cloth toys for children in a homeless shelter.

481

The Sewing Lab and Equipment

WORDS TO KNOW

pinking shears
sewing gauge
bobbin
stitch regulator
presser foot

DISCOVER...

- the keys to success in the sewing lab.
- how to use and care for small sewing equipment.
- how to operate a sewing machine.

Amelia likes sewing because it gives her a chance to be creative. In her free time, she enjoys making her own clothes and pillows and other items for her room. Before Amelia started sewing at home, she learned how to sew and how to operate sewing equipment in the school sewing laboratory.

The Sewing Lab

Your school's sewing lab is a great place to learn and practice basic sewing skills, including how to cut out a pattern and how to use a sewing machine. You will also learn how to work cooperatively with others and how to manage your time wisely.

Safety in the Sewing Lab

Learning how to use the supplies and equipment in the sewing lab involves learning how to operate them safely. Follow these simple safety rules:

- Keep scissors and sharp objects closed when not in use.

- Pass sharp objects with the handle toward the other person.

- Put pins and needles in a pincushion, never in your mouth.

- Keep your fingers away from the path of the sewing machine needle.

- Do not attempt to operate the machine if it is jammed or is making an unusual noise.

Managing Your Time

When you sew in the school lab, you have only a limited amount of time. The keys to making the most of your time are organization, preparation, and consideration.

- **Organization.** Put your supplies in a small container, with your name on it. If you keep your supplies neat and organized, they will be ready to use when you need them.

- **Preparation.** Bring in required fabric or supplies on the first day of the lab. That

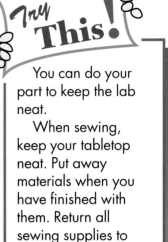

Try This!

You can do your part to keep the lab neat.

When sewing, keep your tabletop neat. Put away materials when you have finished with them. Return all sewing supplies to the proper place.

If you are having any problems with your sewing machine, tell your teacher immediately. What might happen if you try to use a machine that is not working properly?

way, you won't lose valuable lab time. Before you start to sew, read through the instructions for each step. If you are not sure of how to do a step, ask your teacher.

- **Consideration.** When you finish with an item, return it to where it belongs.

Sewing Equipment

To complete most projects, you will need a variety of small sewing tools in addition to the lab sewing machine and steam iron. If you buy quality tools and take care of them, they will last a long time.

Small Sewing Tools

To complete any sewing project successfully, you have to know which tools to use and how to use them. **Figure 17.1** describes some of the most basic sewing tools used for pinning, measuring, cutting, and hand sewing.

SHEARS, SCISSORS, PINKING SHEARS Shears are a large pair of scissors that frequently have a raised handle for easier cutting. Scissors are used for trimming, clipping, and cutting threads. Pinking shears are scissors that have a zig-zag edge.

SEWING GAUGE A sewing gauge is a 6-inch (16-cm) ruler made of metal, with an adjustable pointer. Use it to measure short spaces, such as hems and seam widths.

NEEDLES Use needles for hand sewing. Many people prefer size No. 8 because the eye of the needle is easy to thread.

SEAM RIPPER This is a pen-shaped tool with a small blade at one end for removing stitches.

THIMBLE A thimble protects your finger while you're hand sewing and makes it easier to push the needle through the fabric.

THREAD Select a color that matches your fabric.

PINCUSHION The wrist pincushion is a convenient way to hold pins and needles when you're sewing.

PINS Dressmaker pins are slender, sharp-pointed, smooth, and rust-proof.

TAPE MEASURE A flexible tape is used to take body measurements.

Figure 17.1
Basic Sewing Tools
These tools will make sewing easier. Which ones have you used?

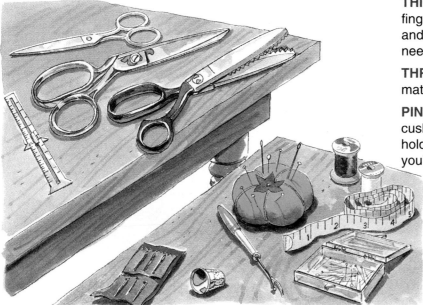

The Sewing Machine

Most sewing machines have the same basic parts, as identified in **Figure 17.2.** Sewing machines all operate in the same way: a needle moves up and down through the fabric, and two sets of threads interlock to form stitches.

Sewing machines vary greatly in what they can do and how much they cost. All machines sew straight stitches forward, and most sew backward too. Many sew a zigzag stitch, which can be used to finish seam edges and apply designs to a garment. Some machines can sew buttonholes, zigzag stitches, and decorative stitches.

Before using any sewing machine, be sure to read the instruction book. You can use it to find the parts on your sewing machine, and how to use its special features.

Using Your Machine

Familiarize yourself with the machine in the school lab. It is a good idea to practice winding the bobbin, threading the

**Figure 17.2
The Parts of a
Sewing Machine**
You can learn the basic parts of a sewing machine by studying this diagram and reading the instruction book for your machine. Why is this important?

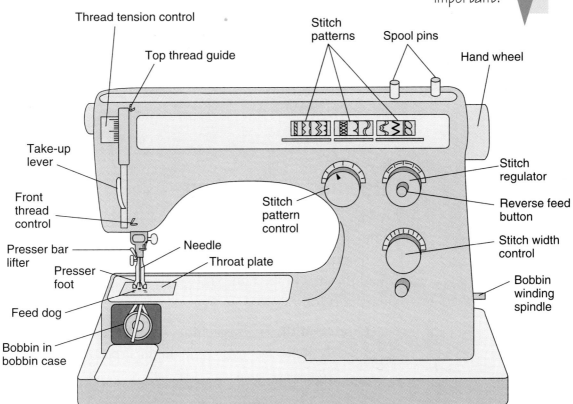

Thread tension control · Top thread guide · Stitch patterns · Spool pins · Hand wheel · Take-up lever · Front thread control · Presser bar lifter · Presser foot · Feed dog · Bobbin in bobbin case · Needle · Throat plate · Stitch pattern control · Stitch regulator · Reverse feed button · Stitch width control · Bobbin winding spindle machine, and setting the stitch regulator. Try stitching on scraps of fabric before sewing on a project.

Winding the Bobbin

Before you can begin sewing on a machine, you must complete a few steps. The first is winding the thread you will be using from your spool onto the bobbin. A **bobbin** is *a small metal or plastic spool that holds the thread inside the machine.* Because each machine may have a slightly different procedure for winding the bobbin, you should check your instruction book to see how to do it. After you have threaded the bobbin, insert it in the bobbin case. Then insert the bobbin case into the sewing machine.

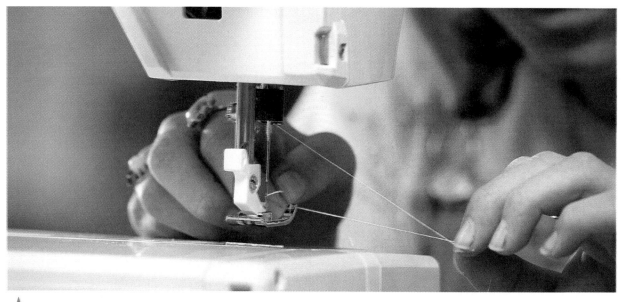

Don't try to guess how to thread an unfamiliar sewing machine. Where can you get information on the correct procedure?

Threading the Machine

The second step is threading the machine. Each type of sewing machine is threaded slightly differently. There should be a diagram in the instruction book that shows you how to thread the machine. The basic procedure for all sewing machines is as follows:

• Before you thread a machine, use the hand wheel to move the take-up lever to its highest point.

• Begin threading with the spool of thread on the spool pin located at the top of the machine.

- Then put the thread through the tension control, the take-up lever, and the needle. Use the thread guides along the way to hold the thread in place. When you thread the needle, be sure that the thread goes through the needle in the direction indicated for your machine.

Types of Stitches

The final step to complete before you can begin to sew is determining what kind of stitch to use. There are four main types of stitches:

- **Regular stitch**—a medium-length stitch (about 10 to 15 stitches per inch) used for most purposes

- **Basting stitch**—a very long stitch used for holding layers of fabric together temporarily; can be removed easily

- **Reinforcement stitch**—a short stitch used to strengthen the stitching area at a corner or a point

- **Zigzag stitch**—a sideways stitch used to make button-holes, finish seam edges, and sew special seams

To set the stitch length on your machine, you will need to use the stitch regulator. A **stitch regulator** is *a dial or lever that controls the length of the stitches*. Machines label stitch lengths differently, but the smaller numbers are always longer stitches. For example, a stitch length of 7 would be longer than one of 14. Check the length of the stitch on a scrap of the fabric you will be using to determine if it is correct.

You can also change the tightness of the stitches with the tension control. If one thread lies flat against one side of the fabric while the other thread forms loops on the other side, you need to adjust the tension.

Operating the Sewing Machine

As with any piece of equipment, operating a sewing machine properly takes practice. Before you can begin sewing, you need to lower the needle into the fabric and drop the presser foot. The **presser foot** is *the metal piece at the end of the needle that holds the fabric in place*.

Skills IN ACTION

Pressing Fabrics

Whenever you sew, you will need to use the iron to press seams and other work. Follow these safety tips:

- Always rest the iron on its heel.
- To see if the iron is hot, try it on a scrap of fabric, not on your finger.
- Unplug the iron when you finish.
- Coil the cord so that no one trips over it or pulls the iron off the ironing board.

Now you are ready to sew! Learning how to coordinate several actions at the same time can be difficult at first. You want to operate the machine at an even speed. That will produce the best stitches. To control the speed, you use either a foot pedal or a knee pedal. The harder you press, the faster the machine runs.

As you stitch, the fabric is automatically pulled through the machine. You need to use your hands to keep it straight. With practice, you will learn how to use your hands to guide the fabric and to follow the pattern markings accurately.

Keeping your tools and equipment in good order will make sewing easier and more enjoyable. How has this teen organized her work?

LESSON ONE *Review*

Using complete sentences, answer the following questions on a separate sheet of paper.

Reviewing Terms and Facts

1. List Give three safety rules for the sewing lab.

2. Vocabulary What is the function of a *bobbin?* Where is the bobbin located?

3. Describe Name two types of stitches and describe the purpose of each.

Thinking Critically

4. Analyze Why is it important to work efficiently in the sewing lab?

5. Compare and Contrast What are the differences among shears, scissors, and pinking shears? For what purpose would each tool be used?

6. Evaluate What are two benefits of learning to sew?

Applying Concepts

7. With a partner, practice basic sewing skills on the sewing machine at school. You should become familiar with how to wind the bobbin, thread the machine, and set the stitch regulator. Then use scraps of fabric to practice operating the machine. Have your partner check your work. Then check your partner's work.

LESSON TWO
Choosing a Sewing Project

DISCOVER...

- what to look for when choosing a sewing project.
- what you can learn from the pattern envelope.
- how to determine your correct pattern size.

What do you like best about sewing? For many people, sewing is a way to express themselves. You show your individuality in the styles, fabrics, and finishing touches you choose. You can personalize your garments or even create your own designs. The key to enjoying your sewing projects is to choose ones that are suitable for your sewing ability.

WORDS TO KNOW

pattern
view
darts
alteration

How to Select a Pattern

Most sewing projects call for a pattern. A **pattern** is *a plan for making a garment or project.* It contains the paper shapes of the various pieces and gives the directions for sewing. Your success in completing your project depends in part on the pattern you choose.

When you choose a sewing project, you will want one that matches your abilities and the time you have to complete it. Before you choose a pattern, consider the following:

- **Purpose.** Do you want to make clothing for yourself, a household item, or a specialty item, such as a backpack?

- **Sewing skills and experience.** If you have never worked on a project before, choose a simple pattern with few pieces.

- **Time.** Do you have enough time to complete the project? This is especially important if you are sewing at school and are sharing a sewing machine.

- **Cost.** How much money are you willing to spend?

By considering these factors, you can decide on the best pattern for your needs.

What to Look for in Patterns

When you are shopping for a pattern, start by browsing through a variety of pattern books. When you find a pattern that you like, make a note of the brand name and pattern number. Then you can find the pattern and look at the envelope for more information.

The pattern envelope provides you with all of the information you need to plan a sewing project. The front of the envelope shows a picture of the completed project. Sometimes more than one **view,** or *version of the garment,* is shown. For example, a shirt pattern may show one view with short sleeves and another with long sleeves.

The best way to find a sewing project is to look through pattern books. What information will you find in these books?

On the back of the envelope, you will find the following:

- A detailed sketch showing the pattern pieces and construction features. For example, the sketch will indicate where darts are located. **Darts** are *tapered V-shaped seams used to give shape.*

- A chart that tells you how much fabric to buy for the style and size you are making

- Recommendations on the types of fabrics that can be used and additional materials you will need, such as thread and buttons

Salespeople in the fabric store are often experienced sewers. Who else could you ask for help when choosing a project?

Multisized Patterns

Some patterns may be styled to fit a range of sizes. For example, a single pattern for a belted tunic may fit sizes small to large. Loose-fitting styles such as this may be a good choice for beginning sewers, since small mistakes will matter less.

Finding Styles That Are Easy to Make

How can you find an appropriate pattern for your first project? Pattern books indicate which patterns are simple to sew and even have special sections for quick and easy projects.

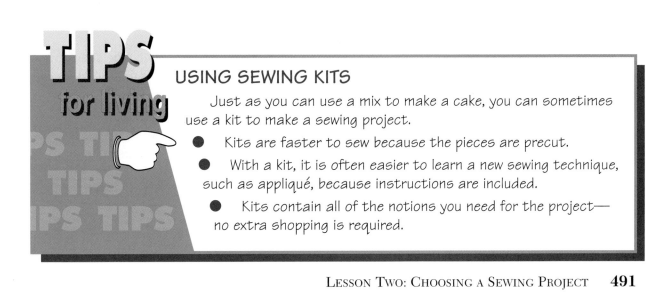

TIPS
for living

USING SEWING KITS

Just as you can use a mix to make a cake, you can sometimes use a kit to make a sewing project.

- Kits are faster to sew because the pieces are precut.
- With a kit, it is often easier to learn a new sewing technique, such as appliqué, because instructions are included.
- Kits contain all of the notions you need for the project—no extra shopping is required.

In addition, look for these features to help you choose an easy-to-make pattern:

- **Number of pattern pieces.** Fewer pattern pieces mean fewer pieces of fabric to cut out and stitch.

- **Number of seams.** Seams join two pieces of fabric together. The fewer seams involved, the easier it will be to complete the pattern.

- **Fit of the garment.** Loose styles are easier to sew than snug or close-fitting styles.

- **Closures.** Elastic waists, snaps, or hooks require less advanced sewing skills than do zippers and buttonholes.

**Figure 17.3
How to Take
Measurements**
Follow these guidelines to take your measurements. Why are accurate measurements important?

Determining Your Pattern Size

Patterns, like ready-to-wear clothing, come in different sizes. They are grouped by figure types.

FOR MALES

NECK Measure around the base of the neck and add ½" (1.3cm), or buy pattern by the shirt size you regularly purchase.

CHEST Measure around the fullest part of the chest.

ARM Take measurement from back base of neck along shoulder to wrist.

WAIST Measure around the natural waistline over a shirt, but not over pants.

HIPS Measure around the fullest part of the hip.

FOR FEMALES

BUST The measuring tape should be placed over the fullest part of the bust and continue under the arms and straight across the back.

BACK WAIST LENGTH Measure from the prominent bone at the base of the neck to the waistline.

WAIST The measuring tape should be held snugly at the natural waistline.

HIPS The measuring tape should be held snugly over the fullest part of the hips. For taller figure types (misses', women's, and junior) this is usually 9 in. (23 cm) below the waistline; for shorter figure types (young girls/teen, junior petite, and misses' petite) this is usually 7 in. (18 cm) below the waistline.

Pattern sizes for female clothing are based on four measurements: bust, waist, hip, and back waist length. Females need to use their measurements to determine which pattern type—girls', teens', junior, petite, or misses'—will fit best. Patterns for male clothing are based on five measurements: chest, waist, hip or seat, neck, and sleeve length. **Figure 17.3** shows you how to take your measurements. When doing so, be sure that the measuring tape is snug and held parallel to the floor.

▲ Your finished product doesn't have to look exactly like the picture on the pattern. How might you personalize a sewing project?

Finding the Correct Pattern Size

After you have taken your measurements, compare them to the measurements on pattern envelopes. You want to select a size that requires very little **alteration,** or *change to make a certain size fit.* Choose the size that has the closest measurements. Use the following guidelines to decide which measurement is most important for a particular type of garment:

- For blouses and tops, fit the bust measurement.

- For shirts, fit the chest and neck measurements.

- For full skirts, fit the waist measurement.

- For pants and semifitted skirts, fit the hip measurement.

LESSON TWO *Review*

Using complete sentences, answer the following questions on a separate sheet of paper.

Reviewing Terms and Facts

1. Recall Name the factors you need to consider before choosing a pattern.

2. List Identify three pieces of information that you can find on the back of the pattern envelope.

3. Name What features should you consider when looking for easy-to-make patterns?

Thinking Critically

4. Explain Why is it important to evaluate your time and skill level before deciding on a sewing project?

5. Evaluate What are some advantages of making your own clothes? What might be some disadvantages?

Applying Concepts

6. Look through fashion magazines or advertisements for clothing styles you like. Identify several garments that you think would be the easiest to make. Then look through pattern books to find similar styles. Present your findings in the form of a chart, showing the style and listing the pattern brands and numbers that come closest.

LESSON THREE
Choosing Fabrics and Notions

WORDS TO KNOW

notions

nap

ravel

interfacing

DISCOVER...

- how to select the best fabric for your sewing project.
- which types of fabrics to avoid.
- how to choose notions that match your needs.

Once you have decided on a project and a pattern, you need to choose the materials with which to make the project. When you select fabric, you should consider more than just the color and texture. You also want to be sure that the materials are of good quality and are appropriate for your project. Then you are ready to choose **notions,** *the small items that are part of the construction of the garment.*

How to Choose Fabrics

Fabrics come in many different colors, textures, designs, and finishes. How do you know which fabric to buy? You will want to evaluate the fiber or fiber blend, how the fabric is made, and any finishes that have been added. In addition, you should check the grain for quality.

When selecting fabric, you can use the information on your pattern envelope. The back of the envelope provides a list of suggested fabrics and how much fabric you will need. The pattern envelope provides special instructions for fabrics with **nap,** or *one-way texture,* such as corduroy.

How to Recognize Quality Fabrics

When you shop for fabrics, you will notice that they come in many price categories. How can you tell which ones are high quality? Keep in mind that you don't have to buy the most expensive one to get a good fabric. When judging quality in fabrics, examine the following:

- **Crosswise threads.** They should be straight and at right angles to the lengthwise threads.

- **Pattern.** If you are considering a printed fabric, make sure that the pattern runs straight with the grain. If the

Check fabric carefully for flaws before you have a salesperson cut the amount you need. Why is this important?

fabric is not printed properly, the garment will look off grain.

- **Weave.** Is it firm and durable?

- **Color.** Is it uniform throughout?

- **Finish.** Does it feel comfortable and pleasing to the touch?

- **Label.** Read the label on the end of the bolt of fabric. It gives facts about fabric width, fiber content, shrinkage, finishes, and care.

How to Select Fabric

When choosing a fabric, think about the requirements of your project. Although woven fabrics are generally the easiest to handle and sew, you should consider the following factors:

- **Whom the project is for.** If you are making something for yourself, look for colors that can be mixed and matched with other clothes you own.

- **When the garment will be worn.** The time of day and the season of the year in which the garment will be worn may affect the type of fabric and the color you choose.

- **How the item will be used.** If you are making a non-clothing item, such as a tote bag, a dark-colored fabric that doesn't show dirt may be a good choice.

- **Type of care needed.** Look for fabrics that are machine washable and that require little or no ironing.

Fabrics to Avoid

Some fabrics are difficult to work with. For example, lightweight, flimsy, and extremely soft fabrics are slippery and hard to sew. Loosely woven fabrics may not be a good choice because they tend to **ravel,** or *have threads pull out of the cut edge.* Patterns in fabrics can make a project more complicated too. For example, plaids, stripes, and large prints need to be matched at the seams.

Expressing Yourself Through Fabric

Sewing can be a way to express your individuality. One way to make a garment uniquely "you" is to use fabric creatively. Try some of these ideas the next time you sew:

- Add a dash of color by using contrasting fabric for facings and undercollars or for collars and cuffs.
- Use interesting prints for the lining material of vests and jackets.

Selecting Notions

After you have chosen a fabric, refer to the back of the pattern envelope for a list of the type of notions you will need. Commonly used notions include the following:

- Thread

- Fasteners, such as zippers, snaps, hooks and eyes, buttons, and hook-and-loop tape

- Elastic

- Hem tape

- Interfacing. **Interfacing** is *a layer of special fabric placed between two pieces of fabric to give more shape to the garment.* It is often used in waistbands, cuffs, and collars.

When you buy notions, use your fabric to match colors. Thread should be the same color as the fabric or slightly darker because it will appear lighter when stitched.

The notions you will need for your project are listed on the pattern envelope. How can you make sure that they match your fabric?

If you calculate the total cost of fabric and notions before you buy them, you can determine whether your choices are within your budget. What can you do if they are too expensive?

Making Choices

The materials you choose will affect the cost and the success of your sewing project. Begin by reading the information on the back of the pattern envelope. Then follow the guidelines for selecting fabric and notions that you learned in this lesson. Now you're ready to start sewing!

LESSON THREE *Review*

Using complete sentences, answer the following questions on a separate sheet of paper.

Reviewing Terms and Facts

1. Recall How would you know the amount of fabric to buy for a particular sewing project?

2. Identify When judging fabric quality, what elements should you examine?

3. Vocabulary Explain what happens when a fabric *ravels*. Which type of fabric ravels easily?

4. Give Examples Name five commonly used notions.

Thinking Critically

5. Analyze Should you buy the most expensive fabric that you can afford? Why or why not?

6. Recommend How could you use notions to update your clothing? Give two examples of items from your wardrobe.

Applying Concepts

7. Estimate the cost of a sewing project you are interested in making. Be sure to include the cost of the pattern, fabric, and notions. How does your total cost compare with that of a similar item you could buy ready-made? What factors, besides cost, should you consider when deciding whether to make or buy this item?

Chapter *17* Activities

SEWING AT HOME

When selecting an area for sewing at home, consider that the ideal sewing area should be well lit and able to accommodate a sewing machine, an ironing board, and a cutting table. Where you sew also depends on when you sew and the schedules of other family members.

TRY THIS!

Think about where you could set up a sewing area in your home. Keeping in mind family schedules, when would be the best time for you to sew there?

A Gl🌐bal View

SEWING AROUND THE WORLD

In some cultures, appliqué sewing has developed into an art form. India is famous for its *shisha* appliqué in which tiny mirrors are sewn onto a fabric backing. In Benin, appliqué has been used for centuries on banners and ritual clothing to record the deeds of battles and the powers of kings. Cuna Native Americans are well known for their molas.

TRY THIS!

Find a picture of or additional information about one of the types of appliqué work described here. Share your findings with the class.

Consumer Focus

Sew or Buy?

The next time you're trying to decide whether to make or buy an item, consider the following factors. Would it take more time to shop for the item or to sew it? Is it less expensive to sew? Do you have the sewing skills?

Try This!

Considering time, money, and sewing skills, would it be better for you to sew or buy? Write a paragraph explaining your answer.

MATH CONNECTION

PRODUCT PRICING

Shannon Reed was sewing ten dolls for an upcoming craft fair. Her costs for materials were $68, and the entry fee to the craft fair was $10.

Each doll had taken three hours to make, and Shannon hoped to earn at least $5 per hour making and selling the dolls. Competitors charged between $20 and $30 per doll.

Follow Up

1. How much would Shannon have to charge per doll to make $5 per hour?

2. How much should Shannon charge per doll if materials cost $85 and she showed the dolls at two craft fairs, each with a $10 entry fee?

3. Why do you think that it was important for Shannon to check the prices of similar dolls before deciding what price to charge for her dolls?

Chapter Summary

- When working in the sewing lab, it is important to follow safety procedures and to organize your time and supplies.

- Basic tools for sewing include needles, pins, a pincushion, a sewing gauge, a seam ripper, shears, scissors, pinking shears, a tape measure, a thimble, and thread.

- Before using any sewing machine, read the instruction book.

- A pattern is a plan for making a garment or project. The pattern envelope provides information about fabric, notions, sizes, and difficulty level.

- If you learn how to take accurate measurements, you can determine your pattern size and ensure that your completed garment will fit well.

- When judging quality in fabric, examine the crosswise threads, pattern, weave, color, finish, and label.

- Some fabrics are easier to work with than others. Woven fabrics are a good choice because they are the easiest to handle and sew.

- Notions are the small items that are part of the construction of a garment. Thread, fasteners, elastic, hem tape, and interfacing are examples of notions.

Words to Know

Using complete sentences, answer the following questions on a separate sheet of paper.

1. What does a *stitch regulator* control?

2. Describe the function of the *presser foot* on a sewing machine.

3. What is a sewing *pattern*?

4. Define the term *view* as it applies to patterns.

5. Why would a garment be designed with *darts*?

6. What is nap? Give two examples of fabrics with *nap*.

7. Define the term *interfacing*. What are three common uses for interfacing?

Review Questions

Using complete sentences, answer the following questions on a separate sheet of paper.

1. List three basic sewing tools, and explain the purpose of each.

2. Describe the basic procedure for threading a sewing machine.

3. What do you use to control the speed on a sewing machine?

4. Using "1" for easiest to sew and "5" for the most complex, rank in order the following five styles: a close-fitting shirt with buttons and gathered sleeves; a collarless shirt with buttons and gathered sleeves; a collarless, sleeveless shirt with snaps; a close-fitting shirt with snaps and gathered sleeves; a

loose shirt with a band collar, snaps, and short sleeves.

5. How do you measure the back waist length? The arm length?

6. Identify which measurement is most important for each of the following types of garments: blouses and tops, shirts, full skirts, pants, and semifitted skirts.

7. Why is it a good idea to buy fabric and notions at the same time?

Thinking Critically

Using complete sentences, answer the following questions on a separate sheet of paper.

1. Evaluate When choosing a sewing project, which of the following factors do you think is most important: purpose, sewing skills and experience, time, or cost? Explain your answer.

2. Analyze Why do you need to consider so many factors when choosing a fabric for a sewing project? What might happen if you make a selection without giving it enough thought?

Cooperative Learning

1. In small groups, brainstorm some classroom rules for the sewing lab. Take into account safety, efficiency, and consideration for others. Compare lists from each group, and combine them to make a master list. Post the rules on a bulletin board in the classroom.

2. In small groups, research one type of sewing notion (for example, snaps, hem tape, or thread). Each group should explain

to the rest of the class the different types of products available within that category and the advantages and disadvantages of each type.

Family & Community

1. Think of a sewing project that you could make as a gift for a friend or a family member. Write a paragraph or two describing the person and the factors you would consider in choosing the best pattern and fabric for the project. If possible, make the item and give it to the person you chose!

2. Find out where in your community you could buy a sewing machine. Visit one store, or obtain brochures about the machines sold there. Find out whether the store offers classes in how to use the machines. Which sewing machine features do you think would be most useful? Share your findings with the class.

Building A Portfolio

1. Use a sewing machine to practice sewing various stitches on small pieces of different types of fabric. Attach notes to each piece, evaluating which stitch you would use for what purpose and how well each is suited to the type of fabric. Place the samples and notes in your portfolio.

2. Choose one item of clothing from your wardrobe. Analyze how many pieces of fabric went into its construction. Make a sketch of the pattern pieces required, labeling where each fits into the completed garment. Add the sketch to your portfolio.

CHAPTER 18

Sewing Skills

TEENS MAKING A DIFFERENCE

Sewing for Dolls

Twelve-year-old Kristi Makita loves to sew. When she was younger, she made clothes for her dolls. Now Kristi makes outfits for her younger sister's dolls. Sometimes she follows a special pattern. Other times she creates her own designs.

A few months ago Kristi displayed some of her doll clothes at a neighborhood craft fair. Several parents were impressed with Kristi's work and offered to pay her to make clothes for their children's dolls. Since then she has received more orders. Kristi has turned her hobby into a moneymaking, customized sewing business!

Try THIS!

Think of a way that you could use your sewing skills to earn, or save, money. Discuss your ideas with a classmate.

LESSON ONE
Preparing Your Pattern and Fabric

WORDS TO KNOW

guide sheet

layouts

markings

ease

grain

selvage

raw edges

bias

DISCOVER...

- how to use a guide sheet.
- how to check pattern pieces and measurements.
- how to prepare your fabric.

Evan thinks he is ready to begin his sewing project. He bought the pattern, fabric, and notions yesterday. He plans to start laying out the pattern pieces and pinning them to the fabric today. Do you know what steps Evan has left out? Do you know what he needs to do to prepare his pattern and fabric before he begins to sew?

Using the Guide Sheet

Before you begin sewing, you need to study the guide sheet inside your pattern envelope. A **guide sheet** is *a set of step-by-step instructions for sewing a pattern.* The guide sheet contains general information on how to use the pattern, a diagram of the pattern pieces, an explanation of the pattern markings, and layouts. **Layouts** are *diagrams of how the pattern pieces should be placed on the fabric.*

If you use the guide sheet, you will be able to sew more quickly and efficiently. For best results, follow these steps:

- Study the diagram of the pattern pieces.

- Circle the letters of the pieces needed for the view that you plan to make.

- Circle the layout diagram that you will use for your size and style.

- Read through *all* of the pattern directions before you start to work.

- As you make your project, put a check mark next to each step after you complete it.

To start preparing the pattern pieces, unfold them and cut them apart. Why shouldn't you trim the pieces?

Preparing the Pattern Pieces

After you have read through the guide sheet, you are ready to start preparing the pattern pieces. Follow these steps:

- Cut apart the pieces you will use, but do not trim them. You will cut off the margins later, when you cut the fabric.

- Put the pattern pieces that you will not use back in the envelope.

- Study each pattern piece, and refer to the guide sheet to find out what the markings mean.

Markings are *guides on the pattern pieces for making a project*. **Figure 18.1** explains common pattern markings.

- If the pattern pieces are wrinkled, iron them with a warm, dry iron.

Checking the Pattern Measurements

Before you place a pattern on fabric, you need to make sure that the pattern you selected fits your body. To do that, compare your measurements with the body measurements listed on the pattern envelope. Determine if the pattern is too long or too short or if any measurements don't match up. If you need to make any alterations to the pattern, now is the time to do so—*before* you cut the fabric.

To make length adjustments, use the two parallel lines labeled "lengthen or shorten." Your teacher can show you how to do this. Be sure that you make the same changes on both the front and back pieces of the pattern.

To make width adjustments, you may need to measure the pattern pieces with the help of your teacher. Then you need to determine how much actual ease is included in the pattern. **Ease** is *the amount of fullness added to a pattern for movement and comfort*. Each part of the pattern requires a different amount of ease, depending on the stress put on that part of the garment when it is worn.

When choosing a pattern, keep in mind that a full design allows for more flexibility and requires fewer alterations. Why would one of these patterns need to closely correspond to body measurements?

How to Prepare the Fabric

You can run into problems if you don't prepare your fabric *before* you begin sewing. Just imagine how you would feel if, after you spent hours sewing a shirt, it shrank when you washed it! To avoid such problems, take the time to preshrink your fabric and check the **grain**—*the direction in which the threads run.*

Figure 18.1
Pattern Markings

Why do you need to under-stand what these pattern markings mean?

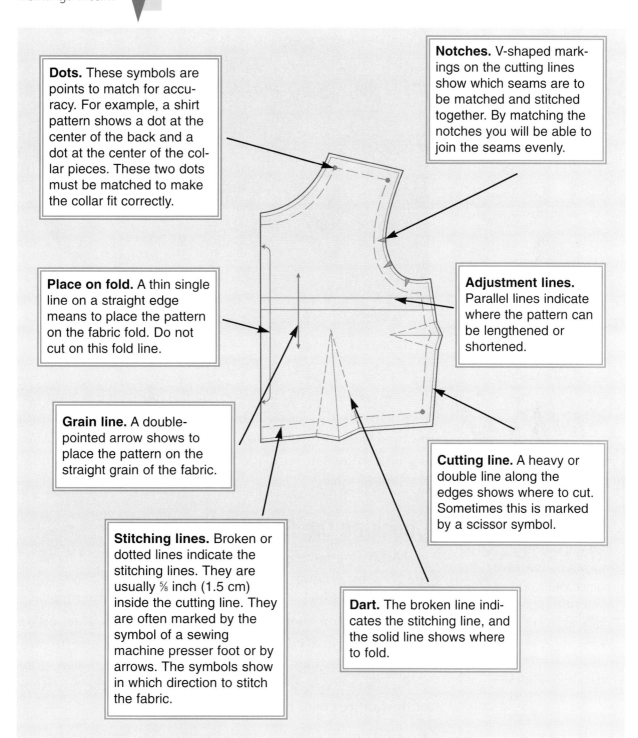

Dots. These symbols are points to match for accuracy. For example, a shirt pattern shows a dot at the center of the back and a dot at the center of the collar pieces. These two dots must be matched to make the collar fit correctly.

Notches. V-shaped markings on the cutting lines show which seams are to be matched and stitched together. By matching the notches you will be able to join the seams evenly.

Place on fold. A thin single line on a straight edge means to place the pattern on the fabric fold. Do not cut on this fold line.

Adjustment lines. Parallel lines indicate where the pattern can be lengthened or shortened.

Grain line. A double-pointed arrow shows to place the pattern on the straight grain of the fabric.

Cutting line. A heavy or double line along the edges shows where to cut. Sometimes this is marked by a scissor symbol.

Stitching lines. Broken or dotted lines indicate the stitching lines. They are usually ⅝ inch (1.5 cm) inside the cutting line. They are often marked by the symbol of a sewing machine presser foot or by arrows. The symbols show in which direction to stitch the fabric.

Dart. The broken line indicates the stitching line, and the solid line shows where to fold.

Preshrink fabric by following the cleaning instructions given on the bolt of fabric. Why is preshrinking important? ▶

Preshrinking the Fabric

Before putting your pattern on the fabric, it is a good idea to preshrink the fabric. To do this, use the same cleaning method that you would use for the finished garment. Cleaning instructions are provided on the care label on the end of the bolt of fabric.

Checking the Grain

After you have preshrunk the fabric, you need to check the grain by looking at the fabric and locating the two selvages along the lengthwise edges. The **selvage** is *the tightly woven edge of the fabric that has no visible loose threads.* **Raw edges** are *the unfinished edges of the fabric that have loose threads.*

To test the grain, fold the fabric along the *lengthwise* grain so that the selvages are on top of one another. If the raw edges of the fabric do not line up, follow these steps:

- For woven fabrics, clip the selvage and pull a crosswise thread. Cut along the line made by the pulled thread.

- For knitted fabrics, cut along one crosswise row of loops to straighten the edges.

Now test the grain again by folding your fabric and matching selvages. If the crosswise ends match exactly and are at right angles to the selvage, the fabric is straight. The fold will be smooth and unwrinkled. If the edges do not match, the fabric is not straight.

You can straighten the fabric by pulling it on the true **bias,** or *diagonal.* To do that, open up the fabric and pull the two opposite corners that are too short.

You can straighten fabric by opening it up and pulling the two opposite corners. When is it necessary to straighten fabric?

LESSON ONE *Review*

Using complete sentences, answer the following questions on a separate sheet of paper.

Reviewing Terms and Facts

1. Vocabulary What is a *guide sheet?* What information does it contain?

2. Identify List five common markings on patterns.

3. Describe How would you adjust a pattern that is too long?

4. Explain Why should you preshrink fabric? How would you know what procedure to follow when preshrinking?

Thinking Critically

5. Explain Why is it important to read through all the directions on a pattern and to think through each step before beginning to work?

6. Summarize Outline the steps that you would take to prepare a pattern before beginning to sew.

7. Contrast Explain how to tell the difference between the selvage and the raw edge.

Applying Concepts

8. With a partner, compare the directions for two different patterns. What are the similarities and differences? Are the instructions for both clear and easy to understand? If not, how could they be improved?

LESSON TWO
Starting to Sew

WORDS TO KNOW

backstitching
seam finishes

DISCOVER...

- how to pin, cut, and mark fabric.
- how to stitch straight and curved seams and how to turn corners.
- ways to finish seams.

Learning how to sew can be both fun and rewarding. Your sewing projects will be more successful if you practice new techniques before you begin. By carefully completing each step—from laying out the pattern pieces to hemming the finished garment—you will be able to make projects that you are proud of.

Using Pattern Pieces

After you have prepared the pattern pieces and your fabric, make sure that you have all of the notions, tools, and equipment that you need for your project. If you are sewing at school, it is a good idea to write your name on your supplies.

Pinning

Look at your circled layout to see how to fold your fabric. Most layouts show the right sides folded together. Lay the pattern pieces on the fabric. The lengthwise grain markings must be parallel to the selvage. Check them with a ruler as you pin. Don't cut out any pieces until they have all been pinned in place and checked by your teacher. Follow these tips:

- First, pin the large pattern pieces that belong on the fold.

- Next, pin the pattern pieces that have a grain-line arrow. To check the grain line, place a pin at one end of the grain-line arrow. Measure from the arrow to the selvage or fabric edge. Position the pattern so that the other end of the arrow is exactly the same distance from the edge. Then pin the piece in place.

- Place the pins diagonally inside the cutting line. This keeps the fabric flat and makes it easier to cut.

- Place pins about 3 to 6 inches (7.5–15 cm) apart.

- Double-check your layout against the layout on the pattern.

Use the circled layout on the guide sheet to see how to fold the fabric and how to place pattern pieces on the fabric. How does it help you to have first circled the layout?

Cutting

Before you begin to cut out your project, practice cutting on fabric scraps. If you cut the edges of the fabric evenly, it will be easier to sew straight seams.

Follow these guidelines:

- Place the fabric flat on the table. Use one hand to hold the fabric in place and the other hand to cut.

- Cut with long, even strokes.

- Cut in the direction of the arrows printed on the pattern seam-line markings. In this way, you will be cutting with the fabric grain, and you will not stretch the fabric.

- Cut around the outside of the notches. Cut double and triple notches together with one long edge across the top.

- Leave the pattern pieces pinned to the fabric until you are ready to stitch.

Using the proper tools can help make the task of marking fabric easier. Which color of tracing paper would you use on light-colored fabric?

Marking

After you cut out your pattern, you need to transfer construction markings from the pattern to the fabric. Markings include darts, dots, fold lines, the center back, and buttonholes. The quickest and most accurate way to mark fabric is to use a tracing wheel and dressmaker's tracing paper. Practice until you can make a light, straight, continuous line. Seam lines don't need to be marked, because you can use the markings on the sewing machine to help you stitch a straight seam. Follow these suggestions when transferring markings:

- Use a color of tracing paper that will show up on the fabric.

- Always test the markings on a fabric scrap to make sure that they don't show through on the right side.

- Slip the tracing paper in place with the carbon next to the *wrong side* of the fabric.

- Press down lightly on the tracing wheel as you mark. You can use a ruler to guide the wheel for straight lines.

- Mark dots with an X. Mark the ends of darts with a short line.

- Mark each line or symbol so that you will know exactly where to stitch.

Basic Sewing Skills

Before you can start sewing a project, you need to know how to stitch a straight seam. To sew a seam, place two pieces of fabric together with right sides facing each other. Line up the edges so that they are even. Match all markings and notches, and pin the two pieces together. The heads of the pins should be near the outside edges of the fabric. For most sewing, pins should be placed about 2 inches (5 cm) apart.

Now look at the throat plate on your sewing machine. The line markings show how far the needle is from the seam edge. Most seams are ⅝ inch (1.5 cm) wide. Find the line on the machine that is this far from the needle. If you line up the fabric edge against this mark as you sew, your seam will stay straight.

Stitching Straight Seams

To complete a project successfully, you need to stitch straight seams. Follow these steps:

1. Use the hand wheel to carry the needle down into the throat plate and up again. When it comes up, a loop of bobbin thread will come with it. **Figure 18.2** shows how to pull up the bobbin thread. Separate the threads, and pull them under the presser foot to the back.

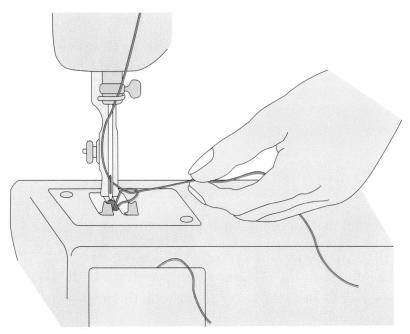

Figure 18.2 Pulling the Bobbin Thread

Pull up the loop of bobbin thread with the thread from the needle. Where do you place the two threads?

To practice sewing safety, keep your eye on the needle when sewing. Don't look away from the machine while sewing, and keep your fingers away from the path of the needle.

2. Place the pinned fabric pieces between the presser foot and the feed dog. Line up the outer edge of the fabric with the ⅝-inch (1.5-cm) marking on the throat plate. Position the fabric so that about ½ inch (1.3 cm) lies behind the needle. Lower the presser foot to hold the fabric.

3. Use the hand wheel to lower the needle into the fabric. Sew backward to the edge of the fabric. Then change the machine to forward, and stitch over your first stitching. This is called backstitching. **Backstitching** is *the technique of stitching over ½ inch (1.3 cm) of a seam at the beginning and end to lock the threads so that the seam won't pull out.* If your machine does not have a backstitch, you can tie the threads together after you have completed the seam.

4. As you stitch, guide the fabric with both hands, but do not push it. Keep your eyes on the fabric edges and guideline markings, and operate the machine at an even speed.

5. At the end of the seam, backstitch again. Then lift the presser foot, remove the fabric, and clip the threads close to the fabric.

Stitching Curved Seams

With curved seams, you must learn to guide the fabric with your hands so that the curves are smooth. You must also keep the stitching an even distance from the edge of the fabric. The best way to learn how to sew curved seams is to practice. Start by stitching curves drawn on a piece of paper. Then practice on scraps of fabric.

Turning Corners

Learning how to turn corners, or pivot, when you sew is another skill that takes practice. Follow these steps:

1. When you come to a corner, slow down the sewing machine. Sew the last few stitches by turning the hand wheel. The last stitch should position the needle exactly at the corner.

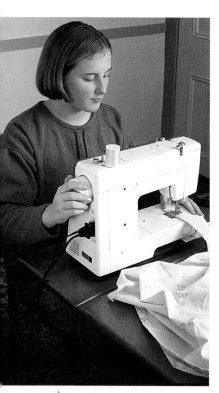

When you approach a corner, sew the last few stitches by turning the hand wheel. What should you do next?

2. Lift the presser foot. Turn the fabric, with the needle still in it, so that you can stitch the next side. Put the presser foot down again.

Adding Seam Finishes

After stitching your project, you may need to add a seam finish. **Seam finishes** are *treatments used on the seam edges to prevent the fabric from raveling.* The most effective seam finish depends on the type of fabric being used. If the fabric ravels only slightly, pink the edges with pinking shears. For greater protection, stitch ¼ inch (6 mm) from each edge before pinking. If your fabric ravels easily, use a zigzag finish. Some fabrics do not ravel and, therefore, do not need seam finishes.

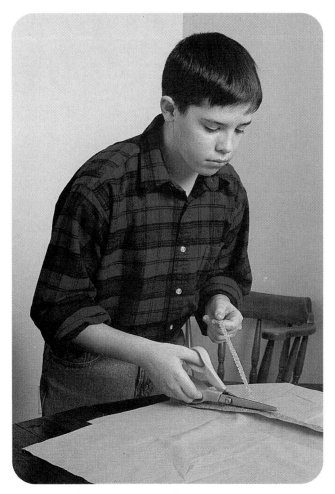

A seam finish can prevent fabric from raveling. Why are there different types of seam finishes? ▶

LESSON TWO *Review*

Using complete sentences, answer the following questions on a separate sheet of paper.

Reviewing Terms and Facts

1. Recall List four guidelines that you can follow to learn to cut accurately.

2. Identify Name the tools needed to mark fabric.

3. Vocabulary What is *backstitching?* Why is it wise to backstitch at the beginning and end of each seam?

4. Identify Describe briefly three finishes that may be used on seam edges to prevent raveling.

Thinking Critically

5. Explain Why isn't it necessary to mark seams?

6. Predict What might happen if you don't practice sewing techniques before beginning a project?

Applying Concepts

7. With a partner, practice pinning, cutting, and marking a few old pattern pieces on scraps of fabric. Follow the instructions in this lesson. Compare your results, and discuss what you found easy or difficult to do.

LESSON THREE
Using a Serger

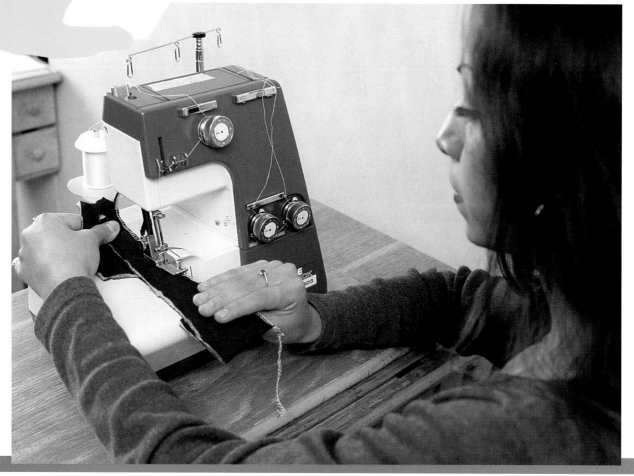

 **WORDS TO KNOW**

serger

cones

loopers

feed dogs

tail chain

stitch finger

DISCOVER...

- what a serger is.
- the uses for a serger.
- how to operate a serger.

Take a look at the seams of the clothes you are wearing. If you made these clothes, each seam is probably a simple line of stitches. If you purchased the clothes, however, the seams probably resemble tiny tubes of fabric wrapped in thread. Seams of this kind are made by a special kind of sewing machine known as a serger.

What Is a Serger?

A **serger** is *a high-speed machine that sews, trims, and finishes a seam in one step.* Although sergers were first designed for factory use, they are now available for home sewing. A serger is a very useful piece of sewing equipment because it can save time and handle a variety of fabrics, from slippery silks to stretchy knits.

Figure 18.3 on the next page shows the parts of a serger. You can see that a serger feeds several strands of thread through guides that are placed above the machine to prevent tangling. **Cones** are *the large, rounded cylinders used to hold thread.* Sergers use cones instead of spools because sergers use more thread than sewing machines do. A cone is much larger than a spool and can hold up to five times more thread.

Sergers are known as two-thread, three-thread, four-thread, or five-thread, depending on the number of threads used to make the stitch. Each thread passes through its own tension dial. Sergers do not have bobbins. Instead, they have **loopers,** which are *rounded parts that hold the thread inside a serger.* The looper threads loop around each other and are interlocked with the needle thread or threads. Depending on the model, sergers may have one or two needles. The remaining threads are wrapped by the loopers.

TIPS for living

SERGER TERMS

Before you use a serger, it is helpful to understand these additional terms.

- **Tension dials** are like the tension control of a sewing machine. Instead of just tightening the stitch, however, you can change the pattern of the stitch by adjusting these dials.

- **Thread guides** help with the threading. To change threads, each new thread can be tied to the old one and pulled through the thread guide. Sergers need as many as eight thread guides for each strand of thread used by the machine.

- **Thread guide holders** look like antennas on the back of the machine. Each thread goes through a loop on this holder before it goes through its own set of tension dials.

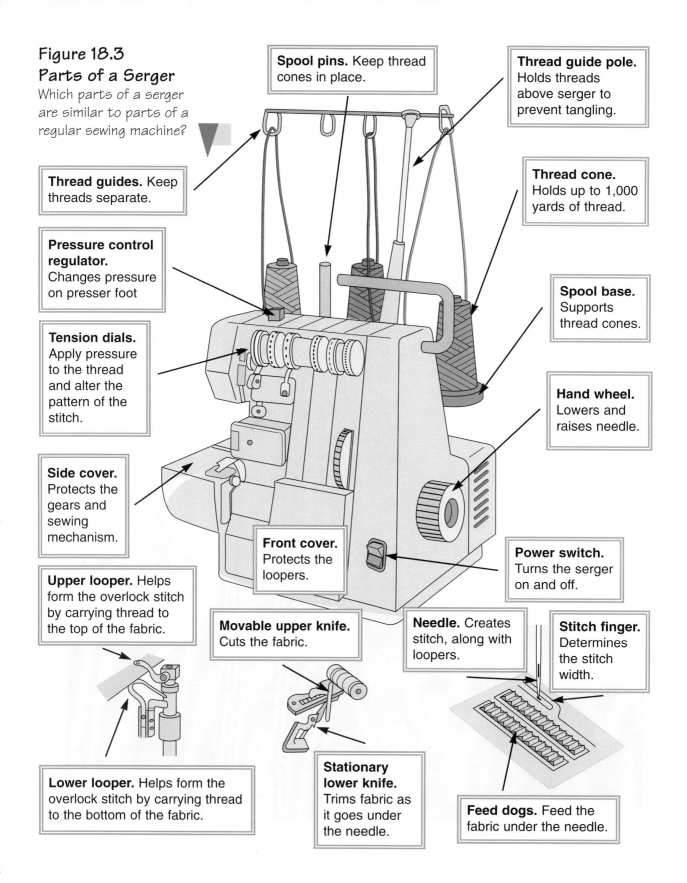

Figure 18.3
Parts of a Serger
Which parts of a serger are similar to parts of a regular sewing machine?

Spool pins. Keep thread cones in place.

Thread guide pole. Holds threads above serger to prevent tangling.

Thread guides. Keep threads separate.

Thread cone. Holds up to 1,000 yards of thread.

Pressure control regulator. Changes pressure on presser foot

Spool base. Supports thread cones.

Tension dials. Apply pressure to the thread and alter the pattern of the stitch.

Hand wheel. Lowers and raises needle.

Side cover. Protects the gears and sewing mechanism.

Front cover. Protects the loopers.

Power switch. Turns the serger on and off.

Upper looper. Helps form the overlock stitch by carrying thread to the top of the fabric.

Movable upper knife. Cuts the fabric.

Needle. Creates stitch, along with loopers.

Stitch finger. Determines the stitch width.

Lower looper. Helps form the overlock stitch by carrying thread to the bottom of the fabric.

Stationary lower knife. Trims fabric as it goes under the needle.

Feed dogs. Feed the fabric under the needle.

Small knife blades are located inside the serger. These knives, which are positioned like the blades of scissors, trim the fabric as it passes through the machine. The result is a seam allowance that is exactly the width of the serger's stitch. As you serge, the entire seam allowance is wrapped inside the stitch.

Types of Stitches

You can produce a variety of stitches with most sergers by using different numbers of threads (from two to five) and adjusting the stitch length and tension dials. Generally, inexpensive sergers produce fewer types of stitches than expensive ones do. Some of the most common stitches are as follows:

- **Overlock stitch**—combines three threads and is most often used on stretch seams and fabrics of moderate to heavy weight. It is also used to finish seams on knits and woven fabrics.

- **Overedge stitch**—uses two threads to secure the edges of fabric and prevent raveling. On some sergers, the overedge stitch wraps around the fabric to produce a decorative finish. This stitch is sometimes used for lightweight seams.

- **Chain stitch**—uses two threads to baste fabric.

- **Safety stitch**—uses four threads to create a stable seam on lightweight woven fabrics. The extra threads help to limit how much the fabric will stretch.

You can use a serger to sew a variety of stitches. Have you seen this stitch on any of your clothes?

- **Flatlock stitch**—works well for flat, stretch seams with minimal bulk and for decorative stitches on knits.

- **Rolled hem stitch**—creates narrow hems and seams and is also used for decorative stitching on knit or woven lightweight fabrics.

Uses for Sergers

A serger does not replace a sewing machine because it cannot sew a single line of locked stitches. It does, however, allow you to use a greater variety of fabrics, including stretchy knits and sheers. It also allows you to take many shortcuts without reducing the quality of your sewing project.

Sergers are most commonly used to sew knits. With a serger, you can easily stitch a strong stretch seam. Sergers can also be used to sew conventional skirt or pant hems or narrow, rolled hems, such as those on cloth napkins. You can also use a serger to produce decorative stitching and reversible seams.

Learning How to Use a Serger

The most difficult part of serging is threading the machine. Your teacher can help you learn how to do this. Most sewing

Fabrics that are usually considered difficult to handle can be sewn quickly and easily with a serger. What are some of these fabrics?

stores also provide demonstrations of how to thread the sergers that they sell.

Once the machine is threaded, you are ready to serge. For safety's sake, make sure that the looper cover is closed before you begin. As you work, you will see that only the needle thread enters the fabric. You will also notice that the seam is stitched where the needle enters the fabric, not where the knives cut the fabric.

Starting to Serge

When you first begin serging, try several different settings on fabric scraps. Label each scrap with the setting used to create the stitch. Then put the scraps in order to get an idea of the stitch varieties that you can make with the serger.

When you are ready to begin a project, set the stitch length and tension dials to the desired settings, and test the stitch on a scrap of fabric. For your test, make sure that you sew as you will on the final product—either with or against the grain. Keep adjusting the stitch length and tension until you achieve the result that you want.

When you sew with a serger, you should avoid using pins to keep the fabric in position. Instead, baste the fabric, or tack it with glue. Pins can seriously damage the serger's knife blades.

When you have tested the stitch and basted your fabric, you are ready to serge. Position the fabric for feeding through the machine. Unless the fabric is unusually thick, you should not need to lift the presser foot. The fabric is moved along by the feed dogs. The **feed dogs** are *the parts of the machine that position the fabric for the next stitch.*

You should begin and end each seam with a **tail chain**— *a length of thread shaped like a chain and made without fabric under the needle.* You make a tail chain by serging without passing fabric through the machine. The tail chain is created as the loopers wrap the thread around the **stitch finger,** which is *a metal prong on the needle plate or the presser foot.* The tail chain keeps the fabric from raveling and eliminates the need to backstitch or tie off the threads of the seam.

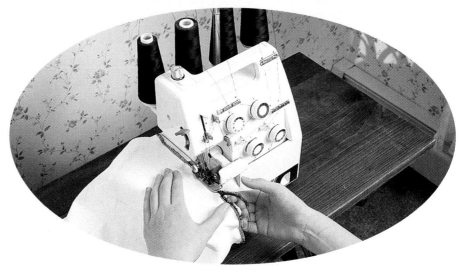

When sewing on a serger, you start and end with a thread tail chain. What does this chain replace?

The Benefits of Serging

Although sergers do not replace sewing machines, they are useful for a variety of sewing jobs. Sergers can stitch, trim, and finish the seam in one step. They are especially useful for sewing straight seams on such garments as sweatshirts. Knowing how to use a serger will help you perform many sewing tasks quickly and easily.

LESSON THREE

Review

Using complete sentences, answer the following questions on a separate sheet of paper.

Reviewing Terms and Facts

1. Identify List the six types of stitches produced by a serger.

2. Vocabulary Define the term *tail chain.* What is the purpose of a tail chain?

3. List Name three sewing techniques that are easily done with a serger.

Thinking Critically

4. Compare and Contrast What is the difference between a seam stitched by a conventional sewing machine and one stitched by a serger?

5. Apply Which serger stitch would you use to do each of the following tasks: make a decorative stitch on a sweatshirt, secure the edge of any fabric, sew a narrow hem on a swimsuit, baste a seam.

Applying Concepts

6. Imagine that you are writing a letter to convince a local fabric store to donate a serger to your classroom. What benefits of serging would you include in the letter?

7. Make a poster showing similarities and differences between the types of sewing that can be done on a conventional sewing machine and on a serger. Display your poster in the classroom.

Making Your Project

DISCOVER...

- basic sewing construction techniques.
- how to finish seams.

Are you ready to begin sewing? Have you laid out, cut, and marked your fabric? Have you practiced sewing both straight and curved seams? Have you checked to make sure that the sewing machine is threaded correctly? If you have completed all of these steps, you are ready to make your project.

WORDS TO KNOW

staystitching

casings

facings

Constructing Your Project

As you begin constructing your project, refer back to the guide sheet that came with your pattern. This sheet lists the steps to follow. Think through each one before you begin.

Staystitching Seams

When you make a garment, the first step is to staystitch the seams. **Staystitching** is *a row of permanent stitching made on or very near the seam line in the seam allowance.* You staystitch by using a regular machine stitch on a single thickness of fabric. This stitch follows the grain, as shown by the arrow on the pattern and guide sheet. Staystitching prevents stretching and helps in turning under edges of hems and bands.

When you have finished stitching a dart, press it flat. Which way should you press vertical darts? Horizontal darts?

Stitching Darts

Darts are used to help shape a flat piece of fabric to the curves of the body. They are usually found at the waistline, elbow, and back of the shoulder. For darts to create the right effect, they must have the correct width and shape. Make sure that they are accurately marked, folded, and pinned before you stitch them. When you are ready to stitch, follow these steps:

- Fold the darts so that the right sides of the fabric are together. Match the stitching lines, and pin them.

- Stitch from the wide end of the dart to the point.

- Stitch the last two or three stitches as close to the fold line as possible. This will make a sharp point without a bubble at the end. Do not backstitch.

- Tie the thread ends securely, and cut about ½ inch (1.3 cm) from the knot.

- Press the dart flat, as stitched. Press vertical darts toward the center and horizontal darts downward.

Gathering Fabric

When you need to fit a longer garment piece to a shorter one, you gather fabric. For example, you might use gathering at the tops of sleeves or at the waist of a full skirt. Gathering gives a soft, full effect. Follow these guidelines when gathering fabric:

- Set the sewing machine for a long stitch of six to eight stitches per inch. Loosen the upper tension.

- Sew two rows of stitches. Stitch one row on the seam line. Stitch a second row ¼ inch (6 mm) closer to the fabric edge. Leave long thread ends. Do not backstitch or tie knots.

- Pin the fabric edges so that the right sides are together and the notches, seams, and markings line up with each other.

- Pull up both bobbin threads from one end. Gently slide the fabric along the threads to gather half the section. Repeat at the other end until the gathered section is the proper length.

- Distribute gathers evenly, and pin about every ½ inch (1.3 cm). Gathers should not bunch up or thin out in any area.

- Stitch with a regular stitch length along the seam line, gathered side up. Make sure that the gathering stitches do not show on the right side of the garment.

- Press the seam allowances flat.

Easing Fabric

When one piece of a garment is only slightly longer than the piece to which it will be joined, easing is used. Easing creates only a slight fullness.

To ease fabric, you need to pin it before you stitch the seam. Place the right sides together, match the notches and ends, and pin every ½ inch (1.3 cm). When you stitch, put the longer seam on top and gently ease in the extra fullness. An eased seam should look smooth and unpuckered, not gathered.

Here are some ideas for storing patterns.
- Before you put the pattern pieces away, press them flat. Then fold them until they're slightly smaller than the pattern envelope.
- As your pattern collection grows, arrange the patterns by category, such as *shirts, pants, crafts.*
- Keep your patterns in a file box or cabinet.

Constructing Casings

If your garment has a pull-on waistband or sleeve band, you may need to sew casings. **Casings** are *fabric tunnels made to enclose elastic or drawstrings.* When you draw up the elastic or drawstring, a gathered appearance is created.

When you sew a casing, make sure that it is ¼ to ½ inch (6 mm–1.3 cm) wider than the elastic or drawstring it will enclose. This will allow the elastic or drawstring to move freely through the fabric tunnel. The two types of casings are fold-down and applied.

- A *fold-down casing* is often used for pull-on pants and skirts. To make a fold-down casing, fold the garment edge ¼ inch (6 mm) to the inside and then again, ¼ to ½ inch (1.3 cm) wider than the elastic. Pin it in place. Stitch close to the inner pinned edge of the casing while leaving a 2-inch (5-cm) opening for inserting the elastic.

- An *applied casing* is often used at the waistline of a dress. To make an applied casing, you need to stitch a separate strip of fabric or bias tape to the garment.

After constructing a casing, use a safety pin to pull the elastic through the opening. How large should the opening be?

If you are inserting elastic into a casing, attach a safety pin to one end of the elastic. Pull the pin through the casing, and be careful not to twist the elastic. Leave the ends of the elastic extending several inches at the opening. Overlap the ends ½ inch (1.3 cm), and pin them. Then try on the garment to make sure that it fits, and make any necessary adjustments. Next, use the sewing machine to stitch the overlapped ends of the elastic securely. Complete the stitching needed to finish the opening.

If you are using a drawstring, you need to make an opening for pulling the ends through to either the outside or the inside of the garment. Refer to your pattern guide sheet for directions.

Constructing Facings

Facings are *fabric pieces used to finish the raw edges of a garment.* Facings are sewn around the edges of necklines, armholes, and waistlines. You stitch them to the right side of the garment and then turn them to the inside. Follow these steps:

- Staystitch the notched edge of each facing piece.

- Stitch the facing pieces together. Trim the seams, and press them open.

- Unless you are using a knitted fabric, finish the outside edge of the facing with zigzag stitching or narrow edge stitching. Knitted fabrics do not require a finish.

- Pin the facing to the garment edge, with the right sides together and the notches and ends matching.

- Stitch the seam. Then trim and grade the seam allowances, and clip the curved areas.

- Turn the facing to the inside. Press it along the seam line, rolling the seams toward the facing side.

- Understitch the facing to help hold it in place. To understitch, open out the facing with the seam allowances toward the facing. Stitch close to the seam line from the right side of the facing through all of the seam allowances. Turn the facing back to the inside, and press it.

- Use several hand stitches to fasten the edge of the facing at each seam.

To achieve a smooth appearance, you need to trim and grade the seam allowance to reduce bulk. **Figure 18.4** on the next page describes the techniques used to reduce bulk. Pattern instructions usually indicate which technique you should use. After you remove the bulk from a facing, you may also need to clip or notch the seam allowance so that the facing can be pressed flat.

Facings can be either extensions of a piece of fabric or fitted pieces cut in the same shape as the garment area to be faced. How do you know which type of facing to use on a garment?

Figure 18.4 Reducing Seam Bulk

How do you know which technique to use to reduce seam bulk?

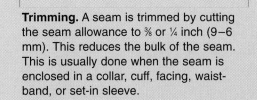

Trimming. A seam is trimmed by cutting the seam allowance to ⅜ or ¼ inch (9–6 mm). This reduces the bulk of the seam. This is usually done when the seam is enclosed in a collar, cuff, facing, waistband, or set-in sleeve.

Grading. A seam is graded by trimming the seam allowances to different widths. Trim the seam allowance toward the inside of the garment narrower than the outside one. This further reduces the bulk. Grading is often done on seams for facings.

Notching. Some curved seams that have too much fabric in the seam allowance may need to be notched. Little Vs or triangles are cut out of the trimmed seam allowance.

Clipping. Curved seams are clipped so that they will lie flat. Slits are cut into the trimmed seam allowance about every ¼ inch to ½ inch (6 mm–1.3 cm). Clip only to within ⅛ inch (3mm) of the seam line, being careful not to cut through the stitching.

LESSON FOUR *Review*

Using complete sentences, answer the following questions on a separate sheet of paper.

Reviewing Terms and Facts

1. Vocabulary What is *staystitching?* Why is it used?

2. Recall Why are darts added to a garment?

3. Identify Name the two types of casings, and give an example of where each could be used.

4. List What are the four techniques used to reduce seam bulk?

Thinking Critically

5. Compare and Contrast What are the similarities and differences between gathering and easing?

6. Explain Why are facings important pattern pieces?

Applying Concepts

7. With a partner, staystitch on various types of fabric scraps. Evaluate how effective the staystitching was on each type of fabric. Which fabrics benefited the most?

Repairing and Altering Your Clothes

DISCOVER...

- when and how to use hand-sewing techniques.
- ways to repair clothing.
- how to recycle clothing.

Although Alexa is just learning how to use a sewing machine in school, she has been hand sewing for several years. She enjoys finding creative ways to personalize her clothes, such as sewing buttons and ribbons on sweatshirts. Recently she cut up a few old pairs of jeans and turned them into a patchwork duffle bag.

WORDS TO KNOW

slip stitch

hemming stitch

shank

Try This!

You can use your hand-sewing skills to help the elderly by sewing on buttons, mending split seams, and repairing hems. Call a nursing home to volunteer, or offer to help an elderly neighbor or relative.

Using Hand-Sewing Techniques

Some sewing jobs require hand sewing. You need to use hand sewing to baste a zipper in place, hem garments, and attach buttons, snaps, and hooks and eyes. Hand sewing gives you more control over the fabric and stitches than you would have with a sewing machine. Follow these guidelines:

- Choose a hand-sewing needle that will pass through the fabric easily.

- Select thread that matches the fabric color.

- Use a short thread—about 18 to 24 inches (46–61 cm) long—so that it won't tangle.

- Make the knot in the thread large enough to keep it from pulling through the fabric as you are sewing.

When you sew a patch over a hole, use a hemming stitch. How else could you cover a hole?

Repairing Clothing

Do you have any clothes that need to be repaired? Maybe you have a sweatshirt that has a hole in the sleeve or a pair of jeans that is missing a button. If you learn some basic hand sewing-techniques, you can easily make these repairs. **Figure 18.5** describes common hand-sewing stitches.

Fixing Small Tears and Holes

It is best to repair tears and holes while they are still small. To fix a split seam, line up the pieces of fabric and pin them in place. Then use a backstitch to sew the seam. To mend small tears, stitch back and forth across the tear to hold the torn edges together. Be sure to begin and end your stitches about ¼ inch (6 mm) above and below the tear. To cover up a hole, apply a fusible patch, or sew on a patch or appliqué.

Replacing Buttons

Replacing lost buttons is probably the most common type of clothing repair job that you will need to do.

Figure 18.5
Hand-Sewing Stitches

How many of these stitches have you used?

Basting stitch. The basting stitch is a temporary stitch used to hold fabrics together for fittings and for matching plaids and seams. To baste, pin fabric layers together. Take even stitches about ¼ inch (6 mm) long and ¼ inch (6 mm) apart.

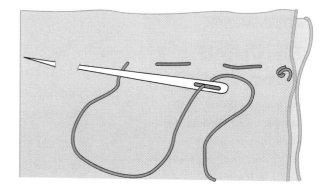

Backstitch. The backstitch is used to repair seams that are hard to reach. Bring the needle through to the upper side of the fabric. Insert the needle back at the beginning of the first stitch, and bring it out again one stitch length in front of the thread. Keep inserting the needle in the end of the last stitch and bringing it out one stitch ahead.

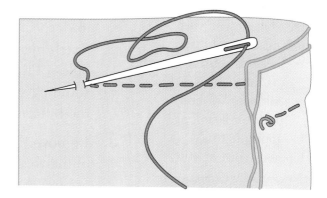

Slip stitch. The slip stitch is a hand-sewing stitch that provides an almost invisible finish. Slide the needle in one folded edge and out, picking up a thread of the under layer at this spot. Take even stitches no more than ¼ inch (6 mm) apart.

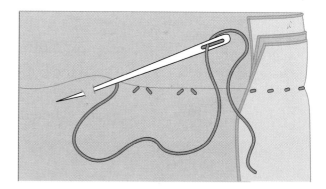

Hemming stitch. As the name indicates, a hemming stitch is a hand-sewing stitch used for hems, especially those finished with hem tape. Take a tiny stitch in the garment, then bring the needle diagonally through the hem tape on hem edge. Take all stitches in this manner, spacing them about ¼ inch (6 mm) apart.

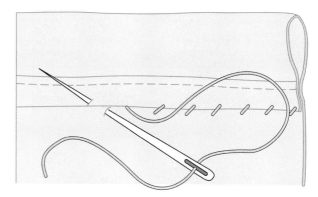

Recycling Your Clothes

You need only your sewing skills and a little imagination to recycle outdated clothes. Here are a few ideas:

- Turn a pair of pants into a pair of shorts.
- Make a jean vest out of an old jean jacket by cutting off the sleeves.
- Add lace, ribbon, buttons, braid, or appliqué to a sweatshirt or vest.

When you sew on a button, select a matching thread color. Double the thread with the ends knotted together for extra strength.

There are two types of buttons: sew-through buttons and shank buttons. A sew-through button has two or four holes through it and no loop on the back. A shank button has a built-in loop on the back. When you hand sew a sew-through button, you need to add a thread **shank,** or *a stem on a button that provides room for the extra layer of fabric around the buttonhole.*

To replace sew-through buttons, follow these steps:

1. Start on the underside of the fabric, and bring the needle and thread to the right side.

2. Bring the needle and thread through a hole in the button. Place a toothpick or a pin across the top of or underneath the button to allow for a thread shank. Stitch in and out several times through the fabric and holes of the button and over the pick or pin. Finish stitching so that your needle and thread are under the button.

3. Remove the pin or toothpick. Pull the button to the top of the thread loop. Wind the thread several times around the stitches under the button to make a shank.

4. Bring the needle back to the wrong side of the fabric.

5. Secure the thread by taking several small stitches in the fabric and then knotting.

If the button you are replacing has a shank, sew it in place using five or six small stitches through the shank and into the fabric. Then fasten the thread securely.

Replacing Other Closures

Other closures commonly used for clothing are snaps and hooks and eyes. Snaps are used to hold together overlapping edges, such as those at the edge of a neckline. There are two parts of a snap—the ball half and the socket half. Follow these guidelines when replacing a snap:

- Place the ball half of the snap on the underside of the overlap, far enough from the edge so that it will not show.

- Secure the ball half by sewing five or six stitches in each hole. Carry the thread under the snap from hole to hole.

- Mark the position of the socket half. Stitch it in place.

Hooks and eyes are often used on waistbands or above zippers, where they are not visible. Attach hooks and eyes by sewing small stitches around each loop. Finish by sewing three or four stitches across the end of the hook to make sure that it lies flat.

Altering Clothes

You can get more use out of your clothes if you learn how to make some basic alterations. One common type of alteration is changing the hem of a garment. Follow these guidelines:

- Use a seam ripper to remove the thread in the old hem. Press out the hem crease.

- Put on the garment to determine the new hem length. Wear the shoes that you plan to wear with the garment. If possible, have someone mark the hem for you. Using a yardstick, place pins every 3 to 4 inches (7.5–10 cm) around the hemline. Stand still, and have the person move around you to place the pins.

- Fold the hem to the new length, and pin it in place. Double-check the length to make sure that it is even.

- Take off the garment, and place it on a table or an ironing board with the hem facing you. Using a sewing gauge or a ruler, mark the proper length of the finished hem with pins or chalk. Most hems are about 2 inches (5 cm) in depth.

- Trim away the excess fabric along the markings. Lightly press the fold of the hem.

- For most woven fabrics, you will need to use some type of hem finish to prevent raveling. The raw edge can be pinked, zigzag stitched, edge stitched, or overlapped with hem tape.

Each type of hook and eye has a different purpose. A round eye is used for edges that meet, and a straight eye is used for edges that overlap. Do you know when a heavy duty eye might be used?

- Stitch the edge of the hem to the garment by hand, using a single thread. Be sure that the stitches do not show on the outside of the garment. Keep the stitches loose so that the hemline doesn't pucker.

- Carefully press the hem.

If you are lengthening a garment and you don't have enough fabric to form a hem allowance, you can use wide bias hem facing. Stitch one edge of the facing to the fabric edge. Then turn the facing to the inside of the garment, and stitch it in place.

After measuring and pinning a new hem, you should look in a mirror to check the length and evenness. What might happen if you don't check carefully?

Recycling Clothes

You can use many of the hand-sewing skills you have learned to recycle garments. If a garment is truly beyond repair, you can cut it into scraps and pieces to be used for other projects, such as a patchwork pillow. You can also save the fabric pieces to use as cleaning rags. Just be sure to remove any buttons or zippers that might scratch surfaces.

LESSON FIVE *Review*

Using complete sentences, answer the following questions on a separate sheet of paper.

Reviewing Terms and Facts

1. Name What types of tasks are best done by hand sewing?

2. Identify When is the *backstitch* a good hand stitch to use?

3. Vocabulary What is a *shank?* How is a shank button different from a sew-through button?

4. Recall How can you determine the new hem length for a garment?

5. Identify What are the benefits of recycling clothing?

Thinking Critically

6. Recommend If you had a tear in your jeans, how would you repair it?

7. Summarize What are the steps for sewing on a sew-through button?

8. Apply Identify three ways to recycle old clothes.

Applying Concepts

9. Find one garment that you own but no longer wear. Suggest ways to repair, update, or change it. Share your ideas with your classmates.

Consumer Focus

On the Mend

Has the zipper in your jacket ever broken? What do you do when you get a hole in your sock? Today, many people don't mend their own clothes. They have their garments repaired or altered at sewing or dry-cleaning shops.

Try This!

Look in the yellow pages and find a shop that repairs and alters clothes. Call the shop, and find out the specific services it offers and how much they cost.

A Global View

SOMETHING BORROWED

To give their designs a new look, American textile and fabric designers often "borrow" the art of various cultures. For example, designers have used the bold geometric designs and brilliant colors found on traditional African cloth to create winter coats, ponchos, and head wraps. Designers have also decorated hats with geometric African designs.

TRY THIS!

Check your wardrobe for clothes or accessories that reflect the art of a particular culture. If possible, show these items to the class.

TECHNOLOGY

Smart Sewing Machines

Electronic sewing machines are now available for use in homes, and they can help make your projects easier. For example, these machines can memorize a buttonhole and then stitch the other buttonholes in exactly the same way.

Try This!

Visit a store that sells sewing machines. Find out the price of an electronic machine, and list its special features. Share your findings with the class.

SOCIAL STUDIES CONNECTION

CLOTHING CUSTOMS

Clothing styles vary from country to country because of climate, available materials, and customs. For example, people in Mexico need clothes to protect them from the heat. People in Australia, a sheep-producing country, wear many woolen clothes. In Middle Eastern countries, where modesty is valued, people wear long robes and coverings.

1. Find information about another country's traditional way of dressing. Try to find out why a particular clothing style developed. Give a brief oral report to the class, and show pictures of the clothing.

2. What countries come to mind when you hear the words *sari, kilt, kimono, clogs,* and *moccasins?* Compare your answers with those of a classmate. Then look in an encyclopedia or a book about clothing to see if you were correct.

Chapter Summary

- Begin your sewing project by reading the pattern guide sheet, which provides a layout and step-by-step directions.

- Learn to identify and understand these pattern markings: grain line, cutting line, place on fold, dart, notches, stitching lines, dots, and adjustment lines.

- To prepare your fabrics, preshrink them and check the grain.

- Follow the correct procedures for pinning, cutting, and marking your fabric.

- To complete a sewing project, you will need to be able to stitch a straight seam and a curved seam, pivot, and finish a seam.

- A serger is a high-speed machine that sews, trims, and finishes a seam in one step.

- With a serger, you can use many types of fabric, including stretchy knits and sheers, that are difficult to sew on a regular sewing machine.

- Basic construction techniques include staystitching seams, sewing darts, gathering and easing fabric, and making casings and facings.

- After a seam is stitched, it may need further treatment to reduce the bulk and give a smooth appearance.

- Hand-sewing techniques are used to repair small tears and holes, sew on missing buttons or snaps, and change hemlines.

- With a little imagination, many garments that cannot be repaired or altered can be recycled.

▶ Words to Know

Using complete sentences, answer the following questions on a separate sheet of paper.

1. Explain the purpose of pattern *layouts*.

2. What are pattern *markings*, and why are they important in sewing?

3. What is *backstitching*?

4. On a serger, what are the *cones* used for?

5. When would you use a *casing*?

6. Define the term *facings*.

7. Describe the advantage of a *slipstitch*.

▶ Review Questions

Using complete sentences, answer the following questions on a separate sheet of paper.

1. How do you determine what pattern alterations need to be made?

2. What are the two steps you should take to prepare fabric for sewing?

3. Give three tips for pinning pattern pieces to fabric.

4. What are four guidelines for transferring markings?

5. Why do sergers use cones instead of spools?

6. For what purpose would you use an overedge stitch? A safety stitch?

7. What is the difference between gathering and easing?

8. Briefly describe two techniques used to reduce bulk in seams.

9. Name four hand-sewing stitches.

10. How would you repair a small split in an underarm seam?

Thinking Critically

Using complete sentences, answer the following questions on a separate sheet of paper.

1. **Apply** Give three examples of sewing jobs that can be done more easily with a serger than with a regular sewing machine.

2. **Explain** What do you think is the meaning of the old proverb "A stitch in time saves nine?" How would you apply it to sewing?

3. **Analyze** What are some benefits of learning how to repair and alter your clothes?

Cooperative Learning

1. Along with several classmates, make a sewing video in which you show the steps for completing a sewing project. Work together to decide what you will include in the video, what materials you will need, and who will do each task. The video can be used to teach other students how to make a garment or a home-decorating project.

2. Working with a small group, decide on something that you could sew for your school. Some ideas include smocks for the art room, covers for the computers, or banners for the entranceway. Each person in the group should sew one part of the project.

Family & Community

1. Design a sewing area for your home. Draw a floor plan, and write a description of the room. Tell how you would organize the space and what furnishings and other materials you would include. Remember to make your space efficient, comfortable, and well-lit.

2. Have a family "sewing bee." Ask family members to gather all their clothes that have missing buttons, ripped seams, holes, broken zippers, and so on. Spend an evening together making repairs.

Building A Portfolio

1. Write a paragraph telling how you can use sewing skills in your life now and in the future. Place your paragraph in your portfolio.

2. Have someone take a photograph of you and a garment, gift, or home-decorating project that you have completed. Write a brief description of your project. Put the photo and the description in your portfolio.

Glossary

A

accessory An interesting item added to make a space more personal; an item such as shoes, a belt, a scarf, a hat, socks, a tie, or jewelry. (8–2), (16–1)

acne A skin condition caused by overly active oil glands. (15–1)

acquaintance A person you greet or meet fairly often but do not have a close relationship with. (5–4)

acquired Learned from the people and things around you. (1–1)

addiction A person's physical or mental need for a drug or other substance. (5–5)

adolescence (a-duhl-E-suhns) The period of great growth and change between childhood and adulthood. (1–2)

advertisement A message to persuade consumers to buy. (7–1)

aerobic exercise Nonstop, repetitive, vigorous exercise that increases breathing and heartbeat rates. (11–4)

alteration A change made in a garment so that it will fit. (17–2)

amino (uh-MEE-noh) acid A chain of building blocks that make up proteins. (10–2)

appetite The desire to eat. (10–1)

appetizer A dish served before the meal. (13–1)

apprenticeship program A formal program that uses on-the-job training to teach job skills. (4–1)

aptitude test A test that predicts a person's ability to learn certain skills. (4–1)

arcing Electrical sparks that can damage a microwave oven and start a fire. (12–4)

assertive Able to explain your needs and opinions clearly while respecting the needs and opinions of others. (5–5)

attention span The length of time a person can concentrate on any one thing. (6–3)

B

backstitching The technique of stitching over ½ inch (1.3 cm) of a seam at the beginning and end to lock the threads so that the seam won't pull out. (18–2)

balanced diet A diet that is made up of a variety of foods with nutrients in the recommended amounts. (11–2)

belonging Feeling included. (5–1)

bias Diagonal to the threads in a woven fabric. (18–1)

biodegradable Able to degrade, or break down, and be absorbed by the environment. (9–2)

bobbin A small metal or plastic spool that holds the thread inside a sewing machine. (17–1)

body language The look on your face, gestures, and body stance. (2–2)

broth The liquid left when meat, poultry, fish, or vegetables have been cooked in water. (14–2)

budget A plan for using your money. (7–5)

C

calcium A mineral that helps build bones and teeth and ensures normal growth. (10–3)

calorie A unit of heat that measures the energy available in food. (10–1)

carbohydrates The starches and sugars that give the body most of its energy. (10–2)

career research The process of finding out all you can about a field of work that interests you. (4–1)

caregiver A person who takes care of a child. (6–1)

casing A fabric tunnel made to enclose elastic or a drawstring. (18–4)

casserole A combination of ingredients cooked and served in a baking dish. (14–2)

chain store One of a group of stores that bear the same name and carry the same merchandise. (7–3)

child abuse Physical or emotional mistreatment of a child. (6–1)

childproof Safe for children to play and explore in. (6–4)

cholesterol (kuh-LES-tuh-rawl) A waxlike substance the body produces and needs in small amounts. (10–2)

citizen A member of a community, such as a city, state, or country. (2–3)

classic style A style that remains in fashion for a long time. (15–2)

cleaning plan A list of daily, weekly, and occasional household jobs and of the family member or members who are responsible for each job. (8–3)

color wheel An arrangement of colors that shows the relationships of colors to each other. (15–3)

commitment Promise. (3–2)

communication The process of sending and receiving messages. (2–2)

comprehension Understanding what you read. (4–2)

compromise (KAHM-pruh-myz) An agreement in which each person gives up something in order to reach a solution that satisfies everyone. (5–6)

conduct To carry electricity. (12–2)

cone A large, rounded cylinder used to hold thread on a serger. (18–3)

conflict Any struggle, disagreement, or fight. (5–6)

conscience The internal moral code that directs people's behavior. (6–2)

consequences (CON-suh-kwen-sez) Results of a choice made or an action taken. (3–3)

conservation The saving of resources. (9–1)

considerate Thoughtful. (5–1)

consistent Reacting the same way to the same situation each time it occurs. (6–1)

constructive criticism Someone's evaluation of you that encourages you and helps you become a better person. (1–3)

consumer A person who buys goods and services. (7–1)

contamination Becoming infected with bacteria. (12–1)

convenience food Food that is already partly prepared to save time. (13–3)

conversation The sharing of ideas, thoughts, and feelings. (2–2)

cooperation Working together for the good of all. (5–1)

cooperative play Play that involves one or two other children and sharing toys. (6–3)

cope Adjust to a difficult situation. (5–3)

cost per wearing The amount of money spent for each time you wear an article of clothing. (16–3)

coworker A person an employee works with. (4–4)

credit A method of payment that lets you buy now and pay later. (7–5)

culture The ways of thinking, acting, dressing, and speaking shared by a group of people. (1–1)

curdle To separate into little particles (curds). (14–4)

customary measurement Traditional units of measure. (13–4)

D

dairy food Food made from milk. (14–4)

dart A tapered V-shaped seam used to give shape to a garment. (17–2)

debit card A card that is issued by a bank and is used to withdraw money directly from a person's bank account. (7–5)

decision A choice a person makes about what action to take. (3–3)

decompose To break down. (9–2)

default To fail to make a decision, leaving the outcome to chance. (3–3)

defrosting Thawing or unfreezing frozen food. (12–4)

dehydrated Dried so that all or most of the liquid has been taken out of a food. (14–2)

department store A store that carries a wide range of merchandise. (7–3)

dermatologist A doctor who treats skin disorders. (15–1)

design The art of combining elements in a pleasing way. (8–2)

developmental task An achievement or milestone, such as walking or talking, that can be expected of children at a certain age or stage of growth. (6–2)

diagonal On an angle. (8–2)

diet Everything you regularly eat and drink. (10–1)

Dietary Guidelines Advice on what Americans should eat to stay healthy. (11–2)

digestion The process of breaking down food into a form the body can use. (10–1)

discipline The task of teaching a child which behavior is acceptable and which is not. (6–1)

discount store A store that carries a limited selection of items at low prices. (7–3)

dough A thick mixture of flour, liquid, and other ingredients. (14–3)

dovetailing Fitting different tasks together smoothly and efficiently. (12–5)

dressing A sauce that adds flavor to a dish. (14–2)

dry-heat cooking Cooking without liquid. (14–5)

E

ease The ability to move freely in a garment; the amount of fullness added to a garment pattern for movement and comfort. (16–2), (18–1)

emotion A feeling such as happiness, fear, or love. (1–2)

empathy The ability to put yourself in another person's place. (2–1)

employee manual A book of rules that employees must follow. (4–4)

empty-calorie food A food that is high in calories but low in nutrients. (11–3)

energy efficient Made to use less energy. (9–1)

enriched Having nutrients that were lost in processing replaced in the same quantity or in greater quantity than the unprocessed food originally contained. (10–3)

entrepreneur A person who starts and runs his or her own business. (4–4)

environment All the living and nonliving things that surround you. (1–1)

evaluate To determine the value of what you have accomplished. (2–4)

exchange A trade of one item for another. (7–4)

expectation A person's idea of what should be or should happen. (5–4)

expenses The money you spend to buy goods and services. (7–5)

expire To run out. (7–4)

F

facing A fabric piece used to finish the raw edge of a garment. (18–4)

factory outlet A store that carries only one manufacturer's products. (7–3)

fad A fashion that is very popular for a short time. (15–2)

fad diet A diet that promises quick weight loss through unusual means. (11–4)

family A group of two or more people who care about each other and are committed to each other. (5–2)

fashion Style of clothing that is accepted as popular at a particular time. (15–2)

feed dogs Parts of a serger that position the fabric for the next stitch. (18–3)

fiber The tough, stringy part of raw fruits, vegetables, and grains that the body cannot digest; one of the tiny strands that make up yarns. (10–2), (16–2)

first impression An instant opinion, or image. (2–1)

fitness The ability to handle day-to-day events in a healthy way. (11–4)

fixed expenses Expenses that are always the same. (7–5)

flammable Capable of burning easily. (12–2)

flexibility The ability to adjust easily to new conditions. (4–4)

flexible expenses Expenses that vary. (7–5)

floor plan A diagram of a room arrangement. (8–2)

flossing Pulling dental floss back and forth between the teeth at the gum line to remove food particles. (15–1)

focal point Center of interest. (16–1)

food group A category of foods on the Food Guide Pyramid. (11–1)

Food Guide Pyramid A set of guidelines to help you choose what and how much to eat to get the nutrients you need. (11–1)

function Use. (8–1)

G

garnish A small amount of a food or seasoning added to decorate a food. (13–1)

generic product A product with a label listing only the product name and nutritional information. (13–2)

goal Something you want to achieve. (3–4)

goods Products made for sale. (7–1)

gossip Talking about other people and their personal lives. (2–2)

grade labeling A measurement of food quality using standards set by the government. (13–2)

graduated measuring cups Set of measuring cups in commonly used sizes. (13–4)

grain The direction in which the threads run in a fabric. (16–2), (18–1)

group play Play with several other children. (6–3)

guidance Direction. (6–1)

guide sheet A set of step-by-step instructions for sewing a pattern. (18–1)

H

habit A behavior pattern that is repeated without thinking about it. (3–3)

hard-cooked egg An egg that is left in hot water, covered, for 15 to 18 minutes. (14–5)

hazard A danger. (9–3)

hemming stitch A hand-sewing stitch used for hems. (18–5)

heredity The passing of traits or characteristics from parents to their children. (1–1)

hue The name of a color. (15–3)

hunger The physical need to eat. (10–1)

hygiene Practices that promote health. (15–1)

I

illusion A feeling that something is different from the way it really is. (8–2)

image ad An ad that connects a product or service to a lifestyle that consumers would like to have. (7–2)

impression An image you present or others present to you. (2–1)

impulse buying Making a sudden decision to buy. (7–3)

incineration Disposing of waste by burning it. (9–2)

income The amount of money you earn or receive regularly. (7–5)

independent play Play during which an infant plays alone and shows little interest in interacting with other children. Also called solitary play. (6–3)

infomercial An extended-length informational commercial that appears on television. (7–2)

information ad An ad that describes the features of a product or service and gives facts about its price and quality. (7–2)

initiative Taking action without being asked. (3–2)

insulation A material installed in the attic or walls of a building to keep it cooler in summer and warmer in winter. (9–1)

intensity The brightness or dullness of a color. (15–3)

interest A fee paid by a bank in order to use your money. (7–5)

interfacing A layer of special fabric placed between two pieces of fabric to give more shape to a garment. (17–3)

intruder Someone who uses force to get into a home. (6–4)

iron A mineral that is an essential component of blood. (10–3)

J

job applicant A person who wants a job. (4–3)

job application A form on which you supply information about yourself that will help an employer make a hiring decision. (4–3)

job interview A face-to-face meeting between an employer and a job applicant. (4–3)

job opening A job that is not filled. (4–3)

job preparation The learning required to get and keep the kind of job you want. (4–1)

K

knit fabric Fabric made by looping threads together. (16–2)

L

landfill A huge pit where waste is dumped and buried between layers of earth. (9–2)

layaway plan A scheduled payment plan in which you put a small amount of money down and make regular payments until you have paid for an item. (7–5)

layout A diagram of how pattern pieces should be placed on fabric. (18–1)

leader A person with the ability to guide and motivate others. (2–3)

leavening agent An ingredient that makes baked food rise. (13–4)

life change A major way in which your life is altered by events that you may or may not be able to control. (5–3)

logo A company's identification symbol. (15–2)

looper A rounded part that holds the thread inside a serger. (18–3)

M

major appliance A piece of large kitchen equipment. (12–3)

management Using what you have to get what you want, being organized, and planning ahead. (2–4)

marking A guide on a pattern piece for making a project. (18–1)

maturity Making wise decisions, practicing self-control, and acting responsibly. (2–1)

meal pattern Habit people follow that determines when and what they eat each day. (13–1)

meat extender A food added to meat to make a small amount of meat go farther. (14–5)

media The means of communication by which advertisers send their messages. (7–2)

mend Repair. (16–4)

menu A list of all the dishes a restaurant serves, organized by category. (11–3)

metric measurement A system of measurements based on multiples of ten. (13–4)

microwave oven An appliance that cooks by vibrating the molecules in food. (12–3)

mineral Element needed by the body in small amounts for sturdy bones and teeth, healthy blood, and regular elimination of body wastes. (10–3)

moderation Avoiding extremes. (11–2)

modesty Ideas people have about the proper way for clothing to cover the body. (15–2)

moist-heat cooking Cooking in liquid. (14–5)

N

nap A one-way texture in fabric. (17–3)

narrative format A recipe format that provides a paragraph description of the steps and ingredients in order of use. (13–3)

national-brand product A product that you see advertised on television or in newspapers or magazines. (13–2)

natural resource A material that is supplied by nature. (9–1)

need Something that you have to have in order to live. (3–1)

negotiation (ni-GOH-shee-AY-shuhn) The process of talking about a conflict and deciding how to reach a compromise. (5–6)

neutral color Black, white, beige, or gray. (15–3)

nonverbal communication Messages sent without using words. (2–2)

notion A small item that is part of the construction of a garment. (17–3)

nutrient (NOO-tree-ent) A substance in food that is important for the body's growth and maintenance. (10–1)

nutrient-dense food A food that is rich in the nutrients your body needs to stay healthy. (11–3)

nutrition (noo-TRI-shuhn) The study of nutrients and how they are used by the body. (10–1)

O

obesity A condition in which a person's weight is 20 percent or more above his or her ideal weight. (11–4)

open dating The display of a freshness date on packaged food. (13–2)

option Possible choice. (3–3)

osteoporosis A condition in which bones gradually lose their mineral content and become weak and brittle. (10–3)

P Q

parallel play Play that occurs alongside of, rather than with, another child. (6–3)

parenthood The function of being a parent. (6–1)

parenting The process of caring for children and helping them grow and learn. (6–1)

pasta A food made from flour and water and formed into shapes. (14–3)

pattern A plan for making a garment or project. (17–2)

pedestrian A person who travels on foot. (9–3)

peer A person of the same age as you. (5–4)

peer group A group of people of the same age. (5–4)

peer mediation A process by which specially trained students help other students find a solution to a problem. (5–6)

peer pressure The influence you feel to go along with the behavior and beliefs of your peers. (5–5)

perishable Likely to spoil quickly. (12–1)

personality The sum total of a person's traits, feelings, attitudes, and habits. (1–2)

personal style The kind of clothes you like best. (16–1)

pinking shears Scissors that have a zigzag edge. (17–1)

plaque (PLAK) A soft, sticky film on the teeth, created by the bacteria that live in a person's mouth. (15–1)

poison control center A medical facility with a staff trained to help in poisoning emergencies. (6–4)

pollution The changing of air, water, and land from clean and safe to dirty and unsafe. (9–1)

popularity The state of being well liked. (5–5)

potential The capacity to grow and develop. (3–1)

precaution Step taken to avoid danger. (8–3)

precycle To avoid buying products that use more packaging than necessary. (9–2)

prejudice (PRE-juh-dis) An opinion about people that is formed without facts or knowledge about those people. (5–6)

preschooler A child who is three to five years old. (6–2)

presser foot The metal piece at the end of a sewing machine needle that holds the fabric in place. (17–1)

pretreat To apply a liquid detergent or stain remover to spots before laundering a garment. (16–4)

prioritize To rank in order of importance. (2–4)

processed Changed (a food) from its raw form before it is sold. (14–1)

procrastinate To put things off. (2–4)

produce Fresh fruits and vegetables. (14–1)

promotion A move up to a better job with more responsibility. (4–4)

proofread Check for errors in grammar, punctuation, and spelling. (4–2)

protein A nutrient that is needed to build, repair, and maintain body cells and tissues. (10–2)

punishment A way of discouraging inappropriate behavior. (6–1)

R

ravel To have threads pull out of the cut edge of a fabric. (17–3)

raw edge The unfinished edge of fabric that has loose threads. (18–1)

realistic goal A goal that you can reach. (3–4)

recipe A list of ingredients and directions for preparing a specific food. (13–3)

recycling Turning waste items into products that can be used. (9–2)

redirect To turn someone's attention to something else. (6–5)

redress Action taken to correct a wrong. (7–4)

reference A person who can tell an employer about an applicant's character and quality of work. (4–3)

refund A return of money in exchange for an item purchased. (7–4)

refusal skills Ways to say no effectively. (3–1)

resource A source of information or expertise that you can use to help you meet your goals; something you need to accomplish a goal. (2–4), (3–4)

respect Consideration. (3–2)

responsibility Ability to make choices and to answer for those choices. (3–2)

risk To take a dangerous chance. (9–3)

role The way you behave when you interact with another person. (1–1)

role model A person who helps you see what is expected of you and shows you how to act in certain situations. (1–1)

rotating Turning a dish a quarter-turn or a half-turn in a microwave oven. (12–4)

S

salad A food or a combination of foods, usually served cold with a dressing. (14–2)

salmonella (SAL-muh-NELL-uh) Bacteria that are often found in raw or undercooked foods, such as meat, eggs, fish, and poultry. (12–1)

sandwich Two pieces of bread surrounding a filling, such as meat or cheese. (14–3)

sanitary Free from germs. (8–3)

saturated fat Fat found in food from animal sources. (10–2)

scald To bring food slowly to a temperature just below the boiling point. (14–4)

seam finish A treatment used on a seam edge to prevent the fabric from raveling. (18–2)

seasonal More plentiful, more readily available, and less expensive at certain times of the year. (14–1)

security Feeling safe and protected. (5–1)

self-concept A mental picture of yourself. (1–3)

self-confidence Faith in your abilities. (1–3)

self-esteem The ability to respect yourself. (1–3)

selvage The tightly woven edge of fabric that has no visible loose threads. (18–1)

serger A high-speed machine that sews, trims, and finishes a seam in one step. (18–3)

service Work performed by one person for others. (7–1)

serving A portion of food that a person would be likely to eat at one time. (11–1)

sewing gauge A 6-inch (15-cm) ruler made of metal, with an adjustable pointer. (17–1)

shank A stem on a button that provides room for the extra layer of fabric around the buttonhole. (18–5)

shape Outline. (15–3)

shoplifting Taking items from a store without paying for them. (7–3)

shopping plan A strategy for spending the money you have available to purchase the items you need or want. (16–3)

sibling A brother or sister. (5–2)

slip stitch A hand-sewing stitch that provides an almost invisible finish. (18–5)

small appliance A piece of small, electrically powered kitchen equipment. (12–3)

smoke alarm A device that sets off an alarm when smoke is present. (6–4)

snack Food eaten between meals. (11–3)

sodium A mineral that helps regulate the amount of fluids in the body. (11–2)

software A computer program or set of instructions. (4–2)

solitary play Play during which an infant plays alone and shows little interest in interacting with other children. Also called independent play. (6–3)

specialty store A store that carries only a specific type of merchandise. (7–3)

stain A soiled or discolored area. (16–4)

stamina The ability to focus on a single activity or a long time. (11–4)

standard format A recipe format that lists all the ingredients in order of use, followed by step-by-step directions for preparing the food. (13–3)

staple Food that you are likely to use often. (13–2)

status Level of importance. (15–2)

status symbol A piece of clothing or other item that gives the owner a special feeling of importance. (16–3)

staystitching A row of permanent stitching made on or very near the seam line in the seam allowance. (18–4)

stereotype An idea or image formed in advance about all members of a group. (2–1)

stitch finger A metal prong on the needle plate or presser foot of a serger. (18–3)

stitch regulator A dial or lever on a sewing machine that controls the length of the stitches. (17–1)

store-brand product Food or household item that has a store's name or another name used only by that store on the label. (13–2)

stress The body's reaction to changes around it. (5–3)

style The design of a garment. (15–2)

sunscreen A lotion that guards the skin against harmful rays of the sun. (15–1)

supervisor The person who checks an employee's work and evaluates his or her performance. (4–4)

synthetic fiber A fiber made partially or entirely from chemicals. (16–2)

T

tail chain A length of thread shaped like a chain and made on a serger without fabric under the needle. (18–3)

talent Natural ability. (2–4)

teamwork The cooperative efforts of everyone in a group to work together to reach a goal. (2–3), (4–4)

texture The way something feels or looks as if it would feel. (8–2), (13–1), (15–3)

time schedule A plan to make sure that all foods are ready to serve at the right time. (13–1)

toddler A child who is one to three years old. (6–2)

trade-off Something that you give up in order to get something more important. (3–4)

tradition A custom or belief handed down from one generation to another. (5–2)

traffic pattern The path people take to move around and in and out of a room. (8–1)

U

unique One of a kind. (1–1)

unit pricing Showing the cost of a product per unit. (13–2)

unsaturated fat Fat that comes from plants. (10–2)

utensil A kitchen tool. (12–3)

V

value The lightness and darkness of color. (15–3)

values Ideas about right and wrong and about what is important in your life. (3–1)

variable A condition that determines how long a food needs to be cooked and at what power level in a microwave oven. (12–4)

vegetarian A person who eats mainly fruits, vegetables, and grains. (11–1)

versatile Able to be worn for many occasions. (16–1)

view A version of a garment style, as shown on a pattern envelope. (17–2)

violence The use of physical force to harm someone. (9–3)

vitamin Substance needed by the body in small amounts to help regulate body functions. (10–3)

volunteer A person who donates time and energy without pay to do a service for others. (2–3)

W

want Something that you would like to have but that is not necessary for survival. (3–1)

wardrobe inventory A list of all the clothes, shoes, and accessories that you have. (16–1)

warranty A manufacturer's written promise to repair or replace a product if it does not work as claimed. (7–3)

wellness A high level of overall health. (11–2)

whole grain A food that contains all of the edible grain, including the outer layer, the bran, and the germ. (10–2)

work plan A list of jobs that need to be done and the name of the person who will do each job. (12–5)

work record A written record of how well an employee performs on the job. (4–4)

woven fabric Fabric made on a loom by interlacing lengthwise and crosswise threads at right angles. (16–2)

X Y Z

yield The number of servings a recipe will make. (13–3)

Glossary/Glosario

A

accessory/accesorio Un artículo interesante que se añade para hacer un espacio más personal; artículos tales como un cinturón, pañuelo, sombrero, corbata, zapatos, calcetines o alhajas. (8–2), (16–1)

acne/acné Una enfermedad de la piel causada por la producción excesiva de grasa por las glándulas sebáceas. (15–1)

acquaintance/conocido Una persona a quien uno conoce pero con quien no tiene amistad. (15–4)

acquired/adquirido Aprendido de las personas y las cosas que te rodean. (1–1)

addiction/adicción La necesidad física o mental que tiene una persona de una droga u otra substancia. (5–5)

adolescence/adolescencia El período de gran crecimiento y cambio entre la niñez y la adultez. (1–2)

advertisement/anuncio Un mensaje para convencer a los consumidores de que compren. (7–1)

aerobic exercise/ejercicio aeróbico Ejercicio enérgico y repetido sin parar, que aumenta la velocidad de la respiración y de los latidos del corazón. (11–4)

alteration/arreglo Un cambio hecho a una prenda de ropa para que le quede bien a una persona. (17–2)

amino acid/aminoácido Una cadena de componentes básicos de las proteínas. (10–2)

appetite/apetito El deseo de comer. (10–1)

appetizer/aperitivo Un plato que se sirve antes de la comida. (13–1)

apprenticeship program/programa de aprendizaje Un programa para aprender un arte u oficio mientras se hace el trabajo. (4–1)

aptitude test/prueba de aptitud Una prueba que predice la habilidad que tiene una persona para aprender ciertas destrezas. (4–1)

arcing/chispas Chispas eléctricas que pueden dañar un horno de microondas y provocar un incendio. (12–4)

assertive/firme Capaz de explicar con claridad las necesidades y opiniones propias, manteniendo el respeto por las necesidades y opiniones de los demás. (5–5)

attention span/capacidad de concentración La cantidad de tiempo que una persona puede mantener su atención en una cosa. (6–3)

B

backstitching/pespuntear Volver a coser ½ pulgada (1.3 cm) al principio y al fin de una costura para que no se deshile. (18–2)

balanced diet/dieta balanceada Una dieta compuesta de una variedad de alimentos, con los distintos nutrientes en las cantidades recomendadas. (11–2)

belonging/pertenecer Sentirse incluido. (5–1)

bias/biés En diagonal a los hilos de la tela. (18–1)

biodegradable/biodegradable Que se puede descomponer y ser absorbido por el medio ambiente. (9–2)

bobbin/bobina Un carretel pequeño que sujeta el hilo dentro de una máquina de coser. (17–1)

body language/lenguaje corporal La mirada, los gestos y la postura de una persona. (12–2)

broth/caldo El líquido que queda cuando se cocina carne, ave, pescado o vegetales en agua. (14–2)

budget/presupuesto Un plan para usar tu dinero. (17–5)

C

calcium/calcio Un mineral que ayuda a formar los huesos y los dientes y que asegura el crecimiento normal. (10–3)

calorie/caloría Una unidad de calor utilizada para medir la energía disponible en los alimentos. (10–1)

carbohydrate/carbohidrato La fécula y el azúcar que le dan al cuerpo la mayor parte de su energía. (10–2)

career research/investigación de carreras El proceso de averiguar todo lo posible sobre un campo de trabajo que te interese. (4–1)

caregiver/cuidador Una persona que cuida a un niño. (6–1)

casing/doblez Un tubo de tela que se usa para cubrir un elástico o cordón del que se tira. (18–4)

casserole/guisado Un conjunto de ingredientes que se cocinan en una cazuela de hornear. (14–2)

chain store/tienda de cadena Una de un grupo de tiendas que llevan el mismo nombre y la misma mercancía. (17–3)

child abuse/abuso infantil El maltrato físico o emocional de un niño. (6–1)

childproof/a prueba de niños Asegurar un sitio para que los niños puedan jugar y explorar en él. (6–4)

cholesterol/colesterol Una substancia parecida a la cera que el cuerpo produce y necesita en pequeñas cantidades. (10–2)

citizen/ciudadano Un miembro de una comunidad, tal como una ciudad, un estado o un país. (2–3)

classic style/estilo clásico Un estilo que se mantiene de moda por mucho tiempo. (15–2)

cleaning plan/plan de limpieza Una lista de los quehaceres diarios, semanales y ocasionales de la casa y de los miembros de la familia que son responsables de cada uno. (8–3)

color wheel/rueda de colores Un arreglo de colores que muestra la relación de un color a otro. (15–3)

commitment/compromiso Una promesa. (3–2)

communication/comunicación El proceso de mandar y recibir mensajes. (2–2)

comprehension/comprensión Entender lo que lees. (4–2)

compromise/acuerdo mutuo Un arreglo en el cual cada persona cede algo para llegar a una solución que satisface a todos. (5–6)

conduct/conducir Transmitir electricidad. (12–2)

cone/cono Un cilindro grande y redondeado que se usa para sostener el hilo en una remalladora. (18–3)

conflict/conflicto Cualquier lucha, desacuerdo o pelea. (5–6)

conscience/conciencia El código moral interno que dirige la conducta de las personas. (6–2)

consequences/consecuencias El resultado de una decisión o acción que se ha tomado. (3–3)

conservation/conservación El cuidado de los recursos. (9–1)

considerate/considerado Atento. (5–1)

consistent/consistente Que reacciona de la misma manera a la misma situación cada vez que sucede. (6–1)

constructive criticism/crítica constructiva Una evaluación que hace alguien de ti que te ayuda a convertirte en mejor persona. (1–3)

consumer/consumidor Una persona que compra bienes y servicios. (7–1)

contamination/contaminación Estar infectado por bacterias. (12–1)

convenience food/comida de preparación rápida Comida que ya está parcialmente preparada para ahorrar tiempo. (13–3)

conversation/conversación El intercambio de ideas, pensamientos y sentimientos. (2–2)

cooperation/cooperación Trabajar juntos para el bien de todos. (5–1)

cooperative play/juego cooperativo Juego en el que a dos o más niños comparten juguetes. (6–3)

cope/hacer frente Adaptarse a una situación difícil. (5–3)

cost per wearing/costo por uso La cantidad de dinero que se ha gastado por cada uso de una prenda de vestir. (16–3)

coworker/compañero de trabajo Una persona con quien un empleado trabaja. (4–4)

credit/crédito Un método de pago que te permite comprar ahora y pagar después. (7–5)

culture/cultura Las maneras de pensar, actuar, vestir y hablar que comparten un grupo de personas. (1–1)

curdle/cortarse Separarse en grumos. (14–4)

customary measurement/sistema de medidas estadounidense Unidades tradicionales de medida en Estados Unidos. (13–4)

D

dairy food/alimentos lácteos Comidas hechas de leche. (14–4)

dart/pinza Una costura que se estrecha en forma de "V" y que se usa para darle forma a la ropa. (17–2)

debit card/tarjeta de cobro automático Una tarjeta de banco que se usa para sacar dinero directamente de la cuenta de una persona. (7–5)

decision/decisión Una selección que hace una persona acerca de qué hacer. (3–3)

decompose/descomponerse Separarse en sus elementos básicos. (9–2)

default/a falta de directivas No tomar una decisión y dejar el resultado al azar. (3–3)

defrosting/descongelar Dejar que un alimento congelado se deshiele. (12–4)

dehydrated/deshidratado Secar un alimento hasta sacarle la mayor parte del líquido que contiene. (14–2)

department store/tienda de departamentos Una tienda que tiene una gran selección de mercancías. (7–3)

dermatologist/dermatólogo Un médico que trata las enfermedades de la piel. (15–1)

design/diseño El arte de combinar distintos elementos de una manera agradable. (8–2)

developmental task/tarea de desarrollo Un logro o hito, tal como el caminar o hablar, que se puede esperar de los niños a cierta edad o cierta etapa de su crecimiento. (6–2)

diagonal/diagonal En ángulo. (8–2)

diet/dieta Todo lo que comes y bebes con regularidad. (10–1)

Dietary Guidelines/recomendaciones dietéticas Consejos sobre lo que deben comer los estadounidenses para mantenerse sanos. (11–2)

digestion/digestión El proceso de descomponer los alimentos para que el cuerpo los pueda utilizar. (10–1)

discipline/disciplina La tarea de enseñarle a un niño cuál conducta es admisible y cuál no. (6–1)

discount store/tienda de descuentos Una tienda con una selección de mercancía limitada pero a bajos precios. (7–3)

dough/masa Una mezcla espesa de harina, líquido, y otros ingredientes. (14–3)

dovetailing/organizarse Hacer varias tareas a la vez, de manera ordenada y eficiente. (12–5)

dressing/aliño Una salsa que le da sabor a un plato. (14–2)

dry-heat cooking/cocinar en seco Cocinar sin líquido. (14–5)

E

ease/holgura La habilidad de poderse mover dentro de una prenda; la anchura que se le añade a una prenda para dar movimiento y comodidad. (16–2), (18–1)

emotion/emoción Un sentimiento, tal como la felicidad, el miedo o el cariño. (1–2)

empathy/empatía La habilidad de ponerse en el lugar de otro. (2–1)

employee manual/manual para los empleados Un libro de reglas que los empleados tienen que seguir. (4–4)

empty-calorie food/alimento chatarra Una comida con muchas calorías y pocos nutrientes. (11–3)

energy-efficient/de eficiencia energética Hecho para que use menos energía. (9–1)

enriched/enriquecido Alimento al que se le añaden las mismas o mayores cantidades de los nutrientes que se perdieron al procesarlo. (10–3)

entrepreneur/empresario Una persona que empieza o dirige su propio negocio. (4–4)

environment/medio ambiente Todas las cosas vivas o no que te rodean. (1–1)

evaluate/evaluar Determinar el valor de lo que has logrado. (2–4)

exchange/intercambiar Cambiar un artículo por otro. (7–4)

expectation/expectativa La idea de una persona de lo que debe ser o debe suceder. (5–4)

expenses/gastos El dinero que usas para comprar bienes y servicios. (7–5)

expire/vencerse Cumplirse un plazo. (7–4)

F

facing/vuelta Una pieza de tela que se usa para terminar el borde de una prenda. (18–4)

factory outlet/tienda de fábrica Una tienda que vende sólo los productos de un fabricante. (7–3)

fad/moda pasajera Una moda que es popular por muy poco tiempo. (15–2)

fad diet/régimen de adelgazamiento rápido Una dieta que promete perder de peso rápidamente por medios poco comunes. (11–4)

family/familia Un grupo de dos o más personas que se quieren y están dedicados unos a otros. (5–2)

fashion/moda Estilo de ropa que es popular durante un período de tiempo. (15–2)

feed dogs/dientes La parte de un remalladora que pone la tela en posición para el próximo punto. (18–3)

fiber/fibra La parte dura y llena de hebras de las frutas, vegetales y granos frescos que el cuerpo no puede digerir; una de las hebras pequeñas que forman el estambre. (10–2), (16–2)

first impression/primera impresión Una opinión o imagen instantánea. (2–1)

fitness/salud completa La habilidad de manejar los sucesos diarios de manera sana. (11–4)

fixed expenses/gastos fijos Los gastos que siempre son iguales. (7–5)

flammable/inflamable Que se quema con facilidad. (12–2)

flexibility/flexibilidad La habilidad de adaptarse con facilidad a nuevas condiciones. (4–4)

flexible expenses/gastos flexibles Los gastos que varían. (7–5)

floor plan/plano Un diagrama de la disposición de una habitación. (8–2)

flossing/limpiarse con hilo dental Halar el hilo dental hacia delante y hacia atrás entre los dientes y las encías para quitar los pedacitos de comida. (15–1)

focal point/centro de atención El centro de interés. (16–1)

food group/grupo alimenticio Una categoría de alimentos en la pirámide de los alimentos. (11–1)

Food Guide Pyramid/pirámide de los alimentos Una serie de recomendaciones para ayudarte a escoger los alimentos y las cantidades de ellos que debes comer para obtener los nutrientes que necesitas. (11–1)

function/función Uso. (8–1)

G

garnish/decorado Una pequeña cantidad de comida o aderezo que se usa para adornar un plato. (13–1)

generic product/producto genérico Un producto cuya etiqueta lleva sólo el nombre del producto y la información nutritiva. (13–2)

goal/meta Algo que quieres lograr. (3–4)

goods/bienes Productos hechos para vender. (7–1)

gossip/contar chismes Hablar sobre otras personas y sus vidas privadas. (2–2)

grade labeling/etiqueta de calidad Una medida de la calidad de los alimentos usando las reglas establecidas por el gobierno. (13–2)

graduated measuring cups/tazas de medir graduadas Juego de tazas de medir en los tamaños que se usan con mayor frecuencia. (13–4)

grain/hilo La dirección en que van las fibras de la tela. (16–2), (18–1)

group play/juego en grupo Jugar con varios otros niños. (6–3)

guidance/orientación Dirección o asesoramiento. (6–1)

guide sheet/hoja de instrucciones Una guía para coser un patrón paso a paso. (18–1)

H

habit/hábito Un patrón de conducta que se repite sin pensar. (3–3)

hard-cooked egg/huevo duro Un huevo que se deja en agua caliente, cubierto, de 15 a 20 minutos. (14–5)

hazard/peligro Una amenaza. (9–3)

hemming stitch/punto de dobladillo Una puntada a mano que se usa para coser los dobladillos. (18–5)

heredity/herencia La transmisión de rasgos o características de padres a hijos. (1–1)

hue/tono El nombre de un color. (15–3)

hunger/hambre La necesidad de comer. (10–1)

hygiene/higiene Las prácticas que promueven la salud. (15–1)

I

illusion/ilusión El sentido de que las cosas son distintas a como lo son en verdad. (8–2)

image ad/anuncio de imagen Un anuncio que conecta un producto o un servicio a un estilo de vida que los consumidores quisieran tener. (7–2)

impression/impresión La imagen que tú presentas o que otros te presentan a ti. (2–1)

impulse buying/compras impulsivas Decidir comprar algo súbitamente. (7–3)

incineration/incineración Quemar los desechos para deshacerse de ellos. (9–2)

income/ingresos La cantidad de dinero que ganas o recibes con regularidad. (7–5)

independent play/juego independiente Juego que el bebé hace solo, demostrando poco interés en relacionarse con otros niños. También se llama juego solitario. (6–3)

infomercial/comercial informativo Un anuncio de televisión largo que proporciona información. (7–2)

information ad/anuncio de información Un anuncio que describe las características de un producto o servicio y da información sobre su precio y calidad. (7–2)

initiative/iniciativa Actuar sin que se lo pidan a uno. (3–2)

insulation/material aislante Un material que se instala en el ático o las paredes de un edificio para mantenerlo más fresco en verano y más caliente en invierno. (9–1)

intensity/intensidad Lo brillante o fuerte que es un color. (15–3)

interest/interés Una suma que paga un banco para poder usar tu dinero. (7–5)

interfacing/entretela Una pieza de tela especial que se pone entre dos piezas de tela para darle mejor forma a una prenda. (17–3)

intruder/intruso Alguien que entra a la fuerza en una casa. (6–4)

iron/hierro Un mineral que es un componente esencial de la sangre. (10–3)

J

job applicant/candidato a un puesto Una persona que quiere un trabajo. (4–3)

job application/solicitud de trabajo Un formulario en el que un candidato escribe información sobre sí mismo que ayuda al empleador a decidir a quién dar un trabajo. (4–3)

job interview/entrevista de empleo Una reunión cara a cara entre un empleador y el candidato a un puesto. (4–3)

job opening/oportunidad de trabajo Un puesto que no se ha llenado. (4–3)

job preparation/preparación para el trabajo La enseñanza necesaria para obtener y mantener el tipo de trabajo que quieres. (4–1)

K

knit fabric/jersey Tela que se hace entrelazando hilos. (16–2)

L

landfill/relleno sanitario Un hoyo inmenso donde se echa la basura y se entierra entre capas de tierra. (9–2)

layaway plan/reservación mediante el pago de un depósito Un plan de pagos programados en el cual das un depósito pequeño y haces pagos regulares hasta terminar de pagar por un artículo. (7–5)

layout/distribución Un diagrama que muestra cómo colocar las piezas de un patrón sobre la tela. (18–1)

leader/líder Una persona que tiene la habilidad de guiar y motivar a los demás. (2–3)

leavening agent/levadura Un ingrediente que hace que crezca la masa de una comida hecha al horno. (13–4)

life change/cambio de la vida Una manera importante en que tu vida puede ser alterada por sucesos que tú no necesariamente puedes controlar. (5–3)

logo/logotipo El símbolo de identificación de una compañía. (15–2)

looper/gancho Una pieza redonda que sujeta el hilo dentro de un remalladora. (18–3)

M

major appliance/electrodomésticos Un aparato de cocina grande. (12–3)

management/manejo Utilizar lo que tienes para obtener lo que quieres, ser organizado, y planear por adelantado. (2–4)

marking/marca Una guía en la pieza de un patrón para hacer un proyecto. (18–1)

maturity/madurez Tomar decisiones inteligentes, tener control de sí mismo, y actuar responsablemente. (2–1)

meal pattern/pautas de comidas Los hábitos de las personas que determinan qué y cuándo comen cada día. (13–1)

meat extender/aumentador de carne Un alimento que se le añade a la carne para hacer que una cantidad pequeña alcance para más personas. (14–5)

media/medios de comunicación Los modos de transmitir información que usan los anunciantes para mandar sus mensajes. (7–2)

mend/remendar Reparar. (16–4)

menu/menú Una lista de todos los platos que sirve un restaurante, organizados por categoría. (11–3)

metric measurement/sistema métrico Un sistema de medidas basado en múltiplos de diez. (13–4)

microwave oven/horno de microondas Un electrodoméstico que cocina por medio de la vibración de las moléculas en las comidas. (12–3)

mineral/mineral Elemento que el cuerpo necesita en pequeñas cantidades para que los huesos y los dientes estén fuertes, para que la sangre esté saludable y para que el cuerpo elimine los desechos con regularidad. (10–3)

moderation/moderación Evitar los extremos. (11–2)

modesty/modestia Ideas que tiene la gente acerca de la manera en que la ropa debe cubrir el cuerpo. (15–2)

moist-heat cooking/cocinar en líquido Cocinar los alimentos en un líquido. (14–5)

N

nap/pelo Textura de una tela que va en una sola dirección. (17–3)

narrative format/formato narrativo La presentación de una receta en un párrafo que describe los pasos y los ingredientes en orden de uso. (13–3)

national-brand product/producto de marca nacional Un producto que ves anunciado en televisión, periódicos o revistas. (13–2)

natural resource/recurso natural Un material que proporciona la naturaleza. (9–1)

need/necesidad Algo que tienes que tener para poder vivir. (3–1)

negotiation/negociación El proceso de hablar sobre un conflicto y llegar a un acuerdo. (5–6)

neutral color/color neutral Negro, blanco, beige o gris. (15–3)

nonverbal communication/comunicación no verbal Mensajes que se mandan sin palabras. (2–2)

notion/artículo de mercería Un artículo pequeño que se usa para hacer una prenda. (17–3)

nutrient/nutriente Una substancia en los alimentos que es importante para el crecimiento y mantenimiento del cuerpo. (10–1)

nutrient-dense food/alimento cargado de nutrientes Un alimento que es rico en los nutrientes que tu cuerpo necesita para mantenerse sano. (11–3)

nutrition/nutrición El estudio de los nutrientes y de cómo los utiliza el cuerpo. (10–1)

O

obesity/obesidad Una condición en la cual el peso de una persona está un 20 por ciento o más por encima de su peso ideal. (11–4)

open dating/fecha descubierta La exposición de la fecha hasta cuando está fresca una comida empaquetada. (13–2)

option/opción Selección posible. (3–3)

osteoporosis/osteoporosis Una condición en la que los huesos gradualmente pierden su contenido mineral y se ponen débiles y frágiles. (10–3)

P Q

parallel play/juego paralelo Juego que ocurre al lado en vez de junto con otro niño. (6–3)

parenthood/paternidad y maternidad La función de un padre o una madre. (6–1)

parenting/crianza de los hijos El proceso de cuidar a los hijos y ayudarlos a que crezcan y aprendan. (6–1)

pasta/pasta Un alimento hecho de harina y agua al que se dan distintas formas. (14–3)

pattern/patrón El plan para hacer una prenda o proyecto. (17–2)

pedestrian/peatón Una persona que viaja a pie. (9–3)

peer/contemporáneo Una persona de la misma edad que tú. (5–4)

peer group/grupo de contemporáneos Un grupo de personas de la misma edad. (5–4)

peer mediation/mediación por contemporáneos Un proceso en el que estudiantes con capacitación especial ayudan a otros estudiantes a encontrar la solución a un problema. (5–6)

peer pressure/presión de contemporáneos La influencia que sientes para dejarte llevar por la conducta y las creencias de tus contemporáneos. (5–5)

perishable/perecedero Que se echa a perder con facilidad. (12–1)

personality/personalidad El conjunto total de los rasgos, sentimientos, actitudes y hábitos de una persona. (1–2)

personal style/estilo personal El tipo de ropa que más te gusta. (16–1)

pinking shears/tijeras dentadas Tijeras que tienen filo de zigzag. (17–1)

plaque/placa dental Una capa suave y pegajosa sobre los dientes causada por las bacterias que viven en la boca de una persona. (15–1)

poison control center/centro de control del envenenamiento Centro médico donde empleados entrenados ayudan con las emergencias de envenenamiento. (6–4)

pollution/contaminación del medio ambiente El cambio del aire, agua y tierra de limpio y sano a sucio y malsano. (9–1)

popularity/popularidad El estado de ser favorecido por los demás. (5–5)

potential/potencial La capacidad para crecer y desarrollarse. (3–1)

precaution/precaución Medidas que se toman para evitar el peligro. (8–3)

precycle/preciclar Evitar comprar productos que tienen más envoltura que la necesaria. (9–2)

prejudice/prejuicio Una opinión que se forma sobre otras personas sin tener datos ni conocimientos sobre ellas. (5–6)

preschooler/niño preescolar Un niño que tiene entre tres y cinco años de edad. (6–2)

presser foot/pisacostura La pieza de metal al final de la aguja de una máquina de coser que sujeta la tela en su sitio. (17–1)

pretreat/tratar de antemano Ponerle detergente líquido o quitamanchas directamente a las manchas antes de lavar una prenda. (16–4)

prioritize/priorizar Poner en orden de importancia. (2–4)

processed/procesado Que ha sido modificado (un alimento) de su forma cruda antes de venderse. (14–1)

procrastinate/dejar para luego Dejar las cosas para hacerlas más tarde. (2–4)

produce/productos de granja Frutas y vegetales frescos. (14–1)

promotion/ascenso Avance a un trabajo mejor con mayor responsabilidad. (4–4)

proofread/corregir Revisar y rectificar los errores de gramática, puntuación y ortografía. (4–2)

protein/proteína Un nutriente necesario para fabricar, reparar y mantener las células y tejidos del cuerpo. (10–2)

punishment/castigo Una manera de poner freno a la conducta poco apropiada. (6–1)

R

ravel/deshilar Salírsele los hilos al borde cortado de la tela. (17–3)

raw edge/borde cortado El borde de la tela sin terminar que tiene hilos sueltos. (18–1)

realistic goal/meta razonable Una meta que puedes alcanzar. (3–4)

recipe/receta Una lista de ingredientes e instrucciones para preparar un platillo específico. (13–3)

recycling/reciclar Convertir los desechos en productos que se pueden usar. (9–2)

redirect/desviar Hacer que alguien dirija su atención a otra cosa. (6–5)

redress/compensación Acción que se toma para corregir un error. (7–4)

reference/referencia Un informe acerca del carácter y habilidades de trabajo del candidato a un puesto. (4–3)

refund/reembolso El intercambio de dinero por un artículo que se ha devuelto. (7–4)

refusal skills/habilidades de rehusar Modos de decir que no eficazmente. (3–1)

resource/recurso Una fuente de información o experiencia que puedes utilizar para alcanzar tus metas; algo que necesitas para alcanzar una meta. (2–4), (3–4)

respect/respeto Consideración. (3–2)

responsibility/responsabilidad La habilidad de tomar decisiones y de responder por esas decisiones. (3–2)

risk/arriesgarse Correr peligros. (9–3)

role/papel La manera en que actúas cuando estás con otra persona. (1–1)

role model/modelo de conducta Una persona que te ayuda a ver lo que se espera de ti y te enseña cómo actuar en ciertas situaciones. (1–1)

rotating/dar vueltas Girar un plato un cuarto o media vuelta en un horno de microondas. (12–4)

S

salad/ensalada Un alimento o combinación de alimentos que generalmente se sirven fríos y con aliño. (14–2)

salmonella/salmonella Bacterias que se encuentran con frecuencia en alimentos crudos o no del todo cocinados tales como la carne, los huevos, el pescado y las aves. (12–1)

sandwich/sandwich Dos lascas de pan alrededor de un relleno, tal como la carne o el queso. (14–3)

sanitary/sanitario Libre de gérmenes. (8–3)

saturated fat/grasa saturada Grasa que se encuentra en alimentos que vienen de fuentes animales. (10–2)

scald/calentar sin que llegue al punto de ebullición Calentar despacio un alimento sin dejar que hierva. (14–4)

seam finish/remate Una manera de terminar el borde de una costura para que la tela no se deshilache. (18–2)

seasonal/de temporada Más abundantes, más fácil de conseguir y más baratos durante cierto tiempo del año. (14–1)

security/seguridad Sentirse tranquilo y protegido. (5–1)

self-concept/autoimagen Tu concepto de ti mismo. (1–3)

self-confidence/confianza en sí mismo Seguridad de tus propias habilidades. (1–3)

self-esteem/autoestima La habilidad de respetarte a ti mismo. (1–3)

selvage/orillo El borde de la tela que está terminado para que no se salgan los hilos. (18–1)

serger/remalladora Una máquina de alta velocidad que cose, corta y remata una costura en un solo paso. (18–3)

service/servicio Trabajo que una persona hace para otras. (7–1)

serving/ración Una porción de comida que una persona probablemente comiera en un ocasión. (11–1)

sewing gauge/regla de costura Una regla de metal de 6 pulgadas (15 cm) con un puntero que se mueve. (17–1)

shank/vástago El tallo de un botón que proporciona espacio para la capa de tela alrededor del ojal. (18–5)

shape/forma Contorno. (15–3)

shoplifting/hurto en las tiendes Llevarse artículos de una tienda sin pagar por ellos. (7–3)

shopping plan/plan de compras Una estrategia para gastar el dinero que tienes disponible para comprar los artículos que necesitas o deseas. (16–3)

sibling/hermano Hermano o hermana. (5–2)

slip stitch/punto de dobladillo Un punto a mano que luce casi invisible. (18–5)

small appliance/aparato eléctrico Un aparato eléctrico pequeño para la cocina. (12–3)

smoke alarm/alarma de humo Un aparato que hace sonar una alarma cuando hay humo. (6–4)

snack/refrigerio Alimento que se come entre comidas. (11–3)

sodium/sodio Un mineral que ayuda a regular la cantidad de líquido que hay en el cuerpo. (11–2)

software/software Un programa o unas instrucciones para computación. (4–2)

solitary play/juego solitario Juego que el bebé hace solo, demostrando poco interés en relacionarse con otros niños. También se llama juego independiente. (6–3)

specialty store/tienda especializada Una tienda que tiene sólo un tipo de mercancía en particular. (7–3)

stain/mancha Un área sucia o descolorida. (16–4)

stamina/resistencia La habilidad de concentrarse en una sola actividad por mucho tiempo. (11–4)

standard format/formato típico La presentación de una receta que enumera todos los ingredientes en orden de su uso, seguidos por instrucciones para preparar el alimento paso a paso. (13–2)

staple/alimento básico Alimento que se usa con frecuencia. (13–2)

status/prestigio Nivel de importancia. (15–2)

status symbol/símbolo de prestigio Una prenda de vestir u otro artículo que le da a su dueño un sentido especial de importancia. (16–3)

staystitching/puntadas de fijar Una línea de puntadas permanentes que se cose encima o muy cerca de la costura en el borde de la tela. (18–4)

stereotype/estereotipo Una idea o imagen formada por adelantado acerca de todos los miembros de un grupo. (2–1)

stitch finger/dedo para puntada Una punta de metal en el plato o pisacostura de una remalladora. (18–3)

stitch regulator/regulador del punto Un dial o palanca en una máquina de coser que controla el largo de las puntadas. (17–1)

store-brand product/marca de la tienda Alimento o artículo doméstico que lleva en la etiqueta el nombre de una tienda o un nombre que sólo se usa en esa tienda. (13–2)

stress/estrés La reacción del cuerpo a los cambios a su alrededor. (5–3)

style/estilo El diseño de una prenda. (15–2)

sunscreen/bloqueador solar Una loción que protege la piel contra los rayos dañinos del sol. (15–1)

supervisor/supervisor La persona que revisa y evalúa el trabajo de otra. (4–4)

synthetic fiber/fibra sintética Una fibra hecha parcial o completamente de substancias químicas. (16–2)

T

tail chain/cadeneta Una cantidad de hilo en forma de cadena hecho en un remalladora sin tela debajo de la aguja. (18–3)

talent/talento Habilidad natural. (2–4)

teamwork/trabajo en conjunto Los esfuerzos cooperativos de todos los miembros de un grupo al trabajar juntos para lograr una meta. (2–3), (4–4)

texture/textura La manera en que algo se siente o luce como si se debe sentir. (8–2), (13–1), (15–3)

time schedule/programa del tiempo Un plan para asegurar que todos los platos estén listos para servir en el momento correcto. (13–1)

toddler/niño pequeño Un niño entre uno y tres años de edad. (6–2)

trade-off/intercambio El sacrificio de una cosa para obtener algo de mayor importancia. (3–4)

tradition/tradición Una costumbre o creencia que se pasa de generación a generación. (5–2)

traffic pattern/patrón de movimiento Las sendas que siguen las personas para entrar, salir y moverse alrededor de una habitación. (8–1)

U

unique/único Que sólo hay uno. (1–1)

unit pricing/dar el precio por unidad Mostrar el costo de un producto por unidad. (13–2)

unsaturated fat/grasa no saturada Grasa que viene de plantas. (10–2)

utensil/utensilio Implemento de cocina. (12–3)

V

value/opacidad Lo claro u oscuro que es un color. (15–3)

values/valores Ideas sobre el bien y el mal y sobre lo que es importante en la vida. (3–1)

variable/factor variable Una condición que determina por cuánto tiempo y a qué nivel de potencia se tiene que cocinar un alimento en un horno de microondas. (12–4)

vegetarian/vegetariano Una persona que come principalmente frutas, vegetales y granos. (11–1)

versatile/versátil Que se puede llevar puesto en muchas ocasiones distintas. (16–1)

view/modelo Una de las versiones de una prenda que se ve en el sobre de un patrón. (17–2)

violence/violencia El uso de fuerza física para hacer daño a alguien. (9–3)

vitamin/vitamina Substancia que el cuerpo necesita en pequeñas cantidades para regular sus funciones. (10–3)

volunteer/voluntario Una persona que da su tiempo y energía sin pago como servicio a otros. (2–3)

W

want/deseo Algo que quieres tener pero que no es necesario para sobrevivir. (3–1)

wardrobe inventory/inventario del vestuario Una lista de toda la ropa, los zapatos y los accesorios que tienes. (16–1)

warranty/garantía La promesa por escrito de un fabricante de arreglar o reemplazar un producto que no funciona como se afirma. (7–3)

wellness/bienestar Un alto nivel de salud total. (11–2)

whole grain/grano integral Un alimento que contiene todo lo que se puede comer del grano, incluyendo la capa exterior, el salvado y el germen. (10–2)

work plan/plan de trabajo Una lista de las tareas que hay que hacer y los nombres de las personas que van a hacer cada una. (12–5)

work record/hoja de servicio Un historial de lo bien que un empleado hace su trabajo. (4–4)

woven fabric/tela de telar Tela hecha en un telar entretejiendo los hilos que van a lo ancho con los hilos que van a lo largo, a un ángulo de 90°. (16–2)

X Y Z

yield/número de porciones El número de raciones que rinde una receta. (13–3)

Index

Parenting skills, 152–157

Parents, communicating with, 120–121

Part-time work, 85

Pasta, 404–405

Patterns, sewing, 490–493, 505–506, 507, 511–512

Paying for purchases, 215–216, 467

Pedestrians, 260

Peer groups, 133

Peer mediation, 145, 146

Peer pressure, 136–140, 264

Peers, 133, 191–192

People as resources, 45–46

Perishable foods, 329, 371

Personality, 11

Personal resources, 44–45

Personal safety, 258–264

Personal style, 453

Physical development, 160

Physical needs, 154

Pinning sewing patterns, 511

Planning
    cleaning, 236
    clothes shopping, 467
    meals, 299, 360–365
    work, 351–353

Plaque, 432

Play, 165–170

Playground safety, 173

Poison control center, 175

Poisonings, 175

Pollution, 247–248

Popularity, 138

Positive attitude, 28–29, 62, 73

Positive communication, 155–156

Positive self-concept, 17–18

Posture, 429

Potential, 55

Precycling, 254

Prejudice, 142–143, 264

Preschoolers, 162, 168–169, 181–182

Preshrinking fabrics, 508

Presser foot, 488

Pressing, 475–476, 487

Pretreating laundry, 474

Preventing
    accidents, 172–175, 259–262, 333–336
    conflicts, 143
    fires, 174, 238, 334

Price and quality, 203–204

Print media, 196

Prioritizing, 47, 73

Privacy, 115, 227

Processed food, 392

Procrastination, 48

Produce, 391

Promises, 61, 62

Promotions, 103

Proof of purchase, 205, 210

Proofreading, 89

Proportion, 231

Proteins, 276, 279

Puddings, 411

Punishment, 155

Q

Quackery, 208

Quality
    in fabrics and clothing, 459–462, 495–496
    food shopping tips, 368, 370
    and price, 203–204

Quick breads, 400

Quiet play, 170

R

Rare meats, 416–417

Raveling, 496

Raw edges of fabric, 508

Reading skills, 87–88

Realistic goals, 72

Receipts, 205

Recipes, 373–379. *See also* Cooking
    formats, 374–375
    ingredients, 378
    measuring ingredients, 380–384

organizing, 374
    terms and abbreviations, 375–378

Recycling, 189, 255–256, 427, 534

Redirecting children, 181

Redress, 207

References for jobs, 95

Refrigerators, 342

Refunds, 210–211

Refusal skills, 57, 139

Regular stitch, 487

Reinforcement stitch, 487

Relationships. *See also* Families; Friends
    in business, 98, 100, 102
    conflict resolution, 141–146
    first impressions, 27, 438
    importance of, 112–114, 116
    peer pressure, 136–140, 264
    skills, 114–116

Reliability, 30

Religion and diet, 275

Repairing clothes, 473, 529–533

Researching careers, 82–83

Resolving conflicts, 143–146

Resourcefulness, 18

Resources, 73
    conservation, 246–251
    managing, 43–46
    planning meals, 364

Respect, 38–39, 60

Responsibility, 18, 59–63
    consumer responsibilities, 208–211
    decision-making, 68–69, 138–139
    on the job, 99–101
    parenting skills, 153–157

Restaurants, 312–315

Reusing items, 254–255

Rhythm, 231

Rice, 403

Rights of consumers, 207

Risk taking, 68, 139, 259

Role models, 8, 63

Roles, 8, 125

Soups, 397–398
Space and room design, 230
Speaking skills, 89–90
Special-needs children, 162–163
Sports and safety, 261–262
Stains on clothes, 473, 474
Stamina, 317–318
Standard format recipes, 374–375
Staples, 367
Starches, 280
Status symbols, 435, 469
Staystitching, 524
Steaming, 396
Stereotypes, 27
Stir-frying, 396
Stitch finger, 521
Stitching. *See* Sewing
Stitch regulator, 487
Stitch types, 487, 519–520
Storage space, 226–227
Store-brand products, 367
Storing
    clothing, 476
    food, 370–372
Straightening fabric, 508–509
Straight seams, 513–514
Strangers, 262
Stress, 127–129
Study skills, 88
Style
    of clothing, 436–439, 453, 465,
      491–492
    of room design, 232–233
Success, 74, 98–104, 353–354, 437
Sugars, 280, 281, 288, 307–308
Sunscreens, 430
Supervisors, 100
Synthetic fibers, 459

T

Table manners, 362
Table settings, 361
Tail chains, 521
Take-out food, 314–315
Talents, 44

Teamwork, 37, 40, 101, 351
Teasing, 142
Teeth, care of, 432–433
Television, 179, 195–197
Tension dials of sergers, 517
Terms in recipes, 375–378
Texture
    and clothing design, 446
    and meal planning, 363
    and room design, 230–231
Thoughtfulness, 18, 115–116
Thread guides of sergers, 517
Threading a sewing machine,
    486–487
Time
    in decision-making, 68
    managing, 46–48, 483–484
    meal planning schedule, 364,
      365
    open dating, 370
    as personal resource, 44
    saving in the kitchen, 352
    saving when sewing, 497
Tints, 441
Toddlers, 162, 167–168, 181–182
Tools. *See* Equipment
Tooth care, 432–433
Toys, 166–167, 168, 169
Trade-offs, 73
Traditions, 120
Trust, building, 115

U

Underweight, 319
Uniqueness, 4, 9, 496
Unit pricing, 370
Unsaturated fats, 283
Used goods, 205
Utensils, 338, 382

V

Values, human, 55–58, 67, 161
Values of colors, 441
Variety, 231, 363
Vegetable Group, 300–301, 362,
    394–398

Vegetables
    cooking, 395–397
    Dietary Guidelines, 306–307
    salads, 397
    selecting and preparing, 395
    soups, 397–398
    storing, 371
Vegetarians, 299
Verbal communication, 32, 34–35
Versatile clothes, 453
Views of garments, 490
Violence, 263–264
Vitamins, 276, 285–288
Volunteers, 36, 39, 40

W, X

Want ads, 84
Wants, 55
Wardrobe. *See* Clothing
Warranties, 205, 209
Washing. *See* Cleaning
Waste, 252–257
Water
    conservation of, 248
    used by body, 276, 289–290
Weight
    controlling, 319–322
    healthy, 305, 318–319
Well-done meats, 416–417
Wellness, 303
Whole grains, 281
Work. *See* Careers; Jobs
Work plan, 351–353
Work record, 102–103
Woven fabrics, 460
Writing skills, 88–89

Y

Yeast breads, 400–401
Yield of recipes, 374
Yogurt, cooking with, 408–409

Z

Zigzag stitch, 487

Cover Art:

Front Cover—Kim Robbie/The Stock Market (photo), Diana Ong/Superstock (illustration); Back Cover—Suresh Shivdasani/Magic Photography (top), DBS Stevenson Photography (bottom)

Photographs:

Lori Adamski Peek/Tony Stone Images x, 1; Arnold & Brown Photography 197, 226, 239, 240, 257, 452, 458, 459, 464, 470; Bruce Ayers/Tony Stone Images 108, 109; Brian Bailey/Tony Stone Images 132; Billy Barnes/FPG International 431; Robert Bennett/FPG International 247; Christopher Bissell/Tony Stone Images 140; Robert Brenner/Photo Edit 168; Michelle Bridwell/Photo Edit 134, 204, 395; David Burnett/The Stock Market 99; Cary Buss/FPG International 160; Jose Carrillo/Photo Edit 193, 194, 211, 232, 249, 414; Myrleen Cate/Tony Stone Images 61; Cindy Charles/Photo Edit 172, 174; Ron Chappel/FPG International 223, 335; Stewart Cohen/Tony Stone Images 424, 425; Comstock 136, 294, 295, 326, 327; David Kelly Crow Photography 475, 476, 488, 504, 506, 508, 509, 510, 512, 514, 515, 522, 523, 524, 526, 527, 529, 533, 534; Bob Daemmrich Photography 163, 411, 429, 439, 444, 445, 446; Bob Daemmrich/Stock Boston 466, 438; Bob Daemmrich/Uniphoto 275, 281, 440, 471; Robert E. Daemmrich/Tony Stone Images 60, 84, 96, 143, 298, 400; Donna Day/Tony Stone Images 299; Mary Kate Denny/Photo Edit 4, 12, 27, 34, 37, 48, 62, 80, 103, 125, 141, 153, 156, 166, 237, 277, 284, 331, 345, 349, 350, 354, 409, 428, 465, 432, 532; Laura Dwight/Photo Edit 169; Amy C. Etra/Photo Edit 115, 145, 181, 182, 199; Jon Feingersh/The Stock Market 120; Myrleen Ferguson/Photo Edit 17, 29, 35, 116, 454; Tony Freeman/Photo Edit 15, 16, 85, 93, 114, 192, 279, 315, 328, 329, 467; Stephen Frish/Stock Boston 434; Tim Fuller Photography 43, 91, 157, 158, 171, 186–187, 188, 189, 212, 214, 215, 216, 296, 310, 338, 342, 344, 346, 351, 353, 380, 384, 392, 393, 394, 396, 403, 405, 410, 411, 418, 420, 450, 451, 480, 481, 490, 491, 493, 494, 495, 497, 498, 502, 503; Robert Ginn/Photo Edit 308; Louis Goldman/FPG International 437; Steven Gottlieb/FPG International 388, 389; Jeff Greenberg/Photo Edit 261; Howard Grey/Tony Stone Images 68; Aaron Haupt/Stock Boston 433; Michal Heron/The Stock Market 64; Index Stock 45; Bonnie Kamin/Photo Edit 236, 264; Ronnie Kaufman/The Stock Market 31; Hal Kern/International Stock 74; Steve Leonard/Tony Stone Images 191; James Levin/FPG International 56, Llewellyn/Uniphoto 319; 176; Bill Losh/FPG International 220, 221; Dick Luvia/FPG International 180; David Madison/Tony Stone Images 112, 150, 151; Felicia Martinez/Photo Edit 373; Tom McCarthy/Photo Edit 397; Fred McKinney/FPG International 165; Mug Shots/The Stock Market 52, 53, 71, 86, 412; Michael Newman/Photo Edit 9, 73, 81, 90, 130, 138, 154, 177, 260, 272, 273, 306, 307, 314, 334, 336, 363, 401, 402, 419, 455, 461, 472, 473, 505, 511, 516, 519, 520; Jonathan Nourok/Photo Edit 263; Gabe Palmer/The Stock Market 142; Jose L. Pelaez/The Stock Market 276; Photo Edit 200, 361; J. Pickerrell/FPG International 382; John Pinderhughes/The Stock Market 119; Jon Riley/Tony Stone Images 24, 25; Joel Rogers/Tony Stone Images 222; Elena Rooraid/Photo Edit 235; Andy Saks/Tony Stone Images 113; Chuck Savage/Uniphoto 312; Mark Scott/FPG International 170; Nancy Sheehan/Photo Edit 127, 152, 202, 227; Stephen Simpson/FPG International 2, 3; Steve Skjold/Photo Edit 408; Don Smetzer/Tony Stone Images 337, 406; The Stock Broker 358, 359; Superstock 8, 42, 44, 66, 70, 117, 122, 126, 146, 159, 164, 283; J. Taposchaner/FPG International 32; Ed Taylor Studio/FPG International 413; The Telegraph Colour Library/FPG International 253; Arthur Tilley/FPG International 78, 79, 137, 173, 244, 245, 251, 427; Arthur Tilley/Tony Stone Images 303; Bob Torrez/Tony Stone Images 195; John Terence Turner/FPG International 246, 278; Uniphoto 110, 111; Dana White/Photo Edit 30; Dana C. White/Dana White Productions 11 26 36, 87, 89, 97, 123, 175, 190, 206, 207, 209, 229, 259, 360, 366, 367, 368, 370, 372, 374, 379, 482, 483, 486; Dusty Willison/International Stock 19; David Young-Wolff/Photo Edit 7, 10, 18, 46, 54, 59, 83, 92, 98, 104, 131, 177, 201, 208, 224, 228, 252, 254, 255, 258, 268, 269, 274, 288, 289, 290, 302, 305, 311, 316, 317, 322, 332, 333, 343, 390, 399, 407, 489; David Young-Wolff/Tony Stone Images 38, 133, 270, 271.

Illustrations:

Shirley Bortoli 485, 507, 513, 518, 528; Anthony Cericola 282, 286–287, 304, 321, 365, 369, 375, 378, 381, 416, 454, 462, 468, 492; Sally Davies 430, 443, 456, 463; Steve Henry 256, 297; Jack Kershner 20, 33, 94, 121, 161, 225, 233, 250, 330, 391, 435, 474; Morgan Cain & Associates 442; Scott Ross 40–41, 47, 51, 101, 118, 128, 167; BB Sams 6, 178, 198, 213, 300–301; Dan Siculan 339–341, 376, 377, 383, 404, 415, 484; Margaret Sims 67